Understanding World Religions

A Road Map for Justice and Peace

David Whitten Smith
Elizabeth Geraldine Burr

ROWMAN & LITTLEFIELD PUBLISHERS, INC.
Lanham • Boulder • New York • Toronto • Plymouth, UK

ROWMAN & LITTLEFIELD PUBLISHERS, INC.

Published in the United States of America
by Rowman & Littlefield Publishers, Inc.
A wholly owned subsidary of The Rowman & Littlefield Publishing Group, Inc.
4501 Forbes Boulevard, Suite 200, Lanham, Maryland 20706
www.rowmanlittlefield.com

Estover Road
Plymouth PL6 7PY
United Kingdom

British Library Cataloguing in Publication Information Available

Library of Congress Cataloging-in-Publication Data:

Smith, David W., 1937–
  Understanding world religions : a road map for justice and peace / David Whitten
Smith, Elizabeth Geraldine Burr.
    p. cm.
  ISBN-13: 978-0-7425-5054-4 (cloth : alk. paper)
  ISBN-10: 0-7425-5054-0 (cloth : alk. paper)
  ISBN-13: 978-0-7425-5055-1 (pbk. : alk. paper)
  ISBN-10: 0-7425-5055-9 (pbk. : alk. paper)
  1. Religions. 2. Religion and justice. 3. Peace—Religious aspects. 4. Church and
social problems. I. Burr, Elizabeth G., 1950– II. Title.

  BL80.3.S65 2007
  201'.7—dc22

                                                                                    2007025253

Printed in the United States of America

∞™ The paper used in this publication meets the minimum requirements of American
National Standard for Information Sciences—Permanence of Paper for Printed Library
Materials, ANSI/NISO Z39.48-1992.

Contents

Expanded Contents

Preface

In 1987, the University of St. Thomas inaugurated a minor in justice and peace studies. We decided that it would be important to study how people's worldviews affect the choices they make that promote or inhibit justice and peace. At the time, our program was unusual. Not many people in this country understood why it might be useful to understand other people's worldviews. After the September 11, 2001, attacks on the World Trade Center and the Pentagon, the country started coming around to our point of view. In 1987, there was no textbook available to introduce what we wanted to talk about, so I started to write one. Many people have helped along the way. This book is the result.

In addition to reading and discussing this book, we ask each student to research one worldview that differs from her own, using a series of steps to organize her study. At the end of the semester, students read and discuss each other's projects. When we xeroxed this book in its earlier forms for their use, we included extensive instructions and other aids for that study project. Since we could not predict how many people would be interested both in the content of this book and in the instructions for such a project, we decided to put the instructions on the World Wide Web at www.stthomas.edu/justpeace/rowman. Here we will briefly describe what is available there.

Students are instructed how to study a worldview according to the following eleven steps:

1. Describe your own worldview and presuppositions by answering the nine sets of questions given. This step will help you (a) to think about many things you have taken for granted, (b) to become aware of the variety in our own class, and (c) to accept and value our differences. The step is graded pass-fail.

2. Describe what you know as you begin your study: the worldview you have chosen to study, what you know or don't know about it as you start, what you want to find out.
3. Select a local resource to help you with your study, preferably someone who lives the worldview you are studying.
4. Experience the worldview through a vicarious experience — a narrative such as a novel, memoir, autobiography, film, play, interview, or foreign travel. We are looking here for stories, not yet for academic information or analysis.
5. From academic research, describe the main ideas and practices of the worldview, especially with regard to justice, peace, prosperity, and security.
6. List and describe briefly the main sacred books, classics, and traditions (including oral traditions) of the worldview. Read parts meditatively and report on the experience.
7. Describe how some real person has been influenced by the worldview in their work on behalf of justice and peace, or how some community living the worldview has responded in some real conflict. This step will consider what happens when one person or a group attempts to live out the worldview's ideals in the actual, messy world.
8. Re-write your responses to the questions of step one as if you personally held the worldview you have been studying.
9. Write a utopia which would make sense to someone holding the worldview. What would a perfect world be like, why isn't the world like that, what is the best situation we might hope for in the real world (a "possitopia"), and how might we move toward that better future?
10. Reflect on your study. Compare what you know and believe now with what you did in step 2 when you started. Did your study confirm your expectations, challenge, or surprise you? How helpful was your local resource of step 3? How could this course be improved?
11. Give us a list of the resources you used with comments for future studies indicating how useful each item was, and for what steps it was useful.

OTHER TREASURES ON OUR WEBSITE

Space limitations have prevented us from publishing everything we would like to share. Some of what didn't fit will be available at our website, in particular, greatly expanded suggestions for further reading and additional spokespersons for each worldview. For the last twenty years, we have been assembling the annotated resource lists that our *students* have produced (step

11 above)—you can see *their* comments on books, periodical articles, websites, and more. We expect also to post further web links, study questions, additional diagrams and tables, photographs, and maybe even a PowerPoint presentation or two. Also posted will be an article I wrote which applies many of the things we talk about in the book; it is called "Inspired Authors and Saintly Interpreters in Conflict: The New Testament on War and Peace." Further, we will be updating our ideas on the website in preparation for a revised edition of this book.

A FEW ADMISSIONS

This book is not neutral; it does not treat war, peace, injustice, and justice "impartially." As Johan Galtung points out,[1] peace studies are similar to health studies—both go beyond impartial understanding. Doctors don't study medicine just because they find diseases intriguing; they want to cure people. We don't study worldviews just because they interest us; we hope that understanding them will help us further our work for justice and peace.

Finally, we have tried to make the book interesting rather than comprehensive. We sincerely hope that you will find this book compelling but incomplete, so that you will be moved to explore on your own some of the areas we introduce.

ACKNOWLEDGMENTS

Many people have helped this book take its current shape. Elizabeth Burr has been doing her best to keep me, David Smith, from making a fool of myself. Where she has failed, it has been due to my obstinacy. She is responsible for writing a significant amount of content, in addition to research and editorial work. We are especially grateful to Anne King, who wrote a large part of chapter 7 on Marxist worldviews, and to Jack Nelson-Pallmeyer for his contribution to chapter 5 on Christian worldviews. We are also very grateful to Ross Miller, our editor at Rowman & Littlefield, for his exceptional editorial guidance. Others who have read and offered helpful comments on various chapters, who have taught the course the book was designed for, who have helped me out on my various study trips, or who in other ways have helped us gather significant material and experience that is contained in this book, include Zev Aeloni, D. C. Ahir, Fr. Antonio d'Agostino, A. T. Ariyaratne, Mubarak Awad, Kedar Bahadur Basnet, Fr. Tissa Balasuriya, Jeff Carlson, Dennis Carroll, William Cavanaugh, Michael Cullen, the late David

Dellinger, Lorna Dewaraja, Rev. Noel Dias, Fr. Peter Dougherty, Jay Erstling, H. R. H. Chief Fonkem Achankeng I, Arun Gandhi, the late Fr. Rafael García-Herreros, Ira Gordon, the late Ned Hanauer, Linda Hulbert, the late Abp. Dennis Hurley, Fr. Diego Jaramillo, James Jennings, Michael Klein, Jonathan Kuttab, Carol Schersten LaHurd, John Landgraf, Ramu Manivannan, Patrick Mawaya, Ashok Mehrotra, Jose Miguez-Bonino, Fr. Hugo Montero, Fred Nairn, Michael Naughton, Leuben Njinya-Mujinya, Michael Novak, the late Arsham Ohanessian, Adil Ozdemir, Rev. George Palackapilly, Agapitos Papagapitos, David Penchansky, Fr. Aloysius Pieris, Vivek Pinto, Fr. Greg Schaeffer, Gerald Schlabach, Juan Luis Segundo, Dr. Suniti Solomon, Sr. Florence Steichen, Ahmed Tharwat, Cris Toffolo, Heidi Tousignant, Ted Ulrich, Dr. Solomon Victor, the late Gerald Vizenor, Sr. Liz Walters, Ira Weiss, Susan Windley-Daoust, Fr. Alex Zanotelli, and Fred Zimmerman. I am grateful to colleagues in the American Academy of Religion, the Catholic Biblical Association, the International Peace Research Association, the Peace and Justice Studies Association, and the Society of Biblical Literature; at the University of St. Thomas, the other University of St. Thomas in Rome (the "Angelicum"), the Catholic University of America, the École Biblique et Archéologique Française (Jerusalem), and the European Peace University (Stadtschlaining, Austria). One or another of these people or groups might be embarrassed to be associated with the contents, so I admit that I didn't always understand or agree with their suggestions.

And now the book is in your hands. I pray that God will help you to understand, appreciate, and put into practice whatever we have said that is true and helpful, and to overlook or ignore whatever we have said that is not.

NOTE

1. Johan Galtung, *Peace by Peaceful Means: Peace and Conflict, Development and Civilization*, 1.

Credits

Except where otherwise indicated, translations of the Bible are from the *New American Bible*, including the Revised New Testament and the Revised Psalms © 1969, 1970, 1986, 1991 Confraternity of Christian Doctrine, Washington, D.C. Used by permission.

The lead quotation of chapter 6: Native American Worldviews is reprinted from *Black Elk Speaks: Being the Life Story of a Holy Man of the Oglala Sioux*, by John G. Neihardt, by permission of the University of Nebraska Press. Copyright © 1932, 1959, 1972 by John G. Neihardt. © 1961 by the John G. Neihardt Trust. © 2000 by the University of Nebraska Press.

Other permissions are noted in the footnotes.

Introduction:
The Study of Worldviews

"[Humans] expect from the various religions answers to the unsolved riddles of the human condition, which today, even as in former times, deeply stir [human] hearts: What is [a human]? What is the meaning, the aim of our life? What is moral good, what sin? Whence suffering and what purpose does it serve? Which is the road to true happiness? What are death, judgment and retribution after death? What, finally, is that ultimate inexpressible mystery which encompasses our existence: whence do we come, and where are we going?"

—*Nostra Aetate*, par. 11

When we talk about justice and peace, we can misunderstand each other because my comments make sense only in a worldview (under a set of presuppositions) radically different from yours. We may wonder why the discussion is so frustrating. This is especially true for people from different parts of the world or from groups holding radically different religious or ideological beliefs. But many of the most difficult world conflicts are ostensibly between such groups: Jews, Muslims, and Christians in Israel-Palestine; Hindus, Muslims, and Sikhs in India and Pakistan; Hindus and Buddhists in Sri Lanka; Marxists and Christians in North Korea and Cuba; and so forth. Conflicts also occur between subgroups within a major worldview, for example, Protestants and Catholics in Northern Ireland, or Sunni and Shiite Muslims in Iraq.

This book seeks (a) to help you decide whether it is true that understanding other worldviews promotes justice and peace, (b) to help you learn the most basic elements of some worldviews you are likely to encounter as you pursue justice and peace, and (c) to teach you how to study other worldviews in a sympathetic way so that you can understand why others think, feel, and act the way they do, anticipate their actions, and perhaps enrich your own worldview.

We hope this book will reduce your fear of people who see the world differently from the way you do. We also hope it will encourage you to examine your own worldview more deeply so as to embrace those of its dynamics that promote justice and peace, and to resist or re-shape those that promote selfish privilege and violence.

Much of what you have regarded as common sense held by all reasonable people, you may find is part of your own particular worldview and open to critical challenge. In multicultural societies, people disagree about what constitutes "common sense."

None of the worldviews featured here will be presented completely, but you can become aware of how worldviews influence people's vision and judgment so that you will be less surprised by how other people react. You will know what needs to be investigated to clarify positions: what implicit claims and questions lie concealed beneath the surface of an argument, and what values are at stake in the answers to those questions.

This book will briefly explain seven influential worldviews: Hinduism, Buddhism, Judaism, Christianity, Islam, Native American religions, and Marxism. In chapter 8 we present the Israeli-Palestinian issue as a case study of worldviews in conflict. We also give special attention to Christian social teaching, liberation theologies, active nonviolence, and just war theory because they illustrate how religious beliefs influence attitudes and actions toward justice and peace.

RELIGIONS, THEOLOGIES, AND WORLDVIEWS

A *worldview* is an overall way of seeing and relating to the world we live in and any larger world that may be beyond our world. It asks about the meaning of what we experience and how we should respond to the people, forces, and things that surround us. Some worldviews are called *religions*. Others, like Marxism and secular humanism, are not. Still, secular worldviews act like religions in many ways.

Most Westerners presume that they know what a religion is: it is something like Christianity, or Judaism, or Islam; it believes in something beyond the "ordinary"—in God or gods, some unseen Power or powers, something "beyond" common, everyday experience. But when Western scholars began studying "world religions," they found that many peoples don't even have a word for religion.

How much does a worldview like Hinduism have to be "like" Christianity to qualify as a "religion"? Is there any single "thing" that we might call Hinduism? (Even the word "Hindu*ism*" was invented by Westerners.) For that matter, is there a single thing we can call Christianity? Rather than decide these questions, we will simply study "worldviews" as a more generic reality. We will consider several "dimensions" that are widely, if not universally, shared by worldviews, and we will presume that everyone in the world has *(1) at least some experience of something, (2) at least a shadowy sense of what they are experiencing, and (3) a preferred or habitual way of understanding and relating to whatever that is.*

THE SEVEN "DIMENSIONS"

In his book *The World's Religions*,[2] Ninian Smart proposes seven dimensions that are common to all or most religions. Rearranging his order, the seven dimensions are: (1) Experiential and Emotional, (2) Social and Institutional, (3) Narrative or Mythic, (4) Doctrinal and Philosophical, (5) Practical and Ritual, (6) Ethical and Legal, and (7) Material and Artistic.[3] These seven dimensions interact with each other. They are not "pieces" of a religion or worldview so much as "viewpoints" or "aspects." As a material object has three "dimensions," and all are dimensions of the same thing, so a religion or worldview has various "dimensions." For example, a church institution (2) is governed by particular rules or laws (6) and performs particular rituals (5).

We have placed the dimensions in an order that makes them easier to remember and shows connections between them. Briefly, here are some connections: (1) Experiential and emotional: people gain experience of life; some people have life-changing experiences. (2) Social and institutional: they seek out others with similar experiences and form groups for support; gradually these groups grow in size and complexity. (3) Narrative or mythic: within the group, they pass on their experiences in stories. (4) Doctrinal and philosophical: as people ask questions about the experiences and the stories, they explain them rationally as best they can—some meaning cannot be expressed rationally, but must remain as expressed in the stories themselves. (5) Practical and ritual: if they understand their experiences to relate to powers or beings beyond visible, everyday experience, they work out concrete ways of relating to those powers or beings (for example, liturgy or worship); they also work out formalized ways of relating to *normal* people and things (for example, social etiquette). (6) Ethical and legal: they decide what actions and way of life are appropriate to their experiences and their understanding of those experiences; they also develop laws to govern the communities they have formed. (7) Material and artistic: in living out these six dimensions, they produce material things (buildings like temples, songs like hymns, visual arts) that are appropriate to their experiences and their understanding.

In brief, people *have experiences* (1); *come together* with others (2); *try to share and understand* their experiences in story (3) and reasoned discourse (4); and seek to *live them out* in solemn or sacred acts (5), ordinary acts (6), and the material facilities they create (7). This order has a certain logical attractiveness and was probably the order in which the founders of the worldview and early converts to the worldview experienced these dimensions, but it is not the order in which many later followers experience them. Most people are "born into" a religion or worldview—socialized into a particular religion or worldview within their family. While they begin life with individual experiences, these are not the experiences most central to their parents' worldview. Perhaps the first dimension they experience is (6): "Johnny, don't do that!" When they ask why not, they are more likely to get a narrative (3) than doctrine (4), since they are too young for doctrine. They also experience the social (2), ritual (5), and material (7) dimensions before they understand the reasons for them. As they grow older, they may get a good dose of the doctrinal dimension (4) through some form of religious education before they finally (if ever) share the core experiences (1) that are the basis for all the rest.

When people who were born into a worldview do finally share the core experiences that underlie it, they find that everything has deeper meaning than they had realized—the rest "comes to life." Often they have to re-think it all. This is called "adult conversion"—not conversion from one worldview to another, but conversion of a person from a merely theoretical knowledge of a worldview to a deeply personal relationship with it.

Now let us look at each dimension in more detail.

EXPERIENTIAL AND EMOTIONAL DIMENSION

Many Westerners first encounter "mysticism" in a context of Eastern religious thought, perhaps through the New Age Movement, Hare Krishna, or Transcendental Meditation. Concepts like yogis, reincarnation, the illusory nature of everyday reality, "mind over matter," and astral projection emphasize how foreign these ideas are to Western minds. Some are then surprised to hear that there is a long-standing and widely developed *Christian* mystical tradition represented by people like Benedict of Nursia (the founder of Western monasticism), Hildegard von Bingen, Catherine of Siena, Julian of Norwich, Teresa of Avila, John of the Cross, George Fox, and Thomas Merton. This Christian mystical tradition describes *experiences* often similar to those recounted in Eastern traditions, while it *understands and explains* them differently. You can read about a variety of mystical experiences from many different traditions in *The Varieties of Religious Experience* by the American psychologist and philosopher William James.

Sociological Support

Impressed by James's book, the American sociologist-priest Andrew Greeley decided to add a few questions to one of his national surveys to see whether he could find a few mystics in a national sample of 1,500 average Americans. He asked the following question: "Have you ever had the feeling of being very close to a powerful spiritual force that seemed to lift you out of yourself?" He was astonished to find that 40% of his sample said "yes, at least once"; 20% said "several times"; 5% said "often." He asked them how intense the experience was. Two-thirds put it at the top of a 7-point scale. He gave them a simple psychological test to see whether they were all crazy. They came out healthier psychologically than any other group who had ever taken that test.

He was disappointed when some of his colleagues dismissed his results without discussion and he couldn't attract money for further research. He thought that a group showing superior psychological health was worth investigating. *Other* colleagues—professional sociologists—approached him quietly to ask whether he might be interested in *their* mystical experiences.[4]

Mystical Experience

Mystical experiences are hard to put into categories. But there are some characteristic types.

Numinous Experiences

One type has been called *numinous experiences*. The name comes from the Latin word *numen*, which refers to a local spirit believed to inhabit a brook, grove of trees, mountain, etc. Experiences of this sort bring us into contact with *a presence that (a) attracts us, while at the same time (b) sending a thrill of awe or fear down our spines*. Picture yourself walking through a graveyard at two o'clock in the morning just as a shadowy shape rises from the ground. A number of Jewish prophets describe their visions in ways that seem to fit this type. Isaiah falls flat on his face crying, "Woe is me." Paul falls to the ground when he sees the risen Jesus, his expectations of arresting Christians in Damascus shattered. Fear is not always the dominant element. Some numinous experiences are dominated by the feeling of love and joy. Still, there is a sense of contact with someone or something "different" or "Other."

Pan-en-henic Experiences

Quite different is a mystical experience more typical of Hinduism, though not unknown among Christians. In this experience, technically termed *pan-en-henic* (literally: "all-in-one"), the mystic feels herself united with all of reality. Far from feeling fear or awe in the presence of an Other, the mystic feels almost a loss of the sense of *self*. This loss, of course, can also be frightening. Many yogic exercises are designed to lead a person into a pan-en-henic experience. The yogis believe that such an experience shows us what the world is really like.

Shamanic Experiences

A third pattern of mystical experience is common among *shamans*. These are religious leaders who, either without willing it or through a deliberate vision quest, pass from this world to another, have experiences there which endow them with power, and then return to this world—often carrying the marks of the journey in chronic illness or woundedness. Having made that journey, they can use their power to help others. You can read accounts of shamans' visions in Native American literature, for example the classic book *Black Elk Speaks*.[5]

"Born Again" Experiences

A fourth pattern is the "born again" experience of adult religious conversion, either into one's own religion or worldview, now seen in a new way, or into a completely new worldview. Typically, a surrender of faith leads to intense experiences of conviction and joy and a new clarity about the meaning of doctrines that were previously "accepted on faith" without understanding. There are numerous Christian accounts of the "born again" experience, especially in evangelical and Pentecostal literature. An example of the "born again" experience outside of confessional church contexts is the Alcoholics Anonymous experience of surrender followed by group exploration of the "twelve steps," which suddenly take on new life and new power.

More Subtle Experiences

Many mystical experiences don't fit neatly into any of these categories. Even the 60% of people who answered "no" to Andrew Greeley's question may well experience feelings of more subtle intensity that give meaning and justification to the worldviews they hold. Emotions felt at the birth of a child, at the death of a friend, while walking in nature, during a religious ritual such as Communion at Mass, or when sitting quietly in prayer, perhaps in a holy place, support our deep convictions. Even such a simple feeling as the thrill of hearing one's national anthem played during the Olympic Games grows out of and gives support to our commitment to each other as citizens of our nation, with a whole range of implications based on stories of national founders and heroes living out our national ideals.

If one has such experiences, and if—as is often the case—they don't follow the usual rules of time and space, they may be difficult to describe to others. One usually begins by telling a narrative or myth, our third category below. But first, one may seek out others who have had similar experiences, leading them to create societies and institutions of like-minded people. This leads us to the social dimension.

SOCIAL AND INSTITUTIONAL DIMENSION

When people share a life-changing experience, they come together to support, encourage, and discuss with each other. Their association eventually takes on concrete, institutional forms. Different worldviews produce different types of communities. Islam has been particularly well organized socially. It gives central importance to the *ummah*, or religious community. Since for Muslims every aspect of life should be marked by submission to Allah, there is no reason to separate religion and state.

Institutional Forms within a Religion or Worldview

Religious groups organize themselves socially in a self-conscious way, since their sense of being in contact with a spiritual reality gives them a deep awareness of shared experience and moves them to come together for common worship. Different religious groups prefer different institutional forms. Many Protestant churches have a fairly democratic structure. The Roman Catholic Church has a monarchical international structure, although it is becoming more democratic at the local, parish level. But these are broad generalizations. Major churches change their structures over time, adapting them to local conditions.

Institutional leadership is not the only, or perhaps even the most important, kind of leadership in churches. There is also the leadership of sanctity and spiritual experience. Sufis, prophets, and saints may elicit more reverence than caliphs, priests, and bishops. Respected local churchgoers and activists may be more influential than preachers and pastors. Reflect on the social structures in whatever church or analogous group you belong to. What sorts of things are done in common? Who makes the *decisions*? Do the decision-makers represent one particular group, age, sex, or race to the exclusion of others? Who has the most *influence* on others? In what ways do members depend on each other and relate to each other?

Relation between Religion and Society

Typically, in primitive societies the entire tribe shares the same worldview. No one asks how the tribal society relates to the larger society, because there is no larger society other than outside tribes, which are seen as foreign.

More complex societies may have an official religion, albeit challenged by alternative worldviews; the society may see itself as religious but not committed to a particular religion; or it may think of itself as indifferent to religion—leaving religion to the "private sphere." But societies are never indifferent to worldviews as such: even societies that treasure separation of church and state have widely accepted principles or ideals that derive from a worldview, although that worldview may be unexpressed and unconscious. The conviction that separation of church and state is valuable is itself a value judgment deriving from a particular way of seeing the world. So is the conviction that citizens should be ready to fight to defend the state.

A worldview or religion may see itself as the dominant faith in one geographic area, as one among many in another area, and as an embattled outsider in a third. Islam is dominant in Saudi Arabia, influential in India, and marginal in the United States, though less marginal than it used to be. Some religions or groups are not large enough to be dominant or even major actors anywhere. These are groups such as the Amish, often called "sects" or (by those who are hostile to them) "cults." They relate to society defensively, doubt that they can have much influence on the larger society, and fear the influence the larger society can have on them. Other religions are so extensive that they dominate large areas of the world. These are the so-called major religions, most of which we are studying in this book. Liberal Protestants are an example of a subgroup within a major religion that actively tries to influence the larger society without fearing that the society will overwhelm them.

In general, religions and other voluntary associations (such as Alcoholics Anonymous, Freemasons, Marxist societies, justice and peace groups) both influence society and are influenced by it. The question whether such groups are more "democratic" or more "monarchical" illustrates how church structures are influenced by secular structures. Reflect on your own experience and consider to what extent your church or similar group has felt self-confident or threatened in relation to the larger society. Does your church try to *conform* to the larger society—"to fit in"? Does it try to *influence* or change the larger society? Does it prefer to *separate* from the larger society?

Influence of Religious Structure on Members

Religions and similar groups aim *consciously* to encourage and influence their members. They also influence their members *unconsciously* by the structures they adopt. Sometimes the structures act against the conscious efforts: exhortations to love can be ineffective in a structure of dominance and special privilege, as was true of colonial churches in Africa. It is useful to examine whether the *structures* of a particular group reflect and encourage the *ideals* preached by that group.

NARRATIVE OR MYTHIC DIMENSION

Narrative of an Experience

After a mystical experience, how does one describe what happened? In his book *Life after Life*, Raymond A. Moody describes a woman who became frustrated because she had only "three-dimensional words" with which to describe her near-death experience, while the experience was more than three-dimensional.[6] In *I Have Met Him: God Exists*, André Frossard writes, "All these impressions which I find it so hard to translate into the deficient language of ideas and images occurred simultaneously and were so telescoped the one into the other that after many years I have not yet been able to digest all they contained."[7] After his final vision, Thomas Aquinas quit writing entirely. Still, people explain as well as they can. People's stumbling narratives are understood best by those who have had similar experiences.

Myth

Beyond describing the *experiences*, people want to describe the *sort of world that might explain* such experiences. Often narrative and poetry is better adapted to describe the indescribable than academic speech is.

Modern Westerners use "myth" to mean "false"; for example, the "six myths" of good health, or the "five myths" of weight loss. In this book we are using the term in a different sense. Theologically, myths intend to express truth. Some myths succeed and some fail, just as some scientific theories succeed and some fail. In *Worldviews*, Ninian Smart defines a "myth" as "a story of divine or sacred significance."[8] Scholars of religion like Ernst Cassirer or Mircea Eliade point out that myths are not just *literary* products, although we often meet them, like the myths of Greece and Rome, in written form from the past. Native American tribal societies *act out* myths in sacred poetry, song, and drama. Through the Mass or the Lord's Supper, Christians act out, in sacred readings, song, and drama, the myth of the death and resurrection of Jesus, a myth that they believe is grounded in history and yet transcends history.

Committed participants believe they come into contact with sacred power through the ritual celebration of the myth. They overcome the normal limitations of time and space to encounter personally the primal energy of a historically ancient event, or of a reality that can only be expressed by nonhistorical narratives. Thus, Christians encounter the power of Jesus' resurrection at the Lord's Supper, the power of creation in the Easter vigil, the power of God to transform humans in baptism. Other myths try to explain how the physical and spiritual reality we live in came to be (creation), where human sin and evil came from, and how history as we know it will end (eschatology).

In his book *Myths and Realities*,[9] John McKenzie discusses myths in relation to stories of the Bible such as the creation and flood stories. Speaking of myths and myth-making in general, he points out that *myth intends to express truth, but through symbolic forms of expression*. It tries to represent an insight into a reality that cannot simply be expressed logically. Myth deals with basic questions of importance to all humans that lie deeper than the things we can touch and see: questions like the nature of God or spiritual forces; the purpose, direction, and goal of human existence; the origins of the world, of humans, of sin and evil, of human institutions; how humans relate to spiritual being, to physical nature, to each other. Myth does not "solve" these problems. Rather it suggests to humans what *attitude* they should take in the presence of such mysteries.

Four Characteristics of Myth

McKenzie outlines four characteristics of mythic language and thought:

1. Myth does not expect to *understand* what is unknowable. Rather it expresses the unknowable in symbols taken from experience. What is expressed is an intuition rather than a "fact."
2. Myth believes that the events we see are controlled and energized by a divine or spiritual background that is personal. This is not just a "personification" of natural forces. That is, we do not speak of it *as if it were* personal because the events we see *look* personal; rather the events we see *are* the way they are *because the background is* personal.
3. Myth does not deal with normal historical events (events which take place in a certain time and place), but rather with timeless realities in the "eternal Now" of the spirit world, which is the source of the recurrent events we observe. Even the death and resurrection of Jesus, which in one respect can be fixed in history, in another respect is timeless and eternally effective because it is an action of God who is outside time.
4. Sometimes different myths seem contradictory, not because one of them is wrong, but because no single myth can express the full reality. Several myths are used to try to embrace the reality. They may contradict each

other on the surface level of symbol, but not on the underlying level of what is being signified.

Modern American Secular Examples

This all may seem remote to many Americans, especially secular Americans who don't believe in a spirit world. But before Americans feel superior to "primitive" mythmakers, they might ask themselves what stories they tell each other, and what those stories mean to them. Why do they keep repeating stories about George Washington "unable to tell a lie," "honest Abe" Lincoln, and victorious General Eisenhower? Not to mention victorious sports teams. Do these stories express what Americans are like? And by what sort of "causality" might Americans or sports fans share in the abilities and virtues of their heroes?

Similarly, when we speak of success and the purpose of life, what message do we give and receive from the programs we see nightly on television—dramas like our police and spy shows, "reality" shows, and nasty quarrels (talk shows)? What attitude do we take in the face of opposition? That evil is a temporary mistake caused by a few stupid or evil people, and that strength and cunning will enable us to restore good by destroying those evil people? If so, we are illustrating what the theologian Walter Wink calls the "myth of redemptive violence."[10]

In short, narratives and myths are one way a community passes on its combined experience to the next generation and reinforces its common understanding of what reality is like. If a person gives no attention or authority to the myths and narratives of her tradition, she reduces her understanding of reality to the narrow range of experience that she herself can have. At the same time, one needs to be critical of the myths of one's own society and culture, recognizing that they are but one set of myths, different from those of other peoples and equally liable to be harmful. Prophets challenge myths of their own societies in the name of what seems to them to be a higher authority.

Ritual Enactment of Myths

Finally, how do we act out our myths? Think of parades marking national holidays, major political demonstrations, memorial remembrances of national figures like Martin Luther King Jr., ticker-tape parades for triumphant generals, postage stamps showing national symbols like the Statue of Liberty, anniversaries of historically significant events, and Olympic victories that reinforce our sense of superiority. The acting out can go beyond mere ceremony. It can bring us into contact with power capable of blessing us or saving us from danger. This aspect of myth leads us to the practical and ritual dimension, which we will discuss shortly. But first, consider another response to religious experience. Such experience gives rise to many questions, to which people seek rational answers as far as possible. The response to that quest is the doctrinal dimension.

DOCTRINAL AND PHILOSOPHICAL DIMENSION

Doctrine is a shorthand way of expressing the meaning of religious experiences and narratives. It has several functions: (a) it attempts to explain as clearly as possible what our experience and our narratives mean; (b) by expressing the worldview in as brief and clear a form as possible, it helps us to articulate and pass on to others our new vision of the world; (c) it helps us to see how the different parts of our worldview relate to each other and tries to resolve apparent inconsistencies; (d) it helps us to judge which new ideas and which new explanations of the worldview succeed in expressing, or at least do not do violence to, the central experiences and insights of the worldview; (e) it helps us to relate the worldview to new questions and new ideas in the larger society around us; (f) it helps us to know who is a member of the community, and who is not.

When one understands the doctrine of a particular worldview, one is in a position to understand why its members act the way they do. That is, doctrine influences ritual, ethics, and the social and material shape of the culture that the worldview generates. There is a classic saying in medieval theology: *Lex orandi, lex credendi*. It means that the way we pray (ritual) reveals what we believe (doctrine). So let us consider how doctrine shapes ritual.

PRACTICAL AND RITUAL DIMENSION

Ritual deals with actions that are in some way particular to a worldview; they are not just generic human actions like sleeping, waking, eating, and so on. Generic human actions can be done *in a particular way* as a result of a particular worldview, for example, the Zen Buddhist tea ceremony, which differs from a suburban career woman's microwaved morning tea; and then it takes on the character of a ritual. The meaning of a particular ritual depends on the worldview within which it takes place. When we think of rituals, we are most likely to think of prayer or public liturgical worship, which are forms of ritual common to Jewish, Christian, and Muslim worldviews. In these religions, prayer and liturgical rituals enact conversation with God or other spiritual beings.

Sacrifice

Animal and vegetable sacrifice is—or was—a widespread ritual among humans. Since it seems foreign to many of us, it is useful to examine its meaning. Sacrifice is usually considered to be a gift given to God or other spiritual beings. The primitive sense is that valuable things can be transferred over from this world to the spirit world in a variety of ways. Fire seems a divine medium for such exchange, since it is capable of turning solid, material things into spiritual substance. Killing an animal is another way to transfer value over to the spirit world, since death frees the soul, considered to be the most valuable part of the animal, from matter.

Worshipers transfer gifts to the spirit world in order to develop and maintain a relationship with God and spiritual beings. While to some people such gift giving may look like bribery, at its best it is an attempt to build a relationship of caring and trust: I show my good disposition to God by offering things of value in the confidence that God, now well disposed to me and by nature good, will meet my needs. To create such a relationship, I must not be cheap or deceitful in my gifts. The offerings must be "spotless," of good quality, such as I might offer to people of influence in human affairs. "First" things are especially valuable (first-born animals, the first armful of harvested grain) because the first symbolizes and stands for the whole. When I offer the "first," I am symbolically offering everything to God. More generally, rituals in many worldviews also offer God *nonmaterial* gifts: praise, obedience, service, time, and attention in prayer.

Festivals and Sacred Times

Rituals also celebrate sacred times: annual or recurrent celebrations commemorating key events whose power continues to reverberate in the community. Examples include Jews celebrating their rescue from bondage in Egypt at Passover and their reception of the Law of Moses at *Shavuot* (Jewish Pentecost); Christians celebrating the birth of Jesus at Christmas, his resurrection at Easter, the descent of the Holy Spirit at Christian Pentecost; Muslims celebrating the initial revelation to Muhammad during Ramadan, etc.

The significance of an event depends on the particular meaning that event has for the community celebrating it. The original historical event takes on a mythical aura, which carries its symbolic power down into the present time. For example, Jews celebrate the establishment of the state of Israel in 1948; Palestinians recall the same event as *al-Nakhba*—the catastrophe—because for over 750,000 Palestinians it led to the loss of their homes, farmlands, and political power. Similarly, Protestants of Northern Ireland annually celebrate their victory in the Battle of the Boyne by marching through Catholic neighborhoods; the Catholics experience these victory parades as humiliating.

ETHICAL AND LEGAL DIMENSION

How we choose to act depends on what we think the world is like, that is, on our doctrine. We understand that our actions have consequences. If we think, as Hindus and Buddhists do, that the world is an illusion that perpetuates suffering, we choose actions that separate us from the world. If we think, as some monotheists do, that a punitive God is watching our every move and comparing it with a list of rules, we choose to follow the rules. Religions think through the implications of their beliefs for action and express the results in moral judgments, rules, and laws.

Great Tradition, Little Tradition

The form in which a particular tradition is *taught* by its most enthusiastic leaders and practitioners, *developed* by major writers and apologists (propagandists), and contained in its *sacred and classic texts*, is called the *great tradition.* In contrast, the way common people—often only vaguely committed to its principles—are *actually living out* the worldview is called the *little tradition.* The rules of a religion or worldview make logical sense if you believe in the great tradition. But many members of the religion, even some of those who carefully think through its implications, are not so sure that the great tradition is right. They act on what they think is *really* true, rather than on what they *are supposed to* think is true.

Some religions base their laws and moral judgments closely on the original mystical experiences of the group. They speak of "divinely revealed laws." Muslims make this claim for the Quran, Jews make it for the Law of Moses (especially the core of the law as expressed in the "Ten Commandments"), and Christians make it for the teachings of Jesus of Nazareth as recorded in the New Testament Gospels.

If we think laws are divinely revealed, they may or may not seem logical. If we act against reality, say, by stepping out of a skyscraper's window, there are immediate consequences. But if we act against the arbitrary rules of someone bigger than we are, the consequences depend on whether that person is watching. On the other hand, the divinity that is revealing the laws may be interpreting reality, warning us of natural consequences that we cannot see with our limited vision.

In general, we are more likely to follow laws willingly if they make sense to us. If all we understand is the law and the authority who punishes law-breakers, we may follow the law, but resentfully. In the former case, our motivation is *intrinsic*, in the latter, *extrinsic*. Alfie Kohn has summarized social research showing that extrinsic motivation *reduces* a person's eagerness to do what the motivator is encouraging, even when that action is intrinsically attractive. Thus, high grades and gold stars, as well as low grades and ridicule, *reduce* students' eagerness to read, question, and learn in comparison with those who are not being extrinsically motivated. Young children are always asking, "Why?" By the time they are in college, they ask, "Will that be on the test?"[11] Religious founders, leaders, and sacred texts often say we will be rewarded and punished for our actions, but the founders themselves and their immediate followers weren't primarily motivated by rewards and punishments. They just fell in love with God, goodness, beauty, compassion, and truth for its own sake. Saint Augustine expressed his conviction that God's commands make sense when he said, "Love God, and do what you want." He did not mean that by loving God you can get away with anything, but that when you love God you end up wanting what God wants.

Nonreligious Moral Norms

Trying to avoid the sense that our laws are just the arbitrary whims of some God, and trying to avoid moral arguments between people of different religions, secular thinkers have proposed nonreligious moral norms. More recent thinkers have pointed out that these "secular" norms, too, depend on the worldviews of those who developed them. Still, it is useful to consider some of the norms they suggested.

John Stuart Mill and Utilitarianism

John Stuart Mill (d. 1873) developed a system that he called "utilitarianism." Actions are good because they are useful, principally because they *promote human happiness and prevent human pain. So the norm for good actions is whatever brings the greatest good to the greatest number of people.*

One problem with applying this principle is how to judge a case in which some people benefit at the expense of other people. Is it good to torture one or a few innocent people in order to save a large group of people? This is not an abstract question, since many governments routinely use torture to combat what they see as rebellions that threaten the "common good," even though torture is illegal in almost all countries of the world. After the terrorist attacks of September 11, 2001, the "Patriot Act" expanded the power of the U.S. government to arrest and hold suspects without charge. Supporters argue that these limitations on basic human rights are necessary to combat terrorism. Critics claim that they led to the abuses at Abu Ghraib in Iraq and at Guantanamo in Cuba.

Another problem with applying utilitarianism is determining what causes human happiness and what causes human pain. Do actions that increase one's possessions cause happiness? Possessions by themselves are neutral. It is how they are used that determines whether they increase human happiness. Furthermore, the amount of human pain or happiness contributed by an object or action is difficult to predict. Recent research shows that humans are not very good at predicting what will make them happy. We regularly exaggerate the *degree* of happiness or sadness that various situations will produce, and the *length of time* that these feelings will last. The bad news is that we will not be as happy as we imagine if we actually win the lottery, buy that new product, or get married, nor will our happiness last as long as we expect it to. The good news is that we won't be as devastated as we expect to be if we actually get fired, fail that test, or experience the death of a family member or close friend, nor will our grief last as long as we expect it to.[12]

Finally, it is especially difficult to *compare* the relative happiness we will experience from different situations. Which causes more human happiness: material, social, artistic, intellectual, or spiritual goods? Who causes more human happiness, a volunteer at a food shelter or a tutor who helps children? In order to answer these questions, one has to consider societal values and moral ideals, both of which vary from person to person and from group to group. For these reasons, utilitarian principles are difficult to apply to social questions and situations.[13]

Kant's Categorical Imperative

Immanuel Kant (d. 1804) developed a principle that he called the "categorical imperative." It has two parts: (1) we must act in such a way that our action could be a universal law for everyone; and (2) we must treat other human beings as ends in themselves, never as a means to something else. Note that the second part would answer the question about torture (see above) in the negative: torturing a few innocent people to bring good to others is using them as means to an end, not as ends in themselves.

John Rawls' Thought Exercise

John Rawls (d. 2002) has suggested a moral thought-exercise that can help us apply the first part of the categorical imperative. If you want to judge whether a particular law or way of acting is moral, imagine that you are determining it for a society that you are not now a part of but that you will become a part of; only you don't know in advance who you will be in that society. For example, if you are determining income-tax laws, you don't know whether you will be rich or poor, healthy or ill, young or old, employed or unemployed. Now, what kind of income-tax laws would you write?

Utilitarianism has been criticized for being based too exclusively on individualism, the belief that the individual is prior to society. In contrast, *Marxism* thinks that society is prior to and more important than the individual. The difference is important because rules are necessary to make a society work. Do we choose our morality simply on the basis that "if no one is hurt, it must be okay?" Or do we establish rules that will help create a cohesive society in which individual humans can be supported and brought to maturity?

MATERIAL AND ARTISTIC DIMENSION

People build and decorate material objects to help them live out in community the insights they have gained from their mystical experiences, which they celebrate in myth and understand according to their doctrine. For example, Greeks thought that gods lived in their temples, so the focal point of the temple was the central room at the far end of which a cult statue of the god was placed. Worshipers did not gather as a body *inside* the temple, so their temples were small compared with later Christian churches. The *Jewish* temple in Jerusalem followed this general pattern, although it did not have an image of God in the central room. When Jews gathered for worship, they did so in the courtyard *in front of* the temple. In contrast, *Christians* believe that God is present in the midst of their *assembly*. Their churches are places where the assembly gathers, so they have large interior spaces for that purpose. Muslims, like Christians, concentrate on the assembled faithful, so their mosques provide large indoor spaces for the faithful to gather, along with courtyards and other facilities.

Decorations on religious buildings do more than just make the building beautiful. They are designed to put worshipers in a prayerful state, or to affect them in other ways. Medieval Gothic architecture draws the eyes of worshipers skyward, encouraging them to think of God and heavenly things. Stained glass windows move the feelings of worshipers with the play of light and color while offering pictures of basic Christian narratives—the "Bible for the illiterate." In contrast, the bare meeting rooms of New England Congregational churches avoid distractions and concentrate the worshipers' attention on the preacher (or on God). Jewish and Islamic religious buildings avoid images of God and, in most cases, even of human beings. Muslim sacred art concentrates on geometric and floral designs and on the decorative effects of Arabic calligraphy.

Eastern Orthodox Christians have a particularly mystical understanding of religious art. They consider their paintings of religious figures, called icons, to be more than just reminders of holy people or illustrations of sacred stories. They are windows on the spirit world, windows through which a person can gain a spiritual experience. A painter needs a long period of apprenticeship painting secular subjects before he is allowed to paint an icon. When the apprenticeship is over, the painter fasts and prays before producing his first icon. After the icon is finished, it is shown to the congregation. Only if the congregation senses that the icon has the appropriate spiritual power is the painter allowed to exercise this ministry. Once he has entered into the ministry of painting icons, he no longer paints secular subjects.

Objects used in sacred worship—chalices, candlesticks, scrolls and books, altars, vestments (sacred clothing)—are beautifully made to reflect the value of the spiritual realities which they reflect and serve. The material dimension is closely linked with the ritual dimension. Rituals make use of material places, buildings, objects, sights, sounds, actions, and smells (like incense).

Music, Dance, Drama, and Recitation

Another material dimension is sound, alone or in combination with movement. Hymns, processions, dances, sacred drama, and sacred poetry are frequently used by religions to dispose worshipers to prayer and to inspire them to action. Native Americans and Africans make extensive use of dance as a religious act. Muslim Sufi dervishes use dance to induce a religious trance. Secular nations, too, make use of parades, national anthems, and patriotic songs to inspire citizens to sacrifice for the common good. Even silence can be a material dimension, for example, in a Quaker meeting.

Holy Places

Besides objects produced by humans, the material dimension also includes sacred *places.* Worshipers seek to come into contact with the power of key events by visiting the places where they happened. *Jews* claim that God gave them the land of Israel. Many of the narratives in their sacred books took place there, and their laws presuppose that Jews are living there along with other peoples. *Muslims* make the hajj to Mecca because the events that took place there in the time of Muhammad are central to Muslim identity. They venerate Jerusalem because Muhammad ascended to heaven from Jerusalem in his mystical visionary experience called the "night journey." *Christians* also value holy places, encouraging pilgrimages to the "Holy Land" and to other shrines, although their theology claims that God has overcome limitations of place, time, and persons. Mount Rushmore in the Black Hills is sacred to the *Dakota*: the carvings of four United States presidents on the side of the mountain are worse than just an insult—they desecrate a sacred place.

We will draw attention to these seven dimensions throughout the coming chapters on worldviews. But first, a few general cautions should be noted about this study.

TWO DANGERS

There are two dangers associated with studying other people's worldviews. One danger is failing to understand the other's worldview because we never see it in its own right, but only as an "error" in comparison with our own. If we fail to understand someone else's worldview, we will probably not understand why they think, feel, and act the way they do. As a result, we may act stupidly because we miscalculate their likely responses to our actions. The other danger is failing to understand that worldviews make claims on us: they want to be received as truth. Some people become so confused by the diversity of worldviews that they end up doubting that *any* worldview can be true — *without noticing that they are still living by a worldview:* a worldview that says the world is too complex to understand *and that it doesn't matter whether they understand it.* They still implicitly make choices on the basis of what they consider most valuable. They just don't *examine* their values.

1. Can We Be "Objective"?

In the past, scholars were confident that they could be "objective." "Postmodernism" has made us aware that earlier writers were influenced by unconscious presuppositions. Today, it is widely acknowledged that we are all influenced by our experiences and learning. The best we can do is to acknowledge our starting point as clearly as possible, make *an effort* to "set it aside" or "bracket it out," and try for a period of time to comprehend another's worldview as if it were our own. *Is it possible* for us to "set aside" our own presuppositions long enough to understand someone else's viewpoint well? Most of us know people who don't do this very well; they are constantly judging everything piece-by-piece on the basis of what they already "know to be true." You can be quite critical of an airplane if you compare it piece-by-piece with an automobile without knowing the airplane as a whole and understanding its purpose: the wings are too wide to go under the highway bridge, the wheels don't steer well. Other people seem able to *approximate* the ideal: to listen carefully to others long enough to see their point of view as a whole. In the end, they may not agree with it. (Sometimes, in fact, they do agree.) But they will *understand* it a lot better.

Many Muslim peace activists and scholars have been urging Westerners to work toward understanding Islam as a whole in relation to issues like just war, violence, and nonviolence. See chapter 5 on Muslim worldviews for a discussion of Chandra Muzaffar from Malaysia (president of JUST: the International Movement for a Just World). We need to understand not only *faraway* worldviews that we learn about from books, but also *"far-out"* worldviews held by friends and co-workers.

2. Can We Be Serious?

Although we "set aside" our own presuppositions long enough to understand someone else's, we should not leave our own convictions "set aside" forever. This book deals with some of the most important questions people ever ask. We encourage you to make the pursuit of these questions and their implications a personal quest. You may not be sure *what you* believe at the beginning of this study. Such a state of mind is common in the late teens and early twenties. We predict that, by the end of this book, the consideration of other people's worldviews will have helped you to clarify your own.

IS STUDYING OTHER RELIGIONS DANGEROUS TO ONE'S OWN FAITH?

Some people worry whether it is safe or morally right to study alien worldviews—whether they are being unfaithful to their own religion by reading about other religions. Some Christian churches teach that other religions are misguided human creations, or, worse, demonic. Historically, the Catholic Church considered itself to be the "one true Church" and the only way to salvation. Both of these attitudes affected the way colonial powers treated indigenous people and their traditions in the areas that they colonized. Certain groups within Islam have strongly resisted Western cultural and religious influences, calling the United States "the Great Satan." For the Catholic Church these attitudes began to change under the influence of worldwide missionary experience interpreted in light of new theological insights. These new views were published in documents of the Second Vatican Council, especially the *Declaration on the Relation of the Church to Non-Christian Religions (Nostra Aetate)* and the *Dogmatic Constitution on the Church (Lumen Gentium)*, which make positive comments on many of the worldviews we will be studying.[14]

COMPLEXITIES

With the exception of several Chinese and Japanese worldviews (Confucianism, Taoism, and Shinto), we will be studying together the classical religious patterns of the majority of the earth's peoples. But the picture is complicated by at least three factors:

1. The major classical worldviews interpenetrate each other: India is heavily Hindu, but many Muslims and Christians live there, too. The United States is thought of as Christian, but many other classical worldviews are strongly represented here, and their influence is growing.
2. All major worldviews exist in a multitude of forms. Expect to be frustrated in your attempt to determine the "*real*, or *true* form" of any worldview you examine.
3. Church leaders, scholars, and saints don't speak for all their members. Even some leaders, while *claiming* to accept the classic formulations of their worldview, often base their concrete actions on quite different principles. An early Christian writer reflects that pagans are impressed when they read that Christians love their enemies. Then they observe the lives of Christians they know and find that they don't even love their friends — and they laugh at us. So don't presume that what you read in the books is what people really believe and live out. Test the ideals against real lives.

When comparing worldviews, it is important to compare the great tradition of one with the great tradition of the other, and the little tradition of one with the little tradition of the other. I have heard students exclaim, "Hindus are *so* impressive! They apply their worldview to every aspect of life, not like Christians who go to church now and then and ignore their religion in the rest of their lives." In fact, many members of *all* worldviews are lax about their religion's core beliefs, while the "saints" in *all* religions or worldviews, even Christianity, apply their worldview to every aspect of life. We learn about our own worldview mostly from everyday, common folk, whereas we learn about other worldviews mostly from books written by or about the most committed members of those worldviews.

Be careful not to confuse "great tradition" with "important, educated people," and "little tradition" with "ordinary, everyday people." Some people who appear to be very "pious" may actually be living lives of selfish hypocrisy, seeking human approval and admiration. Many scholars and religious leaders live their lives based on the "little tradition" (what they consider "practical," what Walter Wink calls the "myth of redemptive violence"),[15] while some very ordinary people—laborers, peasants, office workers, unemployed—live their lives totally committed to and shaped by the "great tradition." They live the deep insights of the great tradition while suffering lives marked by inequities, discrimination, oppression, injustice, and violence, tempted and burdened by emotions of sadness, fear, and anger.

DO RELIGIONS CAUSE VIOLENCE?
CAN THEY PROMOTE PEACE?

Many people, especially since the end of the Cold War with the Soviet Union, claim that religion is more problem than solution, that religious convictions cause or intensify communal violence, that the major danger today is "fundamentalist" religious nationalisms, especially Islamic fundamentalism.[16] Here are some examples of religion used to justify violence:

> I will always be a warrior, this is the nature of a real Jew—the soldier is always under the skin. . . . Our goal is simple and absolute, it is set out in our scriptures, we must possess the land and conquer it. . . . There can be no debate about the word of God, [for God] defines the land as ours, His gift to us.[17]
>
> Violence is our only means of safeguarding the Protestant heritage. . . . The [Roman Catholic] Church sanctions terrorism, gunmen are given the last rights [*sic*], murderers are not excommunicated. . . . There is no such thing as an ordinary Catholic: because of their religion they are in league with the republican movement . . . if you scratch any Catholic you'll find a terrorist sympathizer under the surface.[18]
>
> The evil in the modern world is a result of weakness and the love of luxury. It is not a part of true Islam; it has spread from the outside world and tainted our leaders, who in turn lead the people into corrupt ways. . . . I will kill my own brother with the same force as I would any nonbeliever who opposes the war against evil.[19]

But we also find *peacemakers* motivated by religion: Mohandas K. Gandhi, Khan Abdul Ghaffar Khan, Martin Buber, Mother Teresa, Martin Luther King Jr., Dorothy Day, Thomas Merton, Marc Ellis, Farid Esack.

Douglas Johnston and Cynthia Sampson have edited a book titled *Religion, the Missing Dimension of Statecraft*, which has become influential in the U.S. Foreign Service. The book claims that secular prejudices have prevented international relations experts and practitioners from noticing the key role that religious individuals and groups have played in international crises. Influenced by their belief in the separation of church and state, U.S. scholars and practitioners of international relations have been embarrassed to talk about religion in *public* affairs. Restricting religion to *personal* affairs, they don't realize how much people in other parts of the world integrate religion with politics. This blind spot leads to uninformed policy decisions: diplomats fail to understand what is happening. A prime example is the 1979 American failure to anticipate Iranian students taking American diplomats hostage.

Johnston and Sampson's book gives seven case studies. Three involve nonviolent struggles which would have turned violent without church influence:

1. Cardinal Sin in the Philippines, when President Marcos lost power to Corazon Aquino. The Catholic Church helped to mobilize opposition and protect opposition leaders, while maintaining commitment to constitutional government.
2. Lutheran and other Christian churches in East Germany in 1989, as Communist rule was challenged. They offered sanctuary and aid to dissidents. Most of the "round tables" were chaired by Lutheran pastors.
3. The end of apartheid in South Africa. The Dutch Reformed Church had originally justified apartheid and helped to develop and implement its policies. The English-speaking churches, with a few notable exceptions, resisted *verbally,* but accepted apartheid *in practice.* At a 1990 interdenominational church meeting. the Dutch Reformed spokesman said, "Apartheid is a sin; my church has been guilty of distorting scripture to defend it; we ask your forgiveness." His confession began a process of confession and forgiveness, although a sizable black faction called it "cheap grace" and asked, "Where's the restitution?"

Three of the case studies involve ending wars that were already in progress:

4. The war between the Sandinista government of Nicaragua and the East Coast Mesquito Indians. The Moravian Church, whose pastors often served as mayors of Indian villages, mediated.
5. The Nigerian civil war when the eastern part of Nigeria tried to secede and form an independent state called Biafra. Several groups and individuals wanted to mediate, including Henry Kissinger and Lord Carrington, but only the Quakers were seen by both sides as having no political agenda. Operating on the belief that there is "a spark of God in everyone," the Quakers respected everyone on both sides. Their mediation did not prevent war entirely, but it did avert a bloodbath and led in the end to a magnanimous settlement and reconciliation.
6. The Rhodesian Civil War. The Catholic Church, Quakers, and Moral Rearmament mediated. Moral Rearmament had put together a "cabinet of conscience." The day before the government was to pass from Ian Smith to Robert Mugabwe, Ian Smith was poised to initiate a white coup. A nephew

of Mugabwe in the inner circle suggested that the two leaders meet. Ian Smith's son was also a member of the group. He persuaded his father to meet Mugabwe that night. The atmosphere was highly charged, but Mugabwe was a gracious host. Smith shared his concerns; Mugabwe accepted some of them, and the coup was averted.

The seventh case study concerns reconciliation after a major conflict ended, namely the reconciliation of France and Germany at the end of the Second World War:

7. Moral Rearmament held meetings of French and German leaders following World War II in Caux, Switzerland. Starting in 1946, they brought two thousand French together with three thousand Germans over a three-year period. The meetings also deliberately brought together union leaders and industrialists to mediate *class* resentments. The participants shared personal stories, cooked and washed dishes together (the hotel where they were meeting had no staff), and came to know each other as human beings. Konrad Adenauer and Robert Schumann, who met there, later developed the European Coal and Steel Community—the forerunner of the European Common Market and eventually of the European Union.[20]

Finally, note that religious worldviews are not the only ones that justify violence. Both Adolf Hitler and Josef Stalin appealed to anti-religious or secular worldviews to justify their oppressive governments and major wars. President George H. W. Bush justified the first war in the Persian Gulf by appeals to secular concepts of "human rights" and to free market economics (oil supplies and their influence on Western economies). So as we study worldviews, religious and secular, be attentive to the characteristics that may promote violence and to those that may promote reconciliation.

WHAT LIES AHEAD

In the chapters that follow, you will read primarily doctrinal descriptions of the major worldviews, along with some indication of how that doctrine influences action. Doctrine is the fastest way to encapsulate the meaning contained in a worldview. As you read, try to imagine what experiences lie behind those doctrines—what experiences they have grown out of. Then ask whether *your* worldview has been influenced by similar experiences, and what meaning *your* worldview may have given those experiences. Such an exercise can keep the worldviews you study from being reduced to just words. We will be paying special attention to the way doctrines influence actions toward justice and peace.

SUMMARY

Everyone lives their life on the basis of a particular worldview, although some worldviews are not religious, and some people have not thought their worldview through very well. The seven dimensions can help us understand worldviews—our own, and others that differ from ours. In order to understand other worldviews, we set aside our own worldview long enough to see the world through someone else's eyes. We can never be completely objective, but we can seriously consider other worldviews without fear. Worldviews interact with each other and appear in various forms. The worldview that actually determines how one acts (the "little tradition") may be quite different from the "official" worldview that one claims to espouse (the "great tradition"). Worldviews can sometimes be used to encourage violence. At other times, they can provide positive energy and insight to promote justice and peace. Many seemingly intractable conflicts have been resolved with the help of religious people committed to compassion and justice. Our study hopes to encourage such results.

KEY TERMS

categorical imperative
extrinsic motivation
great tradition
intrinsic motivation
little tradition

numinous
pan-en-henic
shaman
utilitarianism

DISCUSSION QUESTIONS

1. How would the seven dimensions of worldviews apply to the worldview your parents taught you as you were growing up? How did that worldview relate to the larger society—was it dominant, influential, or marginal?
2. How would the dimensions relate to the *official* worldview you currently hold (its *great tradition*)? How would they relate to the *actual* worldview you currently hold (its *little tradition*), including all the qualifications you make or disagreements you have with the official worldview you may be associated with?
3. What attitude do you hold toward "mystical experiences"? Do you know someone well who claims to have had one? (Include "near death" experiences and "born again" experiences.) Do you trust what they say? Have *you* had a mystical experience?

4. Do you find John Stuart Mills' "utilitarian ethic" helpful in deciding how to act? Kant's "categorical imperative"? How about John Rawls' "thought exercise"? What else do you use as criteria for determining your actions?
5. Do you know of examples where religion has been harmful, or where it has been helpful, in working for justice and peace? Can you explain why it has had one or the other effect?

NOTES

1. Second Vatican Council, *Nostra Aetate: Declaration on the Relationship of the Church to Non-Christian Religions*, par. 1.
2. Smart, *The World's Religions*, 11–26. See also Smart, *Worldviews*.
3. For an alternative set of principles, see Cannon, *Six Ways of Being Religious*.
4. You can read further details, including descriptions of the type of people having such experiences, some characteristics of the experiences themselves, and the effects on their lives, in chapter 6: "Are We a Nation of Mystics?" of his book *Death and Beyond*.
5. Neihardt, ed., *Black Elk Speaks*.
6. Moody, *Life after Life*, 26.
7. Frossard, *I Have Met Him*, 119–20.
8. Smart, *Worldviews*, 79.
9. McKenzie, *Myths and Realities*, 182–200.
10. Wink, *Engaging the Powers*, 13–31.
11. Kohn, *Punished by Rewards*.
12. Gertner, "The Futile Pursuit of Happiness." Based on research by the psychologists Daniel Gilbert of Harvard and Tim Wilson of the University of Virginia, the economist George Loewenstein of Carnegie-Mellon, and the psychologist (and Nobel laureate in economics) Daniel Kahneman of Princeton.
13. For several of the preceding points, I am indebted to Joseph Schultz, one of my students.
14. For *Lumen Gentium*, note especially sections 13–17.
15. Wink, *Engaging the Powers*, 13–31.
16. See, for example, chapter 6, "Why Religious Confrontations Are Violent," in Juergensmeyer, *The New Cold War?*
17. Hinde and Watson, *War: A Cruel Necessity? The Bases of Institutionalized Violence*. Used by permission of I. B. Tauris © 1995.
18. Hinde and Watson, *War: A Cruel Necessity?*, 172. Used by permission of I. B. Tauris © 1995.
19. Hinde and Watson, *War: A Cruel Necessity?*, 174. Used by permission of I. B. Tauris © 1995.
20. Johnston has founded the International Center for Religion and Diplomacy to develop and apply his ideas: www.icrd.org/ (accessed March 2, 2007). See also his new book, *Faith-Based Diplomacy: Trumping Realpolitik*.

SUGGESTIONS FOR FURTHER READING

Cannon. *Six Ways of Being Religious: A Framework for Comparative Studies of Religion.*

Ferguson. *War and Peace in the World's Religions.*

Frossard. *I Have Met Him: God Exists.*

Gertner. "The Futile Pursuit of Happiness."

Greeley. *Death and Beyond.*

Hinde and Watson, eds. *War: A Cruel Necessity?*

James. *The Varieties of Religious Experience: A Study in Human Nature.*

Johnston, ed. *Faith-Based Diplomacy: Trumping Realpolitik.*

Johnston and Sampson, eds. *Religion, the Missing Dimension of Statecraft.*

Juergensmeyer. *The New Cold War? Religious Nationalism Confronts the Secular State.*

Kohn. *Punished by Rewards: The Trouble with Gold Stars, Incentive Plans, A's, Praise, and Other Bribes.*

McKenzie. *Myths and Realities.*

Mill. *Utilitarianism.*

Moody. *Life After Life: The Investigation of a Phenomenon—Survival of Bodily Death.*

Neihardt, ed. *Black Elk Speaks.*

Rawls. *A Theory of Justice.*

Schuhmacher, et al., eds. *The Encyclopedia of Eastern Philosophy and Religion: Buddhism, Hinduism, Taoism, Zen.*

Second Vatican Council. *Lumen Gentium: Dogmatic Constitution on the Church.*

———. *Nostra Aetate: Declaration on the Relationship of the Church to Non-Christian Religions.*

Smart. *Worldviews: Crosscultural Explorations of Human Beliefs.*

———. *The World's Religions.* 2nd ed.

Wink. *Engaging the Powers: Discernment and Resistance in a World of Domination.*

Chapter One

Hindu Worldviews

"The Spirit is neither born nor does it die at any time. It does not come into being, or cease to exist. It is unborn, eternal, permanent, and primeval. The Spirit is not destroyed when the body is destroyed."

—*Bhagavad-Gita 2:20*

"Just as a person puts on new garments after discarding the old ones; similarly, the living entity or the individual soul acquires new bodies after casting away the old bodies."

—*Bhagavad-Gita 2:22*[1]

EXPERIENTIAL AND EMOTIONAL DIMENSION

Many Westerners first hear about "mysticism" in a context of Eastern religious thought, perhaps through the New Age Movement, Hare Krishna, or Transcendental Meditation. Foreign ideas like yogis, reincarnation, the illusory nature of everyday reality, "mind over matter," and astral projection tease Western minds.

Hinduism is familiar with the *pan-en-henic* experience in which the mystic feels united with all reality. Many yogic exercises are designed to produce such an experience. Rather than fear or awe in the presence of an Other, the mystic loses the sense of self as distinct from the rest of creation. Yogis believe this shows what the world is really like. Here is an example from Yogananda's *Autobiography of a Yogi*:

The flesh was as though dead; yet in my intense awareness I knew that never before had I been fully alive. My sense of identity was no longer narrowly

1

confined to a body but embraced the circumambient atoms. People on distant streets seemed to be moving gently over my own remote periphery. The roots of plants and trees appeared through a dim transparency of the soil; I discerned the inward flow of their sap.

The whole vicinity lay bare before me. My ordinary frontal vision was now changed to a vast spherical sight, simultaneously all-perceptive. Through the back of my head I saw men strolling far down Rai Ghat Lane, and noticed also a white cow that was leisurely approaching. . . .

All objects within my panoramic gaze trembled and vibrated like quick motion pictures. . . . An oceanic joy broke upon calm endless shores of my soul. The Spirit of God, I realized, is exhaustless Bliss; His body is countless tissues of light. A swelling glory within me began to envelop towns, continents, the earth, solar and stellar systems, tenuous nebulae, and floating universes. The entire cosmos, gently luminous, like a city seen afar at night, glimmered within the infinitude of my being.[2]

HISTORICAL PERIODS

Diversity of Hindu Thought

Western writers invented the term "Hinduism" to denote a religion. The adjective "Hindu" simply refers to the Indian subcontinent. Hinduism encompasses the highly diverse beliefs of the majority of the people who live there. Despite this diversity, certain concepts and viewpoints are widely held. In the 19th century, Ramakrishna and Vivekananda developed a synthesis of Hindu thought which more closely resembles Western ideas of a "religion."

The Early Vedic Period (3000–1000 BCE)[3]

The earliest stages of religion in India are not well known. The first stage for which we have much evidence is the aftermath of invasions by *Aryans* from the Northwest. The invaders gained control over the local inhabitants, the *Dravidians*. The Aryan priests, the *Brahmins*, offered sacrifices and guarded the secret, inspired revelations called *Shruti*.

Originally the Brahmins worshiped and sacrificed to many gods—traditionally 330 million. The Brahmins were the religious specialists who could, by their sacrifices, gain power (*brahman*) for those who employed them. Among key early gods were Indra, god of war; Varuna, god of cosmic order and judgment; Agni, god of fire (who transformed sacrifices so that they could pass over from our world to the world of spirits); and Soma, god of an intoxicating juice used in rituals.

The Pre-Classical Period (1000 BCE–100 CE)

In a later period, the key gods were three: *Brahma*, the creator god; *Vishnu*, the protector—a kindly deity who appears on earth in diverse forms (such as *Krishna* and *Rama*); and *Shiva,* the destroyer, who is also associated with storms. The three relate to the natural cycle of living things: birth, living and dying. All living things not only decay but also remain as the eternal source for the regeneration of life. These three gods form a sort of trinity called the Trimurti or *trivarga*.

Gradually in the pre-classical period, under the influence of *sramanas* or wandering ascetics, religious thinkers began to believe in one God who appeared in a multitude of forms. Thinking of this God as the foundation of everything, they named him *Brahman* (Power). This change illustrates how *doctrine,* which explains *narrative or myth*, can change over time. It also illustrates the difference between the "great tradition" as taught by the sramanas and the "little tradition," which survives among many common people today. The situation is complicated: beliefs vary widely from place to place and among different peoples.

Terms Clarified

There are five terms that are easily confused because their spellings are similar and their meanings may overlap:

Brahma: creator god, early period (capital B);

brahman: spiritual power (small b, small p), for example, the ability of a Brahmin to make sacrifices and prayers that would effectively control spiritual reality on behalf of those who ask for his help;

Brahman: Power (capital B, capital P), the one source or ground of being in the universe which manifests itself in the many gods of tradition;

Brahmana: two meanings: (1) Brahmin, a Hindu priest; (2) part of the Shruti: inspired traditions used by the Brahmins to regulate their rituals; and

Brahmin: a Hindu priest = a Western form for the term Brahmana in its first meaning, an attempt by Westerners to avoid confusion.

Later Historical Developments

In the *classical period* of Hindu development (100–1000 CE), *Buddhism* (the subject of chapter 2) challenged the views of the Brahmins, initially flourished in India, moved out to other countries, and finally withered in India where it had begun. In part Indian Buddhism became too formalistic, and in part the Brahmins took over many of its elements in a new period of Hindu creativity. Thus Buddhist insights in India were absorbed into the larger Hindu worldview.

In the *medieval period* (1000–1750 CE), *Islam* (the subject of chapter 5) entered India and became very influential, first in the north but eventually under the Moghul empire (1520–1857) over much of the subcontinent. The Moghul emperor Akbar (d. 1605) encouraged Hindu-Muslim integration as well as interfaith dialogue in his House of Worship.

In the *modern period* (from about 1750 to today) Great Britain gained first economic and then political control over India, and Christian missionaries exercised a strong influence on Indian society. In the 20th century, Mohandas Gandhi developed *satyagraha,* or "truth-force," as an active nonviolent way of life that overcame British rule and led to Indian independence and the creation of Pakistan in 1947.

NARRATIVE OR MYTHIC
DIMENSION—INCLUDING SACRED WRITINGS

After a mystical experience, *myth* attempts to *describe* what happened. The *doctrinal* dimension comes later as theologians try to *explain* that mystical literature. The *narrative/mythic* dimension gave rise in Hinduism to secret, inspired literature, the *Shruti*, and more public, noninspired but still sacred writings, the *Smriti*.

The Shruti were for centuries handed down orally. They included first of all the *Vedas* (inspired hymns), which are hymns to various gods (in the *Rgveda,* collected about 1000 BCE); hymns for ritual reenactments of cosmic events (in the *Yajurveda)*, for example, rituals designed to ensure the authority and power of the king; and practical charms and prayers used by the Brahmins to exercise spiritual power on behalf of those who sought their help (in the *Atharvaveda*).

Later the *Brahmanas* were developed (prose instructions for the use of the hymns, rather like Catholic "rubrics" for the liturgy, but also containing legends). Much later, between about 800 and 400 BCE, the *Upanishads*, also known as the *Vedanta* ("End of the Vedas"—esoteric teaching), were composed, radically reinterpreting the Vedas under the impact of Buddhist and Jain thought. Much of what we think of today as Hindu doctrine is based on the Upanishads.

Of the noninspired Smriti, the most important are the great national epic poems the *Ramayana* and the *Mahabharata*, which recount the lives and exploits of gods and heroic humans. The *Bhagavad-Gita*, probably the most widely read Hindu scripture, is part of the *Mahabharata*.

DOCTRINAL AND PHILOSOPHICAL DIMENSION: BASIC DOCTRINAL POSITIONS

When we ask how Hindus *explain* their mystical experiences and their mythical narratives of the reality behind these experiences, we are moving into the area of doctrine and philosophy: the Upanishads and modern commentaries, for example, commentaries on the *Bhagavad-Gita*. These *explanations* change and develop over time even as the *experiences* and their mythical representations remain the same. In the Christian experience, these changes are called the *development of doctrine*.

In the pre-classical period, a number of concepts important to modern Hinduism developed, influenced by the new and challenging worldviews of the Buddhists and the Jain. Among these concepts are *reincarnation,* or the *transmigration of souls*, *karma*, *maya*, *samsara*, and *moksha*, and the unity of *Brahman* and *Atman*.

Reincarnation

A key concept very widely held in India is the *transmigration of souls*, often called *reincarnation*. This is the belief that when a person dies her soul enters another body and is reborn as a baby. *Reincarnation* refers to the transition from one *human* body to another. *Transmigration* more generally refers to the transition from one *physical form* to another, where the forms may be human, animal, vegetable, or even mineral (what Westerners would consider "nonliving"). The Hindu word for this cycle of transmigration through many lives—in fact, millions of lives—is *samsara*. One is not always reincarnated immediately after death. There are heavens of varying degrees of happiness and hells of varying horror. But one cannot remain forever in any of them. One's "merit" (or "demerit," negative karma) gets gradually used up, and we need to be reincarnated to earn more merit, or to escape the cycle of merit and demerit entirely through the liberation called moksha.

Karma

The "merit" or "demerit" that we accrue as the result of our good or bad actions in life is called karma. More generally, karma is our actions and the results they cause in us. Good actions produce good results, bad actions, bad results. These results stay with us and continue to affect our present and future lives. What form we are reincarnated into, or what heaven or hell we spend time in, is determined by our karma at the time of death.

Maya, Samsara, and Moksha

According to the Hindu "great tradition," the world of our sense experience, despite its apparent solidity and reality, is an illusion in comparison with the reality of God. *Maya*, or "playful illusion," deceives us into thinking that what we see is ultimate reality. The goal of human life, then, is not an infinite series of reincarnations, not even progressively more desirable reincarnations, but escape from the depressing round of births and deaths (*samsara*). This escape is called *moksha*. It leads to a permanent union or merger with God as a result of which one will no longer be reincarnated.

The proper way to attain moksha is a matter of dispute among Hindus. The answer depends in part on what they think the nature of reality is—and there are variations among Hindus over this point. In any case, the search for God and union with God is called *yoga*, and the person who undertakes this search is called a *yogi*. An aspiring yogi needs the help of a more experienced elder yogi (similar to a Christian "spiritual director") called a *guru*. The mystical experience of Yogi Paramahansa Yogananda described above was triggered when his guru Sri Yukteswar "struck gently on [his] chest above the heart."[4] There are as many types of yoga as there are theories about the nature of reality and the way to attain moksha. This diversity illustrates the connection between *doctrine* on the one hand, and *practice and ritual* on the other.

Many common people consider the escape of moksha to be beyond their grasp in their current state; therefore, they concentrate on gaining merit so that they will be reincarnated in a more desirable state, such as that of a rich male. Others use their religious prayers and rituals primarily to improve their fortunes and guard against misfortune in this present incarnation, as in the charm quoted below, to secure the love of a woman. Many prayers of the *Atharvaveda* speak to these goals, while the later philosophical explanations of the Upanishads tend toward moksha as a goal. "The rituals enjoined in the Vedas are applicable to the realm of dharma, but the one who seeks liberation does not merely desire a place in heaven; he is in search of ultimate Reality itself."[5]

PRACTICAL AND RITUAL DIMENSION

Brahmins and Brahman

Brahmins use sacrifices and incantations to wield spiritual power on behalf of their clients. This power can assure success in business, gain the attention of a lover, or protect one from attack. Here is an example from the *Atharvaveda*:

Book VI, Hymn 8. Charm to secure the love of a woman.

Figure 1.1.   Hindu Temple of Shiva, Mylapore, near Chennai (Madras), India. Courtesy David Whitten Smith, 26 January 1998.

1. As the creeper embraces the tree on all sides, thus do thou embrace me, so that thou, woman, shalt love me, so that thou shalt not be averse to me!
2. As the eagle when he flies forth presses his wings against the earth, thus do I fasten down thy mind, so that thou, woman, shalt love me, so that thou shalt not be averse to me.
3. As the sun day by day goes about this heaven and earth, thus do I go about thy mind, so that thou, woman, shalt love me, so that thou shalt not be: averse to me.[6]

The success or failure of these prayers and rituals is part of the experiential or mystical dimension which leads followers to have or lose confidence in their god or gods.

How to Gain Moksha

Deeply spiritual Hindus are more concerned to attain moksha than to gain advantage in this life. In general, Hindus believe that moksha can be attained through works (*karma*), devotion (*bhakti*), or knowledge (*jnana*).

One attains moksha through *works* (*karma*) when one learns how to act well but without "holding on to the fruits" of that action. That is, one acts well without attempting to manipulate or control other people or circumstances, and without being anxious about what the results of the action will be. One *cares* about what the results will be, but one *does not fret* about it. One is not *attached* to the action or its results, so one does not develop either good or bad karma as a result of that action. This is a key insight of the *Bhagavad-Gita*, and we will see Gandhi reflecting on this insight below.

Note that *good* karma prevents moksha by sending one to a heaven or a better incarnation, just as *bad* karma prevents moksha by sending one to a hell or a worse incarnation. It is our "attachment" to the ego-centered attractions and desires of this life that keeps our atman from uniting with Brahman.

Bhakti refers to fervent *devotion* and surrender to God (seen as personal) or to a particular god. The path of bhakti, combined with the pursuit of good karma and the avoidance of bad karma, is the path followed by most Hindus. Many Hindu rituals and feasts, in the temple and at home, are expressions of bhakti to particular gods, and most Hindus center their spiritual practice around these traditional rituals and feasts."Worship of the Personal God is recommended as the easier way open to all, the weak and the lowly, the illiterate and the ignorant. The sacrifice of love is not so difficult as the tuning of the will to the Divine purpose or ascetic discipline or the strenuous effort of thinking."[7]

"The weak and the lowly, the illiterate and the ignorant" are not the only people who make use of Hindu rituals. When I visited Nepal, my host—a practicing lawyer—knelt down before a niche in a temple we were visiting. When I asked him to explain the significance of his action, he replied that he was kneeling at the shrine of a god associated with skill in speech and argument, and he was asking the god to share that skill with him so that he could more effectively defend his poor clients.

What kind of *knowledge* (*jnana*) might lead to moksha depends on our doctrine or understanding of what reality is like. A major tendency today, which probably developed under the influence of Buddhism, is called *Advaita Vedanta*.

Advaita Vedanta[8]

While it is only one of several possible Hindu ways to understand reality, Advaita Vedanta has had a major influence on modern Hindu theology. Advaita Vedanta argues that (a) all humans share one soul or Self (called *atman*: the eternal and imperishable part of each human), (b) all gods are appearances of one God (this one God behind all gods is called *Brahman*), and (c) God (Brahman) and Self (atman) are identical. The name of this group indicates its key belief: *A-dvaita* ("un-divided," or nondualistic) *Vedanta* (end/explanation of the Vedas). (Note that Sanskrit and English, as "Indo-European" languages, share common roots: *dvaita*/divided and *anta*/end.) "Nondualistic" means that there is no dualism or distinction between my atman and Brahman. Those who hold this doctrinal position express their insight by saying that Brahman is identical with atman.

For those who follow Advaita Vedanta, moksha is attained by jnana when one realizes through a *personal experience* that her *atman* (as well as everyone else's *atman)* is identical with Brahman. One actively seeks this experience through the practice of meditation best learned with the guidance of a *guru* (a sort of "spiritual director"). This insight is not evident to sense perception. Having come to this experiential realization, the person will no longer be reincarnated at death.

Remember, not all Hindus hold this view of reality: there are also adherents of Dvaita (dualistic) Vedanta, who maintain that there is an eternal and real distinction between Brahman, the cosmos, and the individual atman. A. C. Bhaktivedanta Swami Prabhupada, the founder of the Hare Krishna movement (International Society for Krishna Consciousness), seems to hold this position.[9] There are also other, more complex, positions on this relationship.

The Advaita identification of Brahman and atman offers an argument in favor of absolute *ahimsa* or nonharm to sentient beings: if my deepest reality (atman) is identical with yours and with the ground of all being, then when I injure you I injure myself as well. But the argument is weakened by the observation that nothing I do to you can truly injure your atman because the "atman" is the eternal soul that is unaffected by the death and destruction of the physical body. In the *Bhagavad-Gita*, this is one reason Krishna tells Arjuna not to shrink from killing in battle.

Note that the attainment of this state of moksha must occur through our actions in a life on earth, as opposed to our actions in one of the many temporary heavens or hells. If moksha has not been attained by the time of death, one will eventually have to be reincarnated to continue one's progress toward moksha. Periods spent in any of the various heavens or hells gradually *use up* good karma (in heaven) or bad karma (in hell). Only in the human stage on earth is one capable of *overcoming* the formation of karma through disinterested action according to one's dharma (duty of one's caste and state in life) or of gaining the required knowledge (*jnana*) to enter moksha.

SOCIAL AND INSTITUTIONAL DIMENSION

The Caste System

When the Aryans conquered the earlier population of India, the Dravidians, they introduced or intensified a division of society into four distinct classes that tended to maintain the new power structures. These classes are called *varna*, translated as "caste" in English. But the English word "caste" is also used of a later and much more complex division. Here we are using the word in the earlier sense. The root meaning of the word "varna" is "colors." It seems to refer to differences between the light-skinned Aryan invaders and the dark-skinned Dravidian earlier inhabitants. This connection relates caste divisions to race divisions as found in other societies like that of the United States.

The *Brahmin* priests were the highest caste of the new society. Under them were the *Kshatriya* or warrior caste (which included politicians and civil authorities) and the *Vaishya* or merchant, artisan, and farmer caste. Members of these three castes became "twice-born" by an initiation at adolescence. The fourth caste was the *Shudra* or servant caste. Under all four castes were the *outcastes* or "untouchables," today usually referred to as the "scheduled caste" (pronounced in the British fashion as "sheduwuld"), or as the "Dalits."

The name *untouchable* developed from the fear of caste members that they would be polluted by contact with the outcastes—in some cases even by contact with their shadows. In reaction to this notion, and in resistance to its practical effects, Gandhi devised the name *Harijan,* meaning "Friends of God." The late colonial British and post-colonial Indian secular governments coined the term *scheduled caste* as a neutral name that carries no opprobrium and indicates that they are eligible through affirmative action to receive certain benefits. The government similarly uses *scheduled tribe* to refer to indigenous tribes that continue to follow their animist hunter-gatherer way of life. About 16% of Indians are members of the "scheduled caste"; 7% belong to "scheduled tribes."

Members of *scheduled tribes* call themselves *adivasi,* which means "original dwellers" and is roughly equivalent to the term *indigenous.* (Note that Ojibwa Native Americans call themselves *Anishinaabeg*, meaning "original people.") The *adivasi* are proud of their native cultures and do not consider themselves to be second-class. Some wealthy, upper-class conservatives say the so-called *adivasi* are only *vanavasi* ("forest dwellers"), thus denying their claim to be "original dwellers" with the rights which that claim might imply.

The members of the *scheduled caste* have themselves decided that none of these terms accurately describes them. Even Gandhi's attempt to raise their dignity with the term *Harijan* seemed to them to be patronizing. They refer to themselves as *Dalit*—a strong word that means "oppressed, ground down"—to emphasize that their condition is the result of unjust actions by others. We will most often refer to them by the name they themselves prefer.

In general, it was the successful Aryan invaders who made up the Brahmin, Kshatriya, and Vaishya castes. The conquered population provided the Shudra caste and the outcastes.

Some conservatives dispute this history, claiming that the light-skinned Aryans were the original inhabitants of India and the darker Dravidians were outside immigrants. They also maintain that the system of varna or caste is of divine origin and thus unchangeable. Therefore light-skinned Indians should have a higher status because they are the "real" or "original" Indians. The dispute illustrates how theology and history can be used or abused to support one party's claim to status and power.

Caste is often related to karma. The thought is that one's caste and one's good or bad experiences in the present life are the results of karma from previous lives. This belief attempts to explain the serious inequalities of opportunity and fortune which we observe in the world. (Note the relation between experience and doctrine.) It tends to support the status quo, favoring those in positions of power and privilege.

Marxist thinkers, judging Hinduism from outside through their own worldview, might well claim that the concept of karma was invented by Aryan elites to justify their control and to suppress resistance by the lower classes. If I can convince myself and others that the poor are only working out their bad karma from misdeeds in previous lives, I have little incentive to share my wealth and power with them. Such sharing might even reduce their ability to "use up" bad karma and thus cause their next incarnation to be worse than it would otherwise be.

On the other hand, it would be a mistake to conclude from the concept of karma that one need do nothing to help suffering people. Yet many Hindus do draw that conclusion. Some of them accuse Christians of only helping poor Hindus so that they can convert them to Christianity. They feel that the Christian church is exploiting the poverty and the social discrimination of the caste system to serve its own agenda of expanding its religious base in India. Christians could challenge Hindus with the following considerations: we earn good karma from good acts, and helping suffering people is a good act. Ignoring or oppressing suffering people is a bad act. People who oppress the poor could well develop bad karma, which could lead them to share the ill fortune of the poor when they are reincarnated.

Another way to challenge Hindus is to point to the examples of Mohandas Gandhi and Vinoba Bhave (see below), who appealed to Hindu principles to support their commitment to the poor. Yet Gandhi supported the caste system, which put him at odds with B. R. Ambedkar, a Dalit who converted to Buddhism. Gandhi supported Indian laws of "reservation" that assigned a certain quota of school and government positions to depressed classes (a form of affirmative action). Ambedkar wanted to abolish the caste system altogether — he was one of Gandhi's most vocal and articulate critics.[10]

Some worldviews, such as that of Burmese Buddhism, which we will study in the next chapter, believe that helping others earns good karma only if those we help are good people. Such a belief leads laypeople to help holy monks but not poor people, who presumably are to blame for their own suffering.[11]

Four Stages of Life

One tradition in India supposes that the members of the twice-born castes (Brahmin, Kshatriya, or Vaishya; but not Shudra or Dalit) go through four ideal stages of life. The first stage is youth as a student, where one is under the direction of others. The second stage is marriage, where the procreation and rearing of children and participation in society, including the attainment of comfortable affluence, is the center of attention. The third stage is withdrawal to the forest for study of the Vedas and meditation—a sort of retirement that allows younger people to take over active control of society. The fourth stage is that of the detached pilgrim or *sannyasin* (a sort of end-of-life *sramana*), who wanders as an ascetic seeking God or moksha.

ISSUES FOR JUSTICE AND PEACE

The Vedic worldview accepted war as the responsibility or duty (*dharma*) of the Kshatriya or warrior class and as essential to good order. Killing in animal sacrifice and in war were not considered to violate *ahimsa* (nonharm to living things). In fact, the *Bhagavad-Gita* seems on the surface to justify war in the face of various pacifist arguments.

The *Bhagavad-Gita* is, for many Hindus, the most influential of their holy books. Technically it is part of the *Smriti,* or noninspired traditions complementing the *Shruti,* or inspired books. As noted earlier, among these Smriti are two great national epics, the *Ramayana* and the *Mahabharata.* The *Bhagavad-Gita* (often abbreviated as just the "Gita," literally "The Song") is one section of the *Mahabharata.* It has been the basis for many commentaries that explain Hindu beliefs.

In the *Gita*, Arjuna the hero is contemplating a battlefield just before the battle begins. He tells his chariot driver, Krishna (who happens to be an *avatar*, or earthly manifestation, of the god Vishnu), that he will not fight because he does not want to harm his kin even though they are attacking him. In response, Krishna instructs Arjuna that it is right for him to fight, using the following arguments among others: (a) You are Kshatriya, and so it is your dharma or duty to fight. If you disobey your dharma, you will suffer bad karma. (b) The soldiers you kill today will not really die. Only their bodies will die—their atman will survive untouched and be reincarnated. You cannot pierce, hack, burn, or in any way harm the atman. (c) Even if you hold back and refuse to fight, the soldiers you would have killed will still die in some other way, because it is their fate (decreed by Vishnu) to die today. So they will still die, but you will fail your dharma.

As the *Gita* continues, we do find that there are rules about war that are similar to Western just war principles but differently justified. If the soldiers are fighting to carry out their dharma, they must do it correctly. So, for example, cavalry may attack other cavalry, but they must not attack foot soldiers. Most Hindus have thought that the *Gita* and other Hindu traditions allow and even urge war in certain circumstances. This fact is illustrated by the history of Hindu civilization. Most Hindu rulers have used war, and most of their citizens have supported it. But some Hindus believe that ahimsa is absolute and forbids both war and animal sacrifice under any circumstances. These Hindus gain their conviction from the ascetic, or *sramanic,* traditions, especially those influenced by Buddhist or Jain thought.

The best known of these anti-war Hindus was Mohandas K. Gandhi. Another was Vinoba Bhave, the most famous of his followers and successors. Note that discussion of "just war" (the use of war to end a war or injustice, as advocated by Krishna to Arjuna) implies that "the ends justify the means." Gandhi reversed the causal order, claiming that "the means justify (or shape) the end." As an example, he gave the relationship between the seed and the tree.

SPOKESPERSONS FOR JUSTICE AND PEACE

Mohandas (Mahatma) Gandhi

Gandhi is remembered especially for his highly successful campaign of active nonviolence to free India from British rule. As his success and fame grew, he came to be called "Mahatma," a term of respect which means "great soul."

He grew up in a Hindu family in close contact with Muslims and in an area where Jains were also influential. (*Jains* are followers of Jainism, which has a strong commitment to nonviolence similar to that of Buddhism.) He studied law in England, where he had to confront Christianity and Western ideas. It was also here that he read the *Bhagavad-Gita* for the first time—in English translation. After his studies he returned as a lawyer to India, where he had very little success in law. He then went to South Africa to defend Indian citizens who were being mistreated. There he came to see the injustices of the South African laws, discovered how powerfully ahimsa could confront those laws, and directed a successful resistance movement against them.

Gandhi interpreted *ahimsa* in a broad sense to rule out killing in war. He had to deal with the *Bhagavad-Gita* because it seemed to demand war.

1. First, he interpreted the *Gita* as a spiritual message dealing with the inner human struggle within each individual, not with physical, external war. We

need to overcome our resistance to internal struggle and our reluctance to "put to death" habits and tendencies that are so familiar to us that they seem to be "family" or "relatives." Gandhi shares this interpretation with many other interpreters.[12]

2. Second, the *Mahabharata as a whole*, in dealing at length and in detail with the historical Mahabharata war, illustrates the futility of war as a means of solving problems and bringing justice because, at the end of the war after much death and suffering, the situation is worse than it was at the beginning. Thus, it illustrates the conviction that resorting to violence, by the bad karma it produces, outbalances the good karma that one is attempting to achieve.[13]

3. Third, Gandhi notes that Arjuna is not opposed to killing other humans *in general*, since he has willingly fought in other wars. He is just opposed to killing *his relatives*. This is selfish favoritism. If war is acceptable, then it must be acceptable even if our family and relatives are among those killed.[14]

To those who objected that Gandhi had no qualifications for interpreting the *Gita*, he agreed in terms of scholarship, but maintained that the more important qualifications for interpretation are not scholarship but personal commitment to *live* the message of the *Gita* and one's experience in attempting to do so. He said, "I have something far more powerful than argument, namely, experience . . . an effort to enforce the meaning [of the *Gita*] in my own conduct for an unbroken period of forty years" and, "It is a misuse of our intellectual energy and a waste of time to go on reading what we cannot put into practice."[15]

Gandhi's justification raises the interesting question of which is more important for understanding religious traditions and convictions: careful scholarship or personal spiritual commitment. Modern Western scholars seek knowledge that is dependent only on careful study, not on the holiness or personal life of the scholar, and that can thus be repeated by any scholar carefully using the same scholarly methods. Others claim that you can't really understand what the words mean unless you have personally experienced the reality they are talking about. Our conviction is that both careful scholarship and personal spiritual engagement are essential to understand spiritual realities. We have experienced the weakness of people who have one without the other; perhaps you have, too. At the same time, everyone has something valuable to teach us.

Gandhi held that the eternal truths contained in the *Gita,* like those contained in all sacred writings, are filtered through two imperfect media: (1) a human prophet, and (2) the interpreters who attempt to explain the prophets.

So Gandhi felt justified in re-interpreting the prophets based on his own experience. He went so far as to say, "I believe that the teaching of the *Gita* does not justify war, even if the author of the *Gita* had intended otherwise" and,

> Let it be granted, that according to the letter of the *Gita* it is possible to say that warfare is consistent with renunciation of fruit. [That is to say, the *Gita* claims that one can engage in warfare while remaining detached from emotions like greed, hatred, rage, and fear; and from concern for victory or defeat.] But after 40 years of unremitting endeavor fully to enforce the teaching of the *Gita* in my own life, I have, in all humility, felt that perfect renunciation is impossible without perfect observance of ahimsa in every shape and form.[16]

Positively, Gandhi believed that the essence of the *Gita* was contained in the last twenty stanzas of chapter 2. This section describes how one gains perfect control over self along with inner peace *by learning how to remain detached* from what is pleasing and what is displeasing. Thus we can act without the influence of selfish desire or fear. If we can. As Gandhi might say, it is simple, but not easy.

To those who believed that the historical Krishna was an avatar or incarnation of the god Vishnu and therefore was perfect in all respects, Gandhi responded that *every* human is potentially an incarnation of the Absolute God because every atman is God. Krishna was not "ontologically" different from any other human, just more developed. The *literary* Krishna is perfect, but this literary figure is imaginative. The *historical* Krishna, like any human, despite his immense merit and consequent state of moksha or near-moksha was still only in the final stages of being "on the way" to perfection. Thus, the literary Krishna urges *inner spiritual* battle against evil, and this advice is perfect. The historical Krishna urged *outer, physical* battle, and this advice was flawed, as is evident from the long-term effects of the war.

Gandhi's interpretation of the *Gita* is unusual, and few Hindu scholars have followed him so far as to de-legitimize war. But his theory and practice of nonviolence have been much more successful and influential.

Returning to India with these new ideas and considerable fame, he began to use the techniques of ahimsa to challenge the British colonial rule of India. For Gandhi, ahimsa was more than a technique; it was a way of life. He learned how to use provocative actions to force a confrontation, and how to make imprisonment and fasting work in his favor. It was in prison that Gandhi had the time to study the *Gita* at length. As a result of Gandhi's nonviolent campaigns, carried on for more than twenty-five years, the British left India by their own choice in 1947 and on good terms with the Indians.

Unfortunately, the internal power struggle in India was not yet resolved. Hindu and Muslim tensions led to widespread rioting, the transfer of ten to twenty million people, and hundreds of thousands of deaths over the partition of the former colony into Hindu India and Muslim Pakistan. Gandhi went on a "fast to death" or until the violence stopped. His influence and spiritual power did lead to an end of that violence. But then a right-wing Hindu who thought that Gandhi favored Muslims assassinated him.

Once the power in India passed over into the hands of those who had co-operated with Gandhi, the new rulers did not maintain a consistently nonviolent approach to power. For many of them, ahimsa had been a tactic for the circumstances, not a consistent way of life. In Gandhi's terms, they had been using a "nonviolence of the weak" rather than a "nonviolence of the strong." *Nonviolence of the strong* is practiced even when one has the power to force one's way violently, because it is based on a way of life and believes that the means we choose shape the end we achieve. It requires courage and strength of character to accept suffering. *Nonviolence of the weak* is merely a prudent tactic of those who have insufficient power to use violence effectively. When they develop enough power to use violence, they use it. This nonviolence reveals cowardice and weakness of character.

Gandhi urged nonviolence of the strong and made ahimsa a way of life, but for many of his followers, ahimsa was just a tactic to be used in certain circumstances. To be fair to them, there must be a great temptation to use violence when one inherits an existing government and army.

Satyagraha

To explain the power that ahimsa can yield when used correctly, Gandhi coined the new word *satyagraha*. It is often translated "truth-force" or "soul-force" (the translation Martin Luther King Jr. preferred) to emphasize its power. More literally it is *satya*/"truth" plus *graha*/"holding." It refers to the powerful influence that honesty and integrity have when they are courageously maintained and expressed in the face of threats and violence without attacking in return.

Satyagraha combined with ahimsa—holding courageously to truth in threatening situations without harming the opponent—acts powerfully to transform oppressive situations. When an opponent realizes that I am not going to hurt him but that I will accept torture and death rather than cooperate in a line of action I consider unjust, his conscience is deeply touched. If on the other hand I threaten him with harm, he will feel justified attacking me in self-defense.

Key Principles of Satyagraha

Gandhi outlined several key principles of satyagraha as follows: While there is an absolute Truth, our *understanding* of Truth is relative: no one has it all.

We must not force others to accept our view because we're never sure our view is right. We must respect the humanity of our opponents and offer them an honorable solution that does not shame them. In even the most desperate situation we always have good choices. We can always (a) refuse to cooperate with actions we consider evil, and (b) suffer. Innocent suffering has the power to touch hearts and convert people.

Violence is better than cowardice. Satyagraha requires bravery. Cowardly people give in to threats of violence and cooperate with what they know is wrong. Thus they fail to practice satyagraha because they do not act in truth, and they fail to practice ahimsa because they cooperate in harming their neighbor, at least by failing to confront those who cause harm.

Rules for a Satyagraha Campaign

Gandhi proposed the following rules for a campaign of satyagraha:

1. *Self-reliance.* The practitioners must not depend on outsiders; they must maintain their independence of action. As a result, they must be modest in their goals.
2. *Initiative.* The resisters must keep the initiative in the struggle by constantly analyzing the situation and beginning new actions that keep the opponent off guard.
3. *Communication.* The resisters must communicate clearly to educate their followers, mobilize outsiders in their support, and speak their demands clearly to the opponent.
4. *Reasonableness.* The resisters must demand no more than truth and integrity require. They must be ready for reasonable negotiation. Even if they have the power to force excessive concessions, they should not use it.
5. *Advance by stages.* The resisters must understand the progress of the campaign so that they can choose the steps toward their goal.
6. *Self-examination.* Morale and discipline require that the resisters keep examining their own strengths and weaknesses and acting to purify themselves.
7. *Respect for opponent.* The opponent must be able to see that the resisters seek a solution that respects both sides and does not seek to humiliate the opponent.
8. *Holding on to essentials.* Despite the willingness to negotiate fairly taught in step four, there must be no compromise of the essentials demanded by truth and integrity.

Gandhi's "Constructive Program"

Besides his program of provocative nonviolence to make it impossible for the British to govern India, Gandhi also promoted a "constructive program" designed to teach Indians how to rule themselves. He wanted to help the poor masses of India overcome their sense of powerlessness. This program centered on small-scale technology and a village-based economy, symbolized by village health, cleanliness (sanitation and hygiene), education, industry, and especially by the campaign to encourage all Indians to spin cotton, weave cloth, and wear clothing made by themselves or by local artisans (*khadi* or homespun cloth) rather than to buy factory clothes imported from England.

Gandhi considered it bad economics to have millions of Indians out of work while British workers made clothing for Indians to wear. An economy that fails to use local resources and wastes the talents and energies of local people is not a good economy. Many of his ideas continue to influence those who urge "sustainable development." In India, they continued to be applied especially in the famous land reform campaigns of his follower Vinoba Bhave.

Vinoba Bhave

The most famous of Gandhi's followers was Vinoba Bhave. He first joined Gandhi when he was twenty-one, just after he graduated from college. He studied and taught Sanskrit and Indian literature, and was very active in Gandhi's "constructive program." When Gandhi was assassinated, Vinoba became the leader of his movement.

Bhoodan and Gramdan (Land Distribution)

In 1951 Vinoba met a group of Dalits who wanted him to help them purchase eighty acres of land. He called a public meeting and presented the problem. A rich landowner offered to donate one hundred of his five hundred acres. Inspired by this act of generosity, Vinoba began a national campaign to encourage voluntary donations of land (*Bhoodan*), and later of villages (*Gramdan*), money, time, and other contributions. Vinoba traveled around India organizing public gatherings at which the wealthy were invited to make such donations. In addition to meeting the needs of the poor and teaching the poor how to "stand on their own feet" to meet their own needs, this campaign was designed to heal owners of their "slavery to money" and to promote a unity of hearts between all classes. By the time of his death, over four million acres of land, and all the property in over 170,000 villages, had been donated to the poor or the public good.

Vinoba related these activities of Gramdan and Bhoodan with the *Gita* by noting that the *Gita* teaches especially the importance of *bhakti* or worship of God. But *if God is in all of creation, especially in every human, then worship of God includes service to other humans, especially those in need.* The *Gita* says that we pay our debt (a) to the universe that sustains us by practicing sacrifice *(yajna),* (b) to the society of humans that we depend on by giving alms *(dana)*, and (c) to our own bodies by spiritual discipline *(tapas)*. But these are just three more forms of service. By donating excess land or resources, we (a) express our devotion to God through service, (b) sacrifice to the universe in service, (c) give alms to society through service, and (d) exercise spiritual discipline through service.

The concept of action without desire for personal results (fruits) Vinoba also connects with service. One lets go of control over the results of one's actions and dedicates the action and its effects to the Lord. Thus it is easier to let go of land, resources, money, time, and use of talents if one is not hoping to gain something from the loss. One should not act generously in hopes of getting something in return, not even fame or prestige.[17]

THE GREAT TRADITION AND THE LITTLE TRADITION

Mahatma Gandhi and Vinoba Bhave are unusual in the degree to which their expressed, religious ideals shaped the way they lived their everyday lives in every detail. Many other people claim membership in religious groups without being very reflective about their religious traditions, and often without those traditions having much influence on their lives. Their lives *are* shaped by their deepest convictions, but often those convictions are more societal or selfish than religious.

In *Some Trouble with Cows,* the sociologist Beth Roy describes a village conflict in Bangladesh between Hindus and Muslims. The trouble began when a Muslim's cow got loose and ate some of the lentils in the neighboring field, which belonged to a Hindu. When the Hindu complained, the Muslim tied his cow carelessly in the same field the next day. It got loose again and ate more Hindu lentils. The Hindu then took the Muslim's cow home and held it. When the Muslim came to retrieve it, the Hindu would not give it back. As he left without his cow, the Muslim insulted the Hindu by saying in anger, "Why do you want to keep the cow? Do you want to eat it?"

This deliberately offensive remark to his Hindu neighbor is one of the few actions in the whole adventure that can be directly related to either worldview. Nevertheless, the village was divided between its low-caste Hindus and its Muslims. Note that the quarrel could well have divided the village differently, for example between peasants (low-caste Hindus and poor Muslims) on the one hand, and landowners and political leaders (high-caste Hindus and wealthy Muslims) on the other. The result was three days of tension, with tens of thousands of people from miles around sitting on the ground in a face-off;

scattered "raids" from one side to the other resulting mostly in cuts, bruises, and a burned building; and finally shots fired by the regional police that killed two Hindus and two Muslims.

Religious convictions mainly gave people a sense of identity; they identified friends and enemies. Yet Roy questions why it was *religion* that was chosen as the identifying factor. She suggests three reasons: (1) religion provided a powerful sense of community over against the secular, political community, which villagers saw as "outsiders"; (2) religion had recently played a key role in the 1947 political changes —religious identities had been used to determine privilege or oppression—when East Pakistan (majority Muslim) separated from India (majority Hindu);[18] and (3) the particular daily religious practices of the two groups set up certain cultural differences—Hindu practices centered on the home and thus reinforced family ties, whereas Muslim practices centered on the public mosque, reinforcing communal religious ties.

Another interesting division that cut across the religious divide was between the men and the women. In general, the women refused to support the disturbance, declining for example to prepare food for the men while the conflict was underway. Roy comments:

> Men meet more in public spaces, in marketplaces and fields, for instance, where sources of competition and conflict are common. Women meet more on domestic and ritual grounds [visiting neighbors on holiday and other occasions, and attending to births, marriages, illnesses, and deaths] where they have voluntarily sought each other out and therefore approach with a more assured sense of friendliness.[19]

Religious differences are often blamed for conflict, for example, in India, Northern Ireland, and the Middle East. Some suggest we would reduce much violence if we could just put religion aside. In situations of conflict, it is useful to consider to what extent religion is a *cause* of the conflict, to what extent it is the *organizing principle* that helps people in a conflict "choose sides" and establish identity, and to what extent its teachings and practices actually *shape* the course of the conflict and the actions of the participants. Without religion would conflicts cease, or would they just organize themselves differently?

This question has become more urgent in India since the 1998 election victory of the BJP party. That party responded to Hindu feelings of disadvantage by declaring that "India is for Hindus." In several cases it supported Hindus in conflicts with their Muslim neighbors. Its party platform promised nuclear tests. Soon after gaining power it kept that promise, to the surprise of most of the world. Pakistan followed suit, not to be outclassed by its neighbor nation.

SUMMARY

Hindus believe that the world of sense experience is illusory compared with the spirit world of their atman. They pray and sacrifice to many gods, seeking advantage in this world of sense experience, but see these gods as various manifestations of the one Brahman. They explain suffering as a natural result of a person's own past bad actions. Understanding that humans are caught in an endless cycle of reincarnation, they seek to escape this dreary round by choosing to act well, but without anxiety about the effects of their actions, hoping thus to enter moksha. They attempt not to harm life, but Gandhi and his followers are unusual in applying that ahimsa to every form of life, including violent opponents. By contrast, most Hindus see warfare and violence as a normal part of life, especially for kshatriyas.

KEY TERMS

Advaita Vedanta
ahimsa
Atman
Bhagavad-Gita
bhakti
Bhoodan
Brahma
Brahman (capital B)
brahman (lowercase b)
Brahmana
Brahmin
caste
constructive program
Dalit
Dalit theology
dharma
Gramdan
Harijan
jnana
karma
Kshatriya
Mahabharata

maya
moksha
nonviolence of the strong
nonviolence of the weak
outcastes
Ramayana
reincarnation
samsara
satyagraha
scheduled castes
scheduled tribes
Shruti
Shudra
Smriti
transmigration of souls
untouchables
Upanishads
Vaishya
Vedanta
Vedas
yoga
yogi

DISCUSSION QUESTIONS

1. If we were to apply the four Hindu castes to our own society in the United States, which caste would you and your family fall into? In which caste would your future plans (profession or work appropriate to your major field of study) place you?
2. Which of Gandhi's *principles* of satyagraha do you agree with? Which do you disagree with? Explain your reasons.
3. Think of a campaign or struggle that is important to you (violent or non-violent). Explain which of Gandhi's *rules* for a satyagraha campaign are being observed in that campaign. Would the struggle be more or less successful if it followed his principles more closely? Explain.
4. How important do you think a "constructive program" is when a group is struggling for freedom or self-determination? If you think it is important, identify a struggle that is important to you and suggest a constructive program for that struggle.
5. Identify a current conflict that is thought to be based on religious differences. Then ask yourself to what extent religion is a *cause* of the conflict, to what extent religion is the *organizing principle* that helps people "choose sides" and establish identity, and to what extent the teachings and practices of religions actually *shape* the course of the conflict and the actions of its participants. Alternatively, do you think the conflict is essentially unrelated to religion?
6. Mohandas Gandhi and Vinoba Bhave strongly opposed war and embraced simple lives of poverty in order to help the poor. These are not typical Hindu reactions to the world's suffering. Can you name some members of *your own* worldview who interpret your worldview in such striking and unusual ways? Are such people impractical dreamers, dangerous crackpots, or helpful reminders to the rest of us?

NOTES

1. www.sacred-texts.com/hin/gita/agsgita.htm (accessed March 3, 2007).
2. Yogananda, *Autobiography of a Yogi*, 166–67. Used by permission.
3. We are using the periodization from Smart, *The World's Religions*, 45.
4. Yogananda, *Autobiography of a Yogi*, 166.
5. www.advaita-vedanta.org/avhp/mimved.html#ved (accessed January 26, 2005).
6. "VI, 8. Charm to Secure the Love of a Woman." In *Hymns of the Atharva-Veda*.
7. *The Bhagavadgita*, Radhakrishnan, 59.
8. The most famous advocate of Advaita Vedanta was S(h)ankara, who lived somewhere between 500 BCE and 800 CE [*sic*]. See www.advaita-vedanta.org/avhp/ (accessed July 9, 2006).

9. Prabhupada, *Bhagavad-Gita As It Is*, 35–36.

10. www.ambedkar.org/.

11. Spiro, *Buddhism and Society: A Great Tradition and Its Burmese Vicissitudes*.

12. Gandhi, *Bhagvadgita* [sic], 15, 29–30.

13. Gandhi, *Bhagvadgita*, 12.

14. Gandhi, *Bhagvadgita*, 18, 24–28. Radhakrishnan makes the same point in *The Bhagavadgita*, 68.

15. Quoted in Jordens, "Gandhi and the *Bhagavadgita*," 88–109. See 89, 91f, 97.

16. Jordens, "Gandhi and the *Bhagavadgita*," 97.

17. Wilson, "Vinoba Bhave's *Talks on the Gita*," 110–30.

18. This dispute took place before Bangladesh—the former East Pakistan—separated from West Pakistan in 1971.

19. Roy, *Some Trouble with Cows*, 168.

SUGGESTIONS FOR FURTHER READING

The Bhagavadgita, with an Introductory Essay, Sanskrit Text [Transliterated], English Translation and Notes by S. Radhakrishnan.

Bhave. *Revolutionary Sarvodaya.*

——. *Talks on the Gita.*

Bondurant. *Conquest of Violence: The Gandhian Philosophy of Conflict.*

Erikson. *Gandhi's Truth: On the Origins of Militant Nonviolence.*

Gandhi. *An Autobiography: The Story of My Experiments with Truth.*

——. *The Bhagvadgita.*

——. *Non-Violence in Peace and War.*

——. *Non-Violent Resistance (Satyagraha).*

Jordens. "Gandhi and the *Bhagavadgita*."

Minor, ed. *Modern Indian Interpreters of the Bhagavadgita.*

Nanda. *Mahatma Gandhi: A Biography.*

Prabhupada. *Bhagavad-Gita as It Is.*

Radhakrishnan. *Indian Philosophy.*

Roy. *Some Trouble with Cows: Making Sense of Social Conflict.*

Sharp. *Gandhi as a Political Strategist: With Essays on Ethics and Politics.*

Spiro. *Buddhism and Society: A Great Tradition and Its Burmese Vicissitudes.*

Vasto. *Gandhi to Vinoba: The New Pilgrimage.*

Weber. *Gandhi's Peace Army: The Shanti Sena and Unarmed Peacekeeping.*

Wilson. "Vinoba Bhave's *Talks on the Gita*."

Yogananda. *Autobiography of a Yogi.*

Zaehner. *Hinduism.*

Chapter Two

Buddhist Worldviews

"Now, this, O bhikkhus, is the noble truth concerning suffering: Birth is attended with pain, decay is painful, disease is painful, death is painful. Union with the unpleasant is painful, painful is separation from the pleasant; and any craving that is unsatisfied, that too is painful. In brief, bodily conditions which spring from attachment are painful."

"Now this, O bhikkhus, is the noble truth concerning the origin of suffering: Verily, it is that craving which causes the renewal of existence, accompanied by sensual delight, seeking satisfaction now here, now there, the craving for the gratification of the passions, the craving for a future life, and the craving for happiness in this life."

—Buddha, "The Sermon at Benares"[1]

EXPERIENTIAL AND EMOTIONAL DIMENSION

When Siddhartha Gautama, who had been raised in a privileged and highly protected environment, first encountered an old man, a sick man, a corpse, and an ascetic, he was deeply shaken. When traditional Hindu doctrine, asceticism, and meditation failed to explain the problem to his satisfaction, he committed himself to meditating under a single tree until he arrived at a satisfactory answer. After forty-nine days, he was suddenly *enlightened.* We will outline the intellectual understanding of that enlightenment below under the doctrinal dimension; the meditative search for the experience itself, and the peace and joy that enlightenment brings, are the experiential and emotional center of the Buddhist faith. Buddhist writings discuss meditation techniques at length, but Buddhists generally believe that nothing can take the place of experience: one's own, and that of a guide or *guru* who has already achieved enlightenment.

HISTORICAL PERIODS[2]

1. The initial period of Buddhism, including the life and teaching of Siddhartha Gautama, extended from about 550 to 450 BCE. During much of that period, the Buddha taught his new insights and organized his disciples into committed communities.
2. From about 450 BCE to the 1st century CE, various Buddhist schools of thought argued over the correct interpretation of the *dharma* (Buddhist teaching).
3. From the 1st to the 7th centuries CE, a new form of Buddhism called *Mahayana* developed, even as the earlier *Theravadan* form was being more completely developed. This period is considered the classic period.
4. Beginning in the 7th century, the form of Buddhism called *Vajrayana* emerged and evolved, especially in Nepal and Tibet.
5. From the 13th century on, Buddhism basically died in India—or rather was co-opted by a Hindu renewal that adapted many of its ideas—although it maintained a strong presence in Sri Lanka just off-shore, and continued to grow in Nepal and Tibet to the North, and to the East as far as China and Japan. Ninian Smart calls 4 and 5 the "Medieval Period."[3]
6. Finally, from the 18th century CE to the present, Buddhism experienced the impact of Western colonization.

For further discussion of the three major forms of Buddhism, see the doctrinal and philosophical dimension below.

SACRED WRITINGS

Buddhism does not claim that any of its sacred literature has been inspired by a god, since it sets aside the question whether a god or gods even exist. It offers the experience and insights of Siddhartha Gautama and later Buddhists; then it encourages people to try out those ideas and see for themselves. Learning what other people have said is useless unless one validates it with one's own experience. Still, there are some classical writings. The *Tripitaka* (or "Three Baskets") represents the Buddhist canon of scripture. The first basket (*pitaka*) gives a history of the Buddhist *sangha* or community of monks and the rules it follows, the second claims to recount the Buddha's teaching sessions, the third is a collection of Buddhist philosophy and psychology. The *Jataka Tales*, while not considered part of the canon, narrate stories of the Buddha in his earlier lives. Thus the *Tripitaka* relates mostly to the doctrinal and practical dimensions, the *Jataka Tales* to the narrative dimension.

NARRATIVE OR MYTHIC DIMENSION

Life of Siddhartha Gautama

Tradition holds that Siddhartha Gautama was born in 563 BCE:[4] the last rebirth of the one who was to become the Buddha—the "Enlightened One." The *Jataka Tales* describe many edifying experiences he had in previous lives— human and otherwise—that prepared him for this last round of samsara, in which he was to attain *nirvana* (nibbana[5])—the cessation of all suffering— and leave us the *dharma* (dhamma)—the "teaching of the Buddha"[6]—which can help us follow him into nirvana.

Siddhartha was born a member of the Sakyas, so he is also remembered as Sakyamuni: sage of the Sakyas. Early in his marriage he was moved by four striking experiences to abandon his family and join a small group of *sramanas*, or wandering ascetics, in search of truth. After many adventures, including near collapse from excessive fasting and other disciplines, he realized the importance of moderation, which he called the "middle way." At this point he came to enlightenment (*bodhi*) while meditating for forty-nine days under a particular tree afterward called the Bodhi Tree.

Filled with this new enlightenment and with enthusiasm for the truths it revealed, the Buddha returned to his companions, instructed them in the "four noble truths"—his revolutionary discovery—and founded the *sangha,* or community of disciples who would pass on knowledge of the true way to nirvana. He lived for forty-five more years, during which he traveled and taught. Finally he attained *parinirvana,* a mysterious state from which he would never be reborn into this world, but in which it is not correct to say that he exists, nor that he does not exist, nor both, nor neither. His followers cremated his body.

Siddhartha was not the only Buddha; he was the last. He restored the true faith after its decay. Progress in the world is negative: there is less and less enlightenment as time goes by.

DOCTRINAL AND PHILOSOPHICAL DIMENSION

Buddhism's Challenge to Hinduism

Doctrines play an especially important role in Buddhism because the core of the Buddhist message was a new view of the nature of life and reality which challenged Hindu doctrinal views and the authority of the Hindu Brahmins. It claimed that enlightenment came from personal discovery and that tradition, especially the Vedas and the authority of the Brahmins, was of no help. Buddhism also denied the reality of a self-subsisting eternal human personality, of an imperishable atman or soul that could come into personal relationship with a god after death.

The Four Noble Truths

As mentioned above, the key "experience" explained by Buddhist doctrine was an experience of enlightenment that came from meditating on the tragic and unsatisfying experience of life itself.

1. *The truth of suffering. All life is suffering* (dukkha: *ultimately dissatisfying because nothing is permanent*). This insight can be explained as follows: What we *dislike* causes suffering because (a) we hate it when we have it, and (b) we fear it when we don't have it. But what we *like* causes suffering too, because (c) we want it when we don't have it, and (d) we fear losing it when we do have it. Even when we seem to have a firm grasp on good things, we realize that everything, even life itself, even our "personality," is impermanent and we will eventually have to let everything go.
2. *The cause of suffering. Suffering is caused by our* "attachment": *yearning, desiring, holding on to things* both *material* and *spiritual*—and *even to existence itself. Everything* is impermanent.
3. *The cessation of suffering.* Since suffering is caused by yearning and desire, *we could overcome suffering if we could overcome yearning and desire.*
4. *How to overcome yearning and desire. We overcome yearning and desire by following the eight-fold path.* This path leads us eventually to nirvana (see below).

Table 2.1.

Things, both material and spiritual	We have them	We don't have them
Things we like	fear losing them	want them
Things we dislike	want to get rid of them	fear getting them

The Eight-Fold Path

The eight-fold path divides into three groups:
  Group A. *Relating to wisdom (panna or prajna).*

1. *Perfect understanding* about the four noble truths, the reality of impermanence and suffering, and the fact that there is no human soul or atman.
2. *Perfect resolve* to trust and follow the perfect understanding by renouncing desire, loving all beings, and harming none.

  Group B. *Relating to morality (sila) in daily life (ethical and legal dimension).*

3. *Perfect speech.* Don't lie, slander, gossip.
4. *Perfect conduct.* Follow the right ethical observances. (There are various
   opinions on what constitute right observances, expressed in different lists.)
5. *Perfect livelihood.* Avoid professions like butcher, hunter, or bomb maker
   that conflict with Buddhist values because they cause harm or injustice to
   sentient beings.

  Group C. *Relating to concentration (samadhi), meditation, yoga (practical
and ritual dimension).*

6. *Perfect effort.* Do what will help your karma, avoid what will hurt it. Keep
   out new evil, throw out old evil; bring in new good, cultivate old good.
   The purpose is self-perfection.
7. *Perfect mindfulness.* Meditative practice that centers attention in turn on
   body, emotions, mind, and ideas produced by the mind (mental objects).
   The purpose is to be aware of our inner states.
8. *Perfect concentration.* Meditative practice of concentration on a single
   physical or mental object, realizing that all is impermanent, unsatisfying,
   without substance. The purpose is to lead the mind through four stages of
   progressively deeper absorption and detachment into enlightenment.

While this is the traditional order for arranging the eight-fold path, one is
not likely to pass successively through each path in this order on the way to
enlightenment. Actual progress will be circular. Although one may first be
impressed by the vision (paths 1 and 2) and make an initial commitment to
try it out (path 2), it is not likely that one will understand that insight very
well if one is living a corrupt life (paths 3 and 4) thoughtlessly (paths 6–8) in
a wretched job (path 5). As one works to reform one's moral life (paths 3–5),
meditation becomes easier (paths 6–8) and wisdom becomes less frightening

and threatening (paths 1–2). Meditation helps one experience the truth of Buddhist wisdom (paths 1–2). Deeper insight into that wisdom strengthens one's practice of morality and meditation, and the circle goes on.

Analogues in Other Traditions

Without too easily claiming agreement, it is useful to consider whether the experience and traditions of other religions express similar ideas. For example, Christian tradition says we should be detached from desire for material things, trust God's will rather than our own, and love even our enemies. Similarly, Islam urges self-surrender to God's will. In your own experience, have you felt relief when you let go of some desire or goal that you could not attain? When you let go of resentment and forgave someone who had hurt you, did your feelings toward them change?

Here are two Christian examples:

1. A Russian Christian Starets, or spiritual director, Starets Silouan, quotes Paissy the Great, who was trying to overcome anger. God spoke to this holy man in his prayer: "Paissey, if thou dost not wish to get angry, desire nothing, neither criticize nor hate any man, and thou wilt have no anger."[7]
2. An American Jesuit priest in prison in Moscow during the Second World War, Walter Ciszek, had a deep experience of frustration which tempted him to commit suicide: he was unable to convince his interrogator that he was telling the truth. Then he realized he didn't need to be so frustrated. The interrogator was not frustrating God's will—the interrogation itself was at this moment God's will for him. God wanted him to let go of all attempts to control the situation, then to speak naturally and honestly what felt right at the moment: what happened next was God's responsibility. This realization freed him from his agony and radically changed the situation.

These Christian examples are not encouraging us to be cowards. When we truly hold onto nothing but God, we are freed to risk ourselves totally for God.

Anatman and Nirvana

Buddhist doctrine affirms that the individual ego or soul is just as impermanent as the rest of the reality we experience, although the Buddha never affirmed this clearly. The assertion that ego is also part of the illusion of maya is called *anatman* from the negative "a" and the word "atman." The

doctrine of anatman complicates Buddhist teaching about karma and rebirth (see below).

Nirvana is escape from all suffering, which is attained when we overcome
desire, hatred, and delusion. It frees us from the effects of karma, the constant
progression of birth, growth, decay, and death—"arising, subsisting, changing, and passing away."[8] Those who achieve this state by the time they die escape from the round of births and deaths called samsara. Nirvana means "extinction of *suffering*." It does *not* mean "*annihilation*," but rather "entry into
another mode of existence." The true nature of nirvana is beyond our capacity to understand; it cannot be adequately described in human words. It is not
located in space. It is not true to say that the person who attains nirvana
"ceases to exist." The Buddha thought that efforts to *describe* it would be a
distraction from the spiritual practice that can *lead one to attain* it—it should
be enough to know that it extinguishes all suffering.[9]

Since for Buddhists there is no *atman* or individual, independent, eternal
soul to survive death, *nirvana* differs from Hindu *moksha*. Buddhists believe
there is a human *ego,* but it is dependent on and arises out of five impermanent and constantly changing human "aggregates"—form, sensation, perception, mental formations, and consciousness—which together make up the human "personality." There is also no God or Brahman or universal soul (in the
Hindu sense) with whom the atman of Hindu nondualistic theology could
merge.[10]

Students—and scholars—sometimes ask, If there is no soul, how can there
be rebirth? What is born again? What we experience as our ego is just a combination of energies of various types—the "aggregates" mentioned above.
These energies arise from the desires that trap us in the round of samsara. It
is this impermanent collection of energies that produces the new birth. To call
this new birth a "reincarnation" (as Hindus do) would be inaccurate, since
there is no "eternal soul" to be "en-fleshed" or "em-bodied" (the meaning of
"in-carnation"). Buddhists rather speak of "re-birth."

To put it another way, every present moment is caused by the immediately
preceding moment. We like to think that there is some permanent "thing" that
connects the present with the past. But in reality the only connection is the
karmic causation of the present collection of energies by the immediately preceding collection of energies. Since this process has been going on forever,
every new moment is in causal connection with every past moment, since the
immediately preceding arrangement of energies was shaped by what preceded *it,* and so on back down the line. When a person dies, the process continues without interruption. In other words, there is no more discontinuity between the moment before death and the moment after death than there is
between any other two moments in one's life. So the "shape" of the collected

energies just before death determines what happens at the moment of death and then in the next moment, and the process continues.

In your own life, if you experience pain which you connect consciously with past bad choices that "you" made (although the Buddhists claim there is no unchanging "you" to connect the past with the present), the same will be true on the other side of death, with the exception that your memory of the past before your new birth may be dulled. You can decide whether it is safe to amass bad karma on the gamble that it won't be "you" who suffer the consequences when "your energies" are reborn. Was it not "you" who made the bad choices earlier in "your" life which you are suffering from now? If you hit your thumb with a hammer, will it be "someone else" who feels the pain?

Note that in Christian theology, the human being—body and soul—is a *creature.* At every moment we are dependent on God for every aspect of our existence. Yet God lives within the *redeemed* human, by God's grace. So the Christian, like the Buddhist, does not believe in a human atman which is a "piece" or "spark" of God, eternal in the same sense that God is eternal, but the Christian *does* believe that the eternal God lives in intimate union with everyone who has surrendered to God's will.[11]

Moving from the great tradition to the little tradition, it is doubtful that very many Buddhists have internalized the concept of "no atman." To judge from the sociological study of Melford Spiro in Burma, most Buddhists there concentrate on gaining merit so that "they" will experience a better rebirth—as a rich male. They lack enthusiasm for nirvana.[12]

Three Forms of Buddhism

Theravada

Originally Buddhism concentrated on liberating the *individual* through meditation and the monastic life. Nonmonks could gain good karma through their actions, in the hopes of being reborn as monks. Among the actions that promoted good karma was material or financial support of monks and their monasteries. This individualistic emphasis continues in the *Theravada* Buddhism that is dominant today in Southeast Asia: Sri Lanka, Burma, Thailand, and Indochina, with the exception of Vietnam.

Mahayana

Another emphasis developed in the *Mahayana* school, dominant in China and Japan. Zen is derived from the Mahayana school. "Mahayana" means "great vehicle." The followers of this school called the older school of Theravada Buddhism "Hinayana," or "lesser vehicle." Mahayana sees Theravada as selfish in its individualism. Instead, Mahayana proposes to liberate the whole world. One who achieves enlightenment should have the compassion to wait and reach out to others, as Siddhartha did, before entering nirvana. This new insight is expressed in the figure of the *Bodhisattva*: a person who has the enlightenment to pass into nirvana but postpones doing so in order to teach the dharma and bring others into nirvana as well. As the tradition developed, these Bodhisattvas were thought to exist in a state between this world and nirvana and to be capable of helping those who were still in this world. People began to offer devotion to the Bodhisattvas, hoping to gain merit that would move them toward nirvana. The possible danger in this position is thinking that one can attain nirvana by the merit of others without going to the trouble and discipline of seeking enlightenment oneself.

In contrast to Theravada, Mahayana proposes that people in the world can attain nirvana without becoming monks, thus making enlightenment more widely available. If the world is ultimately empty, they argue, there is no need to leave it and enter monastic life.

The validity of the four noble truths and the emptiness of the world are not simply *intellectual* affirmations. They have to be *realized in a true mystical experience* before they will have the power to transform us and lead us to nirvana. This shows the connection between the *ritual*, *experiential*, and *doctrinal* dimensions: the *ritual* leads one to *experience the reality* described by the *doctrine*; it is this mystical grasp that enlightens one and brings one to nirvana.

Vajrayana

In Tibet, Mahayana Buddhism incorporated "magical" practices: pronouncing mantras and using rituals to put the worshiper into contact with spiritual powers. This form of Buddhism is called *Vajrayana*, or "Diamond Vehicle." By visualizing and "becoming" various Buddha-emanations (gods and goddesses who embody different energies), practitioners overcome obstacles on the path to enlightenment. The Dalai Lama is thought to be the most recent incarnation of Chenrizig, the Buddha of Compassion. The various Buddha-emanations act as "patron saints" to preserve the community. After Buddhism declined in India, many of the early Indian Buddhist texts were translated into Tibetan and preserved there, along with later Vajrayana texts. When the Maoist Chinese invaded and occupied Tibet and began to suppress Tibetan worship, many Vajrayana Buddhists fled to the West, taking their literature and practices with them.

PRACTICAL AND RITUAL DIMENSION

Buddhist doctrine shapes Buddhist ritual to be quite different from Jewish, Christian, and Muslim ritual. Most religions use rituals to develop a relationship with God and spiritual beings. What, then, can ritual mean in a worldview like early Buddhism which has little or no relationship with a god or spiritual beings? Theravada Buddhists do not depend on a god for their future, but on their own enlightenment. Their rituals, then, are designed to incline them toward enlightenment, weaning them from dependence on and preoccupation with things that might distract them from reality. Their prayer is designed to still our desire, to concentrate our attention, and thus to open us to enlightenment. For classical Buddhists, sacrifice would only attach us more closely to material appearances.

A Japanese Zen tea ceremony, for example, can last four hours in a garden and an adjoining simple room with tatami mat flooring. Each action is carried on slowly, with attention to what is being done and to the simple objects being used. Rather than acting from habit, one concentrates on the present moment—on each movement and on the sights, sounds, and feelings of simple material objects like charcoal fire, light, poured water, lacquered bowls, pottery, crafted wood, flower arrangements, poetry, and calligraphy. Even the simplest object receives attention, since there is no clutter to distract attention. The host concentrates on each guest, seeking to help all enter into a state of tranquility.[13]

In short, most Buddhist rituals are designed to transform a person without reference to one's relationship with a god or spiritual being. However, Vajrayana Buddhism and some forms of Mahayana Buddhism (such as the Pure Land sect) do use rituals designed to connect the practitioner with spiritual beings who can help them gain enlightenment.

The "Little Tradition" in Ritual

The situation becomes more complex when we look at the "little tradition." Despite the Buddhist conviction that our fate is determined by karma which cannot be avoided, Spiro[14] found that Burmese Theravada Buddhists practiced rituals designed to protect them from dangers, and that these rituals are based on a *paritta* or prayer-spell *composed by the Buddha himself*, as preserved in the Buddhist canon. There is a spell to protect one from snakebite—a prayer designed to "let one's love flow out over the four royal breeds of serpents." Unfortunately, the spell will not work if it is one's karma to die, nor if one is living a bad moral life without faith. But if one's karma leaves the question open, the spell will keep snakes from biting, robbers from striking, elephants from charging, and so on. Numerous other parittas, taken from early Buddhist writings, are used in such rituals.

It is not clear how these spells work, according to Buddhist teaching. Spiro found that most Burmese he questioned were vague and uncertain on the

Figure 2.1. Biggest Buddhist stupa in Nepal: Kathmandu. Note [all-seeing] eyes between dome and pitched roof tower. Courtesy David Whitten Smith, 16 February 1998.

subject. They used the spells regularly without questioning how they worked until he asked them. Then their answers were confused and varied. One lay group gave the "correct" response that the Buddha was dead. When he asked who would then respond to the ritual offering they were preparing for the next day, they carried on quite a discussion among themselves, concluding that, since it was the Buddha who answered the prayers, he must be alive after all.[15] Other responses Spiro received were that the prayers are answered because the words have power, because the Buddha is "alive in his message," by the power of the Buddha's relics, because the person who built the pagoda had great faith, because there is power in the Buddha image, because the worshiper's faith or confidence is increased, because the worship is a meritorious act that improves not only future karma but present karma, or because the person is helped by one or another of the *devas,* or minor gods.

ETHICAL AND LEGAL DIMENSION

Consider a common list of ethical observances which explain "perfect conduct"—the fourth of the eight noble truths. Although there are variations among different lists, the first five points are fairly consistent. For comparison, the ten Christian commandments (in their Catholic division) have been placed alongside (see table 2.2). The Christian love command has also been stated in its negative form: you shall not hate. There are more than ten Buddhist observances because three lists have been combined. The Buddhist and Christian lists are traditionally expressed in different order—here the order has been varied to match up a few of the items for you.

Buddhists set aside the question of gods, so they have no parallel to the Christian (and Jewish) commands "You shall not (1) worship other gods, (2) blaspheme, (3) dishonor the Sabbath."

The "Little Tradition" in Ethical Life

In his sociological study of Burmese Theravadan Buddhists, Spiro[16] found three rather different attitudes:

1. The "orthodox" Theravada emphasis on overcoming karma (bad *and* good karma) in order to enter nirvana at the end of one's current life. For this goal, both good and bad karma are barriers—each leads to rebirth. Even rebirth as a *deva* (minor god or good spirit) holds one back from nirvana by causing one to be reborn in a temporary heaven. People who hold this view try to live "indifferent" to merit. This position was held by very few.

Table 2.2.

Buddhist: I undertake to abstain from . . .	Christian: You shall not . . .
harming living beings	kill
taking the not given	steal
sexual misconduct	commit adultery
false speech	lie in law court
using intoxicating drink or drugs	——
harsh speech	(hate)
useless speech	——
slanderous speech	lie in law court
covetousness	covet other's wife
covetousness	covet other's goods
——	dishonor parents
animosity	(hate)
false views	(heresy)
And from a list for monks— *I undertake to abstain from . . .*	*Christian monks and nuns also live simpler* *lives than laity. They vow themselves to . . .*
solid food after noon	poverty
music, dance, etc.	chastity
perfume, jewelry	obedience
high, soft beds	
money, valuables	

2. An emphasis on overcoming the effects of bad karma and increasing good karma by gaining merit, especially by making donations to monks and other holy people. The degree of merit was in proportion to the holiness of the recipient—donations to "unworthy" needy people had little or no value. The goal was to be reborn in a more pleasant state: perhaps as a *deva,* or at least as a rich male. In contrast to the first position, some believed that eventually lots of good karma would lead one to nirvana.
3. An emphasis on gaining worldly goods and avoiding worldly sufferings in the *present* life, with the help of spells and incantations, without worrying about the next life.

SOCIAL AND INSTITUTIONAL DIMENSION

The Sangha

The Buddhist community is called the *sangha.* In a narrower sense, the term refers to its communities of monks, nuns, and novices; in a wider sense, it includes all Buddhists. The *Vinaya-Pitaka* contains instructions and rules for these groups. In heavily Buddhist societies such as Sri Lanka, monks and nuns exercise strong political influence.

Political Stability

For many Buddhists, the doctrine of karma encourages passivity in the presence of "fate." Yet this doctrine can also encourage political *coups d'état*, as Spiro found in Burma. When one's good or bad karma has been "used up," one's fate can change abruptly even in this life. So a person whose karma was leading him to be ambitious might attempt to seize control of the government, reasoning that, if the coup were successful, it would mean that his own karma had led to his new good fortune and the deposed ruler's karma had led to his or her fall from power. The general public, accepting this explanation, would quickly switch its allegiance to the new ruler. So the doctrine can produce general stability punctuated by sudden instabilities. It also produces lots of new pagodas built by leaders who hope that the merit derived from these gifts will make up for the bad karma they accumulated by the lies they told and the people they killed. This last ploy does depend on the belief that good karma blots out bad karma. Unfortunately, there is an alternative belief that bad karma must be overcome by suffering no matter how much good karma one has—even saints have to spend time in hell to overcome the bad karma accrued from their sins.

ISSUES FOR JUSTICE AND PEACE

Buddhism in its origins was pacifist. War and political power were seen as dangerous to one's progress: the attachment to this world that power, wealth, and violence express and promote yields bad karma and inhibits enlightenment. Worse, political and economic power is often the result of trampling on the rights of others.

There is an incident in the life of the Buddha that illustrates this pacifism. Two peoples, the Sakyans and the Koliyans, lived on opposite sides of the river Rohini. They shared the river as a source of water for their crops. One year there was a drought: there was not enough water in the river for both groups. In this situation of emergency, each laid claim to *all* of the water. Competition led to insults, then to anger, and both groups prepared for war.

The Buddha was the son of a Sakyan father and a Koliyan mother. He happened to be in the area at the time. When he heard of the dispute, he placed himself between the two armies. Both armies saluted him. He then began a discussion to clarify the dispute, which by this time had been lost in mutual insults. When he realized what the dispute was about, he asked the two sides which was more valuable: water or warriors. They agreed that warriors had more value than water. So why were they about to sacrifice the more valuable to get the less valuable? As a result of this intervention, the war was averted and the Sakyans committed themselves to nonviolence.

Some years later the Sakyans were attacked by the king of Kosala. (Note: this is a *third* group, not the Koliyans.) The Sakyans maintained their nonviolent commitment and were slaughtered. Oops. Does that prove that nonviolence is impractical? In Buddhist terms (if you believe in karma, rebirth, and nirvana), which is worse: to be slaughtered or to slaughter? Note also that the initial resolution required the Buddha to come between the two hostile armies. That is normally an uncomfortable place to be. But if you are truly detached from this world . . .

Warrior Buddhists

With this background, it is surprising to find that some later Buddhists were warriors. There were even professional Buddhist soldiers who claimed that true detachment would free one to be a warrior without anxiety either for oneself or for the enemy. If this life is illusion, how can ending it cause bad karma? And why fear death?

Before and during World War II, these attitudes produced widespread Buddhist support in Japan for the war with China, England, and the United States, including even the "Rape of Nanking," in which between 250,000 and 300,000 Chinese were slaughtered after the surrender of the city: "[If ordered to] march: tramp, tramp, or shoot: bang, bang. This is the manifestation of the highest Wisdom [of Enlightenment]. The unity of Zen and war . . . extends to the farthest reaches of the holy war [now under way]" (Zen Master Harada Daiun Sogaku, writing in 1939),[17] and "Warriors who sacrifice their lives for the emperor will not die. They will live forever. Truly they should be called gods and Buddhas for whom there is no life or death. . . . Where there is absolute loyalty there is no life or death" (Lieutenant Colonel Sugimoto Goro).[18]

There has also been a vigorous war in Sri Lanka between the Buddhist government and a Hindu minority group, the Tamils. When I asked a Tamil refugee how the Buddhists justify warfare according to their worldview, he replied that Sri Lankan Buddhists appeal to an ancient chronicle of how Buddhism came to Sri Lanka. According to the chronicle, the first Buddhist monks entered Sri Lanka in the very hour that the Buddha was dying. The Buddha had a vision that this Buddhist settlement would be the one guarantee of the future purity of Buddhism. Therefore, they feel it is essential that

Sri Lanka remain an explicitly Buddhist society with an explicitly Buddhist government in order to guarantee the survival and purity of Buddhism.

How Buddhism can retain its original purity if its followers torture and kill Tamil dissidents is a disturbing question. Buddhists I questioned in Sri Lanka in 1998 responded by saying, "You have to defend yourself when others attack you," which didn't sound to me like a Buddhist principle. After I had asked three or four Buddhists, my Buddhist hostess complained, "Why do you keep asking that question? You can't expect us to live our *whole* life according to Buddhist principles." This is an example of the little tradition and the great tradition not coinciding—a reality experienced in all major religions.

INDIVIDUAL INNER PEACE

A *Metta Bhavana* Meditation

There is an important relationship between large-scale peace among groups and inner peace within individuals. One way of promoting inner peace is through a meditation called *metta bhavana*. *Metta* means kindness; *bhavana* is meditation. The kindness meditation proceeds in a series of steps as follows:

1. Concentrate on *yourself*. Think kind thoughts toward yourself, concentrating on your good qualities and on times when you felt best about yourself. Let yourself feel appreciated and valued. This basis is important if you are to have the energy to love anyone else.
2. Develop similar positive feelings toward *somebody you like* and feel close to but not in a self-interested way (not, for example, a family member or lover).
3. Now let your good will go out toward *someone you feel neutral toward*.
4. Now do so for *someone you don't like,* someone you feel negative toward.
5. Finally, let your good will expand so that it includes not only the previous groups but gradually *all humans, everything in the world, and all being throughout all space and time*.

Other Peace Meditations

Joanna Macy writes and offers workshops teaching spiritual exercises and meditations for aspiring peacemakers.[19] Two of these exercises are called "Breathing through the World's Pain" and "The Great Ball of Merit."

Breathing through the World's Pain

We tend to block out the pain of the world, to numb ourselves, because we don't have solutions. But pain is part of the web of life. If we block pain out, we block out our connection with the world. If we can let it through, we become more resilient.

Relax, breathe. Imagine we are breathing in the world's pain in concrete images. Imagine it coming in through mouth and nose, passing through us, and out through a hole in the bottom of our heart back into the web of life. Observe the painful images without fear, and without feeling we have to do anything special about them at this moment beyond recognizing them. Let sorrow ripen and our hearts expand. We don't need to rush off and inflict the world's pain on others who are not so involved at this moment. They will observe and respond in due time.[20]

The Great Ball of Merit

The previous meditation helps us deal with the *pain* of others. This one helps us deal with their *good fortune* without resentment or envy. We learn to take joy in others' joy (Buddhist *muditha*). We begin by opening ourselves to a power beyond ourselves. Buddhists speak of a "ball of merit," roughly similar to Christian concepts of "grace," the "cloud of witnesses," and the "treasury of merit." The idea is that the good fortune of others is not loss to us, but gain.

Meditate on the merit of all humans, past, present, and future. All had some. We imagine that we are heaping it into a huge ball. Rejoice in it; roll it back into the world for healing. We look at the person across from us — perhaps someone in conflict with us. What does this person add to our ball of merit? stubborn endurance? imagination? love? kindness? courage? healing? Inhale awareness of that person; experience gratitude. We practice observing the good in others without being jealous. We take pleasure in their goodness, aware that it adds something to us. We imagine ourselves to be detectives spying out riches. When we find some, we congratulate ourselves on our insight. As others begin to sense our visions for them, they tend to respond by acting out those positive visions.[21]

SPOKESPERSONS FOR JUSTICE AND PEACE

Nagarjuna (2nd century CE, India)

Nagarjuna, advisor to the Satavahana king Yajnasiri Satakarni, wrote the *Jewel Garland of Royal Counsels* for the king. His recommendations show

how Buddhist principles could influence social and political life. He begins
by inviting the king to resign, since perfecting oneself is more important than
anything else.[22] He points out that key Buddhist virtues are not individualistic: they have specific *social* expressions:

1. *Individual transcendence or enlightenment* is at the base of all social activism, since everyone's final goal is to enter nirvana, and people do that
   one by one. Further, once the king and others are liberated and compassionate, they won't need *detailed* instructions for social policies—right
   policies and actions will come naturally.[23]
2. *Tolerance, detachment, and pacifism:* Overcome lust by meditating on ug-
   liness, the filthy body. Don't hunt; animals don't like it, and you won't like
   what it does to you.[24] Judges should be compassionate to criminals, especially murderers. Judges should imprison humanely, with compassion, or
   they should banish criminals.[25] Nagarjuna mentions several reasons why
   Buddhists should not practice capital punishment:
   a. Buddhists should be compassionate, especially to those who don't de-
      serve it.
   b. Capital punishment would suggest that sometimes killing is all right.
   c. Because nothing is permanent, a criminal's mind can always change.
   d. Because there is no "self," and everyone's actions are conditioned by
      circumstances, any person is reformable.
   e. Every life is precious, especially a human life, because it is so rare to
      be born as a human, and it is only in the context of human existence that
      one can come to enlightenment.[26]
3. *Universal education:* Educate to create Buddhas; support sound teaching
   (dharma) and the monastic community (sangha).[27] People should be educated to attain enlightenment-liberation, not to prepare them to provide
   services for selfish rich and powerful people. (Here it is worthwhile thinking about modern higher education. How many of our "professions" are
   designed to service wealthy people?) Selfish rulers should be afraid of being exposed by the teachings of Buddhist education, and so led to reform.
   This education should be free for all, no matter what the cost to the society.[28] Teachers must be examples in their own lives of what they teach.[29]
4. *Compassionate socialism:* The king must provide for every member of society, making specific provisions especially for the needs of the poor, such
   as special shelters for beggars and cripples. The instructions become very
   detailed: "Provide water fountains on arid roadways . . . At the fountains,
   place shoes, umbrellas, water filters, tweezers for removing thorns, nee-
   dles, thread, and fans."[30] The king should keep taxes low. Police should
   counter thieves and bandits.[31]

People are afraid that there isn't enough wealth to go around. But experience shows that generosity creates abundance. A main source of wealth is the rulers' gifts of resources to their people. If the wealthy clutch their wealth, then love, optimistic confidence, and the creativity of people will all be destroyed.[32] Once basic needs are met, humans are free to contemplate higher needs.

Did these teachings make any difference? Ideals of this sort need to be checked against history: fine ideals are often ignored in practice. Based on the accounts of contemporary Chinese pilgrims, however, the program of Nagarjuna does seem to have been effective.

Contemporary Counsels[33]

The modern scholar Robert Thurman draws some contemporary counsels from Nagarjuna's writing. He says most Americans don't want to hear that:

We are being waited on and served by developing peoples.

We shouldn't consume so much.

Death, the ill, and the poor should be *seen*, so that we can see that life is impermanent and impure.

All beings are of as much value as we ourselves and those dear to us are.

There is no self, no absolute property, no absolute right.[34]

We must face our obligations to other peoples, other species, and nature itself. The wealth of nations today has come from:

1. The work and invention of former generations;
2. The exploitation of peaceful nations in Asia, Africa, and Latin America; and
3. The generosity of the earth, sun, ocean, and wind.

If we are not generous, we will lose our wealth. *We must* restrain consumption to invest in the future for future generations, to restore resources to the exploited, and to heal our environment—*or we will face disaster!*[35]

Thich Nhat Hanh (1926– , Vietnam, in Exile in France)

The Buddhist monk Thich Nhat Hanh founded the Tiep Hien order in 1964 in Vietnam to "study, experiment and apply Buddhism in an intelligent and effective way to modern life, both individual and societal"[36] (that is, to practice "*engaged Buddhism*") and to resist the Vietnam War. The order started with six persons. It organized demonstrations, wrote and distributed literature, offered social services, organized an underground for draft resisters, and cared for the victims of the war.

Under very difficult circumstances the Tiep Hien order practiced social action based on these Buddhist principles: (a) emptiness and nonego in action, (b) the impermanence and insubstantiality of reality, (c) the lack of real separation between myself and my opponents, (d) remaining aware and in a state of compassion, (e) having the courage to see the nature of suffering in its concrete reality, and (f) working to liberate all beings.[37] Members experimented first with themselves, seeking to develop understanding and compassion in ways that could be verified by experience.[38]

There were four foundational principles of the order. Note the relationship of these principles to the war in Vietnam, which was underway at the time:

1. *Nonattachment to views* in a time when everyone around them was killing in order to force their views on others.
2. *Direct practice-realization* rather than intellectual speculation, whereas the war was being justified on the basis of speculative ideologies.
3. *Appropriateness* in meeting the "needs of people and reality of society" rather than the desires of the elite, yet in conformity with the basic tenets of Buddhism.
4. *Skillful means*, or the importance of choosing means that are effective, in contrast with the ineffective means chosen by the warring parties.

The Fourteen Tiep Hien Precepts

The order maintained its spiritual core in the midst of its social service by meeting about every two weeks and publicly and meditatively reciting the following fourteen precepts, which illustrate well the connections between one Buddhist worldview and social action.[39] As you read the precepts, consider how they would have applied in the midst of the Vietnam War, as well as how they might apply to our own situation today.

1. Do not be idolatrous about or bound to any doctrine, theory, or ideology, even Buddhist ones. All systems of thought are guiding means; they are not absolute truth.
2. Do not think the knowledge you presently possess is changeless, absolute truth. Avoid being narrow-minded and bound to present views. Learn and practice nonattachment from views in order to be open to receive others' viewpoints. Truth is found in life and not merely in conceptual knowledge. Be ready to learn throughout your entire life and to observe reality in yourself and in the world at all times.
3. Do not force others, including children, by any means whatsoever, to adopt your views, whether by authority, threat, money, propaganda, or even education. However, through compassionate dialogue, help others renounce fanaticism and narrowness.

4. Do not avoid contact with suffering or close your eyes before suffering. Do not lose awareness of the existence of suffering in the life of the world. Find ways to be with those who are suffering by all means, including personal contact and visits, images, sound. By such means, awaken yourself and others to the reality of suffering in the world.

5. Do not accumulate wealth while millions are hungry. Do not take as the aim of your life fame, profit, wealth, or sensual pleasure. Live simply and share time, energy, and material resources with those who are in need.

6. Do not maintain anger or hatred. As soon as anger and hatred arise, practice the meditation on compassion in order to deeply understand the persons who have caused anger and hatred. Learn to look at other beings with the eyes of compassion.

7. Do not lose yourself in dispersion and in your surroundings. Learn to practice breathing in order to regain composure of body and mind, to practice mindfulness and to develop concentration and understanding. [This seventh precept is the heart of Tiep Hien life. It deals with delusion = *avidya*.]

8. Do not utter words that can create discord and cause the community to break. Make every effort to reconcile and resolve all conflicts, however small.

9. Do not say untruthful things for the sake of personal interest or to impress people. Do not utter words that cause division and hatred. Do not spread news that you do not know to be certain. Do not criticize or condemn things that you are not sure of. Always speak truthfully and constructively. Have the courage to speak out about situations of injustice, even when doing so may threaten your own safety.

10. Do not use the Buddhist community for personal gain or profit, or transform your community into a political party. A religious community, however, should take a clear stand against oppression and injustice and should strive to change the situation without engaging in partisan conflicts.

11. Do not live with a vocation that is harmful to humans and nature. Do not invest in companies that deprive others of their chance to live. Select a vocation which helps realize your ideal of compassion.

12. Do not kill. Do not let others kill. Find whatever means possible to protect life and to prevent war.

13. Possess nothing that should belong to others. Respect the property of others, but prevent others from enriching themselves from human suffering or the suffering of other beings.

14. Do not mistreat your body. Learn to handle it with respect. Do not look on your body as only an instrument. Preserve vital energies (sexual, breath, spirit) for the realization of the Way. Sexual expression should not happen without love and commitment. In sexual relationships, be aware of future suffering that may be caused. To preserve the happiness of others, respect the rights and commitments of others. Be fully aware of the responsibility of bringing new lives into the world. Meditate on the world into which you are bringing new beings.[40]

The Dalai Lama (1935– , Tibet, in Exile in India)[41]

Tenzin Gyatso is the 14th Dalai Lama (meaning "Ocean of Wisdom"), or re-birth of the Buddhist Bodhisattva of Compassion. He was born in the village of Takster in Tibet, into a peasant family. Tibetans call him the "wish-fulfilling gem" or "the presence."

After he was discovered to be the successor of the 13th Dalai Lama, he was taken to Llasa, the capital of Tibet, to begin his education. In 1950, while still a teenager, he assumed the political office of Head of State and Government for Tibet. Four years later he met with Chinese leaders, and two years after that with the Chinese premier and India's Prime Minister Nehru regarding Tibet. Before being awarded a Doctorate of Buddhist Philosophy, he was examined by numerous scholarly monks in logic, the "middle path," monastic discipline, and metaphysics.

As a result of China's military occupation of Tibet in 1959, he moved from Tibet to India, where Dharamsala has served as the capital-in-exile of the Tibetan government. The Dalai Lama's work on behalf of Tibetan independence has taken the form of (among others) a draft constitution, the founding of Tibetan "educational, cultural, and religious institutions," and his Five-Point Peace Plan (1987–1988), according to which an autonomous, democratic Tibet would be established "in association with the People's Republic of China."

In 1989 the Dalai Lama received the Nobel Peace Prize. Much traveled in the West as well as the East, he has met with Catholic, Anglican, Jewish, and other religious leaders. For example, in early February 2006, he spoke with an ecumenical Korean women's group and went to Israel to promote Israeli-Palestinian dialogue. He supports having a plurality of religions in the world, and stresses the importance of feeling the suffering of others.

A. T. Ariyaratne (1931– , Sri Lanka)

This Sri Lankan Buddhist layman has begun a movement of Buddhist social and spiritual development called *Sarvodaya Shramadana* ("the awakening of all through labor for the common good"), which has touched the life of over eleven thousand villages in Sri Lanka. He seeks to develop a "no poverty, no affluence society." That may not seem attractive to the affluent—unless they reflect on how poorly their affluence satisfies them—but imagine how it sounds to the poor.

Ariyaratne calls the current world system a "vicious, power-oriented political system" in which affluence is an addiction. He explains that consumerism is against the Buddhist middle way, because it makes everyone want to join the small, affluent elite. The free-market economy provides nonessential but tempting goods. As a result, malnutrition, crime, bribery, and corruption go up; teenagers loot; and so forth. People see the consumer society, but find themselves unable to take part in it.[42] Quoting Gandhi, to be nonviolent requires us to desire nothing that the poorest can't have. We need to resist the "hypnotic dazzle" coming with "violent force from the West."[43]

In contrast, Ariyaratne uses the traditional Buddhist "four sublime abodes" to explain how his program leads people to live happier lives:

1. *Metta* (loving kindness) gives one respect and compassion for all lives, especially the lives of the very poor.
2. *Karuna* (compassionate action) leads one to change those things that cause others to suffer; to help those in great need by shared labor; and to fight evil—not the evil-doer. As a result, one experiences
3. *Muditha* (altruistic joy)—the joy of service; one rejoices in the happiness of those one helps, and as one makes such actions habitual, one comes gradually to experience
4. *Upekka* (equanimity).

He also promotes four principles of *group* behavior:

1. Sharing resources with all to overcome selfishness and craving (*thanha*);
2. Pleasant speech;
3. Constructive activity, material and spiritual—activities conducted together for everyone's benefit; and
4. Equality.[44]

He relates social action to the four noble truths as follows:

1. All life involves the suffering of egoism: "possession, competition, hatred, harsh speech, destructive action, inequality."
2. This suffering has causes such as *avidya* (ignorance), *thanha* (grasping and greed), "disunity, oppression, disease, poverty, and stagnation."
3. The causes can be removed by "awareness building and awakening" through common effort and action for the common good.
4. One should work out a path or concrete plan for doing so.[45]

With regard to appropriate development, he speaks of ten basic human needs:

1. "A clean and beautiful environment";
2. "A safe and adequate supply of water";

3. "Basic . . . clothing";
4. "A regular balanced diet";
5. "A simple abode";
6. "Basic Health Care Services";
7. "Transport and Communication facilities";
8. "Fuel";
9. "Continuing education for all" through the whole human cycle of births and deaths; and
10. "Cultural and spiritual development."[46]

Note that employment and income are not on the list. They are *only means* to the attainment of these ten needs. In different circumstances there may be alternative means to attain them.

He also lists four essential components of a good economic system:

1. Efficiency in production;
2. Protection of what is produced, for example, preservation of food;
3. The "social environment in which production takes place"; and
4. Balanced consumption patterns.[47]

Throughout his teaching, he emphasizes the key Buddhist concepts of overcoming one's ego self-centeredness (*anatman*) and one's craving (*thanha*) for impermanent, unsatisfying things. We need to overcome our pre-occupation with "I, me, and mine," which leads to anger, hatred, and greed.

A war has been going on in Sri Lanka since the 1980s between Sinhalese Buddhists and Tamil Hindus. Ariyaratne has been very active in peace-making endeavors there. One of his most successful efforts has been a program to bring together Sinhalese and Tamil youth—fifty of each—for a common workshop in which the youth are matched up in pairs. After the workshop they live together for two months and work together in their respective communities: one month in the home of the Sinhalese youth, the next month in the home of the Tamil youth. Recently he has had to suspend the follow-up to the workshop because life in the Tamil area has been too dangerous. But he has continued the seminars themselves. At the end of a seminar, one of the Tamil youth got up and said, "My father was killed by Sinhalese. I vowed that in retaliation I would kill seven Sinhalese. But this weekend I have come to know a Sinhalese boy, and I publicly renounce my vow."

Ariyaratne relates the experience of a Buddhist monk who was captured by terrorists, beaten, and abducted. The monk thought to himself:

Owing to some wrong information I am being beaten and questioned by these foolish people. Perhaps some past karma of mine might even lead to my death.

Therefore, there is no point in my hating these people or even generating self-pity toward myself. Rather, I should have loving-kindness for them. Perhaps loving-kindness will bring them to their true senses. At the same time I might be strengthened to bear my suffering with equanimity like a true disciple of the Buddha, and die with loving-kindness in my heart.[48]

During his ordeal, he concentrated on the teachings of the Buddha and on *metta*. The group which had abducted him came to realize their mistake. They asked him to forgive them, treated his wounds, and released him.

Ariyaratne's work has been quite dangerous at times, and he himself has faced death. Once a Sri Lankan president gave orders to have him murdered. One evening, while he was praying his Buddhist devotions, he felt a strong force push him forward—a sort of spiritual energy. He went out of his house into the garden and found himself facing a man who was pointing a gun at him. He said, "Go ahead. Shoot. But tell whoever sent you that I die with no hatred in my heart." The man dropped his arm and said, "I can't shoot you. Please go hide."[49]

Aung San Suu Kyi (1945– , Burma; President-Elect under House Arrest)

Suu Kyi was born in Rangoon, Burma. Her father, General Aung San, led Burma's struggle for independence from Britain; he was assassinated in 1947, when Suu Kyi was two years old, and her mother, Khin Kyi, served as the Burmese ambassador to India, beginning her term in 1960.

After studying in India and at Oxford University, Suu Kyi worked as Assistant Secretary of the Advisory Committee on Administration and Budgetary Questions of the UN secretariat in New York from 1969 to 1971. In the same period she volunteered as a reader and companion to poor hospitalized patients. At the beginning of 1972, she married Michael Aris (who died in 1999) and had two sons with him. She continued her scholarly work at Kyoto, Simla (northern India), Oxford, and London.

In the spring of 1988 Suu Kyi left England and returned to Burma to care for her mother, who had suffered from a stroke. She has remained in Burma since then, dedicating herself to the transformation of Burma's government from military dictatorship to popular democracy. When the National League for Democracy won the general elections called by the military junta in 1990, although she was already under house arrest, Suu Kyi should have become prime minister, but the junta did not allow this to happen. In 1990 she was awarded the Sakharov Prize, and in 1991 the Nobel Peace Prize. Suu Kyi has spent the decade and a half since her landslide election victory under house arrest or other restriction by the former government, which refuses to yield

power. Her writings include *Freedom from Fear* (1995), in which a biograph-
ical essay about her father is reprinted, and *Voice of Hope: Conversations*
(1997). She leads an explicitly nonviolent pro-democracy and human rights
movement in Myanmar/Burma.[50] To the 1995 global women's conference in
Beijing, she said: "It is not the prerogative of men alone to bring light to the
world: women with their capacity for compassion and self-sacrifice, their
courage and perseverance, have done much to dissipate the darkness of intolerance and hate, suffering and despair."[51]

SUMMARY

The doctrinal core of Buddhism is expressed in the four noble truths, all of
which relate to human suffering. Buddhists concentrate on overcoming suffering by letting go of the desire to hang on to impermanent material and spiritual things, including existence itself, through meditation and appropriate, or
right, living. If we fail to do so, we will continue to experience re-birth and
re-death. Clinging to one's ego produces the main barrier to enlightenment.
In practice, few Buddhists pursue nirvana single-heartedly and love other humans unselfishly, but those who do have been very effective in promoting justice and peace. The ultimate authority validating Buddhist teaching is one's
own experience as one meditates on and enacts what one has learned.

KEY TERMS

anatman	Hinayana
avidya	*Jataka Tales*
bodhi	Mahayana
Bodhisattva	metta
Buddha	metta bhavana
deva	nirvana
dharma	parinirvana
dukkha	sangha
Engaged Buddhism	Theravada
enlightenment	Vajrayana

DISCUSSION QUESTIONS

1. Do you agree with the first noble truth, that all life is suffering—or perhaps, that there is an element of dissatisfaction in every aspect of life? Do

you agree that suffering comes when we try to hold on to impermanent things? Have you ever experienced relief when you let go of something you had been trying unsuccessfully to hang on to?

2. "Perfect livelihood" is one component of the "eight-fold path." How well does your present or anticipated occupation meet its criteria?

3. The chapter shared some ideas of five Buddhist workers for justice and peace: Nagarjuna, Thich Nhat Hanh, the Dalai Lama, A. T. Ariyaratne, and Aung San Suu Kyi. If you had the time and opportunity to read about the life of one of them, or to read his or her writings, which would you be likely to choose first? Why might you choose that one? Was there something in the textbook description that particularly caught your attention and interest? Was there something you especially agreed with? Something you especially disagreed with?

4. If you had to choose one of their lives as your own, whose life would you most like to have led? Whose life would you most like *not* to have led? Why? Do their lives suggest any activities or insights that you would like to incorporate into your own life? If so, which activities or insights, and how?

5. The modern scholar Robert Thurman draws some contemporary counsels from Nagarjuna's writing. Which of his observations and counsels seem right to you? Which do not? What should we do about them?

NOTES

1. Gautama, "The Sermon at Benares." In *Buddha, the Gospel.* www.sacred-texts.com/bud/btg/btg17.htm (accessed March 3, 2007).

2. The periodization here is based on the article "Buddhism" in *The Encyclopedia of Eastern Philosophy and Religion*, 50.

3. Smart, *The World's Religions,* 59.

4. Traditional dates for his life are 563–483 BCE. Smart, *The World's Religions* suggests ("possibly") the date 586 for his birth.

5. The first term given is the Sanskrit word; the term in parentheses is its Pali equivalent.

6. This Buddhist use of the word "dharma" should not be confused with the Hindu sense of the same word. For Hindus, "dharma" means "duty based on the true nature of things and our place in that nature (caste)." For Buddhists, it means the "teaching of the Buddha."

7. Siloan and Sophrony, *Wisdom from Mount Athos,* 98.

8. Schuhmacher and Woerner, eds., *Encyclopedia of Eastern Philosophy and Religion*, 249.

9. For a fuller discussion of various Buddhist views of nirvana, see Schuhmacher and Woerner, eds., *Encyclopedia of Eastern Philosophy and Religion*, 249–50.

10. Some Buddhists deny the existence of God. Others hold that God might or might not exist, but the search to prove God's existence is a distraction from the search for enlightenment. Buddhism arose in dialogue with Hinduism and so denied the Hindu characterizations of God. The pamphlet *Twelve Principles of Buddhism*, by the Corporate Body of the Buddha Educational Foundation, says "Reality is indescribable, and *a God with attributes* is not the final Reality" (p. 8, emphases added). You might think through the implications of this statement in view of Thomas Aquinas' conviction that no positive statement about God can be anything more than an analogy.

11. This connection between the Christian notion of the human creature and the Buddhist notion of *anatman* is noted by Pieris, *Love Meets Wisdom*.

12. Spiro, *Buddhism*.

13. See the description at www.us.emb-japan.go.jp/jicc/spottea.htm (accessed January 26, 2005).

14. Spiro, *Buddhism*, chap. 6.

15. Spiro, *Buddhism*, 149.

16. Spiro, *Buddhism*.

17. Victoria, *Zen at War*, 137.

18. Victoria, *Zen at War*, 121. See also Victoria, *Zen War Stories*.

19. Macy, *Despair and Personal Power in the Nuclear Age*.

20. Macy, *Despair and Personal Power*, 155f.

21. Macy, *Despair and Personal Power*, 156–58.

22. Thurman, "Nagarjuna's Guidelines for Buddhist Social Action," 121–22.

23. Thurman, "Nagarjuna's Guidelines," 125.

24. Thurman, "Nagarjuna's Guidelines," 126.

25. Thurman, "Nagarjuna's Guidelines," 138.

26. Thurman, "Nagarjuna's Guidelines," 139.

27. Thurman, "Nagarjuna's Guidelines," 127.

28. Thurman, "Nagarjuna's Guidelines," 135.

29. Thurman, "Nagarjuna's Guidelines," 137.

30. Thurman, "Nagarjuna's Guidelines," 128.

31. Thurman, "Nagarjuna's Guidelines," 128, 139.

32. Thurman, "Nagarjuna's Guidelines," 139f.

33. Thurman, "Nagarjuna's Guidelines," 130.

34. Thurman, "Nagarjuna's Guidelines," 131.

35. Thurman, "Nagarjuna's Guidelines," 132. For likely disasters caused by resource depletion, especially hydrocarbons, see Diamond, *Collapse*; Heinberg, *The Party's Over* and *Power Down*.

36. Nhat Hanh, *Interbeing*, 16.

37. Nhat Hanh, *Interbeing*, 8.

38. Nhat Hanh, *Interbeing*, 17.

39. For the current, updated version of these principles, now called "The Fourteen Mindfulness Trainings," see the publisher of the book *Interbeing*, now in its third (2005) edition, at www.parallax.org/about_oi.html (accessed July 9, 2006), or the

website of Plum Village Meditation Center, founded by Thich Nhat Hanh, www
.plumvillage.org/ (accessed July 9, 2006).

40. Nhat Hanh, *Interbeing,* 27–36.

41. nobelprize.org/peace/laureates/1989/lama-bio.html (accessed January 19,
2006).

42. Ariyaratne, *Buddhism and Sarvodaya: Sri Lankan Experience.*

43. Ariyaratne, *Buddhism and Sarvodaya,* 66.

44. Ariyaratne, *Buddhism and Sarvodaya,* viii, 7–11.

45. Ariyaratne, *Buddhism and Sarvodaya,* 74.

46. Ariyaratne, *Buddhism and Sarvodaya,* 38f.

47. Ariyaratne, *Buddhism and Sarvodaya,* 49f.

48. Ariyaratne, *Buddhism and Sarvodaya,* 126.

49. Smith, interview with Ariyaratne.

50. See her website at www.dassk.org/index.php (accessed January 24, 2007).

51. www.dassk.org/contents.php?id=127 (accessed January 24, 2007).

SUGGESTIONS FOR FURTHER READING

Ariyaratne. *Buddhism and Sarvodaya.*

Aung San Suu Kyi. *The Voice of Hope.*

Chappel, ed. *Buddhist Peacework.*

Dalai Lama. *The Buddhism of Tibet.*

Diamond. *Collapse.*

Eppsteiner, ed. *The Path of Compassion: Writings on Socially Engaged Buddhism.*

Galtung. *Buddhism: A Quest for Unity and Peace.*

Heinberg. *The Party's Over.*

———. *Power Down.*

Macy. *Despair and Personal Power in the Nuclear Age.*

Nhat Hanh. *Being Peace.*

———. *Interbeing: Commentaries on the Tiep Hien Precepts.*

———. *Vietnam: Lotus in a Sea of Fire.*

Queen, ed. *Engaged Buddhism in the West.*

Queen and King, eds. *Engaged Buddhism.*

Rinpoche. *Selected Writings and Speeches.*

Silouan and Sofronii. *Wisdom from Mount Athos.*

Sivaraksa. *Conflict, Culture, Change: Engaged Buddhism in a Globalizing World.*

———. *Socially Engaged Buddhism for the New Millennium.*

Spiro. *Buddhism and Society: A Great Tradition and Its Burmese Vicissitudes.*

Thurman. "Nagarjuna's Guidelines for Buddhist Social Action."

Victoria. *Zen at War.*

———. *Zen War Stories.*

Chapter Three

Jewish Worldviews

"Hear, O Israel! The LORD is our God, the LORD alone! Therefore, you shall love the LORD, your God, with all your heart, and with all your soul, and with all your strength."

—Deuteronomy 6:4–5

"I, the LORD, am your God, who brought you out of the land of Egypt, that place of slavery. You shall not have other gods besides me."

—Exodus 20:2–3

"You have been told, O [Mortal], what is good,
and what the LORD requires of you:
Only to do the right and to love goodness,
and to walk humbly with your God."

—Micah 6:8

EXPERIENTIAL AND EMOTIONAL DIMENSION

The central experience giving rise to the Jewish worldview is rooted in history far more than were the two previous worldviews. Not only have Jewish experience and beliefs varied *throughout* history, as is the case for all religions; Jews also experienced God *through God's acts in* history. Jews believe that their ancestors escaped slavery in Egypt and entered the land at the eastern end of the Mediterranean through a powerful act of God, who chose them to be his own people and enabled them to settle the land in the face of its indigenous inhabitants. God established a unique covenant with them, calling them to be faithful to God alone (in a world that worshiped a multitude of gods), to live justly, and to be a light to the nations. God accomplished this remarkable act through key leaders—prophets, judges, and kings—who would speak and act for God. When the people accepted and kept the words that God spoke through the prophets, they prospered; when they turned away to worship other gods, they experienced disaster. God's instructions eventually included sacrifice exclusively at one Temple in Jerusalem.

Yet for long periods of Jewish history, they found themselves scattered from the land that God had promised them, the Temple in Jerusalem destroyed. As they tried to understand the meaning of this disaster, they maintained their sense of being a separate people and gradually developed alternative ways of worshiping God and following his directions. For the most part, they lived as foreign communities within the various countries where they found themselves. Previously, their contact with God had been mediated through prophets and through the Law which the prophet Moses had received from God. But prophecy waned, and they centered their devotion on the Law itself, written and oral. Eventually, this was supplemented by a form of mystical union with God called Kabbalah. Some Jews never entirely gave up their expectation that God would restore their own kingdom in their ancestral land through a messiah—an anointed king—sometime in the future.

As they entered the modern period and began to be accepted in modern nation-states as full-fledged citizens, yet with worrisome episodes of persecution, they were torn between their sense of separateness and their desire to belong to the larger society. Toward the end of the 19th century, some Jews concluded that they should return to their ancient land and reestablish a Jewish society there without waiting for God to anoint a messiah; others thought such a move was premature, and even a rejection of God's will. In the middle of the 20th century, the Holocaust shook their confidence that they understood their relationships with God, with non-Jews, and with their own community. This crisis accelerated the establishment of the state of Israel and continues to haunt its domestic and foreign policy, especially in relation to the Palestinians, hundreds of thousands of whom were driven from their homes when the state was established in 1948. The majority of Jews remain outside Israel, where they discuss and practice various ways of being Jewish in their varied circumstances and of relating to the state of Israel, which claims all Jews throughout the world as potential citizens.

HISTORICAL PERIODS[1]

Jews usually divide their history into four main periods:

1. The Biblical Period (from the "beginning" to the Babylonian Exile, which destroyed the kingdom of Judah and the first temple in 587 BCE and lasted about fifty years). Depending on when you think this period "began," it could be divided into two or three sub-periods: (a) from Abraham (ca. 1800 BCE) to the Exodus (ca. 1300 BCE)—during which Abraham, his extended family, and his descendants lived as foreigners in Canaan or Egypt, (b) from the Exodus to the kingship of Saul (ca. 1000 BCE)—the entry into Canaan of twelve tribes called Israelite and their occasional common defense against enemies, and (c) the period of the kings of Israel and Judah. During this biblical period, most of the Hebrew Bible (roughly equal to the Christian "Old Testament") was written. The term "Jews" in this period refers only to those who lived in the kingdom of Judah, not the larger number who lived in the kingdom of Israel. Although the Hebrew Bible "great tradition" insistently demanded that the people worship only one God, its own text shows that many of them were polytheists. The community later attributed the tragedy of the exile to this fact.
2. The Second Temple Period (from the restoration after the exile through the Roman destruction of the second temple in 70 CE). For all but a brief period, the community had limited autonomy under foreign rule. Ritual centered on animal sacrifice exclusively at the Second Temple in Jerusalem. During this period, the community became more exclusive and began to develop the detailed observance of the Law which characterized later Judaism, although different parties disputed the proper interpretation of the Law.
3. The Period of Rabbinic Judaism (from the destruction of the Second Temple to the beginning of the "Modern Period"; the modern period began at widely different dates in different countries: by about 1800 in the United States and France; as late as the 1950s in Yemen). The Roman destruction scattered many Jews outside their homeland in the *Diaspora*; the scattered communities maintained their cohesion because they were allowed limited autonomy exercised through local rabbis. As they lost hope that they could come home to restore political freedom and animal sacrifice, they centered their Jewish identity on detailed observance of the Law. During this period, the Jews also developed a complex mysticism called Kabbalah.
4. The Modern Period. Starting around 1800, some nations began to accept Jews as full citizens rather than as a foreign subculture. As a result, the

authority of their rabbinic leaders declined. At the same time, some Jews sought to adapt their traditional Law to modern conditions. The tensions that developed within the Jewish community and with the larger world outside will be discussed in this chapter and in the case study of chapter 8.

SACRED WRITINGS

Jews refer to the inspired scriptures of the Second Temple Period as the *Tanakh*. They also call them the *Bible* or the *Hebrew Bible*—meaning, approximately, what the Christians call the *Old Testament*. The word *Tanakh* is the acronym made up from the first letters of the words for the three major sections of that collection: (1) *Torah ("Law" or, better, "Teaching"):* Genesis through Deuteronomy—the Pentateuch, (2) *Nevi'im:* the Former and Latter Prophets (the Former Prophets are listed by Christians as "historical books"— for example the books of Kings), and (3) *Ketuvim:* the "Writings"—everything that doesn't fit under the first two categories. In a broader sense, *Torah* can mean the whole *Tanakh*, or even the whole of Jewish moral teaching.

In addition to the *Tanakh*, Jews have many other sacred traditions. In the time of Jesus, a major group of exclusively oral traditions promoted especially by the Pharisees discussed how to live the *Torah* in every aspect of daily life. Traditional rabbis claim that these traditions are as old and as authoritative as the *Torah* itself, that Moses received both the written *Torah* and the oral *Torah* from God himself on Mount Sinai. After several centuries, these oral traditions were written down in several collections. The first collection was called the *Mishnah*. A later and much expanded version, a sort of commentary on the *Mishnah*, is the *Talmud*, which exists in two quite different forms, the Jerusalem and Babylonian Talmuds. In form, each page of the Talmud contains several blocks of text: the Mishnah in one block surrounded by several different blocks of commentary. Those commentaries taken altogether are called the *Gemara,* so it is commonly said that Mishnah plus Gemara makes Talmud.

Another way of dividing the content of Torah is the distinction between *halakhah* and *haggadah*. Halakhah refers to the specifically *legal* materials; the word is derived from the word "to walk" and means "how you walk." Haggadah refers to *all the rest*, consisting largely of narrative materials like stories, legends, folklore, anecdotes, short sayings, and homilies on biblical passages.

Study of the Talmud has accustomed Jews to divergent interpretations of their sacred texts: the very form of the Talmud—a collection of abbreviated rabbinic discussions—and the way it is taught develops in them a flexibility and openness to contrasting interpretations.

Other traditions include the *Targums*, which are rather free translations of the Tanakh from Hebrew into Aramaic. In the time of Jesus, Hebrew had become a religious and classical language, like Latin in our day, and Aramaic was the everyday language of most Jews in Palestine; the Targums were exclusively oral. Later some Targums were written down. There were also expansions and explanations of the Tanakh (including the Nevi'im and the Ketuvim, which are largely absent from the Talmud), called *midrashim* (plural of *midrash*), that functioned as commentaries. Besides these more or less authoritative writings, there are also many Jewish stories, such as the Hasidic tales collected by Elie Wiesel and others.

NARRATIVE OR MYTHIC DIMENSION

As the Jewish community passes on its history in which God reveals himself and through which they believe God has entered into a special relationship with them, several themes stand out.

Covenant and Chosen People

Very strong among Jews is the sense of *covenant* or solemn agreement between themselves and God, who has revealed himself to them and formed them into a community. This conviction gives Jews a strong sense of being a special or "chosen" people, which has been very important to them, because historically Jews have been a small group and often threatened by more powerful neighbors. This sense has also led to misunderstanding, as their neighbors have accused them of being clannish and uncooperative. Their sense of being a chosen people should not lead to arrogance: it is not for their personal glory that God chose Jews, but to be the bearers of God's revelation, God's glory and holiness, and the suffering that the world visits on God's followers. This sense of being chosen also explains why Judaism cannot be understood apart from its history. The Holocaust and the state of Israel are not "just political"—they are part of Jewish self-understanding.

Promised Land

In the 13th century BCE, Hebrew tribes identifying themselves as the twelve tribes of Israel moved into Canaan, later called Palestine after the Philistines. At first the Israelites lived on the margins of the urban society—most of the largest cities remained Canaanite. Over a two-hundred-year period, the Israelites gradually gained control over the country: King David captured

Jerusalem about 1000 BCE. From that time until 587 BCE, Israelite kings (of the kingdoms of Israel and Judah) controlled significant parts of the Near East. From 587 until about 140 BCE the Israelites were under foreign control (Babylonian, Persian, Greek, Syrian), but at first the majority of them still lived in Palestine-Israel-Judah. As time went on, a larger percentage lived outside the homeland. The people came eventually to be called Jews after their base in Judea. They attributed their earlier successes to God's help and their later failures to their failure to obey God's commands.

After the successful (Jewish) Maccabean revolt against Syria in the 2nd century BCE, the Jewish Hasmonean kingdom maintained independence for about eighty years, attributing their success to God's support. Then Rome arrived and incorporated Palestine into the Roman Empire. In response to vigorous Jewish revolts against Rome in 70 and 135 CE, Rome banned Jews from Jerusalem and made life difficult for them elsewhere. Over the course of time, more and more Jews moved out of Palestine to other areas of the Greco-Roman world. On the other hand, there never was a time when all the Jews were gone: centers like Safed, Tiberias, and Jerusalem maintained Jewish populations to the present day.

The communities of Jews scattered throughout the world outside Palestine made up the Diaspora. Most of the earliest Christian mission activity was carried on among these Diaspora Jews. These Diaspora communities kept the memory of the Holy Land alive, praying at each Passover, "Next year in Jerusalem." For the drama of the Jewish restoration in our day and its implications for other communities living in that same land, see chapter 8 on the Israeli-Palestinian Conflict.

A Holy People

Given their historical experience, Jews needed a sense of identity to survive as a community. With the destruction of the temple and exile from Jerusalem, which was rebuilt as a Roman city, Jews could no longer sense God's presence in the *temple* and the *city*. Instead, Jews developed a sense of God present among the *people,* reflected in their holiness expressed in a special way of life. Study of the Torah and the living out of that study in daily life, ritual, and ceremony became a safeguard of Jewish identity and a guarantee that Judaism would go on.

A Sense of Persecution

Judaism has often struggled to maintain its faith under the pressure of external forces. For example, in the 2nd century BCE the Seleucid king Antiochus

IV Epiphanes of Syria had tried to force all his subject peoples to conform to the religious, philosophical, and scientific ideas of Greece. He prohibited Sabbath observance, circumcision, use of the Torah, and worship of the God of Israel. Antiochus rededicated the (second) temple in Jerusalem to the head of the Greek pantheon: Zeus. He arrested women whose children had been circumcised, paraded them around with their dead children hung around their necks, and then killed them.

A revolt against these measures began in 167 BCE in a village near Jerusalem, where a Jewish priest (Mattathias) refused to obey the orders of Seleucid officers. He and his sons—the Maccabees (or, in Greek, Hasmons)—then led a guerrilla operation to end Seleucid control of Palestine. In 164 BCE they reclaimed the temple for Jewish worship. The festival of Hanukkah celebrates the re-dedication of the temple. Eventually the Maccabees (Hasmons) established the (Jewish) Hasmonean kingdom, which endured until 63 BCE, when quarreling factions invited Roman intervention, effectively ending their independence.

Foundations of Rabbinic Judaism

Christian readers are familiar with Pharisees and Sadducees from the Gospels, where they are presented in a generally hostile light. Essenes and Zealots add two more groups. First-century Christians could be considered a fifth Jewish group. Most Jewish inhabitants of the Roman province of Palestine did not belong to any of these groups, although they might have been sympathetic to one or the other of them. It has been estimated that the peasants ("people of the land"), the artisans, the unclean, and the homeless comprised 90% of the Jewish population at that time.

By 66 CE, the Zealots convinced the Jewish leaders, mainly Sadducees, to revolt against Rome. The Romans crushed Zealots wherever they found them, considering them to be terrorists and the main instigators of the revolt. They removed the Sadducees from power, since the Sadducees had been the political leaders in the revolt. They destroyed the Essene community at Qumran, as it lay athwart their supply lines and the Essenes had allied themselves with the rebels. The Christians had refused to join the revolt, but they were not yet numerous enough to be much noticed by the Romans. Of all the dominant Jewish groups, the Pharisees were the least implicated in the revolt.

The main center of the Sadducees' power had been the temple with its sacrificial priesthood, which they lost when Rome destroyed the temple and suppressed Jewish sacrificial worship. The Pharisees, in contrast, had already developed alternative forms of piety centered on prayer worship in synagogues—prayer meeting halls. This form of piety had first appeared in Babylonia during the Babylonian exile after 587 BCE. The exiles were far from Jerusalem and the *first* Jerusalem temple had been destroyed, so the exiles had developed another form of worship requiring only a congregation of at least ten Jewish men to study the Torah, pray, and sing hymns. Now that Rome had destroyed the *Second* temple, the Pharisees expanded this piety into what became rabbinic Judaism. Rabbis thought out ways to preserve Judaism without the temple or its sacrifice. In their place, they put the written *Torah*, the *oral* traditions (which the Pharisees believed also went back to the Sinai revelation), scriptural commentary, and a calendar of sacred festivals. Places of meeting for prayer became known as synagogues.

Premodern Jewish Experience in Europe and Russia

In medieval Christian Europe under feudalism, Jews were not allowed to own land. In Italian and German cities from the mid-16th century on, Jewish inhabitants had to live in urban *ghettos*—quarters assigned exclusively to Jews, since Jews were not allowed to live anywhere else. Jewish rabbis were allowed to regulate these ghettos internally in accordance with rather authoritarian Talmudic law, but they were not pleasant places to live. For their part, medieval Jews on the whole avoided social relations with Christians or Muslims. The Jews were protected by the local rulers, who often employed them

Figure 3.1. "Western Wall" with Temple Mount—site of destroyed Second Temple—in background. Note Muslim Dome of the Rock on the Temple Mount. Courtesy David Whitten Smith, about 1975.

as agents or buffers between themselves and the peasants—as tax collectors, merchants, artisans, and money lenders. Even rulers sought out Jewish money lenders to finance their schemes, since Christians were not allowed to charge interest and so had little interest in lending money. The Jews often found themselves to be convenient targets of peasants' resentment toward their lords.

Persecution by Christians

For centuries Jews in Europe learned to stay indoors and out of sight on Christian holy days, because at those times it was not unusual for mobs of Christians to beat up Jews and burn their homes. This kind of active persecution is sometimes called a *pogrom*: a late-19th-century Russian word. Christians felt threatened by Jews because they kept the ancient faith rather than becoming Christians, thus challenging the Christian faith. The mobs accused Jews of being "Christ-killers." Martin Luther, in 1543, wrote a famous tract entitled *Against the Jews and Their Lies.*

Besides this unofficial, popular persecution, there were also official persecutions of Jews. As cultural and moral habits changed and *Christians* began to finance at interest, Jews no longer filled that vital societal function. As a result they were expelled from a number of countries between 1290 and 1569. Christians remember 1492 as the year that Ferdinand and Isabella of Spain sponsored Christopher Columbus's voyage which discovered the New World. Jews remember it as the year that Ferdinand and Isabella, having conquered the last Muslim resistance in Spain, expelled all Jews and all Muslims from Spain. Especially in Spain and Portugal, the *Inquisition* used torture to seek out "heretics" (including not Jews as such, but those Jews who had publicly converted to Christianity while secretly retaining their Jewish practices), expel or execute them and expropriate their property. Some of these Jews had been baptized and "converted" to Christianity by force. Many of the Jews driven from Spain in 1492 went to North Africa or Turkey, both under Muslim government. Besides expulsions, there were a number of massacres, pogroms, and forced conversions to Christianity.

The expulsions led to a major population shift of Jews from Western to Eastern Europe, in particular Poland. There they lived *without* ghettos, and often with few or no non-Jews in their midst. These Yiddish-speaking Jews enjoyed freedom of religious expression. (Yiddish is a combination of German and Hebrew.) However, in the mid-17th century, rebelling Russian Orthodox Cossacks targeted Jews as well as Roman Catholics; huge numbers of Jews were massacred.

From the Jewish standpoint, then, the *Holocaust* (*Shoah* in Hebrew)—Nazi Germany's program to exterminate all Jews and thus eliminate the need to

relate to them—was the action of a Christian country and just the most murderous example of a common Christian attitude. Hitler was not a practicing
Christian, but most of the people who voted him into office and who continued to support him were; and many Christians, especially in Eastern Europe,
cooperated with Hitler's persecution of Jews. On the other hand, there were
German and other Christians who risked their lives to save Jewish lives; So-
phie Scholl and Dietrich Bonhoeffer are two examples.

DOCTRINAL AND PHILOSOPHICAL DIMENSION

Jews believe that there is only one God—personal, loving, and just—who created the physical and spiritual worlds and demands that his creatures act justly.
This God has full power, and intervenes in behalf of those who love him. He
chooses whomever he wills to receive his blessings, but has special love for
the small, the weak, and the oppressed. He chose Abraham and formed from
his descendants a chosen people. He rescued this chosen people from slavery
in Egypt, revealed his law to them through Moses at Sinai, empowered them
to take possession of the promised land, and protected them so long as they
acted justly and worshiped God alone. But he allowed them to be defeated by
their enemies when they strayed away from the path he had pointed out to
them. He sent prophets to speak his word to them so that they would be re-
called to the proper path. Because the non-Jewish world did not know God or
understand his will, it persecuted his people, but they were called to withstand
the persecution, trusting God to be their protection and bring justice.

Orthodox Judaism believes in a spiritual survival of the soul after death, a
later resurrection of the body, and a judgment involving punishment or reward according to one's deeds in life. Reform Judaism has raised questions
about some of those beliefs. Jews in general spend much less time thinking
and talking about personal survival after death than Christians do: it is not at
the center of Jewish self-consciousness. Ashkenazic Jews, for example, think
of the afterlife more in terms of memory. They will name a child after someone who has died in order to maintain her memory. They recount her life to
the one who bears her name. On the anniversary of her death, they affirm their
belief in God.

In reflecting on human sin, a Jewish tradition speaks of two tendencies in
every human, two urges. One is called the *yetzer ha tov*, or good inclination,
the other the *yetzer ha ra'*, or evil inclination. The evil inclination is present
already at birth, and humans must keep it in check with the help of the good
inclination. But this tradition, too, is not discussed among Jews as often as is
"original sin" among Christians. The Jewish notion of sin is communal as

well as individualistic, as illustrated by the communal confession of pre-scribed sins at the ceremonies of Yom Kippur.

The Thirteen Articles of Maimonides

Moses Maimonides (d. 1204), Spanish physician and Jewish religious philosopher, sought to combine Aristotelian philosophical reasoning with re-ligious revelation. Persecution forced him to move to Egypt. His best-known work is *The Guide for the Perplexed.*

In his commentary on the Torah, he spelled out thirteen articles of Jewish faith that by the 14th century were incorporated into Jewish liturgy at morn-ing prayer: (1) the existence of God as the perfect creator and primary cause of all that exists, (2) the absolute unity of God, (3) God's nonphysicality, (4) God's eternity, (5) the exclusive worship of God, (6) God's communication with humans through prophecy, (7) the priority of Moses' prophecy, (8) the divine origin and (9) immutability of the Torah, (10) divine omniscience (all-knowledge) and providence, (11) divine reward and retribution, (12) the ar-rival of the Messiah and the messianic era, and (13) the resurrection of the dead.[2]

PRACTICAL AND RITUAL DIMENSION

The Jewish faith expresses itself in a rich life of festival and ritual and a strong sense of community. Its feasts embody the main Jewish themes we have seen, especially trust in God in the face of persecution and insecurity.

Passover (Pesach)

Pesach commemorates God's rescue of the Israelites from slavery in Egypt under Pharaoh. On the night of their rescue, the destroying angel *passed over* the Israelite houses, which had been marked with the blood of the lambs sac-rificed to God. It is a reminder that they depend on *God* for their freedom, not on their own virtue or power. Jews today celebrate a *seder* ("order of ser-vice") at home on the first night. Participants eat unleavened bread and bitter herbs; they drink four cups of wine and recite prayers, rituals, songs, and readings from their sacred traditions. The ceremonies remind Jews that life is fragile in this world of empires, and invite them to be grateful to God for their rescue. Unleavened bread called *matza* (plural *matzot*) is eaten for a week. Jewish tradition recalls that the Israelites fled from Egypt so abruptly that they did not have time to leaven the bread they were making. Since ancient leaven was a kind of sourdough that easily symbolized corruption, leaven was a sign of sin in our life and unleavened bread was a sign of a fresh start.

Pentecost (Shavuot)

Pentecost comes fifty days (seven weeks and a day) after Passover. This feast was associated with receiving the Torah (Law of Moses) from God at Mount Sinai, after the rescue from Egypt and before the conquest of the Promised Land; thus, it commemorates their special relationship as God's chosen people and the Law as their grateful response. Jews decorate their synagogues with greenery to celebrate this feast, and read the Ten Commandments and passages from the Book of Ruth.

Tabernacles or Tents (Sukkoth)

Tabernacles falls exactly half a (lunar) year after Pesach, beginning in the fall at the full moon of the seventh month (Tishri). Agriculturally, Tabernacles represented the fall harvest; the feast is also called the *Ingathering.* During the week-long celebration people live in fragile huts (*sukkot*) made of branches, commemorating the period of their wandering in the desert before they entered the Promised Land. Religiously, the fragility of these huts reminds participants of the fragility of life on earth, and memories of the desert wanderings remind them that it is often in the desert of loss and poverty that we find God. The festival runs seven days, followed by an eighth day for solemn assembly and a ninth day called *Simhat Torah*—a day to "rejoice in the Teaching."

The High Holy Days: New Year and the Day of Atonement

The Jewish New Year is celebrated as the new moon starts the seventh month (Tishri). It consists of ten days of self-examination leading to repentance so as to start the new year out with a renewed spirit. This period as a whole is called the *High Holy Days*, beginning with *Rosh Hashanah* (literally, the "head of the year") and ending with *Yom Kippur* (the Day of Atonement)—a day of fasting and repentance for sin. In modern Judaism, Yom Kippur is the most important holiday of the year. Jews abstain on this day from all food, drink, work, washing, sexual intercourse, and the wearing of leather shoes. In synagogue readings and prayers, they celebrate a humble awareness of God's glory, their own fragility, and their need for God's mercy. Since the Mishnah says that the rituals of this day atone only for one's sins before *God* and not for one's sins against other *human beings*, participants supplement those rituals on this day by seeking reconciliation with each other. Rosh Hashanah and Yom Kippur take place a few days before Sukkoth (the seven-day Feast of Tabernacles), forming with them an extended period of ritual called the *Days of Awe*.

Hanukkah

Hanukkah originated in the 2nd century BCE to commemorate the victory of the Maccabees over the Syrians. The Jews purifying the desecrated temple set up the sacred menorah (lampstand), but found only enough undesecrated oil to fuel the lamps for one day. They lit the fire anyway, and were astonished to see it burn for the entire eight days of the dedication, even growing brighter each day. In memory of that miraculous event, on each night of Hanukkah Jews light one more candle in their nine-branch candlestick (the ninth is used to light the other candles). There are also special games played, foods eaten, and gifts exchanged.

A Few Additional Celebrations

Purim commemorates the story recounted in the Book of Esther, almost certainly fictional in its present form, in which the Jewish communities in Persia, threatened with extinction by a wicked king's advisor, manage to turn the tables on their tormenter and kill, not only him, but scores of other Gentiles. Jews value the story as celebrating victory over persecution. Children dress up in costumes, making the feast a sort of Jewish *Carnevale* or *Mardi Gras*.[3]

Daily and Weekly Celebrations

The Jewish prayer book provides morning, afternoon, and evening prayers to sanctify the day. All males thirteen and older are supposed to pray them.

Perhaps the best known Jewish custom is observation of the *Sabbath*. No work can be done from sundown Friday to sundown Saturday—that time is dedicated to God. Special foods, prepared the day ahead, are eaten. Special attention is given to family and guests. The rest from work is an anticipation of paradise, as well as a sign of trust in God to meet the needs of his faithful people. Special prayers and ceremonies are carried out at home, and services are held in the local synagogue.

ETHICAL AND LEGAL DIMENSION

Some religions connect their laws and moral judgments closely or directly to the mystical experiences that were the origins of the group. Thus, they speak of "divinely revealed laws." Muslims make this claim for the Quran; as do Jews for the Law of Moses, especially the core of the law expressed in the "Ten Commandments."

Judaism, like Islam, is especially marked by its attention to how we *act* as opposed to what we *believe*. While Christians have strongly emphasized "ortho*doxy*" or right *doctrine*, Jews have emphasized "ortho*praxy*" or right *action*.

Central to all Jewish laws is the conviction that they are not just rules, they are the desire of a God who has chosen and blessed the Jewish community. Jews keep the laws not to avoid God's anger, but to show gratitude for what God has done for them. God has initiated a special relationship with the Jewish community: their faithfulness to the Torah is their grateful response.

The character of rabbinic teaching is illustrated by a story about the famous 1st-century CE rabbi Hillel, in contrast with the more conservative rabbi, Shammai. A man asked Shammai to teach him the whole Law while he stood on one leg. Shammai picked up a fireplace poker and drove him out. The unbeliever went to Hillel. Hillel made him a convert by telling him: "What you hate, don't do to your neighbor. That is the whole law; the rest is commentary. Now, go study!" Thus, social justice is a key component of Jewish law and the vast commentary on it. Nevertheless, women could not then participate in formal study of the Torah.

In the period of rabbinic Judaism, the institution of the synagogue meant that Jews could live (usually communally) in any culture and yet be distinguished as Jews by such aspects of their lives as diet and Sabbath observance.

Medieval (and Post-Medieval) Judaism: Babylon, Baghdad, Andalusia

Jews had lived in Babylon since the Exile; many exiles had made new lives for themselves there and did not return to Judah at the end of the exile. Babylon was a major Jewish intellectual center until the 10th century—the Islamic conquest did not alter that status. Two renowned *yeshivot* (rabbinic academies) of Babylon oversaw the completion of the Babylonian Talmud in the 6th century CE. Their leaders also wrote responses to questions from Jews who lived in distant places; these answers took the form of legal opinions.

Baghdad was another center of Jewish life. There Jews functioned as scholars and other professionals (for example, doctors), as merchants and tradespeople, and as artisans. Jews and Christians contributed to the Islamic renaissance under the Abbasids. Overall in Muslim-controlled areas, Jews experienced relatively good treatment, despite occasional examples of oppression and intolerance; Jews and Christians lived as "People of the Book," enjoying local autonomy and exemption from military service in exchange for payment of a tax. Speaking Arabic, Jewish scholars produced religious and philosophical works, scientific works, and Hebrew poetry. In Andalusia (Muslim Spain), Jews also held political office.

INFLUENCE FROM THE EXPERIENTIAL AND EMOTIONAL DIMENSION

Kabbalah and the Zohar

The roots of Jewish mysticism are found in the Hebrew Bible, extra-biblical literature, and the Talmud. Medieval Jewish mysticism is known as *Kabbalah*, and the foremost textual expression of Kabbalah is the *Zohar* ("Way of Splendor") thought to have been written by Moses de Leon (d. 1305). The Zohar is a compendium of stories, visionary accounts, and esoteric (secret) commentary on the Torah. In the Zohar the hidden, transcendent God is connected to the immanent creator God by ten emanations (recalling ancient Gnosticism). The world of sense perception is seen as an inferior reflection of the spiritual world, and the divine life is likewise paralleled in the life of humanity, whose acts influence the cosmos. Through the Kabbalah Jewish mystics sought union with God and the restoration of divine unity. Jewish critics complained that these speculations threatened the unity of God.

Isaac Luria (1534–1572) and Tikkun

An important 16th-century Spanish Kabbalist, *Isaac Luria* taught that the cataclysmic process of creation had shattered God's unity, sending divine sparks into the world that have penetrated all objects and actions. The human task is to collect these divine sparks to help repair the chaotic, evil state of the world, which will not be fully repaired (*tikkun* means "repair") until the Messiah comes. The practices Luria taught included obeying the Torah, asceticism, prayer, and chanting of religious formulas.

Hasidism and the Baal Shem Tov (1700–1760)

The term *Hasidism* can be traced back to the 2nd century BCE and the oppressive reign of Antiochus IV, who attempted to eradicate Judaism in Palestine. The Hasidim were the "pious ones" who stood up to him and willingly preferred martyrdom to apostasy.

Modern Hasidism began as an expression of ecstatic piety originating in the 18th century. Founded in Poland by the *Baal Shem Tov* (d. 1760), it represented a populist devotional and mystical revolt against the learned scholars of the Talmud. The Baal Shem Tov (abbreviated BeSHT or Besht) taught that personal piety as expressed in prayer is more important than intellectual study of the Torah and literal Torah obedience. Since God is omnipresent, we have less need for a messiah. He encouraged ecstatic worship of God, including music and dance, and a joyful consciousness of God in day to day life. Thus the soul aspires to *devekut* (cleaving to God).

A Hasidic teacher named Dov Ber contributed to the phenomenal growth of Hasidism among the Jews of Eastern Europe. He supported the special status of the *tzaddik*, or holy man, as distinguished from ordinary Hasidim. This distinction was opposed by those who supported the spiritual equality of Hasidim. Nevertheless, the tzaddik as charismatic leader has remained a key component of Hasidism up to the present. Modern Hasidism is a continuation of the original movement. Its values include humility and universal love. The Jewish philosopher Martin Buber (d. 1965) was a student and interpreter of Hasidism. The contemporary writer Elie Wiesel has also studied and popularized Hasidic tales.

SOCIAL AND INSTITUTIONAL DIMENSION

Varieties of Judaism

In one sense, Christianity and modern Judaism represent two lines of development from 1st-century Judaism down through the past two thousand years of history to today. But Jews do not consider Christians to be a legitimate branch of Judaism; the two communities diverged very early and have quarreled intensely.

Western Varieties and the Enlightenment

Most Americans are familiar with the division into Orthodox, Reform, and Conservative Judaism. Here is how the division began. In Western Europe, the 18th-century Enlightenment ushered in positive change for Jews with its emphasis on reason and tolerance rather than religious and political authority and tradition. The *égalité* of the French revolution naturally encompassed Jews and set a precedent for Europe more generally. Western European Jews no longer had to live in ghettos. They were given previously unheard-of opportunities for advancement. In certain countries of Western Europe they even received citizenship. Thus began the modern period of Judaism.

Moses Mendelssohn and the Jewish Enlightenment

A German Jew named Moses Mendelssohn (d. 1786) sought freedom of religion, separation of church and state, and Jewish integration into European culture through language, dress, and appearance. Envisioning a society in which the shared humanity of Christians and Jews would transcend their religious differences, he established a movement called the Jewish Enlightenment.

Reform Judaism

As part of this movement toward "modernity," Reform Judaism developed first in Germany, attempting to bring Jewish life and belief more in line with modern thought. It reinterpreted doctrines such as Messiah and resurrection. The Jewish liturgy was modernized or Westernized so that returning to the land, or building a third temple in Jerusalem, was no longer mentioned, and the liturgical language shifted from Hebrew to the vernacular. In some synagogues, men and women could sit together. Jews were told to excel as citizens in the countries where they resided.

Jewish Immigration to the United States from the Mid-19th Century

Jews began immigrating to the United States in significant numbers in the middle of the 19th century—first German-speaking, mostly Reform Jews, then Eastern European and Russian working-class Jews, Orthodox and secular socialist. Today more Jews live in the United States than in any other country. One of the strongest world centers of Hasidism is Brooklyn, New York. The number of American Jews may now be approximately equal to the number of American Muslims.

American Reform Judaism developed in the late 19th century. The Pittsburgh Platform of 1885 dispensed with the dietary regulations of the Torah (kosher laws), as well as purity and dress laws, retaining only the ethical commandments. The emphasis was on Jewish faith in the God of justice and love. In contrast, *Orthodox* Judaism, vigorously supported today by Hasidic Jews, sought to maintain all the historical Jewish traditions and beliefs. *Conservative* Judaism is a mainly American movement that views Reform Judaism as having gone too far, but which allows some deviation from the Orthodox position.

The most recent group in American Judaism is *Reconstructionist* Judaism, founded by Rabbi Mordecai Kaplan in 1983 as an alternative to Conservatism. He rejected the traditional idea of the Torah as supernatural revelation as well as the exclusivist doctrine that Jews are the only chosen people of God. He revised the prayer book to eliminate pejorative comments about women and Gentiles. Women participate equally in Reconstructionist synagogue worship.

Wikipedia gives the following statistics for these groups in the United States: Conservative: 4.5 million, Unaffiliated and Secular: 4.5 million, Reform: 3.75 million, Orthodox: 2 million, Reconstructionist: 150,000—for a total of 14 million [*sic*!].[4]

Ashkenazic and Sephardic Jews

As is true of most major worldviews, Jews have been influenced by the diverse cultures surrounding them. A major cultural split is that between Ashkenazic and Sephardic Jews. Ashkenazic Jews represent a basically Germanic culture, Sephardic Jews a basically Spanish-Arabic culture.

From a German base, Ashkenazic Jews spread through Eastern Europe and Russia; then, under 19th-century persecution in the East, back through Western Europe and the United States. Before the German Holocaust, about 90% of Jews world-wide were Ashkenazim. Since the Holocaust, the percentage has dropped to about 83%.

From a Spanish base, Sephardic Judaism moved beyond Spain after Ferdinand and Isabella expelled all Jews from the country. Since Spain had been for centuries a multicultural Muslim-ruled civilization and the Muslims had given Jews more freedom than Christians had, many Sephardic Jews moved to North Africa and the Middle East. Others moved to the Balkan states. They spoke Ladino, a Romance-based language. Today, many Sephardic Jews have been strongly influenced by Arabic culture.

About half of the Jews in the state of Israel are Ashkenazim, about half Sephardim. Ashkenazim are much more widely represented in the government and in positions of power than are Sephardim. Sephardic Jews complain that they are discriminated against.

Zionism

Zionism in general is an international movement aiming to bring Jews from European and other nations to live together in their ancient homeland. Jewish Zionism in its modern form dates from the late 19th century. It was preceded by a Christian Zionism of the first half of the 19th century. As we will see in the chapter on Christianity, this Christian Zionism is of a very different character from the Jewish form, although politically it strongly supports Jewish Zionism. In its earliest form, Jewish Zionism spoke simply of living together *in one place*, but Palestine soon became the only place seriously considered. Not all Zionist thinkers were planning to create a Jewish *state*. But *some* were, even from as early as Theodor Herzl late in the 19th century.

Throughout the 19th century, many Jews in Western Europe were moving out of the ghettos into the wider society, gaining education, and being accepted into many areas of life which had formerly been closed to them. For many Jews, this integration into the larger culture was more important than maintaining their old traditions and their Jewish identity. Surprisingly, this integration was accompanied by renewed pogroms, especially in Russia. Both secular and religious Jews had hoped their enlightened neighbors would support them. Assimilated Jews (those who were not practicing the Jewish religion or who had converted to Christianity, atheism, or agnosticism) wondered why their neighbors still considered them to be "Jews" and discriminated against them. If Jewishness is not a religion, some thought, perhaps it is a nationality, like French or British. It was a time when Italians and Germans were developing a national character and forming modern nation-states. But Jews, like Kurds and Armenians, had no nation-state to develop. So Zionists began to think that Jews should gather themselves into a single homeland to gain security and develop their potential national character.

Forms of Zionism[5]

Political Zionism thought that the best way to gain Jewish security was to get authorization from the international community or from one or more powerful states to emigrate from their European homes and colonize a Jewish state somewhere else. Theodor Herzl tried to convince the Ottoman Empire, and later Britain, that it should support Jewish colonization in Palestine.

Socialist Zionism thought that waiting for great powers to grant Jews a state would be useless. Jews should simply move into Palestine and begin developing the society that would eventually become a state. Influenced by Marxist theories of class struggle (see chapter 7 on Marxist Worldviews), they thought Jews needed to reform their national character. For centuries they had been forbidden to own land or to farm, so they had become small merchants and money lenders, and eventually with European enlightenment, professionals and financiers. They needed to develop a strong agricultural and manufacturing working class.

Cultural Zionism was not so concerned with creating a Jewish *state,* but rather with restoring and renewing Jewish *cultural and religious life in Palestine*, where history, geography, climate, and other natural factors were most suitable to that project. Some cultural Zionists supported a *bi-national state* — Jewish and Arab — with equal rights for all its citizens, open to the development of Jewish, Muslim, and Christian cultures.

Originally most *Orthodox* Jews resisted Zionism, claiming it was blasphemous to ask politics to accomplish what God intended the Messiah to do. Recently, some have supported Zionism despite its secular roots. This is the origin of *religious Zionism*. Rabbi Abraham Isaac Kook, a leading religious Zionist, argues that

> Zionism was not merely a political movement by secular Jews. It was actually a tool of God to promote his divine scheme and to initiate the return of the Jews to their homeland—the land he promised to Abraham, Isaac and Jacob. God wants the children of Israel . . . to establish a Jewish sovereign state in which Jews could live according to the laws of Torah. . . . Therefore, settling Israel is an obligation of the religious Jews and helping Zionism is actually following God's will.[6]

Religious Zionists are the most tenacious Israeli settlers on Palestinian land in East Jerusalem and the West Bank. They insist that to give back a square centimeter of the Promised Land to *goyim* (non-Jews) would be rebellion against God.

Jewish Fears Grow in Europe

Early movement toward a Jewish community or state began in the middle of the 19th century. A wealthy Jew, Baron Edmond de Rothschild, financed two agricultural settlements in (Ottoman) Palestine in 1882–1884.

The Austrian journalist Theodor Herzl (d. 1904) was responsible for establishing Jewish Zionism as an international *political* movement. In France in 1894, a popular Jewish army officer, Alfred Dreyfus, was falsely accused and convicted of treason—selling military secrets to Germany. "Enlightened" Gentiles failed to defend their Jewish confreres. Some Jews concluded that emancipation might be *increasing* anti-Jewish feelings rather than diminishing them, by increasing contact between Jews and Gentiles. Herzl argued that Jews needed a nation of their own. Perhaps enlightened European Gentiles would support a wholly Jewish state on the enlightenment model somewhere *outside* Europe in order to get rid of the Jews in their midst. He began to urge European states to sponsor such an establishment.

Herzl convened the first Zionist Conference in 1897 in Basel, Switzerland. He considered several possible locations for a Jewish state: Argentina, where Baron Hirsh was already settling East European Jews; the Sinai Peninsula, proposed by Britain as a temporary measure (but Egypt objected); another British offer of some "unoccupied" land in Uganda. But most Jews insisted the settlement had to be "a publicly recognized, legally secure homeland in Palestine," and the Zionist conference formally agreed.[7] The conference also created the World Zionist Organization to further these aims.

Many Jews, both Reform and Orthodox, did not at first agree with Zionism. Reform Jews, inspired by the Enlightenment, thought that Jews should live as full citizens among non-Jews. Orthodox Jews thought that only God could return the Jews to Palestine if and when God chose to do that. The Nazi

Holocaust (see below) drastically changed the balance of Jewish opinion on Zionism. Suddenly it seemed to be a matter of survival.

Kibbutzim and Moshavim

At first, the largest groups of Jews who *did* support Zionism and move to Palestine were socialists or Marxists, not religiously observant Jews. They set up cooperative communities called *kibbutzim* (plural of *kibbutz*) and partial-cooperative communities called *moshavim* (plural of *moshav*). In a kibbutz, the more fully communal of these institutions, *all* property was held in common. Children were raised communally, splitting their time between common dormitories and their parents' homes. Members ate in common dining halls and cultivated fields in common. The first kibbutz was founded on the south shore of the Sea of Galilee in 1910.[8]

Kibbutzim and moshavim at first represented pioneers willing to sacrifice for the good of their community. They supplied the most committed soldiers and politicians to the development of Israel. As they have grown more affluent, they have lost much of their original egalitarianism, and their influence on Israeli society has waned.

To pick up the story of how Zionism produced the state of Israel and the conflict that resulted, turn to chapter 8: the Israeli-Palestinian Conflict.

ISSUES FOR JUSTICE AND PEACE

In the Tanakh, there is frequent mention of war, and God is seen as a warrior. But there is also an urgent call for justice on the grounds that the God who is just calls his people to be just. There is a strong call for peace, represented especially in the prophets and symbolized by Isaiah's vision of a peaceful future in which "the nations" will "beat their swords into plowshares and their spears into pruning hooks" and "the wolf shall be a guest of the lamb" (Isaiah 2:4; 11:6). Jewish daily worship includes a petition for peace in both the morning and evening prayers every day.

Holy War

The concept of Holy War is well developed in the Hebrew Bible. Holy War has important limits:

1. War must be begun and carried on as God orders, not for human glory.
2. God's people win not by force of arms, but by God's strength. In order to keep that reality clear and to avoid human pride, the community must not seek allies, nor multiply soldiers or weapons. Sometimes it is called to reduce weapons (Judges 7:1–8).

3. Isaiah speaks of a "suffering servant"—often identified by Jews with Israel—who carries the sufferings of others for the sake of others. This image suggests that there is purpose in suffering and weakness.

4. While the Hebrews (ancestors of the Jews) did experience God-given victory in the Exodus and conquest of Canaan, they also experienced God-given defeat in the Exile. They discovered that God did not defend them when they failed to trust God and failed to be just and holy, and that in these circumstances God could and would empower their *enemies* against them.

5. In the Maccabean revolt against the Seleucids (Syrians) in the 2nd century BCE, the Jews found that they could win with small numbers when they were faithful to God, but that it could turn out badly when their leaders started seeking personal power.

6. In the revolts of 66 and 132 CE against Rome, the Jews discovered that some revolts are not supported by God even when they presume to be restoring God's control over his nation.

Herem

One of the most difficult concepts of the Tanakh for theologians of peace is the concept of *herem*. This is the claim that God condemned certain groups to annihilation at the hands of his people. Modern liberal Jews consider herem to be no longer of *practical* importance; it is only of *theological* importance in determining what authority the narratives of the Tanakh have to guide current discussions on war. But some religious Zionists equate Palestinians or nearby Arab nations with Amalekites and still think in terms of herem. Questions to think about when researching this issue might include: (a) Does it answer the problem to note that God has ultimate authority over human life and death? (b) Does it answer the problem to speak of moral development in the Sacred Scripture, implying that herem might have been understandable in the ancient period but not later? (Jewish scholars do speak of "development" in scriptural understanding as they interpret the meaning of herem.) (c) How did the Hebrew people know that God was calling for herem in a particular case? (d) Is there any modern analogy to herem? And for those who think there is, how would a modern government discern that God is calling for it?

Talmudic Attitudes toward War and Peace

Many Christians are familiar with war and peace in the Tanakh, because they know it as the "Old Testament." But Talmudic and other traditions are less well known. Leonard Grob surveys the Talmud and concludes that it supports the priority of peace and urges peacemaking, although it does not rule out war.[9]

Note that the Hebrew word *shalom*, often translated "peace," actually has a broader meaning. In grammatical origin, it means wholeness or completeness. In the Tanakh it is used to mean a variety of things, including physical health, safety, long life, prosperity, and military victory—everything politicians promise to give you if you vote for them.

The Shoah (Holocaust)

Many Western Jews since the Enlightenment tried to enter into the modern European culture and distance themselves from their Jewish roots. The Nazi Holocaust was unique in that it refused to accept such choices as valid. Hitler intended to kill every Jew no matter what his or her personal convictions or actions were. Even a single Jewish grandparent was enough to identify a person as a Jew.

It is hard to imagine the horror of the situation. In other persecutions, one could escape by denying the faith, by going along with the oppressor, or by deception. Those who died felt that they were at least witnessing to their convictions. In the Holocaust, in contrast, there was no escape. An entire ethnic group (religion, tradition, and racial stock) was doomed to complete annihilation. The psychological effects on those few who survived are hard for outsiders to appreciate. That is the importance of Holocaust literature.

Also of great importance was the Jewish experience of being often (though not always) abandoned by their Christian friends and neighbors. While the full extent of the Holocaust was kept secret for a long time, it was no secret that Jews were being systematically and cruelly persecuted. Many proposals were made to relieve the situation, but other countries did little to help. At an international conference before the Holocaust had been set in motion, Hitler offered to let all the Jews under German control emigrate. But the other countries at the conference, including the United States, refused to expand their immigration quotas adequately to accept the Jews. So Hitler told his advisors, "You see, no one wants them," and proceeded to implement his program of annihilation. And while the defeat of Germany in the war finally ended the slaughter of Jews, there was no effort to carry on the war effort in a way that would free the Jews of the concentration camps quickly. Even after clear photographs showed the purpose of the camps, proposals to bomb the ovens and gas chambers were rejected. Many Jews concluded from these experiences that they could not afford to trust non-Jews, so Jews must have a country of their own that they could control without sharing that control with anyone else. They must remain a majority in that country and hold uncontested political power.

Jews consider the lessons of the Holocaust to be vital to their survival. They go to great efforts to pass on the memory of their experiences and their conclusions to the next generation, which did not live through them. An example of an author who has been very influential in this remembrance is *Elie Wiesel.* See especially his book *Night:* an autobiographical account of his experiences in the death camp where his father died. In Jerusalem and in Washington, D.C., there are deeply moving museums of the Holocaust. The Jerusalem museum is called *Yad va Shem* ("a memorial and a name," Isaiah 56:5).

Responses to the Holocaust

This section summarizes a small-group interview with Marc Silverman in 1988 at the Holocaust memorial *Yad va Shem* in Jerusalem describing Jewish theologies of the Holocaust under three aspects. He describes a wide range of influential Jewish positions, although some are held by small numbers of Jews.

Theological Explanations. Some ultra-orthodox Jews believe that the Holocaust was a punishment for Jewish failure to live the Law of Moses, and that the state of Israel is a blasphemous attempt to bring in the messianic era without the Messiah. The appropriate response to the Holocaust, then, would be to return to meticulous observance of the covenant law as they interpret it. There is also a claim, very controversial among Jews, that the Jewish community has a special vocation to suffer.

At the other extreme, some secular Zionists, such as the socialist pioneers of the kibbutzim and moshavim, believe that the Holocaust was the natural result of trusting God to protect you when what is needed is human strength. For them, sin is unwillingness to take your history into your own hands.

Some modern Orthodox religious Zionists, represented by groups like the National Religious Party and *Gush Emunim* (the "Block of the Faithful"), see the Holocaust as the first stage of a process of dying and rising. For these Jews the dying was necessary, and the rising is beginning with the state of Israel, which is a sort of human first step toward the messianic kingdom that God will eventually establish. It is "first fruits" of God's kingdom. Jews of this persuasion sometimes advocate the expansion of Israel to include Jordan and parts of Syria: all the territory contained under ancient Israel and Judah at the time of its greatest extent. They promote this expansion concretely by building and moving into Jewish settlements in the occupied Palestinian territories. Christian Zionists support this position, but with the expectation that Jews will eventually be converted to Christianity, an expectation that Jews do not find supportive.

Silverman strongly rejected any idea that the Holocaust was punishment for sin, or necessary to produce God's kingdom, pointing out that no sin is great enough to justify the Holocaust, and "six million Jews are not the cost of this country." He called such theories "beneath contempt."

Social-Cultural Aspects. The dominant reaction of Israeli Jews who visit the Holocaust museum *Yad va Shem* is, "We must do all in our power so that Jews are no longer powerless." Jews born in Israel, when visiting the Holocaust museum, feel not so much *pity* for the Jews pictured there, as *disgust:* "Why didn't they do something to help themselves? I must not be like that." They insist that the Holocaust must be constantly relived in memory so that it will not be relived in fact. (Some Jews insist that the Holocaust must not be relived by *anybody,* whether Jew or non-Jew.)

Political Aspects. Some take the attitude that all Gentiles are guilty of allowing the Holocaust to happen. Since the Gentile nations failed to prevent it, they all stand accused of moral failure and have no right to criticize the state of Israel. Israel, then, has no need to listen to any criticism from Gentiles.

Enemies who threaten the state of Israel are sometimes compared with the Old Testament neighbor Amalek. God called the Hebrews to destroy Amalek totally because they opposed God's people—a key instance of herem. When local Palestinians, or neighbors like Jordan, Syria, or Iraq, are equated with "Amalek," no pity need be shown and no rules of war need apply. Note that these symbols can operate on an unconscious level. There is little analysis behind the feelings.

SPOKESPERSONS FOR JUSTICE AND PEACE

Ahad Ha'am (Asher Ginsburg, 1852–1927, Russia)

In the early history of Zionism, Ahad Ha'am represented *cultural Zionism* as distinct from Theodor Herzl's *political Zionism.* Russian-born, with a Hasidic background, he believed that Zionism and a Jewish state could culturally and spiritually renew the Jews of both Western and Eastern Europe. In 1890 Ahad Ha'am traveled to Palestine, where he wrote, "Thoughts from the Land of Israel." Noting that Palestine was by no means empty and that its Arab-owned land was entirely cultivated except for "sand dunes or stony mountains," he deplored the Jewish "use of violence and humiliation" against the Arab residents. In 1912 he spoke out against the Jewish "boycott of Arab labor as a strategy to conquer the land," fearing that future "power in Eretz Israel" would bring worse: "If this be the 'Messiah,'" he wrote, "I do not wish to see his coming." Before he died in 1927 in Tel Aviv, he asked, "Is this the dream of our return to Zion, that we come to Zion and stain its soil with innocent blood?" Thus, in his view, was the prophetic tradition being destroyed.[10]

Martin Buber (1878–1965, Austria)

Martin Buber was a philosopher and religious thinker; two of his most famous books are *I and Thou* and *Between Man and Man*. A Zionist, Buber believed that Jews returning to Palestine must relate to the indigenous Arabs as equals, inhabiting a shared Palestine. In his view "modern political Zionism" was "intensified," but not caused, by anti-Semitism. Zionism had been produced by the "unique connection of a people and a country." The Jews had been called to found a just community in Palestine, and from there to spread justice around the world at the behest of their prophets.[11]

Buber recognized three legitimate demands of Zionism: for land, for Jewish immigrants to settle the land, and for Jewish self-determination in the land. He envisioned peaceful coexistence with the Palestinian Arabs and joint development of the land; such cooperation was essential for the successful "redemption of [the] land." He imagined the two peoples as sharing some "spheres of interest and activity" and not others. For Buber, "national rebirth" did not mean "becoming a normal nation." After 1948, he protested consistently against "Israeli nationalism." Supporting confederation, bi-nationalism, and religious socialism, and advocating connection over domination, he ended up living as an exile in the state he had helped to build.[12]

Etty Hillesum (1914–1943, Holland)

After earning a law degree at the University of Amsterdam, Hillesum studied Slavonic languages and eventually psychology. The Germans occupied Holland in 1940. She had worked for two weeks as a typist for the Jewish Council in Amsterdam when she decided to be among the "first group of Jews" to go to the transit camp Westerbork in the eastern part of the country, en route to Auschwitz in Poland. For over a year she worked in a hospital in the camp. Despite having the opportunity, she chose not to try to escape. With most of her family she was sent to Auschwitz in 1943, where she and three others died. Marc Ellis calls Etty Hillesum's spirituality, expressed in her diaries, "eclectic and beautiful, though in some ways disturbing." She wrote of being "without the least bitterness and so full of strength and love"; of living in continuous dialogue with God with "tears of gratitude" running down her face; of the Jews helping God even if God could not help them; of safeguarding "that little piece of You, God, in ourselves"; of not exempting herself from "what so many others have to suffer." Far from "empowerment," Hillesum urged "witness" and forgiveness, refusing to hate the enemy yet recognizing the "monstrous conditions" created by humans.[13]

SUMMARY

Through their historical experience as a people, Jews came to believe that the one true God had chosen them for a covenant relationship with Himself and promised them a land where they could live securely and independently in conformity to His will. That belief has been sharply tested throughout history. Prophets, claiming to speak for God, have declared that it is the people's own infidelity to God which has destroyed their security and exiled them from the land. In their exile, they developed a strong tradition of careful fidelity to the Torah, along with a rich Jewish mysticism, through which they have maintained their distinctive identity. In modern times, an outside world open to Jewish assimilation has drawn many Jews away from their ancient faith, and the Holocaust came close to ending the community's very existence. In reaction, many Jews have turned to their own resources to establish the state of Israel, based on a project launched decades before the Holocaust, where they hope to be secure; a few have denounced that move as showing a lack of faith that God will fulfill his promise of a Messiah. Jews are engaged in a vigorous search for a theology that could explain why God allowed the Holocaust to happen and what the community should do now.

KEY TERMS

Amalek
Ashkenazic
Baal Shem Tov
Besht
bi-national state
Conservative Judaism
covenant
cultural Zionism
Day of Atonement
Days of Awe
Diaspora
Gemara
ghetto
Haggadah
Halakha
Hanukkah
Hasidism
herem

Holocaust
ingathering
Kabbalah
Ketuvim
kibbutz
midrash
Mishnah
moshav
Neviim
Orthodox Judaism
Passover
Pentecost
Pesach
pogrom
political Zionism
Purim
Reconstructionist Judaism
Reform Judaism

religious Zionism
Rosh Hashanah
Sephardic
shalom
Shavuot
Shoah
socialist Zionism
Suffering Servant
Tabernacles
Talmud

Tanakh
Targums
tikkun
Torah
tzaddik
yetzer ha ra'
yetzer ha tov
Yom Kippur
Zionism
Zohar

DISCUSSION QUESTIONS

1. Which of the theological responses to the Holocaust do you find most convincing? Which do you find most problematic, or even repellent? If you don't like any of those described, what theological response would you propose?
2. How might non-Jews have responded to Hitler's program so as to prevent the Holocaust without war? Why didn't they? Would their response have been effective?
3. Some Jews believe that there ought to be one nation in the world—Israel—where one's Jewish faith can influence one's entire life, and where Jews can be safe from attack and from proselytization (attempts by Christians or others to "convert" their children away from the Jewish faith and community). Such a nation ought to have a government based on Jewish law. They claim that such a government would allow other faiths to practice their beliefs without interference. Do you agree? If not, on what *should* the laws of Israel be based? How *should* Jews be protected from attack and from proselytization? What if their nation contains a substantial or equal number of non-Jews? How should these non-Jews be treated?
4. This chapter introduced three Jewish workers for peace: Ahad Ha'am, Martin Buber, and Etty Hillesum. Which one of them would you be most interested in reading about further? What caught your attention and interest? With which of their ideas did you particularly agree or disagree?

NOTES

1. Shahak and Mezvinksy, *Jewish Fundamentalism*, 2–4.
2. www.fordham.edu/halsall/source/rambam13.html (accessed August 29, 2005).

3. For party ideas, see the website at www.holidays.net/purim/ (accessed July 4, 2006).

4. "Major religious groups," en.wikipedia.org/wiki/Religions (accessed January 16, 2007).

5. For historical details on Jewish Zionism, see the article by Ami Isseroff at www.mideastweb.org/zionism.htm (accessed July 2, 2006).

6. Quoted in en.wikipedia.org/wiki/Religious_Zionist_Movement (accessed June 15, 2006).

7. www.jewishvirtuallibrary.org/jsource/Zionism/firstcong.html (accessed January 22, 2006); www.wzo.org.il/en/resources/view.asp?id=1057 (accessed January 22, 2006).

8. Wigoder, *Everyman's Judaica: An Encyclopedic Dictionary*, 338.

9. Gordon and Grob, *Education for Peace,* chap. 3.

10. Ellis, *Toward a Jewish Theology of Liberation*, 61–64.

11. Ellis, *Jewish Theology of Liberation*, 187.

12. Ellis, *Jewish Theology of Liberation*, 188.

13. Ellis, *Jewish Theology of Liberation*, 181–87.

SUGGESTIONS FOR FURTHER READING

Arendt. *Eichmann in Jerusalem.*
Buber. *Between Man and Man.*
———. *I and Thou.*
Ellis. *Toward a Jewish Theology of Liberation.*
Gordon and Grob. *Education for Peace.*
Hillesum. *Etty: The Letters and Diaries of Etty Hillesum.*
Potok. *The Chosen.*
Rubenstein. *After Auschwitz.*
Rubenstein and Roth. *Approaches to Auschwitz.*
Vorspan and Saperstein. *Tough Choices: Jewish Perspectives on Social Justice.*
Watterson. *Not by the Sword: How the Love of a Cantor and His Family Transformed a Klansman.*
Wiesel. *Night.*
Wigoder. *Everyman's Judaica.*

Chapter Four

Christian Worldviews

"The beginning of the gospel of Jesus Christ, [the Son of God]."

—Mark 1:1

"For God so loved the world that he gave his only Son, so that everyone who believes in him might not perish but might have eternal life."

—John 3:16

"Love your enemies, and pray for those who persecute you, that you may be children of your heavenly Father."

—Matthew 5:44–45a

"For I am convinced that neither death, nor life, nor angels, nor principalities, nor present things, nor future things, nor powers, nor height, nor depth, nor any other creature will be able to separate us from the love of God in Christ Jesus our Lord."

—Romans 8:38–39

EXPERIENTIAL AND EMOTIONAL DIMENSION

The basic Christian experience was Jesus of Nazareth. His followers saw him heal and exorcize (drive evil spirits out of afflicted people), and heard him preach with astonishing authority. They came to believe that Jesus was the one whom God had promised to send to the Jewish people. Although the religious and political leaders had Jesus condemned to a shameful death, his followers reported that he appeared alive to them afterward—raised from the dead by God, who thus vindicated his ministry and preaching. They came to believe that God would raise *them* from the dead, too—at the end of their lives or when Jesus came again in glory. Early Christians experienced extraordinary power, enabling them to do many of the things that Jesus had done. They understood this power to come from God's own Spirit—a Spirit somehow linked with the risen, living Jesus who now was authorized to act for God.

Christians also understood themselves to be in conscious, personal relationship with the risen Jesus, with God the Father, and with other Christians who had died—especially those who, like Jesus, had been killed because of their Christian lives. In the Catholic and Orthodox traditions, this understanding has continued in ongoing relations through prayer with "saints" who have died. In nearly all Christian traditions, some people have performed acts of spiritual power and experienced mystical experiences. Many Christians have modest spiritual experiences such as unexpected joy and peace, for example at individual or community prayer. Mystical writers usually discourage Christians from actively seeking extraordinary spiritual experiences; one should seek God, not mystical experiences.

HISTORICAL PERIODS

1. *Apostolic*—the 1st century after the death of Jesus, approximately 30 CE. Most of the books that became the New Testament were composed during this period.
2. *Church of the Martyrs*—from the early 2nd century until the early 4th century. Christians were periodically attacked, exiled, had their property confiscated, or were killed by local authorities or the Roman state. "Martyr" means "witness." The Christian martyrs witnessed to the fact that their Christian faith (commitment to Jesus and to God) was more important than their lives and wealth. People often joined the church despite the danger of martyrdom because of what they observed in the extraordinary lives of their Christian neighbors.
3. *Roman Empire after Constantine*—the Roman emperor Constantine (d. 337) made the Christian faith legal. Soon it became advantageous to be Christian, resulting in many weakly committed Christians. Some of the more committed tried to recover the earlier vigor by becoming hermits or monks. The main doctrinal explanations of the nature of God, Jesus, and the Holy Spirit were worked out in this period.
4. *Fall of Rome; local control and monasticism*—an overextended Roman empire in the West was destroyed by non-Roman tribes, beginning in the late 4th century. Society became more locally based. Christian monasteries preserved books and literacy.

5. *High Middle Ages and the Crusades*—rise of universities, scholastic theology, Gothic cathedrals. In the Crusades, European Christians invaded Palestine to set up short-lived Christian kingdoms. Christianity was enriched by interaction with the more advanced Islamic culture.
6. *Protestant Reformation*—divergent theologies responding to various church abuses found support from local rulers, producing rival churches to the Roman Catholic Church.
7. *Enlightenment*—the growth of large nation-states, liberal notions of human freedom, and the natural sciences challenged traditional Christian doctrines. Churches responded defensively (fundamentalist movements) or adaptively (liberal churches).
8. *Post-modernism*—the previous search for a neutral standpoint from which one could judge all beliefs was regarded as a delusion; each person is affected by her or his own background and experiences. The best one can do is to be open about one's own starting-point and then to engage in honest dialogue. During this period, ecumenical movements (seeking unity among Christian churches) and interfaith movements (seeking cooperation between all worldviews) developed.

SACRED WRITINGS

Unusual among major worldviews, Christians actively read (privately and in liturgical worship) and study the sacred writings—the Tanakh—of the previous worldview that gave it birth; they call these writings the "Old Testament" to show their relation to the books written by 1st- and early 2nd-century Christian authors. Christians do not generally read the Mishnah or the Talmud, which developed *after* the Christian movement had split from the Rabbinic Jewish movement.

The earliest Christians wrote more books—about Jesus and his teachings (the Gospels), occasional letters to new Christian communities (the Epistles), an account of how the new faith was spread by the apostles Peter and Paul (Acts of the Apostles), and a theological vision (claiming to be based on visionary experience) explaining how Christians should respond to the Roman Empire (the Revelation of John). These books—the "New Testament"—were considered to have authority at least equal to that of the Tanakh, based on the belief that both were "inspired" by God so that, in some sense, God could be said to be their ultimate author.

Christians revere and study many later writings—decisions of church councils, defenses of Christian doctrine, theological investigations, prayers and liturgies, mystical writings, interpretations of the earlier books, histories, and more.

NARRATIVE OR MYTHIC DIMENSION

The New Testament presents Jesus as the Messiah (promised in the Tanakh), the Son of God, sent to introduce the Kingdom of God (indicating that God is taking over control of the world). Jesus gathered and trained twelve intimate followers. He preached with authority (as though he knew from personal experience what he was talking about), healed people of physical disease by spiritual power, drove out evil spirits that were inhabiting and tormenting people, and urged people to trust God. Religious and political leaders sought to kill him, succeeded with the help of one of his inner circle who betrayed him, and had him executed in Roman fashion on a cross. Although guards protected the tomb, Jesus rose from the dead "on the third day" and appeared to his followers. Later, Jesus sent the "Holy Spirit" to "baptize" his followers "in spirit and in fire"—as a result, they lost their fears and spread the "good news" widely despite murderous opposition. The Holy Spirit made the risen Jesus present in power within his followers; they continued to do what he had started. The new worldview spread rapidly far beyond the reaches of its Jewish origins, as Christians spread the word and baptized new believers.

The Kerygma (First Announcement; Mission Preaching)

Christians early developed a common way of announcing what they had experienced and what it meant. In Acts of the Apostles 3:1–11, Peter and John first cure a cripple. Then when they have everyone's attention, Peter gives them a speech—a typical first message to people who don't know what God has just done in Jesus and why it is significant. This is "good news"—a mission speech, technically called *kerygma*. Note that the apostles are *not just telling about what Jesus did,* they are *demonstrating it by doing it themselves.* The healing (act of God's power) provides the occasion for Peter to proclaim the *kerygma* to the crowd by explaining the significance of the healing that has just taken place.

Six key elements turn up over and over again in these speeches. Steps 1–4 have happened already when the apostles are preaching. They expect step 5 to happen very soon, so step 6 had better happen soon, too. (1) God's promise of a Messiah has been fulfilled (2) by the life, death, resurrection, and ascension of Jesus of Nazareth (3) and by his exaltation at the right hand of God the Father. (4) From heaven, Jesus has sent the Holy Spirit on us to transform us. (5) Jesus will soon return to judge the living and the dead. (6) So repent right now while you have the chance.

DOCTRINAL AND PHILOSOPHICAL DIMENSION

Christianity began as a renewal movement within 1st-century Judaism. It shared all the basic Jewish beliefs. As the Church's experience grew, it understood that Jesus, the Spirit, and the Father were all, somehow, God—yet neither three gods, nor parts of one God, nor ways one God expressed itself. Further, Jesus was both divine and truly human. Thinking out how to express this mystery of God, Jesus, and the Spirit engaged the attention of Christians for several centuries. They eventually developed a simple verbal formula: God is three "persons" in one "nature"; Jesus is two "natures" in one "person."

Unfortunately, few people today understand what the terms "person" and "nature" meant to these early Christians. The *modern* word "person" doesn't mean what the 4th-century Latin word *persona* meant. Although God is three "persons," all three persons share one "intellect" or way/center of knowing and one "will" or way/center of choosing.[1] So it would be impossible for there to be any disagreements or disputes among the three "persons" of God. Although Jesus is one "person," that one person has two "intellects" or ways/centers of knowing (one divine, one human) and two "wills" or ways/centers of choosing (one divine, one human). So Jesus might "know" with his divine "intellect" something that he did not know with his human intellect. In fact, if one were to try to put into his human intellect everything he knew through his divine intellect, it would "trip all the circuit breakers." There is also the abstract possibility of Jesus' human will choosing something opposed to his divine will. He does not in fact do so because he *chooses* always to do "his Father's" will (which is identical with his own *divine* will).

Popular piety sometimes misrepresents this understanding of the "Trinity," for example, by speaking of Jesus restraining God the Father from punishing humans. Such misrepresentation also leads Jews and Muslims to suppose that Christians believe in three gods. But they do not. Christians, like Jews and Muslims, believe in only one God.

There are two poles to Christian ideas of salvation: the *birth* (or more properly, the *conception and incarnation*) of Jesus, and his *death and resurrection.* Christians believe that *something radical changed in the nature of creation* through these two events.

Incarnation and Indwelling

The *birth* or *incarnation* of Jesus *connected* humans to God in a new way. God united himself to one human, Jesus, in a mysterious and powerful way

Figure 4.1. Church of the Nativity in Bethlehem. Courtesy David Whitten Smith, about 1975.

that gave all other humans a new capacity to share in God's nature. Humans do so by uniting themselves in faith and confidence to Jesus. As a result he begins to *live within them* and act through them. They become so intimately related to him that they can truly be said to be part of his "body."

Death and Resurrection

Another thing engaged the church's attention for the first three centuries: periodic, deadly persecutions. Christians came to associate their own suffering with that of Jesus. If Jesus did not escape death at the hands of God's enemies, and if they have become "part of his 'body,'" then they should not expect to escape death either. At the same time, as "members of his 'body,'" they could confidently expect to share in his resurrection.

In fact, the church came to understand that it was Jesus' willingness to die, trusting God the Father beyond what Jesus could control, that somehow transformed the rebellious state in which humans found themselves in relation to God. It was Jesus' commitment to truth, goodness, nonviolence, and love of enemies—his insistence on speaking the truth respectfully to those in power even when they threatened to kill him if he didn't shut up—that led to his death. This trusting, loving, faithful death of the innocent Jesus transformed creation itself at its roots, making possible a relationship between humans and God that had not been possible before. A person in such a relation to God could not remain dead for long. Before three days had passed, Jesus sprang back to life by God's power, now no longer subject to death. *Thus, Jesus did far more than bring good ideas to humans. Jesus acted in power to transform radically the nature of reality—to defeat powers of evil that had held humans in bondage to hatred, fear, and death.* This understanding of the effect of Jesus' death is nicely expressed in the Letter to the Hebrews in the New Testament: "Now since the children [whom God has given to Jesus] share in blood and flesh, he likewise shared in them, that *through death he might destroy the one who has the power of death, that is, the devil, and free those who through fear of death had been subject to slavery all their life.*" (2:14–15, emphasis added)

Christian Participation

If Christians wanted to share in what God had done through Jesus, then they too would have to trust God in the face of death. They would have to live and respond as Jesus did: loving their enemies, doing good to those who hated them, praying for those who persecuted them. But they were only able to live this way when they let go of their own selfish wills and chose to trust God in everything. When they did that, God acted through his Spirit, in mysterious connection with the resurrection of Jesus, to unite them with the risen Jesus and give them the power to live this way. He gave this power as a free and unearned gift that no one deserves. They experienced a radical change in their lives—loss of fear, new confidence, and love for people no one else seemed able to love.

"Original Sin"

I wrote above about "powers of evil that had held humans in bondage to hatred, fear, and death," about a "rebellious state in which humans found themselves in relation to God," and about humans learning to "let go of their own selfish wills and choose to trust God in everything." These statements suggested that there is something in human beings that resists goodness, generosity, courage, and trust. In fact, Christian theology has attempted to express and understand the "something that resists" by speaking of an "original sin." The concept is based on passages from the Scriptures, has been taught by nearly all Christian churches, is based on what I believe is universal human experience, and is misunderstood and therefore disbelieved by most students I have taught in the past thirty-five years.

The narrative or mythic way of expressing original sin is found in Genesis chapter 3: God commanded the first humans—Adam and Eve—not to eat the fruit of a certain tree, warning them that they would die if they ate it. A serpent enticed them to eat it, explaining that it would not kill them, but rather give them knowledge of good and evil. They trusted the serpent rather than God, ate it, and became "mortal" (subject to death). God then threw them out of paradise; all their descendants also lost access to paradise and became subject to death.

Doctrinal and philosophical reasoning tries to explain the meaning of that story and relate it to human experience. Recent theologians and ordinary Christians have faced several problems as they attempted to explain it. Students ask, "Why would God create people in sin?" But the point of the teaching is to say that *it is not God* who is responsible for the state we are born into. Students ask, "How can a little baby be guilty?" But "original sin" *is not talking about guilt*.[2] Students say, "It's not fair to be born into a condition of sin, or incompleteness, or woundedness." It probably isn't fair, but it seems to be true. Every day children are born with AIDS or fetal alcohol syndrome, into conditions that will cause them to starve or die of disease before their fifth birthday, into families where they will be beaten, into neighborhoods where they will be attacked and killed, into societies which will kill their parents and destroy their villages. The teaching on original sin says that this situation is the result of *human choices,* not God's desire.

We can get distracted if we try to answer all the related intriguing questions, especially if we insist on answering the question of how it all got started. What is more important is the situation the human race is in and what we can do about it. So let's begin by setting aside the story in Genesis, which too easily gets us confused between the story and the reality it is trying to explain. Let's consider, instead, what the teaching is saying about *us.*

We recognize from experience that we are free to make choices. We also experience an inclination to do things that are mean, selfish, and harmful to ourselves and other people. We find that often, when we have achieved the things we thought we wanted, they turn out to be not what we wanted at all, or at least to be disappointing. As we grow older, we begin to realize that the world we have been born into has serious problems and that many of these problems come about because humans take advantage of each other. When we try to correct these situations, we find that both the world around us and our own inner selves are surprisingly resistant to correction. If we try to go back to find a time when such problems didn't exist, we realize that their origin disappears into the remote past.

The teaching on "original sin" is basically very reassuring. It tells us that the problems we experience are not part of human nature in its deepest layers. God did not create humanity to be like this. Rather, the world is in its current mess because of human choice. Further, it tells us that through Jesus Christ, through his incarnation, death, and resurrection, God has destroyed the power that these realities had to enslave us. God has given us the power to make choices and take actions that will undo the damage. But it is *only* through God's power or grace that we can escape the disintegrative and destructive tendencies of the world around us and of our own inner selves. Without God's help, we are so conditioned by our disordered inner desires and by the way the world around us has affected us that our very efforts to undo the problem are themselves flawed and ineffective.

There is no use deciding who is at fault, because the chain of destructive human choices that has produced the situation extends back so far that its beginning is lost in history. We presume it's back there somewhere, but we can't place the blame, which is why Genesis describes the problem as having begun with the very first human. *It's not our fault* that we are born into a world whose laws, institutions, and habitual ways of acting are so flawed that they systematically mis-educate us and mis-develop us. *But we do have a responsibility* to do what we can to *change* the situation. In particular, once we realize the power that God is giving us to transform ourselves and the world around us, we have a responsibility to cooperate.

The Philippine liberation theologian Vitaliano Gorospe explains the case well: "It's the sinful condition in the world and our own weakened human nature (disorder in our appetites and drives) that we inherit, not Adam's personal sin. . . . God's grace strengthens us to overcome this disorder. . . . Baptism 'takes away original sin' by bringing to the baptized the gift of the Holy Spirit, God's saving, sanctifying, presence."[3] That is, God gifts the infant with the Holy Spirit and (through baptism) initiates the infant into a Christian community where he or she will find the Christian atmosphere needed to grow up as a disciple of Christ. The local church is intended to be a less sinful, more favorable Christian environment.[4] Original sin is only half of the story— God's grace is the other half.

Today there is special emphasis on how the *structures* of the world (institutions, laws, habitual ways of acting) encourage and enforce injustice. At the same time, it is human choices that institute, strengthen, and support those structures. There is a reciprocal relationship: the structures make it easy for us to sin, and our sin strengthens the structures. Similarly our *disordered desires and passions*, especially our pride and self-centeredness, press us to sin, to make bad choices; and the choices we make strengthen the disordered desires and passions and feed our pride. In theological terms, there is a worldwide, constant struggle between sin and grace. And sin is contagious, both through personal example and through the influence of social structures with their commonly accepted values.

Original sin means that humans are lacking the grace that God intended to give, and still intends to give. Humans need a double liberation: personal conversion and transformation of structures. Structures are transformed only through cooperative community action. *There is no permanent solution: struggle against sin is continuous.* As Gorospe says:

> The Christian doctrine of original sin is a realistic reminder that there is no perfect society and we should distrust absolutes and ideologies that posit a perfectly just society. Any concrete proposal for a more just society must seriously take into account not only human greed but the sinfulness of the human situation. . . . We would be totally subject to the power of sin and death, if it were not for the liberating, healing grace of Jesus Christ.[5]

We are called to cooperate with Christ's redemptive love working through the Holy Spirit.

Three Types of Social Sin

To clarify what he means by "social sin" or "structural sin," Gorospe distinguishes three types:[6] (1) "Structures which systematically oppress human dignity and violate human rights, stifle human freedom and impose gross inequality between the rich and the poor." Examples could include martial law, untouchability in India, and poverty in the midst of affluence. (2) "Situations which promote and facilitate greed and human selfishness." He gives corruption as an example. I would add war for national advantage and an exaggerated consumer society. (3) "The complicity of persons who do not take responsibility for evil being done or who silently allow oppression and injustice." For example, those who fail to testify as witnesses from fear of harm. I would add those who fail to resist injustice from laziness or fear of what others might think.

Overcoming social sin requires "conversion"—that is, real change. Gorospe lists two obstacles to *"conversion of the head"*—which means, coming to see things as God sees them: (a) unexamined ideological presuppositions, assumptions, and values, especially unwillingness to question the status quo, and (b) isolation from the pain and suffering of others.[7] Similarly, *"conversion of the heart"*—which means, coming to love people and things as God loves them—requires (a) a radical change in one's lifestyle and (b) a willingness to subvert unjust structures.[8]

PRACTICAL AND RITUAL DIMENSION

To the two key doctrines (incarnation/indwelling, and death/resurrection) correspond two key rituals: *baptism,* which "incorporates" the recipient into the "body of Christ" so that they come to share something of his divine nature, and the *Eucharist*, or *Lord's Supper*, which re-presents or symbolizes the last supper that Jesus shared with his disciples before his death and resurrection. Different Christian churches vary in the way they celebrate and explain the meaning of these rituals.

Most Christian churches also celebrate three key annual rituals: *Christmas,* celebrating the (incarnation and) birth of Jesus; *Easter*, celebrating, with Good Friday, the death and resurrection of Jesus; and *Pentecost*, celebrating the apostles receiving the Holy Spirit, which empowered them to continue what Jesus had started. Catholic, Orthodox, and some Protestant churches precede Easter with forty days of preparation called *Lent.* That preparation used to require significant fasting, but very little of that discipline remains for Catholics. Celebration of Christmas reminds Christians that they are united with Jesus as Jesus was with God, that God was willing to become vulnerable as we are, and that God is present among poor and simple people. Easter reminds them that God loved them enough to die for them, incarnate in Jesus, and that they need not fear death or suffering since they can depend on resurrection with Jesus. Pentecost reminds them that Jesus lives and acts through them, and that they can expect God's power working through them to do things that their own human power cannot do.

Almost all Christian churches practice Sunday of each week as a special day for community and individual prayer, similar to but generally less intensive than Jewish observance of the Sabbath. Christians justify the shift from Saturday to Sunday on the grounds that it was on a Sunday that Jesus rose from the dead. Many celebrate the Eucharist on that day each week; most advise members to abstain from work, although few require it.

Catholic and Orthodox churches celebrate the lives of their deceased who lived holy lives (saints) by assigning one or more saints to each day of the year and encouraging members to pray to them for wisdom and God's help. Some Christian churches object that this "devotion" to saints is a form of idolatry.

ETHICAL AND LEGAL DIMENSION

Old Testament

The Old Testament takes war for granted. It does challenge common *attitudes* toward war: the Hebrews are not to go to war unless God calls them to it; they are not to go to war to enrich themselves; they are not to build up impressive forces, weapons, alliances, or defenses, but rather to depend on God; and if they fail to act justly in their relationships with others and with each other, they should expect God to abandon them to their own (inadequate) resources, as God in fact did when Babylon invaded Judah.

New Testament

In contrast to the Old Testament, the New Testament is predominantly pacifist. Commands to love enemies and not to resist evil people are central. Passages that are sometimes quoted to justify war are marginal or are not primarily talking about war. The strongest pacifist argument in the New Testament is the example of Jesus. He resisted expectations that he should lead an armed revolt. He even allowed himself to be betrayed and executed. The "cleansing of the temple," sometimes quoted to show Jesus acting violently, is a symbolic act rather than a violent seizure of power; at the end of the incident, the temple police were still in control of the temple area. Jesus had caused considerable embarrassment, but he had not seized power.

Strong pacifist statements are found in the Sermon on the Mount in Matthew's Gospel.[9] Many of Jesus' sayings there make people nervous because they seem extreme:

> Blessed are the meek, for they will inherit the land. (5:5)
> You have heard that it was said, "An eye for an eye and a tooth for a tooth." But I say to you, offer no [violent] resistance to one who is evil. When someone strikes you on [your] right cheek, turn the other one to him as well. If anyone wants to go to law with you over your tunic, hand him your cloak as well. Should anyone press you into service for one mile, go with him for two miles. Give to the one who asks of you, and do not turn your back on one who wants to borrow. (5:38–42)
> I say to you, love your enemies, and pray for those who persecute you. (5:44)

These passages have been discussed for centuries, and there are various ways to understand them. Some interpreters explain them in a much weaker form than others do. Here are the major ways people have understood Jesus' Sermon on the Mount:

1. Absolute. *Take Jesus' sayings as they stand and try to live them.* Francis of Assisi interpreted the Sermon this way. He said, in effect, "Scholars may know some special way to explain these sayings. But I am just a simple man. I hope you'll excuse me if I just live the sayings as they stand." And he did. Most of the time. But even he couldn't do it all the time. Mohandas Gandhi was another who tried to live the Sermon literally. The Sermon on the Mount was the part of Jesus' teaching that appealed most to him as a Hindu.

    Note, however, that "as they stand"—a "literal" interpretation—requires us to study the world in which they were said so as to understand what they would have meant to their hearers. A 1st-century Galilean would most likely have been "struck on the cheek" by a person of "importance" who wished to humiliate him with a back-handed slap. Turning the other cheek would reject the humiliation, indicating a refusal to grovel, and it would do so nonviolently, refusing as well to attack or insult the striker. Giving a debtor one's *underwear, too,* when he demands one's suit highlights his injustice with humor, as Francis of Assisi demonstrated when his father challenged his religious commitment to poverty.[10]

The next three interpretations seek to reduce the intensity of these commands:

2. Rhetorical exaggeration. *Preachers exaggerate to make a point. The sayings are challenging enough without being rigid about it.* Under this point we might put two subheadings: (a) General principles. *The sayings deal with types of acts, not rigidly with specific acts.* The saying, "If he slaps you on the right cheek, turn the other cheek" does not allow for punches in the nose. On the other hand, when Jesus was slapped at his trial, he didn't turn the other cheek. Rather he challenged his attacker, saying, "If I have spoken wrongly, testify to the wrong; but if I have spoken rightly, why did you strike me?" (John 18:23). Still he left himself vulnerable to further blows, and in fact got them later. (b) Attitudes, not acts. *The internal attitude is more important than the external act.* Still, if our external act is never the one that Jesus suggests, we might wonder whether our internal attitude is any better. Augustine urged this second view.
3. Reach for perfection. *Jesus knows we can't really accomplish what he says, but if we try hard we'll do better than we would have otherwise.* However, if we think this is what he meant, we may not even try very hard.
4. Impossible demand breaks pride. *Jesus knows we can't keep his commands, but wants us to try so that we will see how sinful we are. Then we won't be able to look down on other sinners.* This explanation has been popular with Lutherans. It avoids the danger of justification by works. But there is nothing in the Sermon on the Mount itself to suggest that Jesus wasn't asking people to do what he said.

The next three interpretations limit the area that the commands apply to:

5. Distinguish precept from counsel. *Some people are called to keep all the demands of the Sermon on the Mount, others only to keep the more basic Christian demands. Hermits, monks, nuns, and similar especially committed people are called to keep them all. The commands that* all *Christians must keep are called "precepts"; those that* only special *people must keep are called "counsels of perfection."* This explanation has been traditional with Roman Catholics. There are some hints in the New Testament that

support this view (Mt 19:16–30; Mt 10–12; 1 Cor 7:38). But it can lead to clericalism and a sense that the laity is second-rate. And there's nothing in the Sermon itself to suggest that any Christians are being left out of the demands.

6. Two realms. *The demands apply to the* spiritual *realm and to the life of the* individual, *but not to the* temporal or secular *realm and the life of the* community. *To know how to live in the secular realm, ask your secular leader. Christians in their individual relationships should turn the other cheek, but Christian nations should not.* This distinction was urged by Martin Luther. It has lost much of its attraction because it led many German Christians to support Hitler.

7. Dispensational. *The Sermon on the Mount was intended to be the new Law for Jews who accepted Jesus as their Messiah. When the Jews rejected Jesus, God put a different plan into action and saved Gentiles through faith. At the end of time when the Jews are finally saved, they will follow the Sermon on the Mount, but in the meantime it doesn't apply to the rest of us.* This position is held by some dispensational Protestants, but not by all of them. Dispensational Protestants believe that God deals differently with different historical periods or "dispensations."

The last two interpretations invalidate the demands of the Sermon:

8. Interim ethic. *Jesus thought that the world would come to an end very soon. He thought that in this special urgent age people could keep the demands of the Sermon for the short time necessary until the end. If he had known how long it would take, he would not have made such difficult demands.* This modern theory arose as biblical scholarship asked how much Jesus actually knew. It is risky to decide what Jesus would have done if circumstances had been different. There is nothing in the Sermon itself to suggest that Jesus would have spoken differently if he thought the time were not short.

9. Harmful. *The demands of the Sermon make Christians weak cowards. Strong men would act with power.* Friedrich Nietzsche proposed this view. Unfortunately his attitudes were influential with Nazis, making many others hesitant to embrace them with enthusiasm. Also, it would be hard to describe Gandhi, Francis of Assisi, and others who embraced the Sermon as weak cowards.[11]

The Sermon on the Mount looks a lot more impractical to affluent people than it does to the poor. Perhaps a large part of our problem comes from our attachment to wealth and comfort. Wealth and comfort bought at the price of anger and resentment are costly. Psychosomatic medicine teaches that anger and resentment which are not dealt with cause physical and emotional illness. So perhaps if we don't want to be ill, we should take seriously Jesus' call to forgive. But how *can* we forgive really obnoxious or evil people?

How to Forgive

I do have a suggestion, based on the writings of Agnes Sanford[12] and on my own experience praying with people for healing. Keep in mind that this is a personal answer, and that each of you must decide for yourself what you think of it.

1. *Put yourself in God's presence.* Find a quiet place and put yourself into a state of prayer. Think how much God loves you, that you can trust God to meet your needs, how much God loves sinners, how Jesus forgave those who crucified him, etc. If you are not Christian, think about whatever in your own tradition may be similar to these thoughts. For example, a Buddhist could think about how the things that cause us to be angry are passing and ultimately unreal.
2. *Choose the person or persons you want to forgive.* This step is harder than it looks. A lot of people have convinced themselves that they aren't angry at anyone. We feel we aren't supposed to be angry, and so we look for other explanations for our feelings. ("I'm not angry. I'm righteously indignant. Besides, I've already forgiven her. I think.") So here's a way to find out whether there is someone you resent who would be a good subject for forgiveness. Imagine that you have found a little space in your busy day. The weather is beautiful. You have time for a walk, or a snack in the local pub. Now, who is the last person in the world you would like to see walk up to you or sit at your table? The person whose presence would make your blood run cold? That's the person you need to forgive.
3. *Put those you want to forgive into God's presence.* This type of prayer makes use of imagination to engage our unconscious in the forgiveness. Our unconscious speaks to us in images (for example, in dreams), so that's the way we're going to talk back to it. So close your eyes and visualize the person you have decided to forgive. Visualize her in God's love and presence, perhaps with Jesus standing by her side with his arm around her. Or imagine his face beside Jesus' face, and then imagine the two faces merging. Or choose some other image which reflects the reality that God loves this person and wants forgiveness and healing for her.
4. *Remember what you are forgiving these people for.* Remember step 2 where we were tempted to think that we had no resentments? Here we are

tempted to think that we have already forgiven the person. So it is important to remember concretely some of the ways the person has hurt us. Otherwise we may forgive them for unimportant hurts while holding on to the
really deep hurts. What has he done or failed to do that hurt? What has she
said or failed to say that hurt? Imagine that the person has just received a
revelation clarifying his life, so that he now knows just what he has done
and how those actions have affected others, while at the same time he is
being overwhelmed by God's love and forgiveness. Then we can imagine
ourselves talking to her about how she has hurt us without her becoming
defensive.

5. *Forgive the person.* Now that we understand what we are forgiving the
   person or persons for, it is time to decide that we want to forgive them.
   This is a moment of choice. We may feel incapable of forgiving. Don't
   worry about that, because we are calling on *God's* power. All that is necessary is to *want* to be able to forgive. So imagine that you are talking to
   the person, that you have just reminded them how they have hurt you, and
   that you now are saying, *[The person's name], I forgive you in the name
   of Jesus, and I thank God that you are being forgiven. Amen.* (If you are
   not Christian, try the prayer in the name of whatever ultimate power you
   trust in—as Alcoholics Anonymous says, "the God of your understanding.") Because you are forgiving them in the name of Jesus (or the God of
   your understanding), you need not feel that your own power is adequate.
   You are calling on a higher power. It is important to thank God that the
   person is being forgiven. It doesn't help much to pray, "I forgive you in
   the name of Jesus, but just wait till God gets hold of you!" At the end of
   the prayer, think a moment to decide whether this is what you really want.
   Then if it is, confirm it by saying "Amen."

6. *Thank God that they are being forgiven, even if it doesn't feel like it.* Once
   you have finished the prayer, you may well feel worse than ever. After all,
   you have just reminded yourself of a lot of hurt. Our feelings may adjust
   slowly to the reality of the forgiveness. It's like a splinter in our finger. At
   first we imagine it's not really a splinter. Then we hope it will fall out by
   itself. Finally, when it begins to fester, we get out the sterilized needle or
   knife and tease it out. Even after it is out, our finger will still hurt because
   we've been jabbing around with that needle. It may even hurt worse than
   before we began. But we know from experience that, once we have the
   splinter out, the wound will heal. We just need to wait. Our pain is swal-
   lowed up by our joy that the splinter is out. So if you still feel bad even
   though you have really chosen to forgive, consider that these are just the
   leftover feelings that will soon heal up, and keep thanking God for the gift
   of forgiveness.

7. *Ask God to bless them.* Over the next few days, think of good things that
   God could do for the person or persons you have forgiven, and ask God to
   do them. You might also find God suggesting things that you could do to
   celebrate the forgiveness.

ISSUES FOR JUSTICE AND PEACE

Especially since the Protestant Reformation, Christian churches vary widely
in their social and institutional practices. The Roman Catholic Church organ-
izes most of the world with (usually) one pope in Rome, a bishop in each major city or geographic area, and one or more priests in charge of each sub-area
of the bishop's charge. At the other extreme, some Protestant churches consist of little more than a minister, a store front, and a congregation. Churches
also vary in their actions for justice and peace. It seems most helpful to consider both elements together through a brief historical survey, with primary
attention to actions for justice and peace.

   In the first three centuries, before the emperor Constantine legalized Christianity, Christians were pacifist *with respect to persecutions*: they did not use
arms to defend their religious rights. Yet their pacifism was active: they demanded their rights. In this early period, Christians *did not exercise state
power,* so they didn't have to decide whether to use force to defend the political state. Most Christian *writers* were pacifist even in regard to *state* power:
they explained why Christians could not serve in the army. Thus, the Christian "great tradition" was pacifist in its primary expression.

   Some scholars have asked how well *ordinary Christians*—the "little tradition"—agreed with their writers. Others have pointed out that *even the writers*
had *a variety of reasons* for keeping Christians out of the army: it was an environment permeated with pagan worship. Few soldiers were Christians. On
those few occasions when a soldier did become Christian, the community was
so happy to get a *soldier* convert that it didn't know quite what to do with him.

   After Constantine legalized Christianity, Christians held state power. How
can or should one remain pacifist when one has the levers of police and army
in one's hands? Ambrose of Milan and Augustine of Hippo adapted pagan just
war traditions to Christian theology, transforming them in many ways. (See
chapter 12 on Just War Theory.) It was a very dangerous time for Roman
power. Barbarian movements were threatening Roman civilization. But Rome
lost to the barbarians anyway—acceptance of just war didn't prevent the fall.
And it wasn't all one sided: Rome didn't act fairly toward the barbarian tribes.
Once the barbarians were in control, just war was even harder to maintain and
pacifism even less likely.

The Middle Ages

In the Middle Ages, power was much more local than it had been in the Roman Empire. Feudal culture valued loyalty to the local lord. Wars tended to be small, local or regional, and fought by professional knights who were so wrapped up in armor that casualties among the knights were light.

The church tried to reduce warfare by instituting the *"Peace of God"* and the *"Truce of God."* The *"Peace* of God" tried to reduce the number of *people* who could take part in war by putting certain categories off limits (not monks, not priests, not peasants . . .);[13] the *"Truce* of God" tried to limit the number of *days* that war could be fought (not Advent, not Lent, not Sundays, not feast days, not Saturdays, not Fridays, not Thursdays. . .).[14]

The pope tried to end petty wars *between Christians* by sending warriors off against a *"worthy"* enemy—the Muslims. He had a pretext: a change of Muslim leadership in the Holy Land had led to laws interfering with Christian pilgrimages. This was the origin of the *Crusades*. By the time the Crusaders reached the Holy Land, another change of leadership had removed the restrictive laws, but by then it was too late to stop the momentum. Sensitive Christians had second thoughts afterward, although even St. Bernard preached a Crusade. Later, there were religious crusades against "heretical" *Christians in Europe*. And during the Protestant Reformation, persecution led to wars among different denominations.

The Inquisition

The *Inquisition* was an effort to deal with religious dissent in the Roman Catholic Church using special church courts. If the church court found people guilty of heresy (religious beliefs that were false according to the Roman Catholic Church), they were handed over to civil authorities for punishment. The inquisition was also used in Spain against Jews who had falsely pretended to convert to Christianity in order to avoid sanctions against Jews, such as the 1492 law expelling Jews (and Muslims) from Spain.

The Inquisition used torture to force confessions, and it often burned its victims at the stake. A 17th-century Anabaptist (see *peace churches* below) gathered historical examples of persecutions from the 1st century through the 15th (thus, up to the Radical Reformation) and published them in 1660 (in Dutch) in a large book called *Het Bloedig Tooneel* (English translation: *The Bloody Theater: or, Martyrs Mirror*), evidently to encourage those who were being persecuted in his own day. Here is a sample account:

> A. D. 1417 . . . M. Raymond Cabasse, D.D. . . . declared . . . that the aforesaid Catharine Saube . . . was a heretic, and that she had disseminated, taught and be-

lieved divers damnable heresies against the Catholic faith, namely, "That the Catholic (or true) church is composed only of men and women who follow and observe the life of the apostles." . . . Again, "That she did not worship the host or wafer consecrated by the priest; because she did not believe that the body of Christ was present in it." Again, "That it is not necessary to confess one's self to the priest; because it is sufficient to confess one's sins to God; and that it counts just as much to confess one's sins to a discreet, pious layman, as to any chaplain or priest." Again, "That there will be no purgatory after this life."

Said town-book . . . contained also four other articles with which Catharine was charged, . . . (1) "That there never has been a true pope, cardinal, bishop, or priest, after the election of the pope (or bishop) ceased to be done through miracles of faith or verity." (2) "That wicked priests or chaplains neither can nor may consecrate the body of Christ, though they pronounce the sacramental words over it." (3) "That the baptism which is administered by wicked priests, is of no avail to salvation." (4) "That infants which die after baptism, before they have faith, are not saved; for they do not believe but through the faith of their godfathers, godmothers, parents, or friends."

Having pronounced this sentence upon her, the vicar . . . delivered her into the hands of the bailiff, . . . The people entreated him much in her behalf, that he would deal mercifully with her; but he executed the sentence the same day, causing her to be . . . burnt as a heretic, according to law.[15]

Colonies

European powers had mixed motives for colonizing the New World: the spread of Christianity, national glory, and personal enrichment. Some Christian leaders resisted the corruption involved. Theologians argued seriously whether the "natives" were really human and had souls, illustrating how theology can be influenced by desire for personal gain and can serve special privilege.

SOCIAL AND INSTITUTIONAL DIMENSION: PROTESTANTS AND THE REFORMATION

Martin Luther

Martin Luther, an Augustinian monk, began the Protestant Reformation in Germany in 1517 by calling for a public discussion of ninety-five theses which questioned points of Catholic faith and practice connected with indulgences and spiritual pardons.[16] Luther's doctrine of justification by "faith alone" contrasted with the Catholic doctrine of salvation by faith in combination with the good works that faith produces. Note that justification and salvation are not identical. Recent Catholic-Lutheran dialogue shows that

Catholic and Lutheran positions are not very far apart. But conditions in the 16th century made that convergence difficult to see.

Luther spoke of "two realms"—church and state—and maintained that the state, not the church, had authority in the political arena. The fact that state power sometimes supported him against the pope may have influenced his judgment.

When a revolt broke out between lower classes and privileged classes (the "Peasants' Revolt") in Germany and surrounding areas in 1524–1525, many elites blamed Luther. In fact, Luther strongly agreed with the lower classes that princes, lords, clergy, and other elites were treating them unjustly:

> Since it is clear, then . . . that the bishops are . . . an accursed people before God—rising up against God's order to destroy the gospel and ruin souls—every Christian should help with his body and property to put an end to their tyranny. . . . One should trample obedience to them just as though it were obedience to the devil.[17]

But when, encouraged by his language, the peasants revolted, Luther denounced their violence and rebellion against the established order. Although their demands were just, social order must be maintained. Christians must obey "even unjust and cruel rulers" as "ordained by God" unless "the gospel [was] in jeopardy." When the peasants continued their armed rebellion, Luther encouraged the princes to slaughter the rebels wholesale as they were already doing:[18]

> It is better that all the peasants be killed than that the princes and magistrates perish, because the rustics took the sword without divine authority. The only possible consequence of their satanic wickedness would be the diabolic devastation of the kingdom of God. Even if the princes abuse their power, yet they have it of God, and *under their rule the kingdom of God at least has a chance to exist.* Wherefore no pity, no tolerance should be shown to the peasants, but the fury and wrath of God should be visited upon those men who did not heed warning nor yield when just terms were offered them, but continued with satanic fury to confound everything. . . . To justify, pity, or favor them is to deny, blaspheme, and try to pull God from heaven.[19] (emphasis added)

In his *Treatise on Christian Liberty*, Luther wrote that Christians should act in a Christ-like way toward their neighbors, becoming "Christs to one another." Such neighborliness would include financial assistance to those in need. Attention to the needs of others was later emphasized by 17th-century German Pietists. In the United States, the Lutheran Social Service exemplifies that teaching, as does the Lutheran World Federation globally.

John Calvin

Another Reformer, John Calvin (1509–1564), placed church power above state power: in Geneva, Switzerland, he established a theocracy based on laws derived from the Bible. Because of the biblical story of the "fall" ("original sin"), Calvinists believed that humans on their own are entirely sinful. The sociologist Max Weber proposed that Calvinist doctrine made European capitalism possible.[20] According to Calvin, God is the all-powerful creator, and God's world order is to be maintained. To that end, humans must practice the virtues of "thrift, hard work, sobriety, responsibility, and self-reliance."[21]

Peace Churches

Some Protestant denominations, especially among "*Anabaptists*" (Christians who insisted that people baptized as infants had to be baptized again as adults),[22] advocated following the Sermon on the Mount literally with regard to violence. This movement was called the "Radical Reformation," and denominations deriving from it became known as "*Peace Churches.*" Examples are the Mennonites, the Amish, and the Church of the Brethren. Although they were not Anabaptists and not part of the Radical Reformation, the Quakers also took this position.

Anabaptist Peace Churches

Here are three positions held by the peace churches that are directly relevant to justice and peace: (1) Christians should separate from the world and the state, and therefore not be involved in politics; (2) Christians should not resist evil, hence they should practice nonviolence and pacifism (which could be understood as a form of separation from the state); and (3) Christians should share their goods, or even should own goods and property in common, as the Hutterites did. Diverging from the beliefs and practices of Catholics and Protestants, Anabaptists were persecuted by both.[23]

A Mennonite relief agency based in Holland was established in the early 18th century. In 1920 North American Mennonites established the Mennonite Central Committee, which in 2003 administered relief projects in more than sixty countries with a budget exceeding $62 million. Most Mennonites seek social and economic justice to alleviate world poverty. They oppose war—especially nuclear weapons—as ineffective for achieving justice.[24]

Quakers

The Religious Society of Friends (nicknamed *Quakers* by their critics) was founded in 17th-century England by George Fox (1624–1691), who wanted to end religious wars and prevent church conflicts. His quest led to his experience of inner peace and his "doctrine of the Inner Light." He held a positive view of human nature in contrast to the negative views of Luther and Calvin; his experience of *direct, inner* revelation offset their emphasis on *biblical* revelation.

Fox and the Quakers were strong advocates of pacifism.[25] They regarded violence as satanic. Early Quakers testifying to their inner religious experiences risked prison, exile, and execution. Socially egalitarian, they addressed others as "thou" and "thee" without honorific titles;[26] they also refused to pay taxes to state churches. Their own meetings were silent except when the Spirit moved one of them to speak. Since the sacraments were internalized, no outer Eucharist was necessary.

In England and North America, Quakers opposed slavery and "most capital punishment."[27] They went to prison and paid fines rather than participate in warfare. Toward the Indians, they practiced reconciliation and friendship. The American Friends Service Committee[28] was founded in 1917 to allow World War I conscientious objectors to serve refugees and war victims. The Depression crystallized Quaker commitment to labor issues and workers' rights. The Friends Committee on National Legislation, established in 1943, works to implement Quaker principles in American public policy. It is the largest peace lobby in Washington, D.C.[29]

Evangelicals and Fundamentalists Battle Liberal Protestants

In the 19th century, many Protestant churches, under the influence of new scientific theories of geology (an earth much older than six thousand years), evolution (Charles Darwin), and psychology (Sigmund Freud), began downplaying traditional theology in favor of humanitarianism. This movement was called "Liberal Protestantism." More conservative Protestant churches resisted, insisting on maintaining the "fundamentals" of the Christian faith, for example, human sinfulness atoned through the bloody sacrifice of Jesus, literal interpretation of an inerrant Bible, and the bodily resurrection of Jesus. These churches called themselves "Fundamentalist." Later, they preferred the term "Evangelical."[30]

As the 20th century was drawing to a close, some politically conservative American Evangelical Protestants joined with similarly conservative members of other faiths—Catholic, Jewish, Mormon, secular—to form the "Christian Right," epitomized in the "Christian Coalition of America."[31] Other Evangelicals did not share their political agenda. Grant Wacker, a professor at Duke University Divinity School, estimates that, while there are only about two hundred thousand core members of the Christian Right, millions more could be enlisted to promote a particular political issue. A recent Evangelical position paper on social issues claims that one-quarter of Americans are Evangelicals! Although they share the concerns of classical Evangelicals and Fundamentalists, the Christian Right can be traced to the 1960s, when civil rights, Vietnam, women's liberation, and sexual freedom were among key societal concerns. In response to what they perceived as the dangerous liberalization of American culture, conservatives such as Jerry Falwell and Pat Robertson "sought to defend traditional Christian values such as the authority of the Bible in all areas of life," catching mainline Protestants and the mainstream media by surprise.[32]

According to Wacker, the "four cornerstones" of the Christian Right are (1) an arsenal of "moral absolutes"; (2) a refusal to firmly separate "the public and private spheres of life" (compare with Muslim beliefs); (3) the conviction that the "proper role [of government] is to cultivate virtue, not to interfere with the . . . marketplace or the workplace"; and (4) the reaffirmation of Judeo-Christian values ("Christian civilization") as the proper foundation for life in the United States. Members of the Christian Right feel defensive in the face of hostile media, public schools, and anti-family forces, including certain government policies. On its website, the Christian Coalition of America presents itself as a pro-family political organization founded in 1989, whose mission is to "represent the pro-family point of view before local councils, school boards, state legislatures and Congress; speak out in the public arena and in the media; train leaders for effective social and political action; inform pro-family voters about timely issues and legislation; protest anti-Christianity bigotry; and defend the rights of people of faith."[33]

Progressive Evangelicals have promoted a different political vision. See the program proposed by the National Association of Evangelicals in chapter 9 on Christian Social Teaching.

The Prosperity Gospel

Some Evangelical writers and television evangelists have proposed a "Prosperity Gospel" based on the premise that God wants Christians to prosper. As Kenneth Copeland explains, Christians short-circuit worldly means of financing by investing in God and trusting in God to provide what they need. God then meets their needs not grudgingly but abundantly. Christians "invest" resources generously and in faith through "tithing, giving to the poor, investing in the Gospel, and giving as a praise to God." Then through the following steps they "draw out" on what they have "invested" spiritually: (1) Decide how much money you need. (2) Get your family or local Christian group to pray with you for that intention, trusting in Matthew 18:19:

"[Amen], I say to you, if two of you agree on earth about anything for which they are to pray, it shall be granted to them by my heavenly Father." (3) Trust in faith that God will give you the money. (4) Pray in the name of Jesus to "bind" the devil and his forces so that they cannot interfere. (5) Pray that the forces of heaven [angels] will be "loosed" to produce the desired effect. (6) Praise God in advance for answering your prayer.[34]

There is much to be said for expecting God to be loving and generous, and for investing money, time, and energy generously in God and in the poor. It is important to keep priorities straight and values clear. If the "laws" of the prosperity Gospel are interpreted as a way to "get ahead of others," there is something un-Christian in that goal. If material wealth is valued for itself, human values are distorted.

Christian Zionism[35]

We spoke in the previous chapter about *Jewish* Zionism, which dates in its modern form to the end of the 19th century. *Christian* Zionism actually began earlier, in the early part of the 19th century. It is exemplified today in *The Late Great Planet Earth* by Hal Lindsey, describing the end of the world, and the *Left Behind* series of books describing the "rapture." Many Evangelical and Fundamentalist Christians are convinced that such beliefs are well founded. Scholars and other members of the Catholic Church and of mainstream Protestant churches disagree.

Christian Zionism began with speculation on the end of the world, which gave rise to scriptural interpretation called "dispensationalism": the view that God deals with different historical ages according to different rules. In itself there is nothing objectionable about this idea—it depends on what one thinks the rules are for different ages. Classical dispensationalists, as represented by the notes in the *Scofield Reference Bible*,[36] think that the Sermon on the Mount was intended by God for Jews who recognized Jesus as the Messiah. When Jews failed to recognize the Messiah, God set up an altogether different set of rules, represented by Paul's preaching on justification by faith. Thus, the Sermon on the Mount does not apply to today's Christians. It will apply to the Jews when they come to accept Jesus as Messiah.

According to Christian Zionist interpretation, when Jesus returns, all those Christians who truly believe in Jesus will be snatched out of this world, *raptured* into the air with Jesus. Everyone else, those "left behind," will have to go through seven years of severe *tribulation* leading to the *Battle of Armageddon*, when Jesus will defeat the *Anti-Christ*. After that battle, Jesus will rule on earth for a thousand years (the *millennium*). During the millennium, Satan will be chained so that he cannot cause any trouble. At the end of the millennium, Satan will reappear for one final battle with God. Satan and his followers will be thrown into hell, and all the saved will join God in heaven.

When believing Christians are raptured out of this world, those left behind will face some short-term problems. If they are flying on an airplane both of whose pilots are believing Christians, the plane could be left without pilots, with predictably unhappy results. Highways will show similar problems, with driverless cars careening this way and that.

What makes such dispensational interpretations "Zionist"? Christian Zionists take their descriptions of the end of the world from Hebrew prophets who anticipated the future as they could understand it. Their predictions described the Messiah coming to an Israel ruled by Jews who sacrificed in the temple. If these prophecies depict end-time events literally, then the end cannot come until (1) the Jews are back in Israel and in control of the government, and (2) there is a Jewish temple in Jerusalem where animal and vegetable sacrifices are being conducted. But there is no Jewish temple in Jerusalem. The Muslim Dome of the Rock may well sit on the spot where the temple stood. Furthermore, the parts of the ancient Holy Land that comprised the ancient northern and southern kingdoms of Israel and Judah are mostly in the West Bank, assigned to the Palestinians by United Nations resolutions and international law. The most likely way to "set the stage" for the second coming of Jesus, if his coming has to look literally like the prophecies, is to kick the Palestinians out of the West Bank, fill it with Jews, tear down the Dome of the Rock, and build the Third Jerusalem Temple in its place. Christian Zionists think that this is exactly what should happen.

Jewish Zionists are not so happy about the Christian Zionists' plans for *them*: when Jesus returns, he will convert about a third of the Jews in Israel to Christianity; the other two-thirds will be destroyed in the Battle of Armageddon. Fortunately, most Jews do not take Christian Zionists' *theology* seriously. But they do take their *political* support seriously. In 2002, when President George Bush objected publicly to Israel's invasion and devastation of the Jenin refugee camp on the West Bank, he received about one hundred thousand angry e-mails, mostly from Christian Zionists, telling him to quit interfering with God's plan for Israel. There are some militant Jews who believe God wants them to rebuild the temple, and some have tried to bomb the Dome of the Rock. So far, the Israeli police have stopped them.

Palestinian Christians wonder what they have done to deserve this treatment from their Christian brothers and sisters. They are proud of their ancestry, which in many cases goes back to the apostles and other 1st-century Jewish converts to Christianity. Christian Zionists say that God gave Israel to the Jews. Palestinian Christians wonder whether God really intended to give Israel only to those Jews who would reject his Messiah, and to force out of

Israel those Jews who would accept his Messiah. In any case, there are other ways to interpret the passages in question—ways that Catholic and mainline Protestant scholars prefer.

The Catholic Church and Mainline Protestant Churches on Justice and Peace

Roman Catholic teaching on justice and peace for the last century has been dominated by strong papal leadership, recently reinforced by national groups of bishops. These sympathies are shared with several politically active liberal Protestant denominations. See chapter 9 on Christian Social Teaching. In recent years there have been important attempts to apply just war principles to conditions of modern warfare. Some question whether such discussions have ever been beneficial, or whether they have just been an excuse to do what those in power wanted. Others claim that just war arguments helped to limit the savagery of war and mobilize opposition to war, for example in the United States during the Vietnam War. See chapter 12 on Just War Theory.

SPOKESPERSONS FOR JUSTICE AND PEACE

Jane Addams (1860–1935, United States, Protestant Christian) founded Hull House in Chicago, an early settlement house for immigrants. Working both to meet *immediate* needs and to uproot the *causes* of poverty, she engaged in political action against child labor and on behalf of immigrants, industrial safety, labor unions, limited working hours, and women's right to vote. Arguing that war destroys social reform, she helped found the Women's International League for Peace and Freedom, of which she was the first president, the National Association for the Advancement of Colored People (NAACP), and the American Civil Liberties Union (ACLU). She received the Nobel Peace Prize in 1931.

Dorothy Day (1897–1980, United States, Catholic Christian)[37] experienced poverty in her childhood when her father, a professional journalist, lost his job. Her connection with poverty never left her—she "had a gift for finding beauty in the midst of urban desolation."[38] She studied journalism at the University of Illinois for two years, then wrote for a socialist newspaper. A vehement opponent of injustice, she picketed the White House in 1917 on behalf of women's right to vote and, when jailed, went on a hunger strike for ten days. After some time as a communist "urging revolutionary [social] change," during which she bore a child to her common-law husband, she became a Roman Catholic in 1928. She was forced to break with the father of her daughter, who objected to her conversion to Catholicism and the birth of their child. She then struggled to reconcile her Catholic identity with her passion for justice.

A major turning point in her life came in 1932 when she met Peter Maurin,[39] a wandering French radical anarchist and former Christian Brother at the settlement house she had founded in New York City. He encouraged her to publish the newspaper that appeared a few months later as *The Catholic Worker*.[40] While Marxists were hawking their paper shouting, "Read the *Daily Worker*," Day would proclaim, "Read the *Catholic Worker* daily." The name came to designate also her settlement house in New York City, and eventually a cooperative farm for the poor which they established upstate. They emphasized disengagement from the power structures of our society and direct mutual aid.

Within the first year, the Catholic Worker movement began to open more "houses of hospitality" for homeless persons; by 1936, thirty-three Catholic Worker houses, urban and rural, had opened nationally.[41] A militant pacifist, Day and the Catholic Worker movement maintained a strictly pacifist position during World War I and all wars since. During the Cold War, she and the Catholic Workers refused to take shelter during New York City's annual civil defense drill, inaugurated in 1955. By 1961, when the protesters numbered about two thousand, the drills were discontinued. She traveled twice to Rome during the Second Vatican Council in the cause of peace, once to express appreciation for Pope John XXIII's encyclical *Pacem in Terris* and once to join a fast until the council made a definite statement against war; such a statement was contained in the document *Gaudium et Spes*. She also supported the civil rights movement and the farm workers movement, and was jailed for twelve days at age seventy-five on behalf of the United Farm Workers. Late in life she was honored with the Laetare Medal from Notre Dame University, which commended her for "comforting the afflicted and afflicting the comfortable."

Martin Luther King Jr. (1929–1968, United States, Baptist minister), was born in Atlanta and earned a doctoral degree from Boston University. As pastor of the Dexter Avenue Baptist Church in Montgomery, Alabama, he was selected to lead the Montgomery Bus Boycott. Strongly influenced by Mohandas Gandhi, he developed the nonviolent strategies of the civil rights movement in the United States. He was jailed, he was stabbed, his home was bombed, and when he began to connect race relations with economics and the war in Vietnam, he was shot dead. He helped found the Southern Christian Leadership Conference and the Student Nonviolent Coordinating Committee, and ran a training school for nonviolence. He received the Nobel Peace Prize in 1964.

SUMMARY

Christians believe that God united God's self with a human nature in Jesus of Nazareth, who invited his listeners to welcome *God's* kingdom in preference to the addictive and violent power structures of their world, confronted the power elites of his day, refused to back down when—under the influence of evil spirits—they threatened to kill him, but also refused to organize violence in his own defense, was killed, and rose or was raised from the dead. Alive today, he joins himself to his followers who, transformed by baptism and the Eucharist and acting in his power through the Holy Spirit, continue his mission to save all humans and their societies from the results of "original sin." Since faithful Christians will be raised from the dead as Jesus was, they are free to love their enemies, do good to those who hate them, and refuse to defend themselves by means of violence. But they will not back down from speaking the truth to oppressors.

Some Christians expect Jesus to return momentarily, first snatching them out of this world and the tribulation that will then occur as Jesus battles the Anti-Christ. These Christians support Israel's project to return all Jews to Israel, even at the expense of Christian and Muslim Palestinians, since they believe it is a precondition for Jesus' return. Other Christians oppose dispossession of Palestinians just as they oppose all oppression. Numerous courageous Christians have taken great risks to work for justice and peace on behalf of all humans, whatever their worldviews.

KEY TERMS

Anabaptists

Armageddon

Christian Zionism

Christmas

conversion of the head

conversion of the heart

Crusades

dispensationalism

Easter

Enlightenment

epistles

Eucharist

Evangelicals

exaltation

Fundamentalists

Holy Spirit

incarnation

indwelling

Inquisition

inspired

interim ethic

kerygma

Lord's Supper

Messiah

millennium

original sin

Peace Churches

Peace of God

Pentecost

Prosperity Gospel

Radical Reformation

rapture

resurrection

Sermon on the Mount

social sin

Son of God

structural sin

tribulation

Truce of God

DISCUSSION QUESTIONS

1. How does this chapter's description of "original sin" compare with your previous understanding of it? If any of these ideas are new, do you find them helpful or disturbing? Do you think the concept of "original sin" in some form is true and therefore beneficial, or false and therefore harmful?

2. Which of the explanations of the Sermon on the Mount comes closest to your own view? If none of the interpretations seems to reflect your view, how would you explain the Sermon on the Mount? Which of the interpretations, if any, do you think might produce *bad* effects?

3. What experience have you had with mainline Christian churches (Catholic and Protestant), Evangelical and Fundamentalist churches, peace churches, Christian Zionists, and/or the Prosperity Gospel? Would you describe any of these groups differently than the textbook has described them?

4. Which of the churches described here, if any, do you think is contributing positively to justice and peace? Which, if any, is contributing negatively? What could be done about that?

5. This chapter introduces three Christian workers for peace. Which of them would you be most interested in reading about further? What details caught your attention and interest? With which of their ideas did you particularly agree or disagree, and why?

NOTES

1. Cory and Landry, eds., *The Christian Theological Tradition*. God is so radically different from any creature that any positive statements about God are inadequate: our words are always (as Thomas Aquinas points out) mere analogies. In particular, God's way of knowing is completely different from the human's way of knowing. But using terms like "intellect" and "will" is the best we can do to approximate what we are trying to say.

2. At least not in the normal English sense of the word, where "guilt" implies that something is "my fault."

3. Gorospe, *Forming the Filipino Social Conscience*, 58.

4. Gorospe, *Forming the Filipino Social Conscience*, 58.

5. Gorospe, *Forming the Filipino Social Conscience*, 65.

6. Gorospe, *Forming the Filipino Social Conscience*, 73–75.

7. Gorospe, *Forming the Filipino Social Conscience*, 83.

8. Gorospe, *Forming the Filipino Social Conscience*, 84.

9. Mt Chaps. 5–7.

10. See Wink, "Jesus' Third Way: Nonviolent Engagement," chap. 9 (pp. 175–93) in *Engaging the Powers*.

11. Wink also refutes this notion in "Jesus' Third Way: Nonviolent Engagement," chap. 9 (pp. 175–93) in *Engaging the Powers*.

12. Sanford, *The Healing Light* and other books.

13. "Medieval Sourcebook: Peace of God—Synod of Charroux, 989," www.fordham .edu/halsall/source/pcofgod.html (accessed July 10, 2006).

14. "Medieval Sourcebook: Truce of God—Bishopric of Terouanne, 1063," www.fordham.edu/halsall/source/tofgod.html (accessed June 16, 2006).

15. van Braght, ed., *The Bloody Theater: Or, Martyrs Mirror*, 343–44. From *Martyrs Mirror* by Thieleman J. van Bright. Published by Herald Press, Scottdale, PA 15683. Used by permission.

16. The theses are available online: "Disputation of Doctor Martin Luther on the Power and Efficacy of Indulgences, by Dr. Martin Luther (1517)," www.iclnet .org/pub/resources/text/wittenberg/luther/web/ninetyfive.html (accessed June 16, 2006).

17. Luther, "Doctor Luther's Bull and Reformation," in *Against the Spiritual Estate of the Pope and the Bishops, Falsely So Called* (1522), 283. Used by permission of Augsburg Fortress.

18. Cory and Landry, eds., *The Christian Theological Tradition*, 268.

19. "Letter of 30 May, 1525, from Wittenburg to Nicholas Amsdorf at Magdeburg," in Smith, *The Life and Letters of Martin Luther*, 164–65. Used by permission of Augsburg Fortress.

20. Weber, *The Protestant Ethic and the Spirit of Capitalism*.

21. Weaver, *Introduction to Christianity*, 105.

22. The Greek prefix *ana* means "again."

23. Weaver, *Introduction to Christianity*, 107.

24. Dyck, "Mennonites."

25. Weaver, *Introduction to Christianity*, 120.

26. Similar to the familiar French *tu* or German *du* used to address family members, small children, and inferiors. The English "you" was equivalent to the formal *vous* or *Sie*—or "Sir"—used to address "people of importance."

27. Barbour, "Quakers."

28. www.afsc.org/ (accessed July 10, 2006).

29. See Barbour, "Quakers," and the website www.fcnl.org (accessed July 10, 2006).

30. Weaver, *Introduction to Christianity*, 159, 176–77.

31. www.cc.org/ (accessed July 10, 2006).

32. www.nae.net/images/civic_ responsibility2.pdf; www.nationalhumanitiescenter .org/tserve/twenty/tkeyinfo/chr_right (accessed June 16, 2006).

33. www.cc.org/about.cfm (accessed July 10, 2006).

34. Copeland, *The Laws of Prosperity*, 76, 103.

35. See the discussions on Christian Zionism by Palestinian Christians and Mennonite biblical scholars available at "Christian Zionism and Peace in the Holy Land," www.mcc.org/peace/pon/PON_200503.pdf (accessed June 19, 2006).

36. 1917, copyright renewed 1945. See also Halley, *Halley's Bible Handbook*.

37. www.cjd.org/paper/dorothy.html (accessed July 6, 2006).

38. vitw.org/archives/317 (accessed June 25, 2006).

39. www.catholicworker.com/maurinjf.htm (accessed July 6, 2006).

40. The paper still costs a penny a copy. You can buy a year's subscription (seven issues), mailed to your home, for twenty-five cents. www.catholicworker.com/cwfaq.htm (accessed July 6, 2006).

41. For general information on the movement, see www.catholicworker.org/ and www.catholicworker.com/index.html (accessed July 6, 2006).

SUGGESTIONS FOR FURTHER READING

Ciszek. *He Leadeth Me.*

Copeland. *The Laws of Prosperity.*

Cory and Landry, eds. *The Christian Theological Tradition.*

Curle. *True Justice: Quaker Peacemakers and Peacemaking.*

Dart. *Marjorie Sykes, Quaker Gandhian.*

Day. *The Long Loneliness: The Autobiography of Dorothy Day.*

Doherty. *The Gospel Without Compromise.*

Eliade, ed. *The Encyclopedia of Religion.*

Gorospe. *Forming the Filipino Social Conscience: Social Theology from a Filipino Christian Perspective.*

Halley. *Halley's Bible Handbook: An Abbreviated Bible Commentary.*

King. *A Testament of Hope: The Essential Writings and Speeches of Martin Luther King Jr.*

Lindsey. *The Late, Great Planet Earth.*

Merton. *The Nonviolent Alternative.*

Peterson. *Martyrdom and the Politics of Religion: Progressive Catholicism in El Salvador's Civil War.*

Sanford. *The Healing Light.*

Scofield and Weston, eds. *The Scofield Reference Bible. The Holy Bible, Containing the Old and New Testaments. Authorized King James Version.*

van Braght, ed. *The Bloody Theater: Or, Martyrs Mirror.*

Weaver, Brakke, and Bivins. *Introduction to Christianity.*

Weber. *The Protestant Ethic and the Spirit of Capitalism.*

Wink. *Engaging the Powers: Discernment and Resistance in a World of Domination.*

Yarrow. *Quaker Experiences in International Conciliation.*

Zahn. *In Solitary Witness: The Life and Death of Franz Jägerstätter.*

Chapter Five

Muslim Worldviews

"In the name of God, Most Gracious, Most Merciful.
Praise be to God, the Cherisher and Sustainer of the worlds;
Most Gracious, Most Merciful;
Master of the Day of Judgment.
Thee do we worship, and Thine aid we seek.
Show us the straight way,
The way of those on whom Thou hast bestowed Thy Grace,
those whose (portion) is not wrath, and who go not astray."[1]

—Sura 1 from the Quran

EXPERIENTIAL AND EMOTIONAL DIMENSION

While meditating in a mountain cave, Muhammad had a powerful encounter with the angel Jibril (Gabriel), who commanded him to "recite/read." He objected that he could not because he was illiterate,[2] but Jibril insisted until he finally *submitted*. This submission to God's will is the central value of Islam and the reason the religion is called *Islam*. Until his death twenty-two years later, Muhammad continued to have similar encounters, during each of which he received verbal revelations from God in Arabic which he was commissioned to recite to others. The Arabs of Mecca prized poetic skills highly. When Muhammad recited the revelations he was receiving from God, the Meccans were in awe at the beauty and power of their language, which no human being could duplicate. Muslims consider the Quran to be the one miracle performed by Muhammad (as sent by God).

117

Once, in what came to be called the *"Night Journey,"* Muhammad was "transported" to Jerusalem on a heavenly winged steed, then taken to heaven where he encountered prophets, angels, and God. Muslims consider this journey and ascension to be a "miracle that no one saw"; its purpose was not to convince others but to reveal religious truths to Muhammad and to test Muslims' faith.

Muhammad's followers, who had previously worshiped multiple gods, became convinced that there is only one God calling them to the straight path of submission to God's will. Muhammad challenged all Meccans, including the wealthy and elite religious-economic establishment, members of his own tribe, to submit to Allah, trusting God rather than possessions, and sharing their wealth with the poor. His followers came to believe that Allah would judge all humans justly after their deaths, rewarding the good and punishing the wicked. These convictions gave them a sense of confidence well expressed in two common sayings: *Allah (hu) akbar* = "God [he] is greater [than anything or anyone else]," and *Hasbuna Allah* = "God is our enough."

HISTORICAL PERIODS

Spread of Islam

After Muhammad's death, the new faith spread rapidly by conversion and conquest. By the Middle Ages it had expanded north through Turkey to Constantinople and across Eastern Europe to just short of Vienna, west across North Africa, across the Mediterranean Sea to Sicily, across the Strait of Gibraltar and north into Spain, east into India and beyond, reaching eventually as far as Indonesia, which today is the world's most populous Muslim nation.

The first four caliphs were companions of Muhammad who lived simple lives as he had. Once the caliphate became dynastic and Islam intercontinental, leadership was more politicized and contested. Uniting the entire Islamic world under one caliph became less and less possible. The last dynasty with a functioning caliphate was the Ottoman Empire centered in Istanbul (Constantinople). After the First World War, when Turkey was going through an explosive process of modernization under Mustafa Kemal (Ataturk), the caliphate was abolished. Since that time there has been no recognized caliphate.

The Umayyad dynasty (Damascus, 661–750) and the Abbasid dynasty (Baghdad, 750–1258) came after the first four caliphs. In the medieval period, three outstanding sultanates flourished: the Moghuls in India, the Ottomans based in Turkey, and the Safavids in Iran. The next major development in the Islamic world was European colonization, which ended in the 20th century. Relations with the West, where millions of Muslims now live, have been an important concern of Muslim countries in the post-colonial period.

SACRED WRITINGS

Muslims believe that their faith is a renewal of the Jewish and Christian revelations. They revere Jewish and Christian prophets but believe that the Bible has become corrupted over time with the Jewish doctrine of the chosen people and the Christian doctrine of Jesus' divinity. The Quran, understood to be God's actual words, restores the true content of the prior revelations, restating Allah's original message to the Jewish and Christian prophets.

The Quran (Koran)

The *Quran* (literally "to recite/read/proclaim") is the miraculously received sacred revelation from God to Muslims. It is believed that the Archangel Jibreel (Gabriel), in a series of spiritual encounters over a twenty-three year period, recited the poetic verses of the Quran in Arabic to Muhammad, indicating also where each verse belonged in relation to those earlier revealed. Muhammad in turn recited the verses to his companions, who repeated them, memorized them, and eventually wrote them down. Because the very language is part of the revelation, no translation adequately represents the Quran—translations are only "interpretations."

After Muhammad died, Muhammad Abu Bakr, the first caliph, assigned Zayed Ibn Thabit, a secretary of the Prophet, the job of assembling a complete, authentic copy of the Quran based on the oral and written materials and on previous instructions by Muhammad as to the correct order. The collection was further standardized under Uthman, the third caliph, by an official commission, also headed by Ibn Thabit. Copies were then widely distributed, and the earlier partial copies were destroyed to assure a uniform and authentic text.

The verses of the Quran are arranged in 114 sections of varying lengths, called *suras*. Muslims refer to each sura by a keyword that reflects something of its content. After the first sura, which introduces the whole revelation, the second sura is the longest. The remaining 112 suras are approximately in order of declining length; the arrangement also makes use of connections between keywords and ideas. The suras are divided into two categories: (1)

Those received earlier, in Mecca, are generally shorter than the second group, and so appear later in the Quran. (2) Those received in Medina after the *hijra*, or flight from Mecca, are generally longer and appear earlier in the Quran. Since Muhammad was invited by Medina to be their judge, these later suras contain many rules and regulations for the Muslim community (*ummah*), which are not found in the earlier suras.

The Sunna and Hadith

Besides the Quran, Muslims venerate the *Hadith*—written collections of the *Sunna*, or traditions that claim to record the words and actions of Muhammad as remembered and passed on by his followers. These texts are considered authoritative, but are subject to criticism in a way that the Quran is not, since the Quran is believed to consist entirely of divine revelation. Each individual hadith has an *isnad*, or chain of authorities, on which the tradition is said to rest. The value of a particular hadith depends on the trustworthiness of the witnesses cited in the isnad.[3]

Here are three examples of hadith, words attributed to Muhammad, minus the isnad: "None of you [truly] believes until he wishes for his brother what he wishes for himself." (#13)

"Fear Allah wherever you are, and follow up a bad deed with a good one and it will wipe it out, and behave well towards people." (#18)

"Whosoever of you sees an evil action, let him change it with his hand; and if he is not able to do so, then with his tongue; and if he is not able to do so, then with his heart; and that is the weakest of faith." (#34)[4]

NARRATIVE OR MYTHIC DIMENSION

Islam began in an Arabian society that was mostly pagan. Muhammad had some awareness of Christianity, but in a form considered heretical by both Rome and Constantinople, the centers of Western Catholicism and Eastern Orthodoxy. He also had some awareness of Judaism, but it was probably not a dominant part of his background.

Muslims insist that Islam was not "borrowed" from or "based on" Judaism and Christianity. Muhammad did not "study" the Bible—he was illiterate. So if Islam is similar to Christianity and to Judaism, it must be because it has a common *source*—God.

Muhammad was born in 570 CE. His father died before his birth. Since his mother was very poor, he was raised at first by his foster mother Halimah.

When he was six, his natural mother died and his foster mother gave him to his grandfather Abd al Muttalib. Two years later his grandfather died, and he was given to an uncle, Abu Talib. Muhammad grew up fairly poor in the trading center of Mecca, a place of strong contrasts between rich and poor, and much injustice.

As a young adult, Muhammad worked for a wealthy widow named Khadijah managing her caravans. Impressed by his success and his integrity, Khadijah offered to marry Muhammad. (The marriage was her idea, not his.) He accepted gratefully, and lived with her as his only wife until she died many years later in 619, when he was about forty-nine. After her death he took other wives, according to the customs of the time. Some of these marriages were intended to strengthen relations with neighboring tribes. By Khadijah he had four daughters and two sons; but only one daughter, Fatimah, had children who lived into adulthood.

At age forty, Muhammad began to have visions and dreams. He spent a lot of time praying alone in a mountain cave. There, during the month of Ramadan, he received the first revelations through Jibril (Gabriel). Khadijah encouraged Muhammad to trust his visions and share them publicly. When he did so, the wealthy and elite religious-economic establishment of Mecca, members of his own tribe, became worried that the new way of living would produce radical changes in the social world, so they tried to bribe Muhammad to keep quiet. He responded that they should submit to Allah's will instead, but they refused.

Like Jesus, Muhammad was a social reformer. The revelations he received became the Quran, which expresses God's will for the community and teaches people how to live out the will of God (the so-called "Quranic mandate"). These are some of the reasons that Meccan elites resisted Muhammad's reforms:

1. Muhammad wanted to replace tribal loyalty with loyalty to the whole community (*ummah*) under one God; this would mean an end to retaliatory, tribal warfare as well as to polytheistic belief and practice. The Meccan elite profited from the annual pilgrimage of polytheists to a shrine called the *Kaabah* and its idols. Muslims believe that the *Kaabah* has been the house of worship from time immemorial. It consists of a sacred black stone within a cubical building. The building is covered with a black cloth and surrounded by a courtyard.

2. Muhammad was disturbed that values of sharing were eroding in Mecca as trade and urban life grew. But the elite establishment gained its wealth from that trade. Two of the five pillars of Muslim faith (alms and fasting)

relate directly to economic justice. See comments below when those pillars are explained.

3. Muhammad opposed female infanticide and introduced reforms that improved the position of women with respect to marriage, divorce, and inheritance. These changes challenged the established patriarchal social order, which the elites wanted to maintain.

In 620, Muhammad experienced the *"Night Journey."* It was during this ascension to heaven that he received the command for all Muslims to pray five times a day.

Hijra to Medina

In 621 Muhammad converted some pilgrims from Yathrib (later called *Medina*: "The City"), about two hundred miles north of Mecca. They urged him to come to Medina as mediator in some local disputes there. Through his mediation he gained authority and respect. In 622, Muhammad and his followers fled from Mecca and escaped to Medina, where he was accepted as city leader. This *Hijra* (*Hegira*), or emigration, began his role as head of state, and the date July 16, 622 CE, stands as the beginning of the Muslim calendar: as Christians measure dates AD—*Anno Domini*, in the year of the Lord [Jesus Christ], so Muslims measure dates AH—*Anno Hegirae*, in the year of the *hijra*. More recently, scholars have begun to use the designation CE (the "common era") in place of AD in an attempt to de-link this most widely used dating system from a particular religion, although its origin was religious.

Muhammad in Medina

In Medina, Muhammad established a new constitution for the *ummah*, or community, which included people of all religious faiths. His diplomatic skills in Medina and new defensive military tactics against aggression from Mecca increased the respect of his followers. The rulers and elite of Mecca mounted three major attacks between 624 and 627, but ultimately failed to thwart the growth of Muhammad's following.

In 630, Muhammad and his followers returned in force to Mecca and took control there with almost no resistance. He proclaimed an amnesty toward his opponents. He purged the sacred black stone, the *Kaabah*, of its 360 idols, thus confirming Mecca's conversion to Islam. The Muslims believed that their ultimate victory and the incorporation of Mecca into the ummah was the fulfillment of God's will. In 632 Muhammad made his final pilgrimage to

Mecca and delivered his farewell sermon. By this time, most of Arabia was united under Islam. In that farewell sermon, Muhammad said: "Learn that every Muslim is the brother of another Muslim and that Muslims constitute one brotherhood. Nothing shall be legitimate to a Muslim that belongs to a fellow Muslim unless it was given freely and willingly."[5]

Final Word on Muhammad

He was highly regarded as a mediator to resolve tribal disputes, and often functioned as such. He was given the name *al-Amin* ("the trustworthy one"), indicating the confidence that his contemporaries placed in him. He is also called "the living Quran," one whose words and actions revealed God's will. Muhammad lived simply and did not want to have a marker placed over his burial site, so that no one would worship him after he died.

DOCTRINAL AND PHILOSOPHICAL DIMENSION[6]

Some Key Muslim Beliefs

1. *There is only one God.* The fundamental human sin (called *shirk*) is to choose something other than God as our ultimate good, or to associate any created thing with God as if it were on the same level of being and importance as God. God is completely self-sufficient; God needs no "help." We must not attempt to make images of God, who is far beyond anything we can imagine. Some Muslims, like the Wahhabi Muslims of Saudi Arabia, claim that we should not even make images of Muhammad or other human beings. This latter belief is not shared by all Muslims. For example, Iranian Muslims erect huge public posters of their Ayatollah. God's will governs every aspect of human life. Religion, state, law, and society compose one reality; hence Islam is a way of life. God is powerful and merciful, ultimately just. God's justice is in dialogue with human accountability, but God forgives those who repent when they have erred.
2. *Prophets.* In addition to other prophets, Islam accepts as prophets those whom Jews and Christians accept. Noah, Abraham, Moses, Isaiah, and Jesus were all prophets in the sense that they spoke God's word. They were also Muslims in the sense that they surrendered to God. Muhammad is the last prophet—no more are to be expected.
3. *Revelation and the Quran.* God has revealed his truth to humans through the many prophets, through Moses (in Torah—the Law), through Jesus (in

the Injil—the oral gospel), and most perfectly through the Quran. Over time, distortions have crept into the Torah and Injil. The Quran, in contrast, was revealed word for word by God through Jibril (Gabriel) to Muhammad and preserved free from error. The purpose of the Quran is to guide those who revere, adore, and fear Allah on the straight path through life leading to final judgment and (if the Quran is followed) paradise in the afterlife.

4. *Angels.* There are angels created by God without bodies, but powerful and intelligent. They help humans surrender to God and come to salvation. One such angel is Jibril, who transmits revelations to prophets—to Muhammad and others. He transmitted Allah's Quran to Muhammad.

5. *Judgment, heaven, and hell.* All humans will rise from the dead and come together at the end of time. Then God will judge each on the basis of his or her actions in life, all of which have been recorded in a "book of deeds." The good and compassionate will go to heaven, which is visualized as an oasis: a beautiful garden with underground sources of water. The evil and selfish will go to hell, visualized as a place of torment and everlasting fire. It is essential to take this life seriously, as it is our only opportunity to do good.

6. *Dignity of humans.* Humans are the highest form of God's material creation. They have a special status as God's representatives on earth. Their purpose is to realize God's will in history, to fulfill the "Quranic mandate" to serve and worship Allah by promoting justice. The Adam and Eve story as told in the Quran does not include "original sin" in the Christian sense. But the reality of Satan does stand behind the human moral struggle between good and evil.

7. *Response: surrender to God (Islam).* The appropriate response of humans is to trust God and surrender to God in faith. This surrender will include believing the Quran and the Prophet (Hadith), keeping the Five Pillars, and seeking through the *"greater jihad"* to overcome one's inner selfishness, and through the *"lesser jihad"* to overcome injustice and unbelief in the world.

8. *Role of the community.* Muslims live out this response in the ummah, or Islamic community, which is based on faith, not on ties of blood, tribe, race, ethnicity, or nation. It is open to all, and serves as an example to the nations (Quran 2:43). The ummah has the moral mission of creating an ethical social order, that is, fulfilling the Quranic mandate. The *"lesser jihad,"* or struggle for justice, requires political-social activism. Belief must lead to action in the world, which means that this message is reformist and could be revolutionary, depending on the situation the community finds itself in.

PRACTICAL AND RITUAL DIMENSION

Repeatedly in the Hadith, Muhammad mentions the basic practices required of Muslims. Muslim tradition has assembled these essential practices into "five pillars."

The Five Pillars

1. *Shahada* is the profession of Islamic faith. You become a Muslim the first time you recite it sincerely. Muslims generally repeat it each day. Here is what they say: *La ilaha illa-allah: Muhammadun rasul Allah.* (There is no God but Allah and Muhammad is his prophet/apostle.) *Allah* is a special form of *al-ilah* = The God—implying "*The Only God.*" (Al-ilah has a plural; Allah does not.) This profession of faith is part of the public "call to prayer" that Muslim chanters, or *muezzin*, proclaim from the *minaret* (proclamation tower) of the mosque five times a day.
2. *Salat* is prayer: remembrance of or devotion to Allah, which every adult Muslim does five times a day on a prayer mat facing Mecca.[7] Salat keeps the believer in contact with God throughout the day and makes the Muslim less likely to act contrary to God's will. The prayer mat on which Muslims kneel for salat is decorated with images of flowers and geometric designs, thus representing a garden in which the believer prays to God.
3. *Zakat* is almsgiving: sharing one's possessions with those in need. *Zakat* is a fixed public tax, typically collected or paid at the end of Ramadan each year.[8] *Sadaqa* is the more private, spontaneous almsgiving. In general, zakat amounts to 2.5% of one's "wealth"—assets over and above basic living expenses like food, clothing, housing, etc. For field crops and animals (not counting work animals and those needed for basic survival) there are fixed percentages depending on the crop, the species of animal, and other factors.

   Zakat helps to redistribute wealth and reduce somewhat the disparity between rich and poor. In addition to helping the poor, zakat "purifies" or legitimizes wealth which one has gained *honestly*, especially by one's own labor. Zakat represents the right that poor people have to the wealth of the rich, which is considered impure until it is shared. In addition to purifying the *property itself*, zakat also purifies the *heart of the giver* from selfishness and greed. At the same time, it purifies the *heart of the receiver* from envy, jealousy, and anxiety; and it builds good will in the community.
4. *Saum or sawm* is fasting (during daylight hours of the month of Ramadan).[9] One fasts from all sense-pleasures: food, drink (even water),

tobacco, sex. One does not just eat and drink *less* (as, for example, Catholics used to during Lent); one doesn't eat and drink *at all* during the day—not even water! Muslims awaken before dawn to eat a meal before the sun rises and do not eat again until after sundown in the evening.

Saum enables one to share the experiences of hunger and thirst, and to express solidarity with those who are actually so poor that they cannot afford sufficient food and drink. It reminds Muslims that they all inhabit one ummah; they care about and depend on one another. It also reminds Muslims that they depend on God for the goods of the earth that sustain them, so it has a joyful character.

The Muslim year is about eleven days shorter than the Western year because it consists of twelve lunar months. So the Muslim calendar drifts backward about eleven days a year, and Ramadan occurs in every season of the year over the normal lifetime of a Muslim. When Ramadan occurs in the summer in high latitudes, the period of fasting from sunup to sundown can be very long.

5. *Hajj* is pilgrimage (to Mecca, required at least once in a lifetime).[10] The hajj is required provided that one can afford the trip from one's own resources. No one is obliged to borrow or depend on others for the costs. At the same time, the Muslim community goes out of its way to make the trip affordable, and Muslims of those areas through which the hajj passes show great hospitality to the pilgrims. The hajj offers a dramatic experience of Muslim unity and equality before God. All wear a common, simple white gown. They eat, sleep, and travel simply. They participate in common ceremonies with up to a million other pilgrims at one time.

Malcolm X made the hajj when he was still an active member of the Nation of Islam, which at that time preached that blacks were superior to other races. His experience of unity and equality was so overpowering that he converted to a more orthodox form of Islam committed to equal value and dignity for every human of any race or ethnicity.

Festivals

The two major feasts of the Islamic year are the three-day *Eid al-Fitr* (Feast of Breaking the Fast) at the end of Ramadan, and the three-day *Eid al-Adha* (Feast of Sacrifice) at the end of the annual pilgrimage, or hajj, in Mecca.

The Eid al-Fitr begins on the first day after Ramadan. In addition to feasting and visiting with family and friends, Muslims give food to the poor for their feast and gifts to children and others. The Eid begins with an Eid sermon and congregational prayer service.

The Eid al-Adha closing the hajj commemorates the story of Abraham's near-sacrifice of his son Ishmael (not his second son, Isaac, as in the Genesis 22 account). The animal sacrifice of cattle, goats, and sheep that precedes the feast alludes to God's substitution of a ram for the boy. The meat that is left over from the feast is given to poor people, who probably eat meat very infrequently. Note how this feast celebrates the key Muslim virtue of trusting surrender to God (Islam). Both Abraham and Ismail (Ishmael) trusted God: Abraham was offering his dream of living on in his descendants, the core of the promises he had been receiving from God. Ismail was offering his very life.

There are additional Shia religious practices, such as the celebration of the birth and death days of the Imams, pilgrimage to tomb shrines including those of the "holy family," and commemoration of the martyrdom of Ali's son Husayn at Karbala (in Iraq) in the year 680 through annual and daily Muharram processions, the recital of sacred stories, and the performance of passion plays. Veneration of martyrs and saints draws attention to their virtues and encourages Muslims to imitate them. Commemorating the martyrdom of Husayn reminds Muslims that trusting confidence in Allah is the core of Islam, and that trust requires sacrifice. It also cautions them against putting trust in political power, which is often corrupt.

EXPERIENTIAL AND EMOTIONAL DIMENSION: SUFISM

Islam began with Muhammad's prophetic experiences. Although it believes that Muhammad was the final prophet, it has produced mystics throughout the centuries. Because mystics claim to have a special closeness to the spiritual world which challenges political authorities and may raise questions about traditional theological or doctrinal explanations, they are esteemed by some but mistrusted and feared by others.

Sufis are Muslim mystics. They get their name from the woolen "suf" or cloak that they have traditionally worn. The Sufi movement began in the 8th century CE. It was a time of flowering intellectual and spiritual development: theological, legal, scientific, and mystical. These developments were reactions against formalism and oppression, especially the un-Islamic focus on power, wealth, decadence, and luxury in the Umayyad court. Muhammad served as the key model of simplicity; since he was married, simplicity or asceticism for Islam did not necessarily include celibacy as it did in Christian monasticism.

The early Sufis sought to avoid hell in the afterlife by renouncing worldliness, following the inner path of self-discipline and purification, and practicing repentance, prayer, meditation on the Quran, and imitation of the Sunna. All Sufis emphasize the unity of creation, interpreting the *shahadah* ("There is no god but God") to mean "There is no reality but the Reality." They seek to know this Reality through perfect surrender to God and through spiritual methods which concentrate attention on the Real.

Fakir (faqir) is the Arabic term for poor, especially religiously poor—those who detach themselves from material things in order to seek God. *Dervish* is the Turkish and Persian equivalent. The Sufi Rumi founded a 13th-century fraternity of dervishes. Fakirs and dervishes are similar to Hindu *sramanas* and *sannyasin*. Some sought ecstatic trance by dancing; these are the so-called "whirling dervishes." Mustafa Kamal (Ataturk) suppressed their order in the 1920s, but they are reviving today. Common practices among Sufis are *dhikr,* or remembrance of God, through recitation, song, and/or dance, and veneration of saints, especially visiting their tombs to receive blessings. A Muslim colleague remarked that Sufis, fakirs, and dervishes are a "fringe part of Islam." The Sufis, fakirs, and dervishes, of course, might not agree with that judgment.

Some Famous Sufis

Rabia of Basra (d. 801, located in modern Iraq) focused the religious life on love and devotion; she refused to marry and had her own disciples. Through her influence, Sufism opened up to a much broader membership, cutting across class boundaries, and gaining ground throughout the Middle East. Here is one of Rabia's sayings: "O God! If I worship Thee in fear of Hell, burn me in Hell; and if I worship Thee in hope of Paradise, exclude me from Paradise; but if I worship Thee for Thine own sake, withhold not Thine everlasting beauty!"[11]

Abu Hamid Muhammad al-Ghazali (d. 1111, Baghdad) gave up a successful career as a professor of theology to become a Sufi, exchanging words for true experience. After traveling for eleven years, he returned to his native Persia and established a Sufi residential community. His synthesis of law, theology, and mysticism helped to shape what today is orthodox Islam.

Sufis were often in tension with the religious establishment (*ulama*), whom they tended to see as illegitimate and contaminated by association with political power. But in *The Revivification of the Religious Sciences,* Ghazali successfully defended the orthodoxy of Sufism to the *ulama*, thus saving Sufism from being driven underground.

Ghazali's mysticism produced reflections like the following, as excerpted from a summary by D. B. Macdonald:

Then, as he sits in solitude, let him not cease saying continuously with his tongue, "Allah, Allah," keeping his thought on it. At last he will reach a state when the motion of his tongue will cease, and it will seem as though the word flowed from it. Let him persevere in this until all trace of motion is removed from his tongue, and he finds his heart persevering in the thought. . . . If he follows the above course, he may be sure that the light of the Real will shine out in his heart. At first unstable, like a flash of lightning, it turns and returns; though sometimes it hangs back. And if it returns, sometimes it abides and sometimes it is momentary. And if it abides, sometimes its abiding is long, and sometimes short.[12]

These ideas are similar to the practice, in Eastern Orthodox Christianity, of the repeated *Jesus Prayer:* "Lord, Jesus Christ, Son of the Living God, have mercy on me, a sinner." Another famous saying of Ghazali (paraphrased here) tells us to be compassionate toward unbelievers just as Allah is. Abraham the prophet refused to receive an unbeliever whom he had unwittingly invited to dinner. But then he heard God's voice contrasting God's own generous feeding of the unbeliever over decades with Abraham's refusal to feed the man a single meal.[13]

Jalal al-Din al-Rumi (d. 1273, born in Afghanistan, worked in Konya [modern Turkey]) wrote the *Mathnawi* (twenty-five thousand rhymed couplets) in Persian, regarded by Sufis as a companion to the Quran. Here he compares the rationalistic theologian with the mystic:

> Do you know a name without a thing answering to it?
> Have you ever plucked a rose from R, O, S, E?
> You name His name; go, seek the reality named by it!
> Look for the moon in the sky, not in the water!
> If you desire to rise above mere names and letters,
> Make yourself free from self at one stroke.
> Become pure from all attributes of self,
> That you may see your own bright essence,
> Yea, see in your own heart the knowledge of the Prophet,
> Without book, without tutor, without preceptor.[14]

SOCIAL AND INSTITUTIONAL DIMENSION

Islam has been particularly well-organized socially. Its worldview gives central importance to the ummah. Ummah (note: *umm* = mother) *in general* means a community or nation. In its *special* use it means a *religious* community in *submission* (*Islam*) to Allah and to Allah's *rasul* (messenger/apostle). Sometimes Muslims say the rasul for the Islamic ummah is Muhammad, the rasul for the Christian ummah is Jesus, and so on for other groups. But Christians and Jews can be thought of as part of the Islamic ummah if they pay two special taxes. (Christians and Jews were not subject to the draft to defend the Islamic society, so they paid for the support of the state with these special taxes.) At other times, Muslims insist that Muhammad was sent for *all*, not just for Muslims. Note also that Muslims believe that Jesus was a prophet.

In Islam, every aspect of life should be marked by submission to Allah, so that there is no reason for a separation of church and state. Muhammad functioned as both a religious and a civil leader, setting a pattern that some Islamic societies have tried to follow. Many modern states with Muslim majorities organize themselves as Western-style secular governments. Egypt and pre-invasion Iraq would be examples. Others, like many of the Gulf States, look more like tribal governments. Some, like Iran and Pakistan, have attempted to create specifically Islamic governments, with mixed results.

Sunni and Shi'ite Muslims

Those who became *Shi'ite* Muslims divided from the main body of Muslims (later called *Sunni*) over the question of who should be the "successor" or *caliph* (*khalifa*) to lead the ummah.

The Shi'ites believe that Muhammad's legitimate successor must be from Muhammad's family. Thus, in their view, the first true successor to Muhammad was Ali, the fourth caliph after Muhammad. (*Shi'a* means "partisans [of Ali].") Tragically, Ali was killed at prayer by a Kharijite Muslim on the grounds that Ali had failed to punish the assassins of Uthman, the third caliph. Kharijite assassins had intended to kill all three potential caliphs: Ali, Muawiya of Syria, and Amr of Egypt, but they failed with all but Ali. Muawiya became widely but not universally recognized as the next (fifth) caliph. In 680, when Muawiya died, Ali's son Husayn attempted to claim the caliphate, but he was killed in battle at Karbala in modern Iraq by forces loyal to Yazid, Muawiya's son. Thus for Shia, the themes of persecution, suffering, and the quest for justice became paramount. The Shia saw themselves as the "righteous remnant" struggling to restore God's rule through the rightful authority of their religious and political leader—the Imam—in opposition to the corrupt rule of one or another Sunni caliph. The Shi'ites commemorate Husayn's tragic death each year in the celebration called Ashurah with passion play performances reenacting the martyrdom.

In contrast, the *Sunni* Muslims claim to hold the true, orthodox tradition. They accept the three caliphs before Ali as true successors to Muhammad, as well as the caliphs since Ali, who were also not from Muhammad's family. Over time other religious, political, and social differences have developed between Shi'ite and Sunni Muslims. Shi'ite Muslims add to the *shahada* the phrase "Ali is the friend of Allah." Today about 85% of the world's Muslims are Sunni, and about 15% are Shi'ite or members of other minor groups. Iran is officially Shi'ite. Other areas where Shi'ite Muslims are numerous include Iraq (60% Shi'ite), Pakistan, India, and the Yemen.

Christian-Muslim Interfaith Dialogue

Since 1965, there has been ongoing dialogue between Roman Catholics and Muslims. In 2001, Pope John Paul II visited Syria and spoke of how much we grow in understanding when we live side by side. Summarizing twenty years of U.S. Muslim-Catholic dialogue, John Borelli noted,

> What [Muslims] are truly looking for in religious individuals is God-consciousness. . . . Muslims are particularly eager to tell Christians about their respect for Jesus. They have difficulty understanding why Christians might not like them, or distrust them, or feel that they are out to get them, or why Christians say what

Figure 5.1. Muslim Dome of the Rock, part of Al-Aqsa Mosque complex, marking spot in Jerusalem where Muhammad ascended to heaven on the night journey. Courtesy David Whitten Smith, April 2004.

they do about Muslim beliefs when Muslims know they themselves have such a wonderful respect for Jesus . . . Christians and Muslims often judge one another by the extremists . . . they each make the mistake of judging the other's worst by their own best.[15]

MATERIAL AND ARTISTIC DIMENSION

Islamic Culture

Medieval Muslim culture was stunning. Muslim scholars translated Greek philosophy, mathematics, and science and developed them further. Thomas Aquinas came to know Aristotle first through Latin translations from Arabic.

Islam developed beautiful architecture. Since it emphasizes the importance of daily prayer for all, it built very large gathering places called mosques. Beside the mosques, tall towers called *minarets* were built from which religious chanters called *muezzins* could proclaim the call to prayer and be heard throughout the city. For religious reasons Muslim artists avoided representing God or human forms. So Islam decorates its large buildings with bright ceramic tiles using elaborate geometric and floral decorations, and calligraphy. The al-Hambra palace in Granada, Spain; the Taj Mahal funeral monument in India; the Blue Mosque in Istanbul; and the Dome of the Rock shrine in Jerusalem are world-famous Islamic monuments.[16]

Music, Dance, Drama, and Recitation

As was mentioned above, Sufis use music and dance to induce an ecstatic religious state. Elaborate recitation of the call to prayer and of the Quran produces a beautiful and prayerful effect. In 1990 I had the privilege to stay overnight above Nazareth on a Muslim holiday. From the town below, we could hear a Muslim leader chanting. After each phrase of his chant, the town's teenagers in the streets enthusiastically and joyfully repeated the chant.

Holy Places

Besides objects produced by humans, the material dimension also includes sacred places. Muslims make the hajj to Mecca because the events that took place there in the time of Muhammad are central to the Muslim experience. Pilgrims circle around the *Kaabah*. Muslims also visit *Medina* after the pilgrimage to Mecca to see where the prophet lived and where the early *ulama* (body of learned Islamic scholars) was established. They venerate *Jerusalem* because Muhammad ascended to heaven from Jerusalem in his mystic-visionary experience called the "night journey." By their pilgrimages, worshipers seek to come into contact with the power of those events.

ETHICAL AND LEGAL DIMENSION

The core of Islamic faith is surrender to Allah. Therefore, Islam emphasizes ethical and legal interpretation of God's revelation in the Quran. *Sharia* (literally "the straight path") is the term for Islamic law, Allah's will. *Iman* means right *faith* or *belief* in Allah (similar to Christian ortho*doxy*). *Amal* means just *action* (similar to Christian ortho*praxis*). Justice itself distinguishes between *adl*: justice that *maintains* an equal balance (proportionate to a person's potential and situation), and *ihsan*: justice (mercy, charity) that *restores* balance by making up for a loss or deficiency. In practice, ihsan often means helping others materially, coming to perfection through sincerity and charity of heart. Thus, ihsan fulfills adl as love fulfills the law. Finally, *haq* means the righteousness or right that gives everyone what they are entitled to; it also means truth.

ISSUES FOR JUSTICE AND PEACE

Islam and War

The early Muslim wars of expansion were relatively civilized. Conquered Christians and Jews were invited to join the ummah by payment of a head tax. This tax took the place of the military and civil obligations which *Muslims* owed to the ummah. Later they were required to pay an "exemption tax" as well. They were allowed to continue their religious practices because they were monotheists and "People of the Book." They did, it is true, experience "social restrictions" in comparison with Muslims. In some periods these were lenient, in others oppressive.

The Crusades[17]

The Crusades were military campaigns in the 11th through the 13th centuries CE, usually called or approved by a pope and officially intended to protect Christian pilgrims by gaining control of Jerusalem and the "Holy Land." The

First Crusade was called in 1095 CE when the patriarch of Constantinople asked the Western church to help him resist Muslim attacks. Popes encouraged participation by offering spiritual benefits to the crusaders, such as indulgences (remission of spiritual punishment for past sins which had already been forgiven). Other factors also drove the campaigns: popes hoped the campaigns would unite all Christians—Eastern and Western—under the pope's leadership; Christians wanted to control areas the Muslims had captured over several centuries—the Middle East, North Africa, Asia Minor, Eastern Europe, Spain; popes urged European knights to stop killing each other and vent their warlike spirits and skills (about the only trade they knew) on a "worthy foe"; Italian port cities profited by shipping knights and war material; and younger sons unable to inherit the family estate dreamt of conquering territory for themselves.

Crusader knights set up kingdoms which survived for less than one hundred years inland, as in Jerusalem, and off and on for another century along the coast, as in Acre. With the fall of Acre in 1291, the last of the Western Christian kingdoms was destroyed. In contrast to the early Muslim wars of expansion, Christian crusaders tended to be butchers and have been long remembered for their atrocities against Muslims, Jews, and even other Christians in their conquest of the Holy Land—especially their massacre of civilians when they captured Jerusalem in 1099. Patriarchs of Constantinople soon regretted having invited in the Westerners, who eventually sacked Constantinople itself. Even in the face of crusader cruelty, the Muslim general Salah ed-Din, who re-captured Jerusalem in 1187, was noted for his chivalry and generosity toward the crusaders he was defeating.

Arab memories of crusader cruelties and injustice continue to affect Middle Eastern politics, a fact that was quickly explained to President George W. Bush when he referred to a "crusade against terrorism" in response to the attacks of September 11, 2001, on the World Trade Center and the Pentagon.

Colonization

European colonization of the Islamic world was driven by economics. Modernization and industrialization impelled Europe to expand their markets for manufactured goods, which were exchanged for the exploitable resources of the colonies; the influx of manufactured goods from Europe severely disrupted the local economies. Moreover, the colonies had to be financially modernized, that is, westernized, as they were incorporated into the colonizers' dominant economic system. The traditional agrarian societies of the colonized world experienced an alien process of transformation, with the result that within those societies most people were left behind while a few prospered. Modernization and westernization appeared to be synonymous to those on whom they had been foisted. Economically annexed to Europe, the Muslim world was also subjected to the colonizers' racist ideology of cultural superiority. Europe's initial colonization of the Muslim world—in Egypt, North Africa, India (including later Pakistan), and the Far East—took place in the 19th century. The First World War extended European control to one of the last areas to resist colonization: the Ottoman Empire. Liberation from colonial rule came mostly after World War II.

Turkey and Armenia

Religions and nations tend to be more tolerant when they are confident in their power than when they fear they are losing power. The Ottoman Empire, centered in Istanbul, had prided itself on its religious diversity and tolerance. During the First World War, the empire had recently lost control over Greece and was in the process of losing to Western colonization or control what today is Iraq, Saudi Arabia, Syria, Lebanon, Jordan, Israel, Gaza, and the West Bank. The ruling faction in Turkey decided that the (Christian) Armenians had the potential to support Turkey's enemies and dilute the "Turkish character" of the country. So they expelled or killed virtually all of their million and a half Armenians through murder and forced marches into the Syrian desert, in what became the first major genocide of the 20th century. Hitler would later point to their success to support his "final solution" of the "Jewish problem."

Turkey denies that what happened to Armenians was a genocide. They describe it rather as a "deportation" due to wartime conditions. They claim that the conflict was mutual, that Armenian groups attacked and killed Turkish neighbors, that all sides suffered in a time of warfare, that foreign witnesses were prejudiced against Turks, that there are no official documents establishing a deliberate campaign against Armenians, and that it is unfair to single out the Armenians as victims and accuse the Turkish government of deliberate genocide.

Most non-Turkish scholars argue that governments rarely describe their genocidal plans in official written documents, that the Turkish archives for that period are still sealed, that even prejudiced witnesses can give valid first-hand testimony, and that a comparison of population figures before and after the period do not support the notion that the suffering was of comparable degree. In addition, the Turkish government has applied significant pressure attempting to influence the historical record, including pressuring Israel to cancel a planned conference on the subject and threatening Microsoft with a lawsuit for including the "Armenian Genocide" in their online encyclopedia.[18]

The Lesser Jihad

In our contemporary "war on terrorism," news reports speak of Islamic *mujahid* waging *jihad* against democratic nations. To keep our terms straight, it is useful to notice the similarity between (a) an Arabic term for an *actor* and (b) the related term for the corresponding *action*. The term for the *actor* begins with the letter "m"; otherwise the *consonants* of the two words are identical. A change of *vowels* distinguishes actor from action. For example, a *Muslim* is a person who practices Islam; *Islam* is self-surrender to Allah. A *mujahid* is a person who practices jihad; *jihad* is the act of striving for justice in Allah's cause (including but not exclusively by war). A *mumin* is a person who practices iman; *iman* is right faith or belief in Allah (*iman* in Arabic is related to *amen* in Hebrew).

Outsiders associate *jihad* with wars of conquest to spread the Islamic faith. Muslims respond that they are not forcing anyone to change their faith. They are merely taking political control to provide *conditions* in which people can *hear* the call to faith. To declare war in order to *force* a nonbeliever to believe is a violation of the Islamic principle that *"there should be no compulsion in matters of religion"* (Quran 2:256).[19] Force *is* legitimate to *keep others from oppressing Muslims or preventing them from believing* (2:190–193). Although *political* leaders have often claimed that one or another of the wars they were conducting should be considered a "jihad," Islamic *religious* leaders have rarely considered any of these wars to be a genuine jihad since the original struggle with Mecca.

No one should be forced to *become* Muslim. However, once one has become a Muslim (either by conversion or through birth), a *rejection* of Islam is seen as a rejection of Allah and a disgrace to family and community. What happens next varies greatly from society to society. Some Islamic legal scholars hold that one who *abandons* Islam should be executed. In March 2006, Abdul Rahman, a Pakistani citizen, was in court seeking custody of his children from his former wife. He was denounced as a convert to Christianity, arrested, and threatened with execution. Western governments put immense pressure on the Afghan government to free Rahman. The Islamic court objected to political pressure, but offered to free Rahman if he would profess faith in Islam. An Afghani Muslim cleric described as "moderate" (in Afghani terms), Abdul Raouf stated, "Rejecting Islam is insulting God. We will not allow God to be humiliated. This man must die."[20] Popular opinion in Afghanistan, where there is much resentment over Christian missionary activity, supported his death. The compromise reached was to drop the case on the grounds that Rahman was mentally unfit for trial. He was released and quickly flown to Italy, which granted him asylum.

Many Muslims would regard such a response as extreme. Although a Muslim man with whom I spoke in Baghdad asserted that he would kill his sister if she became a Christian, another Iraqi Muslim man of whom we heard fully accepted his son's conversion to Christianity.

In origin the word jihad is more general. It means *"striving in the cause of Allah."* That may mean striving to defend Muslims' freedom to practice their faith. Or it may mean striving *to establish justice* in the world. Note also that one can strive *nonviolently.*

Historically, Muhammad at first counseled patience in response to attacks from his opponents in Mecca. When he gained community leadership in Medina, he developed *defensive* tactics against aggression from Mecca. Later he accepted *offensive* military action, seemingly as a concession to the desires of his followers. But the sense of jihad as the means of creating conditions in which Islam can be made available to all nonbelievers throughout the world developed only after Muhammad's death. Many people of other faiths preserved these faiths even under Islamic rule.

Rules for Just War

Islam has *rules for just war.*[21] According to the Quran:

1. The war must be in response to an enemy who threatens the freedom of Islam.
2. One must first seek through faith and prayer to avoid fighting.
3. One must next try through reason and meditation to determine appropriate moral action.
4. Finally, as a last resort, armed action may be accepted.

Later, in regard to wars to extend Islam, the following rules were formulated:

1. The *jihad* must be led by an imam or Muslim political leader.
2. There must be good chance of success.
3. The enemies must first be invited to accept Islam.
4. Monotheists, including Christians and Jews ("people of Kitab"—the book), need not accept Islam as such but need only accept Muslim political rule and pay a special tax in place of the *zakat*, which Muslims pay. Each religious group forms a semi-autonomous community called a *millet*.

The Greater Jihad

All of these meanings above deal with the world *outside* the believer, and are collectively called the *lesser jihad*. The *greater jihad* is the *inner* spiritual struggle. Sufis, and many modern writers, insist that jihad refers *primarily* to the *inner struggle against sin*—the inner religious striving that believers go through in their own spiritual quest.

Travelers in the Sri Lankan jungles in the early 1900s reported meeting a holy man there who seemed to have a deep, sympathetic grasp of the core spiritualities of world religions and an ability to explain himself in their terms. *M. R. Bawa Muhaiyaddeen* (died in the United States in 1986) emerged to author twenty books, although he himself was illiterate. Especially important for our study is his book *Islam and World Peace: Explanations of a Sufi.*[22] He explains the "laws of holy war" as a concession that Allah made to the Arabs when they professed their inability to forgive as Muhammad forgave. He goes on to report that Allah said:

> To convert without force is the way of Islam; to destroy and kill and slaughter people is not. Therefore, tell your followers that the holy war they must wage is one of lifting up those who have fallen into the state of disbelief [*kufr*]. Tell them to use My actions, My words, and My behavior in order to release those who are hidden in satan and buried in illusion. That is the true holy war. That is Islam. Reveal this to your followers.[23]

The Muslim Brotherhood

There are strong movements in the Islamic world challenging Western-style governments as corrupt. The *Muslim Brotherhood* in Egypt ("Al-Ikhwan Al-Muslimun"), founded in Cairo in 1928 by Hassan al-Banna, is a leading example. It objects to the 1924 suppression of the caliphate by Turkey and the fragmentation of what had been the Ottoman Empire into competing countries. It also complains that the governments of these separate countries have abandoned Islamic principles for corrupt Western alternatives. Influenced by Saudi Arabian Wahhabi theology, it wishes to apply Islamic principles of the Quran and Sunna to all areas of life, including government, with special attention to the role of women, promotion of social justice and political freedoms, elimination of poverty and corruption, and an end to colonialism. To further these aims, it supports schools, hospitals, pharmacies, and social services. Its theoretical foundations are found especially in the writings of Sayyid Qutb (see below).

The Brotherhood has supported some Islamic governments and challenged others. Most of these governments have been authoritarian with limited democratic institutions. When members of the Brotherhood tried to assassinate Gamal Abdel Nasser of Egypt in 1954, six were executed, four thousand were arrested, and thousands fled. Since then, the Brotherhood in Egypt has concentrated on nonviolent, reformist politics and grassroots community development.

Barred from running candidates in its own name in Egypt, Brotherhood candidates ran as independents in 2005 and, despite the fact that "government-friendly thugs roughed up Brotherhood supporters, killing one,"[24] gained about 20% of the seats in the legislature, forming by far the largest opposition party. "In Egypt, the risk from the Muslim Brotherhood is that if it gained enough power, some fear it could do away with the secular state, as happened in Iran. Although the Brotherhood long ago renounced violence, defines itself as moderate, and says it respects the ballot box, it also supports the establishment of Islamic law, or sharia."[25] (Muslims consider *sharia* to be the revealed law of God, in contrast to *fiqh*, or jurisprudence, which is the written record of Islamic legal interpretation over centuries.)

The Brotherhood is active in many Middle Eastern countries. Its local organization in the occupied territories of Palestine is called Hamas.

A Theorist for the Muslim Brotherhood

Sayyid (or Syed) Qutb (1906[26]–1966, Egypt) was an Egyptian teacher, writer, and theorist for the Muslim Brotherhood who received a Quranic education in his home village and studied Arabic literature in Cairo. Early in his career he wrote fiction, employed first as a teacher and then as a bureaucrat in the Ministry of Education. From 1948 to 1950, he earned a master's degree at Colorado State College of Education.

Originally Qutb was not anti-Western, but he changed his mind when he saw "what [the West] had done to the world of Islam through colonialist imperialism and [the] export of secularism, sexual immorality, and materialism."[27] While studying at Colorado State, he published *Social Justice in Islam*,[28] where he called on Muslims "to return to their true mission on earth as a just and balanced system of social life, governance, economy, and worship."[29] Disillusioned by what he had witnessed in the United States, he left the civil service when he returned to Egypt and became a major spokesman for the Muslim Brotherhood. He originally supported Gamal Abd al-Nasser's coup against King Farouk, but eventually became equally disillusioned with the Nasser regime. With other members of the Muslim Brotherhood, he was imprisoned in 1954 after a failed assassination attempt against Nasser. He wrote:

> The real struggle is between Islam on the one hand and the two camps of East and West on the other. Islam is the true power which opposes the strength of the

materialistic philosophy professed by Europe, America, and Russia alike. . . . It is Islam which gives to life a spiritual doctrine to link it with the Creator in his heaven, and to govern its direction on earth; and it is Islam which is not content to allow life to be limited to the achievement of purely material aims, even though material and productive activity is one of the Islamic modes of worship.[30]

Except for eight months in 1965, Qutb spent his remaining years in prison. Seeing the torture and murder of prisoners radicalized him as a firm opponent of the regime. From prison he wrote *In the Shade of the Quran* (1954), a 30-volume commentary on the Quran),[31] and his famous work *Milestones*, which decries Muslim societies that are no longer guided by Islamic principles of social justice and outlines the way to establish truly Muslim societies (1964):[32]

> This movement uses the methods of preaching and persuasion for reforming ideas and beliefs and *it uses physical power and Jihaad for abolishing the organizations and authorities of the Jahili system which prevents people from reforming their ideas and beliefs.* . . . [It] does not confine itself to mere preaching to confront physical power, as *it also does not use compulsion for changing the ideas of people.* These two principles are equally important in the method of this religion.
>
> They say, Islam has prescribed only defensive war! . . . depriving it of its method, which is to abolish all injustice from the earth, to bring people to the worship of God alone, and to bring them out of servitude to others into the servants of the Lord. *Islam does not force people to accept its belief, but it wants to provide a free environment in which they will have the choice of beliefs* . . . to abolish those oppressive political systems under which people are prevented from expressing their freedom to choose whatever beliefs they want, and after that it gives them complete freedom to decide whether they will accept Islam or not. . . . No political system or material power should put hindrances in the way of preaching Islam. . . . If someone does this, then it is the duty of Islam to fight him until either he is killed or until he declares his submission.[33]

After a brief reprieve from detention, Qutb was arrested again, accused of treason on the basis of statements in his book *Milestones*, and executed in 1966.[34]

SPOKESPERSONS FOR JUSTICE AND PEACE

Active Nonviolence and Islam

Violent resistance is not the only, or even the most effective, response to corruption and oppression. Here are some prominent Muslims using alternative, nonviolent responses.

Khan Abdul Ghaffar Khan (d. 1988, Afghanistan). One of Mohandas Gandhi's closest associates, called by Hindus the "Frontier Gandhi," was a Muslim leader from the Northwest Province of India, Khan Abdul Ghaffar Khan. As Gandhi was called "Mahatma" (great soul) in recognition of his greatness, so Ghaffar Khan was called "Badshah Khan" (King of Khans). He enthusiastically adopted Gandhi's ideas of *ahimsa* and *satyagraha*, explaining them in terms of *Islam* or submission to God's will.

As a native of the Northwest Province of India, which the British had annexed from Afghanistan to provide an easily defended border for India, Ghaffar Khan grew up resentful of British power. His tribe, the proud Pathan, noted for their fearless fighting, had been split in two by the annexation. They had already given the British reason to regret having annexed them. More recently it was the Soviet Union that had reason to regret its invasion of Pathan territory, and today perhaps the United States—Ghaffar Khan's Pathan tribe is the same tribe that later embraced the Taliban.

But Ghaffar Khan discovered the power of Gandhi's ideas. He not only applied them in his own life, but he also founded a Pathan army without arms. Called the *Khudai Kitmatgars*, they swore themselves to fearless and provocative nonviolence in the face of oppression. For decades in the Northwest Province they supported Gandhi's campaign against the British. Their efforts were strikingly successful and played a major role in freeing India from British rule.

After India was independent, other Islamic leaders committed to a Muslim Pakistan imprisoned Ghaffar Khan and his followers, and the population was less supportive of his ideas of nonviolence now that local Muslim leaders controlled police and army. Yet a recent researcher has found that, a half-century later, many Afghans who took part in the struggle are still deeply influenced by Ghaffar Khan's example and consider their participation in his nonviolent campaign to have been a high point of their lives.[35]

Ghaffar Khan died in 1988 at the age of 95.

Giasuddin Ahmed (d. 1952, Bangladesh)[36] was born in what was then East Pakistan (now Bangladesh). During Bangladesh's struggle for independence from Pakistan, Ahmed witnessed the horrors of the war and in reaction became a volunteer worker in Indian West Bengal's refugee camps distributing rations. He was only eighteen when he went back home, while the war was still raging. He came to recognize that prayer, peace, and wisdom are essential. Only when people truly represent God and, as a result of identifying with others, "practice . . . goodness, forgiveness, and justice," can they "act effectively against social and structural violence."[37] Three years after Bangladesh gained independence (1972), Ahmed earned a master's degree in English literature. He went on to teach and to continue reflecting on Islam, for example, in relation to nonviolence. In 1988 he co-founded the Bangladeshi affiliate of the International Fellowship of Reconciliation, an interfaith organization called Sampreeti[38] (Society for Peace & Development [SPD]),[39] with which he has worked full-time as president since 1992. Sampreeti focuses on inter-religious education involving Hindus, Buddhists, Christians, and Muslims; on nonviolence; and on economic development.[40]

Fatima Mernissi (1940– , Morocco) grew up in Fez, Morocco, in a progressive family. Educated in Morocco, France, and the United States, she teaches sociology at the University of Rabat and advises UNESCO on issues affecting Muslim women. In her view the veil has become a device to silence women and make them invisible. She criticizes the West for suppressing democracy by supporting autocratic Arab governments. Mernissi believes that, through repressive interventions such as the Gulf Wars, the West has reinforced North African and Middle Eastern tendencies to limit the freedom of Muslim women and of Muslims generally. Seeking liberation, she interprets the Quran and Hadith within their historical context, and she studies Islam as a source for both individual freedom and social stability in modern Muslim societies.[41]

Chandra Muzaffar (1947– , Malaysia) was a professor of political science at the University of Malaysia from 1970 to 1983. He was arrested briefly in 1987 while helping direct the Asian Commission on Human Rights. Human Rights Watch nominated him as a monitor in 1988. Currently, he is president of the International Movement for a Just World (JUST), whose webpage describes its purpose as follows:

> For the first time in history, a global empire has emerged. This has had an adverse impact upon humankind. It is an empire that allows a privileged minority to dominate and control the world. Its dominant power is perpetuated through war and violence. It is an empire in which the vast majority of humankind remains poor and powerless. It panders to the unbridled greed of a few but fails to provide for the basic needs of the many. An empire which encourages greed to grow and selfishness to spread is a threat to humanity. It undermines the spiritual and moral basis of civilization. It would be a tragedy if such an empire becomes the inheritance of our children. This is why, all of us, wherever we are, and whoever we are, must do all we can to help create a just world. . . . Today, more than at any other time in the past, human civilization possesses the knowledge and technology to create a just world. . . . This is what makes the present situation conducive for inter-faith, inter-civilizational dialogue. Through dialogue and interaction, we shall discover that the spiritual and moral worldviews and values embodied in all religious and cultural philosophies can offer the human race much needed guidance in our common quest for a just world.[42]

SUMMARY

When Arabian society was in tension between traditional Bedouin mores and the values of urban merchants and traders, Allah sent Jibril to reveal his will to Muhammad through his eternal word. Rejecting the revelation preached by Muhammad, the Meccan elite persecuted Muhammad and his followers. Fleeing to Medina, Muhammad and his followers developed a strong community, defended themselves against Meccan attacks, and eventually returned in triumph to Mecca, where the Prophet dealt generously with his former opponents. After Muhammad's death, Islam spread rapidly around the Mediterranean world and eastward as far as Indonesia.

The core of Islam is surrender to Allah, who protects his followers, calls for justice, and judges all humans at the end of their lives. Surrender involves an internal *jihad* against one's evil tendencies that resist Allah. It also gives Muslims the courage to engage in external *jihad* as may be necessary to overcome injustice and to free people from political and religious oppression. Thus, Islam affects every aspect of one's life, including politics. Some Muslims experience a deep mystical spirituality, but all that is truly necessary is surrender and generous living on the basis of the five pillars.

KEY TERMS

adl	Injil
Allah	Islam
Allah (hu) akbar	isnad
Anno Hegirae	Jibril
Caliph	jihad
Crusades	jihad, greater
Dome of the Rock	jihad, lesser
Eid al-Adha	Kaabah
Eid al-Fitr	Karbala
faqir (fakir)	Khudai Khidmatgars
five pillars	Mecca
Hadith	Medina
hajj	minaret
Hasbuna Allah	muezzin
hijra	mujahid
ihsan	mumin
iman	Muslim

Muslim Brotherhood
Night Journey
Quran
Ramadan
rasul
sadaqa
salaam
salat
saum
shahada

Sharia
Shia
shirk
Sufism
Sunna
Sunni
sura
ummah
Wahhabi
zakat

DISCUSSION QUESTIONS

1. How did Muhammad seek to reform the society in which he lived? What are some measures that he advocated to create a more just society? What obstacles did he face?
2. Sayyid Qutb expresses the position of the Muslim Brotherhood in its struggle against what it regards as destructive Western ideas. Do his ideas sound reasonable? Which would you agree with, and which would you disagree with? To what extent are Muslims who resist what they consider Western imperialism following these ideas?
3. Many Muslims believe that one's faith ought to influence one's politics, and that a Muslim-majority nation ought to have a government based on Islamic law. They claim that such a government would allow other faiths to practice their beliefs without interference. Do you agree? If not, on what *should* the laws of nations be based? Should a nation that is primarily Christian have a government based on Christian principles? What about a nation that is primarily Jewish?
4. This chapter introduces several Muslim Sufis and peace workers. Which would you be most interested in reading about further? What caught your attention and interest? With which of their ideas did you particularly agree or disagree?

NOTES

1. *The Holy Qur'an*, trans. Abdullah Yusuf Ali, sura 1. Accessible at www.sacred-texts.com/isl/quran/00101.htm (accessed March 3, 2007).
2. *Shi'ites* (see below) usually believe that the Prophet was *literate*.

3. For examples, see list.ahad.org/mailman/listinfo/ahad (accessed July 10, 2006) and click on "AHAD Archives" at the bottom of the page.

4. "An-Nawawi's Forty Hadiths (Translation)" www.iiu.edu.my/deed/hadith/other/hadithnawawi.html#hadith34 (accessed March 3, 2007).

5. www.islamonline.net/English/In_Depth/mohamed/1424/kharitah/article02.shtml (accessed March 3, 2007). See also Esposito, *Islam: The Straight Path*, 11.

6. See Rahman, *Major Themes of the Qur'an*, 108, 120.

7. See for example *Quran* 2:3, 43, 177; 4:103.

8. See for example *Quran* 2:43, 110, 177, 277

9. See for example *Quran* 2:183–87.

10. See for example *Quran* 2:158, 196–203.

11. Quoted in Nicholson, *The Mystics of Islam*, 115. Available online at www.sacred-texts.com/isl/moi/moi.htm (accessed June 8, 2006).

12. Nicholson, *Mystics*, 46–48, quoting from D. B. Macdonald (source not clearly specified). Ghazzale's Mishkât Al-Anwar ("The Niche for Lights") is available online at www.sacred-texts.com/isl/mishkat/index.htm; his *Alchemy of Happiness* is at www.sacred-texts.com/isl/tah/index.htm (accessed July 10, 2006).

13. Fadiman and Frager, eds., *Essential Sufism*, 63.

14. Nicholson, *Mystics*, 69–70. Rumi's complete *Mathnawi (Masnavi)* is available at www.sacred-texts.com/isl/masnavi/index.htm (accessed June 8, 2006).

15. Borelli, "Christian-Muslim Relations in the United States," 326–27.

16. islamicity.com/education/culture/ (accessed July 10, 2006).

17. See Esposito, *Islam: The Straight Path*, 58–59; Wikipedia, en.wikipedia.org/wiki/Crusade (accessed July 10, 2006).

18. See Akçam, *A Shameful Act*.

19. www.pakistanlink.com/Religion/2004/Religion-Oct-29.htm (accessed July 7, 2006).

20. en.wikipedia.org/wiki/Abdul_Rahman_(convert) (accessed July 8, 2006).

21. Kelsay, *Islam and War*.

22. Muhaiyaddeen, *Islam and World Peace: Explanations of a Sufi*. His followers maintain a website at www.bmf.org/ (accessed July 10, 2006). The entire book is available online at www.bmf.org/iswp/ (accessed July 10, 2006).

23. Muhaiyaddeen, "Islam and Holy War," in *Islam and World Peace,* www.bmf.org/iswp/laws-holy-war.html (accessed July 10, 2006).

24. "Legalizing the Muslim Brotherhood," *Christian Science Monitor*, November 23, 2005. www.csmonitor.com/2005/1123/p08s02-comv.html (accessed June 7, 2006).

25. "Legalizing the Muslim Brotherhood," *Christian Science Monitor*.

26. Most of our sources gave the year 1906 for his birth, but the Library of Congress classifications for his books give the year 1903.

27. Denny, *An Introduction to Islam,* 349.

28. Qutb [Kotb], *Social Justice in Islam*.

29. Denny, *An Introduction to Islam*, 349.

30. Qutb [Kotb], *Social Justice in Islam,* 278.

31. His commentary on Suras 78–114 is available online at www.youngmuslims
.ca/online_library/tafsir/syed_qutb/ (accessed May 30, 2006).

32. Qutb, *Milestones*. The entire book is available on the web at www.youngmuslims
.ca/online_library/books/milestones/hold/index_2.asp (accessed July 10, 2006).

33. www.youngmuslims.ca/online_library/books/milestones/hold/chapter_4.asp
(accessed July 10, 2006).

34. For an excellent summary of his life and work, see Denny, *An Introduction to
Islam*, 348–51.

35. Banerjee, *The Pathan Unarmed*.

36. Ahmed and the following two people are discussed in the "Islam" chapter in
Berndt, *Non-Violence in the World Religions*.

37. Berndt, *Non-Violence in the World Religions*, 54–55.

38. "Sampreeti" means "friendship." See www.bgyellowpages.com/yellow_page/
detail.php?co_id=5686 (accessed July 10, 2006).

39. www.ifor.org/members.htm (accessed July 10, 2006).

40. Berndt, *Non-Violence*, 55–56.

41. Berndt, *Non-Violence*, 69–71.

42. www.just-international.org/page.cfm?id=3000022 (accessed July 10, 2006).
See also his biography and several articles on nonviolence at www.transcend
.org/t_database/members.php?idm=234 (accessed March 3, 2007).

SUGGESTIONS FOR FURTHER READING

Banerjee. *The Pathan Unarmed*.
Berndt. *Non-Violence in the World Religions: Vision and Reality*.
Borelli. "Christian-Muslim Relations in the United States."
Denny. *An Introduction to Islam*.
Easwaran. *Nonviolent Soldier of Islam: Badshah Khan*.
Esack. *Quran, Liberation & Pluralism*.
Esposito. *Islam: The Straight Path*.
Esposito and Voll. *Islam and Democracy*.
Fadiman and Frager, eds. *Essential Sufism*.
Glasse. *The Concise Encyclopedia of Islam*.
Hovannisian, ed. *The Armenian Genocide in Perspective*.
Kelsay. *Islam and War*.
Khadduri. *War and Peace in the Law of Islam*.
Kotb [Qutb]. *Social Justice in Islam*.
Maalouf. *The Crusades through Arab Eyes*.
Macdonald. *The Religious Attitude and Life in Islam*.
Mahfouz. *Midaq Alley*. (and many other novels)
Muhaiyaddeen. *Islam and World Peace: Explanations of a Sufi*.
Munif. *Cities of Salt*.
Nicholson. *The Mystics of Islam*.

Paige, Satha-Anand, and Gilliatt, eds. *Islam and Nonviolence*.
Qutb. *Milestones*.
Rahman. *Major Themes of the Qu'ran*.
Saadawi. *A Daughter of Isis: [Autobiography]*.
———. *The Hidden Face of Eve: Women in the Arab World*.
———. *Memoirs from the Women's Prison*.

Chapter Six

Native American Worldviews

"Two men were coming from the clouds, head-first like arrows slanting down. . . . Each . . . carried a long spear, and from the points of these a jagged lightning flashed. They came clear down to the ground . . . and stood a little way off and looked at me and said: 'Hurry! Come! Your Grandfathers are calling you!'

"Then they turned and left the ground like arrows slanting upward from the bow. When I got up to follow, my legs did not hurt me any more and I was very light. I went outside the tepee, and yonder where the men with flaming spears were going, a little cloud was coming very fast. It came and stooped and took me and turned back to where it came from, flying fast. And when I looked down I could see my mother and father yonder, and I felt sorry to be leaving them.

"Then there was nothing but the air and the swiftness of the little cloud that bore me."[1]

—The Great Vision of Black Elk

Indigenous groups and their worldviews are highly diverse. In this chapter indigenous worldviews will be represented by Native American tribes partly because they are more familiar to American readers.

EXPERIENTIAL AND EMOTIONAL DIMENSION

The core experience for Native American tribes is the struggle for tribal survival and well-being in a culture that is very close to nature. Mutual cooperation and interdependence are essential, as is a close awareness of natural processes and resources—both material and spiritual.

Natives see spirit present in everything—a view called *animism*. Animals are our "brothers and sisters." Plants, rocks, and earth all have spirit. Before hunting, many tribes ritually ask the animals for permission to kill them, explaining that they will kill only what they need, use all parts of the animal, and leave a tobacco offering to the spirit of the animal. If animals are our brothers and sisters, we should be able to talk with them. The author of the book *Rolling Thunder* describes how her modern Indian host taught her to talk with bees. It would be interesting to compare her description with the results of modern laboratory experiments concerning the effects of talking to flowers and other plants.

HISTORICAL PERIODS

Origins

The traditional explanation for how Native Americans got to the New World is that various Oriental tribes crossed the Bering Strait on dry land when oceans were low because glaciers had locked up so much water in ice. Some scholars have challenged this hypothesis, pointing out that there is no clear evidence for it, whereas there is considerable evidence that human groups moved around the world's oceans by boats of various sorts.

Native American tribes belong to very diverse groups, speak very diverse languages, and have diverse histories, but there are some frequently observed common features. We will illustrate some of those features, using especially the *Dakota* (or *Lakota* or *Wakota*) tribes as an example. But first, here are brief historical descriptions of some leading Native American tribes.

Some Typical Tribes

Aztecs: Our Lady of Guadalupe

The Aztecs in Mexico were highly centralized and had a rich material culture. They thought that human sacrifice was required to keep the sun rising, so each morning they tore the heart out of a living human victim and offered it to the gods. The neighboring tribes whose members supplied those hearts did not appreciate this belief; as a result, they tended to support the Spanish invaders against the Aztecs.

Christian missions in Central America made little headway until an Indian, *Juan Diego,* experienced a vision of the Virgin Mary—an example of the role played by mystical experience in religion. As a sign to the local bishop, in midwinter Mary produced flowers native to the bishop's Spanish homeland

and imprinted on Juan Diego's cloak an image of herself as an Indian woman. This image also made use of native symbols, which convinced the Aztecs and others that the new religion could free them from oppressive features of their indigenous religions. Within a few decades, massive numbers of natives embraced Catholic Christianity. The cloak with its image is displayed today in the shrine to Our Lady of Guadalupe in Mexico City.[2]

Mayans

Mayan tribes in Mexico and Guatemala had a less centralized government than the Aztecs did, yet they built highly-developed cities and developed astronomy, mathematics, and writing. The collapse of their urban culture, which left impressive structures such as the pyramids of the Yucatan Peninsula overgrown in the jungle, has been one of the puzzles of archaeology and ethnology — it now appears that they exploited their resource base unsustainably until their population crashed for lack of resources.[3] There are still many indigenous Mayans living in southern Mexico and the mountains of Guatemala, although they have mostly adopted a type of Catholicism with Mayan features. *Chiapas,* in southern Mexico, is the center of a nonviolent rebellion against the Mexican government and local landowners. The leader of that rebellion, who calls himself (or herself) *Subcomandante Marcos*, makes liberal use of the Internet to explain his or her policies.[4]

The Incan Empire

The *Incas* in Peru, Bolivia, and Chile developed impressive building techniques, fitting stones closely together without mortar, as well as agricultural expertise. They created a large empire that controlled a large population until the Spanish conquerors destroyed their political power. Like the Mayans,

Figure 6.1. Aztec dancers at a Catholic parish in Mexico City. Courtesy David Whitten Smith, 1988.

there remain many ethnic Incans in Bolivia and Peru who speak tribal languages such as *Aymara*, spoken by over a million people in the area around Lake Titicaca,[5] and *Quechua,* the original language of the Incan empire spoken by more than eight million.[6]

Five countries of Latin America have a majority or near majority of indigenous populations, in many cases speaking their native languages rather than, or in addition to, Spanish: Mexico and Guatemala (Mayan, Aztec, and others), Peru, Bolivia, and Ecuador (Incan: Aymara and Quechua).

Cherokee: The Trail of Tears

In the southeastern United States, five tribes (Chickasaw, Choctaw, Creek, Cherokee, and Seminole) came to be known as the *"five civilized tribes"* because they adopted many of the laws, politics, customs, and clothing of the European settlers. Before 1820, the *Cherokee* named Sequoya developed an 85-character "syllabary" to write the Cherokee language. (An "alphabet" represents each sound by one symbol; a "syllabary" represents each syllable, a more complex sound, by one symbol.) In 1821 that syllabary was used to print the *Laws of the Cherokee Nation*, and in 1828 to print the *Cherokee Phoenix*: the first Native American newspaper. The Cherokee set up a European-style government with legislative, executive, and judicial branches.

Unfortunately, these adaptations to the new immigrants were not sufficient to protect the Cherokee. When gold was discovered in the Cherokee territories in Georgia, whites found a small minority of Cherokee willing to sign a treaty—the *Treaty of New Echota*—which sold all the Cherokee territory east of the Mississippi River to whites for five million dollars. At forty-three thousand square miles, that would have amounted to about $116 per square mile (18 cents per acre) for well-developed farmland and potential gold mines. Most Cherokees disavowed the treaty and *John Ross*, the Cherokee chief, took the case to the U.S. Supreme Court, which ruled in favor of the Cherokee. Georgia officials ignored the Supreme Court's ruling, and President *Andrew Jackson,* on whose side the Cherokee had fought against the Creek fifteen years earlier, claimed that he had no right to intervene in a matter pertaining to one of the states. The *Indian Removal Act of 1830* evicted the Cherokee by force on foot under military escort and sent them to Oklahoma. The journey took almost four months and was badly organized; about four thousand of the fifteen thousand Cherokee died on the way. This removal came to be called the *"trail of tears."*

When they arrived at their new territory in Oklahoma, the Cherokee heard news of the potato famine in Ireland. They were so moved by the suffering of the Irish that they took up a collection for Irish relief.

Southwestern Indians

In the southwestern United States, influential tribes included the *Apache, Pueblo,* and *Hopi* Indians. The *Hopi* are especially noted for their relative success in preserving their traditional way of life. The following story illustrates their vigilance in maintaining the secrecy of their traditions. A graduate school friend reported that when he was a seminary student one of his classmates, a Hopi Indian, didn't return from a holiday. When the seminary investigated, they found out that his tribe had killed him because they believed that he had revealed some of their tribal secrets.

Indians around the Arctic

In the far North can be found various tribes such as the *Inuit (Eskimo) and Aleuts.* The Inuit are especially interesting because of their very gentle, pacifist traditions.

New England Indians: Thanksgiving; the Pequot War

Our Thanksgiving traditions introduce us to Indian tribes of what became New England. The *Wampanoag* tribe, which inhabited the area around Plymouth Rock where the Pilgrims settled, had been decimated by diseases caught from European traders sailing the coast. Their numbers fell from twelve thousand before the Europeans arrived to about one thousand by 1675, leaving much idle land available to the Pilgrims and inclining the Wampanoag to view Pilgrims as allies who could strengthen them against their native enemies. They taught the Pilgrims local survival skills, such as how to grow corn, and so helped them to survive the first, difficult winter. But as the settlers increased in numbers, available land and resources became scarce. Indians did not understand the settlers' concept of land ownership: Indians believed that land purchases became null if the land was not utilized. Also, later settlers treated Natives with disdain and dealt with them unjustly.

The first northeastern tribe to resist settlers was the *Pequot.* A contemporary account of the *Pequot War* illustrates how the settlers' religious convictions contributed to the savagery of their war with the Pequot:

> And indeed such a dreadful Terror did the Almighty let fall upon their Spirits, that they would fly from us and run into the very Flames, where many of them perished. . . . Thus were they now at their Wits End, who not many Hours before exalted themselves in their great Pride, threatning and resolving the utter Ruin and Destruction of all the English, Exulting and Rejoycing with Songs and Dances: But God was above them, who laughed his Enemies and the Enemies of his People to Scorn, making them as a fiery Oven: Thus were the Stout

Hearted spoiled, having slept their last Sleep, and none of their Men could find
their Hands: Thus did the Lord judge among the Heathen, filling the place with
dead Bodies![7]

Blessed be the Lord God of Israel, who only doth wondrous Things; and
blessed be his holy Name for ever: Let the whole Earth be filled with his Glory!
Thus the Lord was pleased to smite our Enemies in the hinder Parts, and to give
us their Land for an Inheritance: Who remembred us in our low Estate, and redeemed us out of our Enemies' Hands: Let us therefore praise the Lord for his
Goodness and his wonderful Works to the Children of Men![8]

The Wampanoag Indians who initially aided the Pilgrims also turned
against them after several decades of abuse and were defeated, but not easily,
in the war called *King Philip's War.*[9]

The Iroquois Confederation. In the northeastern area of North America,
there were also forest Indians. Especially notable were the *Iroquois,* a confederation of five nations. Their constitution influenced the content of the
U.S. Constitution.[10]

Anishinaabeg (Ojibwa). As white settlers took over the eastern United
States and southern Canada, *Anishinaabeg (Ojibwa)* tribes were pushed west
from the Lake Ontario region, where they had been (not always peaceful)
neighbors to the Iroquois. The Ojibwa had guns and gunpowder, and used
these innovations to defeat the Dakota tribes in Minnesota. These two tribal
groups were still competing for territory in Minnesota in the middle of the
19th century, at the time the state of Minnesota was admitted to the Union.

Here is the Ojibwa agenda for the cycle of seasons for northern climates:
winter: trap, stay warm; *spring*: make maple sugar; *summer*: fish; *fall*: gather
and process wild rice.

Dakota: The Dakota Uprising. By 1862 in Minnesota, the Dakota had
ceded all but about 2,800 square miles (a bit less than two million acres) of
their land to the U.S. government in the *Treaty of Travers des Sioux.* In exchange for twenty-one million acres of Dakota territory, the U.S. government
promised to pay the Dakota an annual annuity. But the annuity was often late,
forcing the Dakota to purchase on credit from white traders. By the time the
annuity arrived, the Dakota would find virtually all of it going to the traders.

In the summer of 1862, four years after Minnesota was admitted to state-
hood, the annuity arrived so late that the Dakota were starving. The white
traders also refused credit. Several young Indians searching for food attacked
some settlers, igniting an uprising that resulted in the death of over five hundred settlers or their supporters and sixty Dakota. Once the white government
had regained control, it carried out quick trials which resulted in over three
hundred Dakota being condemned to death. President Lincoln, on the urging
of moderates including the Episcopal bishop Henry Whipple, asked for trial

records and pardoned all but thirty-nine Dakota. One more was later acquit-
ted. The thirty-eight remaining condemned were hung at New Ulm, Minnesota, in a single public spectacle: the largest mass execution in United
States history. The Dakota community was then removed from the state,
mostly to South Dakota.[11]

Reservation lands in South Dakota were violated by white settlers and
their armies as populations grew and gold was discovered in the *Black
Hills*. An army expedition led by General George Custer was annihilated
when it grossly underestimated the size of an Indian settlement it planned
to attack. Retaliatory raids shattered Dakota and other communities, with
some attempting to escape to Canada. Wanton slaughter of bison herds also
destroyed one of the tribes' life sources that provided food, clothing, and
bone for tools.

While the Plains Indians were reeling from these defeats, a Paiute Indian
named Wovoka claimed to have had a vision designating him as the messiah
who would restore the Indians to their former prosperity by teaching them a
"*ghost dance*" which would miraculously bury the whites and restore the
prairies, even bringing dead warriors back to life. Indians who wore the special ghost dance shirt, marked with secret symbols, would be protected from
the white man's bullets. Whites saw this as a rebellious movement that called
for a strong response and decided to arrest *Chief Sitting Bull*, who refused to
condemn the dance. The Indian police who were sent to arrest him accidentally shot him dead. Some of Chief Sitting Bull's people decided to seek the
protection of *Chief Red Cloud* because they thought he was at peace with the
whites. As they were on their way to join him and his people, the U.S. Army
caught up with them and forced them to surrender.

The army led them to Wounded Knee Creek and helped them to set up
camp. As the army went through the camp to collect weapons, a gun went off.
Since tensions were already high, the surrounding soldiers began to open fire
on the Indians with Hotchkiss guns, a sort of primitive machine gun. About
three hundred Dakota men, women, and children died as well as twenty-five
U.S. soldiers. Wounded Knee was the last large-scale encounter between the
U.S. Army and Native Americans.[12]

SACRED WRITINGS

Most Native American tribes have no sacred *writings*, since their traditions
are oral. An exception would be the Mayan classics, the *Popol Vuh* and the
Chilam Balam. There are, however, compilations of oral Native tales written
by non-Native scholars.[13]

NARRATIVE OR MYTHIC DIMENSION

Native American oral traditions have numerous stories about the origins of the world, of human beings, and of their own tribe. The stories frequently involve multiple gods and animals. For example, Mayan creation stories say that the gods tried unsuccessfully to create humans from mud (they fell apart) and from wood (they were rather "block-headed" and so unable to learn how to worship the gods); finally, they succeeded by creating them from corn. These stories make more sense to Natives than they might to settlers, since Natives believe that animals have souls and that individual animals relate to animal spirits that represent each animal species or type, such as Bear Spirit or Beaver Spirit.

DOCTRINAL AND PHILOSOPHICAL DIMENSION

Native traditions remain close to their original narrative forms, with very little doctrinal or philosophical elaboration. But they do have ritual, ethical, and social elaboration, as described below.

PRACTICAL AND RITUAL DIMENSION

Vision Quest

Indians treasure spiritual experiences. The adolescent male Indian goes on a *vision quest* seeking relationship with a guardian animal spirit that will share some of its spiritual power, revitalizing his spiritual resources. Individual animals are thought to represent an underlying spirit symbolizing that species of animal; an individual bear, for example, is the visible representative of the spirit of bear. The vision quest usually involves fasting and keeping a vigil (staying awake outdoors wearing minimal clothing) for two to four days. The experience is supervised by a holy man. When the quest is successful, some animal approaches the quester with a message. Thereafter that animal (or, what is the same, its spirit) becomes the Indian's protector and guide.

Shamans

The *shaman* is a human who has mysteriously been to the spirit world and back again, often through an episode of apparent illness or death. The shaman on his return forms a human link with the spirit world through visions. See Black Elk, whose vision is quoted at the head of this chapter, as an example.

Young Indians may seek the advice of a shaman to understand the meaning of a dream or of their quest experience.

Spirits of the dead live in the spirit world, and can transmigrate.

ETHICAL AND LEGAL DIMENSION

Probably the most common image of Indians among whites is a Plains Indian on horseback. There were many Plains Indian tribes. One example is the Dakotas, who developed their plains way of life as they were pushed out of Minnesota by the Ojibwa. The Dakota and other Plains Indians adopted a way of life based on the horse, which was originally brought to the New World by the Spanish.

Five Characteristics of the Dakota Worldview

In 1971 in South Dakota John F. Bryde published a book titled *Modern Indian Psychology* based on his years of working with the Dakota. His discussion seems to have been well received by several Native Americans I have spoken with. His description illustrates some of the characteristics that are widely shared among Native American tribes. Bryde lists five characteristic Indian (that is, Dakota) virtues or values: bravery, individual freedom, generosity and sharing, adjustment to nature, and good advice from Indian wisdom.

Bravery. Bryde defines bravery as "doing a hard thing without showing fear or running from it." One could show bravery by stealing a horse or killing a buffalo. One could also show bravery by the particular way one engaged in warfare.

Dakota warfare emphasized bravery over effective killing. For example, to "*count coup*" (gallop up through a hail of arrows, touch your enemy with a stick, and then get safely away) was considered more glorious and more courageous than killing from a distance, but no one was hurt (if you got away). If you were skilled at counting coup, you were considered to have "strong medicine" (in this case, strong spiritual power that protected you from harm). Another characteristic practice showing bravery was to stake yourself down in battle (attaching yourself to the stake by a cord) as a sign that you would not retreat. Warriors who did this were called "*dog strap soldiers.*"

Whites observed that Dakota males spent a lot of time sitting around letting the females wait on them, only "working" when hunger drove them to hunt or danger drove them to fight. Bryde points out that there was an important reason for this. Hunting and warring were both very dangerous. If the men spent all their time hunting and warring, not enough of them would survive to continue the tribe.

Individual Freedom. As Bryde explains this characteristic, "You yourself decide to do the *right thing* in order to survive"—that is, in order that the *tribe* will survive and the *people* will remain strong. ("To survive" means "to go on living in the best way possible.") No one has the right to force his or her own will on anyone else. But one should let those who refuse good advice get hurt by their choices. One should "respect advice" by "listening all over" (to the elders). Those who ignore commonly respected advice get ridiculed by the whole group.

It is important for the community that its members be able to stand alone; that quality is especially essential as a support to the previous characteristic—bravery. Emphasis on individual combat produced superb individual warriors but less effective group action. Indians loved to set ambushes, but often failed with them because one of the warriors sprang the trap too soon. On the other hand, one white general is said to have welcomed his successor with the caution, "When fighting Indians, beware of three things: Surprise, surprise, and surprise."

Generosity and Sharing. This characteristic is expressed especially with regard to (a) *food and shelter*: seven hunters can support one hundred people, and material goods, like animals captured, belong to everyone—the hunter is just the instrument; and (b) *praise and blame*: praise is shared with the whole group, which means that Dakota do not try to stand out from the group; rather the special talents of any one person and what he or she accomplishes raise the whole group, so there is no need for jealousy.

The concept of the "*Indian giver*," properly understood, is admirable. It means that one gives freely to anyone who is in need without fear of not having enough for oneself, expecting that if one is later in need oneself someone else will provide what is needed. Thus it is not a question of giving something and later taking it back (as whites often misrepresent it) but rather of a free circulation of necessary goods, an unlimited giving and getting, which assures that goods will end up at any moment where they are most needed. Dakota thus get honor by giving things away; their center of attention is group wealth rather than individual wealth.

Adjustment to Nature. Bryde describes this characteristic as "getting along with all things, including humans." First, getting along with things: Dakota revere the earth that all things grow from. (This characteristic makes them suddenly "politically correct" in relation to our new concern for the environment.) Second, getting along with people: the Dakota word *oyate,* translated as "people," includes both humans and animals. So the contrast between "things" and "people" is not so strong as it is among white Americans. Attention focuses on survival for today, on the present. Enjoy what you have to-day. To "get along with someone" includes (a) *loving* that person, (b) *relying on* that person for your needs, and (c) *being responsible* to that person for his or her needs. The Dakota kinship system emphasizes the extended family: the Dakota have eleven different words for "cousin." They "adopt" close friends as brothers or sisters.

In the late-19th and early-20th century, white reformers thought that the Indians' sense of communal responsibility was keeping them in poverty, and that they would benefit from some competition and selfish individuality, which would move them to work hard to "get ahead." The reformers complained that the Indians would rather starve together than abandon the rest of their community to launch out on their own. So they proposed that the reservations be parceled out to individual Indian families in hopes that this would motivate them to work hard. Unfortunately, the lands "parceled out" were too infertile and small to support individual families, and the process of distribution left many families in such debt that they either sold their land or saw it foreclosed to pay taxes or other debts. As a result, large parts of the original reservations have passed into the hands of whites. In recent years, the White Earth tribe of Ojibwa in Minnesota, under the leadership of Winona LaDuke, has begun a program to re-purchase those parts of its original reservation that were lost through such sales and foreclosures.

Good Advice from Indian Wisdom. Natives judge each other by what they are, not by what they have. Before the whites came, they neither had nor used money. Everything is considered to be part of one body: *wakan* (the holy, or mysterious) is contained in (1) living things and (2) things that exhibit power, including (a) active power (such as wind) and (b) passive power (such as a rock). One is invited to listen to things, think about them, and learn from their power. Things "talk." One prays, then uses these powers—lets them flow through one—for human good.

The visible world is a shadow of the real world. Some of the sacred traditions include the pipe and purification through the sweat lodge, the vision quest, and the sun dance. In the *sun dance,* one fasts, dances, and suffers for the sake of the people, to renew the community's strength. The dancers fast for the duration of the dance, which can last several days. The dancing men pass skewers of wood through the skin of their breast and under part of the breast muscle; they then attach these skewers to thongs which are tied to the central pole. As they dance, these lines pull on the skin and muscle until, eventually, they tear loose. Until recently, whites forbade the practice of the sun dance, considering it "barbaric." Today it is again legal. Speaking the truth and being happy with one another are both highly valued. Good people eventually come out ahead.

Comparing Native American and White Values

These Native American values stand in tension with common white American values:

1. Bravery stands in tension with the white emphasis on material achievement and financial success. The Dakota learned to hunt or wage war *when necessary,* whereas white Americans value working every day.
2. Individual freedom stands in tension with material achievement. Material achievement requires daily discipline that may threaten individual freedom.
3. Generosity and sharing stands in tension with material achievement. Dakota acquire things to give them away, first to their own extended families. White Americans acquire things to keep them, and to express their sense of self-worth. Dakota value generosity highly; whites value possession highly.
4. Adjustment to nature stands in tension with scientific progress. Dakota value getting along with nature and with other people. White Americans value conquering nature and competing with other people.
5. Good advice from Indian wisdom stands in tension with white American efficiency and practicality. Dakota seek to live in harmony with people and things. White Americans value making things and money to gain power and possessions.

SOCIAL AND INSTITUTIONAL DIMENSION

Land

Land belongs to God. A human can't "own" it, although one group can give others permission to hunt there. Whoever makes use of any piece of land should use it responsibly in a way that will sustain its resources.

If this seems strange to us, we might compare it with white attitudes toward water and air. Individuals do not buy and sell lakes, portions of the ocean, or rivers. We consider these to be "common property." We might well object to a group that claimed to buy Lake Michigan and to prevent anyone else from sailing on it or fishing in it. While we don't speak of God as the owner of the lakes, we do say they are common or state property: it is the state of Minnesota or the U.S. government that regulates their use. In some states, like Colorado, the water of the rivers is allocated in complex ways so that there is enough water for various users at various locations on the river: if someone upstream uses so much water that the stream dries up farther down (as could well happen in drier years) the government will come and close their access so that the water will be fairly shared. As to air, we have not thought to buy or sell its rights—until air pollution recently brought the problem to our attention.

Our current struggles with air and water pollution, indicating that one person's use may prejudice another person's use, parallel Native American attitudes toward land. White uses of the land, especially their fencing off of and restricting access to certain areas (by both hunters and grazing wild animals) and their decimation of the buffalo herds, disastrously affected Native American users of the land.

Authority and Freedom

Individual freedom is treasured. Followers choose to accept a leader, normally for a particular purpose and limited time (ad hoc). This practice confused whites, who wanted to know who was in charge. So whites settled on someone as "chief" and tended to make all their negotiations with that person. This procedure suited white purposes, not native ones. Worse, whites often deliberately chose natives who would agree with what the whites wanted, and then dealt with that person as the "chief" even if the tribe did not recognize his leadership. The Treaty of New Echota between white settlers and a small group of Cherokee, mentioned above, is an example of this process. Indians tend to drift from one leader to another if they don't approve of the first or trust his abilities. As a result, bad leaders end up with small tribes of followers, good ones with large tribes.

ISSUES FOR JUSTICE AND PEACE

War among Plains Indians

Historically, Plains Indians went to war for two main reasons: (1) to gain territory to live on—if pushed out by others, the tribe tried to annihilate or frighten away an enemy tribe to make space for itself; and (2) to gain glory by displaying manhood—this kind of warfare was mostly carried on by the young.

As already mentioned, Plains Indian warfare emphasized bravery over effective killing, for example, in the practice of counting coup. Also mentioned was the characteristic practice of the dog strap soldier—showing bravery by staking yourself down in battle as a sign that you would not retreat. Finally we noted that emphasis on individual combat reduced the success rate of Indian ambushes; nevertheless, Indians were remembered as masters of ambushes, and they excelled at surprising the enemy.

Whites kept pushing into Indian territory, violated treaties, and finally "concentrated" the remaining Indians on reservations. The Red Lake Ojibwa reservation in Northwest Minnesota is an example of land never ceded to the U.S. government and never parceled out to individual Indian families—this tribe was a holdout. Other tribes ceded land for money and what seemed at the time to be valuable promises. Later experience showed that the promises were mostly broken.

Twentieth-Century Revival

For years, many Indian ceremonies were illegal: not only the ghost dance, but even the sun dance. Indians were corralled on reservations. Then in 1934 the *U.S. Indian Reorganization Act* established tribal councils. These councils did not follow Indian traditions of authority. Many Indians viewed these tribal governments as working the will of the United States, not of the Indians. Sometimes the U.S. government would even "buy out" a tribal council—the Menominee Tribal Council in Wisconsin accepted cash payment to dissolve itself in 1958.[14]

That same year, a Haudenosaunee Indian named Mad Bear led a nonviolent stand against the government of New York State and inspired a resistance movement called the *American Indian Movement (AIM)*. AIM leaders, including *Dennis Banks* and *Russell Means*, established a "Trail of Broken Treaties." Their goal was to expose broken treaties from West to East, ending in Washington, D.C. They organized various resistance activities to support Indian land claims. The secret FBI surveillance and disruption program called *COINTELPRO* began to target the movement. Many AIM leaders were arrested, and many Indians were killed.

Wounded Knee Occupation

In February of 1973 the Oglala Sioux Civil Rights Organization was established on the Pine Ridge Reservation in South Dakota. The Oglala leaders asked AIM to help them make a statement by seizing the town of Wounded Knee. They demanded that a Presidential Treaty Commission be established to conduct hearings on Indian treaty rights, to investigate the practices and procedures of the Bureau of Indian Affairs (BIA), and to inspect all Sioux reservations in South Dakota.[15] U.S. agents surrounded the reservation and a sixty-nine-day siege resulted. The Indians had been promised a meeting with a government official to discuss the 1868 treaty, which the Oglala claimed the U.S. government was violating. That treaty set out the conditions and guarantees under which the Sioux would cede most of their land to the United

States and end attacks on settlers.[16] The official met with Frank Fools Crow, chief of the Oglala, who wanted one question answered: "Will the 1868 treaty be reinstated, yes or no?" He didn't get a direct answer because the official claimed that the Oglala fell under the Indian Reorganization Act of 1934.[17]

This exchange illustrates two different understandings of law: (1) laws are historical, written, and built up on the basis of precedent (white British-American); (2) law is situational, spiritual, and based on the available human wisdom (Indian). Frank Fools Crow said through his interpreter: "They say they can't give us our land back because it was so long ago that they took it, and now so many white people live there, but the Indian doesn't believe that. One hundred years is not so long for us."[18]

Fishing Rights

There have been fishing disputes in Minnesota and Wisconsin lakes. Natives net or spear all fish indiscriminately, both game fish and rough fish. For the most part, they preserve and eat what they catch; sometimes they sell part of the catch. Some of the reservations also stock lakes in their area with game fish. The Minnesota Department of Natural Resources (DNR) has stated that Indian fishing practices improve the availability of game fish. White resort owners claim that those practices threaten game fishing for others.

What would "game fish" mean to an Indian who takes only enough to eat and asks the animal's permission because he needs to eat? The Indian might well wonder about the white practice of "catch and release." Although to the whites this seems humane to the fish, the Indian might well wonder why whites find pleasure in annoying fish that they don't need for food.

SPOKESPERSONS FOR JUSTICE AND PEACE

Bartholomé de Las Casas (1484–1566)

The first Catholic bishop of *Chiapas* in what is now Mexico was *Bartholomé de Las Casas*, a personal friend of Christopher Columbus and instrumental in preserving Columbus's journal. His famous book *The Tears of the Indians* is a moving protest against the cruelty of Spanish conquistadores, for example, their practice of cutting off Indians' hands, stringing the severed hands around their necks, and sending them off to "carry the message" to the other Indians.[19] The book was quickly translated into English (not by Las Casas) and distributed in England and its colonies as anti-Spanish propaganda. As a result, some scholars have doubted its accuracy.

It is also he who records for us the famous sermon of Friar Antonio de Montesinos on the Caribbean island of Hispaniola in 1511, nineteen years after Columbus's first voyage, in which he told his Spanish congregation that they were all in mortal sin because of the way they were treating the Indians, and that the Dominican monks would not hear their confessions or give them communion until they repented. Rather than repent, they protested to the Spanish king and to the Dominican superior in Spain, both of whom told the local preachers to stop upsetting their congregations.[20]

Winona LaDuke (1959–)

Born of an Anishinaabe (Ojibwa) father from Minnesota and a Jewish mother, Winona LaDuke was raised in Oregon, earned a Harvard degree in native economic development, and took a job as high-school principal on the White Earth Reservation in Minnesota. In order to help the reservation buy back thousands of acres of the land which their 1867 treaty with the United States should have guaranteed it, she founded the White Earth Land Recovery Project.[21] She was Ralph Nader's vice-presidential running mate in the 1996 and 2000 presidential elections, representing the Green Party. Author of four books, she has also founded the Indigenous Women's Network[22] and "Honor the Earth."[23]

SUMMARY

Working from a worldview that sees spiritual power working in all material nature, and that treats plants and animals as "people" like ourselves, Native American tribes developed sophisticated ways of surviving and thriving in their environment. European settlers, working from very different worldviews and with more advanced military technology, took control of most of the resources of the Americas, pushing Native Americans onto small and poor reservations in North America, or exploiting them as poverty-level laborers in Central and South America. With renewed awareness of the injustices involved, descendants of the Natives and of the Europeans have taken some steps to compensate, but there remains a wide gap in power and wealth between the two groups. Some Europeans resisted the injustices; some Natives are working to restore appropriate Native culture and resources. As the industrialized United States culture draws down nonrenewable resources and increases unsustainable pollution, Native traditions may have more and more wisdom to offer.[24]

KEY TERMS

Aleuts
American Indian Movement (AIM)
animism
Anishinaabeg
Apache
Aztec
Cherokee
Chiapas
Chilam Balam
COINTELPRO
counting coup
Dakota
dog strap soldier
Five Civilized Tribes
ghost dance
Hopi
Inca
Indian giver
Inuit
Iroquois
Maya
Ojibwa
Our Lady of Guadalupe
Pequot
Pequot War
Pueblo
Quechua
shaman
strong medicine
sun dance
trail of tears
vision quest
Wounded Knee

DISCUSSION QUESTIONS

1. Was the removal of Indian tribes to reservations in the late 19th century an example of "ethnic cleansing"? Was it justified? Is it an appropriate model for Israel to follow in dealing with the Palestinians?

2. If the best model of human justice is for people to share the earth's resources fairly and in the process to re-distribute resources which past injustice has distributed unfairly—land, money, education, etc.—how should the U.S. society compensate Native Americans for the injustices done to them?

3. When should land be individually owned, and when communally owned? What limitations should there be on what an owner can do to the land? For example, should an owner be free to destroy productive farmland when people are starving?

4. When should water be individually owned, and when communally owned? What limitations should there be on what an owner can do to the water? For example, should drinking water supplies like city water systems be privately owned and managed? What if safe water becomes too expensive for the poor?

5. When should air be individually owned, and when communally owned? What limitations should there be on what an owner can do to the air? For example, should factory owners be required to pay for expensive pollution control if the result will be that their product or service has become too expensive to compete in the free market? If so, should they choose not to produce that product or service? If not, who *should* pay for the damage?
6. Do you find some Native American attitudes and practices attractive? If so, how might you integrate them into your own life?

NOTES

1. The Great Vision of Black Elk, from *Black Elk Speaks,* 22.
2. An official website can be seen at www.virgendeguadalupe.org.mx (accessed July 10, 2006).
3. See "The Maya Collapse," chap. 5 in Diamond, *Collapse,* 157–77.
4. www.ezln.org.mx/; www.zapatistas.org/ (accessed July 10, 2006).
5. www.aymara.org/index_eng.php (accessed July 10, 2006). This English version has not been updated since July 2003. The site recommends that you access the Spanish version at www.aymara.org/ (accessed August 29, 2005) and then use any web-translator.
6. www.zompist.com/quechua.html (accessed July 10, 2006). If you would like to learn the Quechua language, check out www.ullanta.com/quechua/#about (accessed July 10, 2006)!
7. Mason, *A Brief History of the Pequot War,* 29–30.
8. Mason, *A Brief History,* 44.
9. www.geocities.com/Heartland/Hills/1094/king.htm (accessed July 10, 2006).
10. www.iroquoisdemocracy.pdx.edu/ (accessed July 10, 2006).
11. www.d.umn.edu/cla/faculty/tbacig/studproj/a1041/siouxup/ (accessed July 10, 2006).
12. users.commkey.net/fussichen/otddak.htm (accessed July 10, 2006).
13. See, for example, www.sacredtexts.com/nam/index.htm (accessed January 25, 2007).
14. Weyler, *Blood of the Land,* 39.
15. Weyler, *Blood of the Land,* 78.
16. Text of the treaty is available at digital.library.okstate.edu/Kappler/Vol2/treaties/sio0998.htm (accessed July 10, 2006).
17. Weyler, *Blood of the Land,* 95.
18. Weyler, *Blood of the Land,* 123.
19. See, for example, sections from de Las Casas at "Bartholomé de Las Casas, Brief Account of the Devastation of the Indies. (1542)," www.swarthmore.edu/SocSci/bdorsey1/41docs/02-las.html (accessed July 10, 2006). See also "The Man, The Issues," www.lascasas.org/manissues.htm (accessed January 25, 2007).
20. "Bartholomé de Las Casas," www.lascasas.org (accessed July 10, 2006).

21. "White Earth Land Recovery Project," www.nativeharvest.com/ (January 25, 2007).

22. "Indigenous Women's Network," www.indigenouswomen.org/ (accessed January 25, 2007).

23. "Honor the Earth," www.honorearth.org/ (accessed January 25, 2007). For further information on LaDuke, see "Winona LaDuke," en.wikipedia.org/wiki/Winona_LaDuke (accessed January 25, 2007).

24. With regard to the radical transformations that our declining inexpensive energy will force, see Heinberg, *The Party's Over* and *Power Down*.

SUGGESTIONS FOR FURTHER READING

Boyd. *Rolling Thunder.*
Brown. *Bury My Heart at Wounded Knee.*
Bryde. *Modern Indian Psychology.*
Casas. *Tears of the Indians.*
Deloria. *God is Red.*
Ebbott. *Indians in Minnesota.*
Gill. "Native American Religions."
Heinberg. *The Party's Over.*
———. *Power Down.*
Niehardt, ed. *Black Elk Speaks.*
Restall. *Seven Myths of the Spanish Conquest.*
Weyler. *Blood of the Land.*

Chapter Seven

Marxist Worldviews

"You are horrified at our intending to do away with private property. But in your existing society private property is already done away with for nine tenths of the population; its existence for the few is solely due to its non-existence in the hands of those nine tenths. You reproach us, therefore, with intending to do away with a form of property the necessary condition for whose existence is the nonexistence of any property for the immense majority of society. . . .

"Communism deprives no [one] of the power to appropriate the products of society; all that it does is to deprive [one] of the power to subjugate the labor of others by means of such appropriation."

— Karl Marx, *The Communist Manifesto*[1]

EXPERIENTIAL AND EMOTIONAL DIMENSION

The experiential basis of the Marxist worldview combines the secularizing tendencies of the Enlightenment, which raised doubts about God and spiritual claims, with the sufferings produced by the Industrial Revolution: destruction of pre-industrial economies, long hours of boring and dangerous work, wages too low to support decent lives for workers and their families, squalid homes in crowded slums close to polluting factories. The gap between these realities and the luxurious lives of industrialists was giving rise to agitation and violence that threatened social stability. Various socialists had sought solutions with limited success. Karl Marx thought his analysis showed "scientifically" what was really going on and where it was all headed.

HISTORICAL PERIODS

Karl Marx (1818–1883) was a German philosopher who became interested in social and economic issues. He was aghast at the sufferings produced by the Industrial Revolution. Banned from teaching because of his radical ideas, he entered a career as a journalist, traveling all over Europe in an attempt to enlighten the workers. He and his family suffered both from the circumstances of the Industrial Revolution itself and from reactions to his ideas which appeared in the press. Why would he take such risks for himself and his family? In his *Theses on Feuerbach* (1845) Marx writes, "the philosophers have only *interpreted* the world in various ways; the point however is to *change* it."[2] Whether or not we ultimately agree with his ideas—or the use to which they have been put—Marx was in his own way seeking justice.

In his study of economics, Marx was influenced by Friedrich Engels (1820–1895): it is their collaboration that produced many of the classic "Marxist" writings, including the essential work *Das Kapital (Capital)* (1867). Engels is also responsible for the wide dissemination of Marxist ideas, for he later supported Marx and his family in England so that Marx could continue his prolific writing.

After Marx's death, Vladimir Lenin (1870–1924) seized on the Russian Revolution to introduce a communist society in Russia. Russia had not reached the developed capitalist stage that Marx thought would be a necessary precursor to socialism and communism, so Lenin tried to bolster Russian communism by encouraging a worldwide revolution, especially in advanced capitalistic societies, but with little success.

Josef Stalin (1879–1953) controlled the (Russian) Soviet Communist Party from the late 1920s until 1953, concentrating on communism in Russia by accelerating the country's industrialization, developing a repressive, centralized bureaucracy, and suppressing alternative voices with purges and draconian policies that resulted in millions of deaths. He led Russia through the German invasion of World War II and consolidated communist control over much of Eastern Europe at the end of that war. Although several Eastern European communist governments then tried to gain freedom from Soviet control, only Yugoslavia succeeded. By the end of Stalin's rule, critics concluded that the "communism" of the Soviet Union bore little resemblance to Marx's dream, having become, rather, "state capitalism" or "bureaucratic socialism."

Nikita Khrushchev (1894–1971) led Russia's program of "de-Stalinization" after 1956. During his presidency, Russia developed intercontinental ballistic missiles with nuclear warheads and launched earth satellites and a manned space station before the United States did, although Russia never put humans on the moon. His decision to send nuclear missiles to Cuba for defense against U.S. threats produced the "Cuban Missile Crisis"; when he backed down to avoid a nuclear exchange, Soviet elites forced his resignation.

Mao Zedong (1893–1976) led the Chinese Communist Party from 1937 until his death, defeating Chiang Kai-shek's government in 1949. Emphasizing a rural-based communism, his party broke with the Soviet Union. When China's "great leap forward" toward industrialization failed, resulting in widespread famine, Mao launched the "Cultural Revolution" to re-establish his authority. He organized a "Red Guard" or militia of activist youth to purge "counter-revolutionaries." Intense struggles produced a disastrous purge of leadership—Deng Xiaoping was sent to work in a factory for "re-education."

Deng Xiaoping (1904–1997) gained power when Mao died, and gradually moved China toward a more capitalist economy. When student agitation pressed nonviolently for wider human rights and more rapid liberation, the government responded with a violent attack on the students gathered in Tianamen Square, followed by a country-wide repression.

Ho Chi Minh (1890–1969) led Vietnam's struggle for national liberation from French, Japanese, and U.S. control. Final victory came in 1975 after his death. Vietnam maintains a communist government, but with significant openness to a free-market economy.

Fidel Castro (1927–) led the Cuban Revolution against the corrupt pro-U.S. government of Fulgencio Batista and developed an advanced communist government (in the face of rigid U.S. embargos and other pressures) that has given Cuba some of the best vital statistics of any American country—better than those of the United States—but at the cost of limited freedoms and a low average standard of living.

Mikhail Gorbachev (1931–) tried to develop a freer society and more market-based economy in the Soviet Union, which resulted in loss of control over most of Eastern Europe along with demolition of the Berlin Wall in 1989, and the final collapse of the Soviet government in 1991. Proponents of capitalism claimed that "capitalism has won"; time will tell whether capitalism itself will eventually suffer a similar fate.

CLASSIC WRITINGS

The core classics of Marxism are the writings of Marx and Engels, especially *The Communist Manifesto* and (the incomplete) *Das Kapital*. In his writings, Lenin adapted Marxist ideas to the new and different situation in Russia. The writings of Lenin's successor, Josef Stalin, have proved to be less enduring. Other important authors include Antonio Gramsci, Peter Kropotkin, Rosa Luxemburg, and Leon Trotsky. Among more recent writers are Mao Zedong and Che Guevara.[3]

NARRATIVE OR MYTHIC DIMENSION

Marx wrote as a philosopher and economist. He described many *types* of oppression in his doctrinal explanations, but did not give much *concrete narrative* of the problems that energized his campaign. Many of the novels of Charles Dickens help to fill in this gap, providing narrative descriptions of the sufferings caused by industrialization in England.

DOCTRINAL AND PHILOSOPHICAL DIMENSION

In order to understand those worldviews that claim to be "Marxist" or "communist," it is necessary to understand some of Marx's own key ideas. Key concepts for understanding Marxism include *alienation*, *dialectical materialism*, *ideology*, and *class struggle*. They are derived from Marx's early philosophy that he sought to put in practice already at the start of his career.

Feuerbach was an early inspiration for Marx. His concept of *alienation* enabled Marx to understand modern working people's profound isolation (see below). Marx came to disagree early in his career with both Feuerbach and Hegel about *why* this alienation existed and how to *remedy* it. From *Hegel* he drew the central idea of *dialectic*, but saw it in a very different way.

Dialectic

Marx accepted Hegel's conviction that a process of *dialectic* moves history itself through three basic stages capable of repetition—*thesis*, *antithesis*, and *synthesis*. A status-quo situation provides the *thesis*. As society begins to change, forces and ideas that challenge the status quo constitute an *antithesis*. As these two battle each other, the tension between thesis and antithesis ultimately results in something new, the *synthesis*. But no status quo is stable forever. The synthesis itself becomes a new thesis. Repeating the process, this new thesis generates a new antithesis, and the continuing struggle produces a new synthesis.

Hegel believed that all of history was moved by *ideas*. Behind these ideas was something he called "*Absolute Spirit*." (His work could be interpreted religiously or not, as he is not himself clear what "Spirit" actually means.) Marx rejected Hegel's assumption that history is moved by ideas—it is far more practical than that. History is moved by *materialism*—there is a constant tension, struggle, and resolution in the *physical*, *material* world, not in the world of immaterial ideas. Thus, he described his theory as *dialectical materialism*.

Thus Marx interpreted the dialectic in *socioeconomic* terms, whereas Hegel had been thinking in terms of *ideas* and religion. Concretely, the (socioeconomic) *thesis,* a particular form of society at one historical period, develops inner tensions as new forms of economic production are not well directed by old forms of political and economic power. In reaction to these tensions, another vision of society is proposed, distributing power differently, called the *antithesis* because it stands opposed to the earlier form.

These two forms struggle against one another. Concretely, people who dominate the old forms of power (such as rural landholders) struggle for power against people who dominate the new forms of power (such as factory owners and managers). The result of these power struggles is a new form of society, the *synthesis* (industrial capitalism) that mediates both sets of powers and interests.

For Hegel, the key example was Christianity: the Jewish Christianity of Jesus was the thesis, the Greek Christianity of Paul was the antithesis, and out of the struggle between these two came Roman Catholicism, the synthesis. For Marx, the struggle between the thesis of feudalism and the antithesis of industrial capitalism was in the process of producing the synthesis of communism.

Alienation

Another concept that is necessary to understand Marx's worldview is *alienation,* as we have mentioned above. Alienation for Marx was not just about the individual self, nor about ideas, but also about the social and economic structure of 19th-century life. To understand the Marxist notion of alienation, we have to look first at the social and economic situation.

Capital (centralized ownership of costly productive resources like factories) causes the alienation of the working class. Thus capitalism is the problem in society, the thesis that needs to be changed. Modern conditions of production like the assembly line make abundant product possible, but at the same time they alienate workers from the products that they produce, from themselves, and from other workers. "Alienate" means to "make alien or foreign."

Workers are alienated from *the product*, which disappears down the assembly line. Part of the worker's self is in it, but the worker can't keep it and has no say over what becomes of it. Workers are alienated from *themselves*: dull, repetitive work can't express self adequately. The worker becomes "just a machine." Workers are alienated from *other workers*: despite the fact that they have to cooperate in their job to build the product, workers are put into competition with each other—when they should be cooperating with each other—*for scarce jobs and low wages*. Competition for low wages leads the worker to see *other workers* as an enemy rather than to see *the system and the managers* as the enemy.

Alienation, then, is the cause of *social and class struggle*, more commonly called *class warfare*. The interests of the middle and upper classes (the bourgeoisie) and those of the working classes (the proletariat) are in tension with each other; they are nearing a breaking point.[4]

What is the root problem that Marx and Engels saw with capitalism?

The "Contradiction" in Capitalism

Capitalism socializes production (humans have to act cooperatively to produce efficiently) but not ownership (one or a few people own the product and control what happens to it). This is a built-in contradiction that can't last. The few individuals who control production compete with each other for profit, producing a boom-bust cycle (over-production leading to depression) because each individual wants to increase his production hoping that the others will limit theirs, and no one is doing overall planning. The solution, according to Marxism, is to socialize ownership as well as production and to institute centralized planning to avoid the boom-bust cycle.

Exploitation and Oppression

Capitalization (gathering enough resources to build machines and factories) is based on exploitation and oppression. Workers would not put so much of the profit from their labor back into a factory that someone else owned if they had anything to say about it. They do not get a fair share of the return from the product they make. According to Marx, an owner does not give a worker the full value she produced, but steals part of it to pay for expansion—which the capitalist or stockholder, not the worker, then owns.

Consider for example a modern leveraged buy-out. The new owner, who borrowed money to buy the company, will need to pay off the loan. Where

Figure 7.1.   São Paulo, Brazil. On right, Ford Motor Company assembly plant; on left, favela, where some of the Ford workers live. Courtesy David Whitten Smith, 1 December 1988.

will he get the money to do that? Was the company's profit big enough before his purchase to add up in a few years to the value of the company? If so, was that a fair profit? If not, how does the profit get made big enough? By reducing wages and increasing prices? Then workers and consumers pay for the owner to buy the company. Are workers and consumers paying for ownership to be concentrated in fewer and fewer hands?

Marx expected the problems of capitalism to keep getting worse until the whole system collapsed and the workers took over. Historically, rather than what Marx predicted, a sort of mixed economy developed that prevented the worst effects of capitalism from developing—at least in the most developed countries. But this mixed economy is being challenged by a new wave of over-production caused by the expansion of manufacturing into previously un-industrialized societies. These newly industrializing societies are producing not so much for themselves (since their wages are too low to allow their workers to purchase their own products) as for citizens of the old industrialized societies whose wages have been historically high enough to produce a mass market. However, as the old industrialized societies are being "de-industrialized" by the move of factories to new areas, their wages are going down, threatening the market on which all the production depends. It is too soon to predict how the world economy will respond to this new situation.

Theory of Value

Many people before Marx, such as Adam Smith, had accepted a theory of value based on worker hours; few made it as central and controversial as Marx and Engels did. This theory is one of the least accepted of Marx's central theories. It states that the value of a product is based on the worker-hours used to produce it. Before dismissing it out of hand, one has to be reminded that in the late 19th century this may have been more plausible than it seems today.

This definition makes sense until you ask about the value of the product *for you*. Three electric typewriters may take more human hours of labor to produce than one word-processor, but are they of more value to you? A lot of expensive typewriters are finding no buyers since microcomputers became available. An ornate horse drawn carriage may take more hours to produce than a small automobile, but who would trade the car for the carriage?

It might be more appropriate to speak of the labor theory of *costs*. The human work used to produce it *does* affect the *cost* of the typewriter or carriage even if that may not determine its value to you or a prospective buyer. A movie studio might be willing to pay the cost of the carriage for a historical movie, while no one would want one for transportation. If something costs more than its value to *anyone*, the logical choice is not to produce it at all.

We also need to include the role of management and of inventiveness in our theory of value. Badly managed companies waste a lot of worker energy doing things that people don't need or want, or doing them inefficiently. So management deserves return, too. In that sense, as we will see in chapter 9 on Christian Social Thought, Pope John Paul II was correct to consider management to be labor, not "capital."

But how much return does management deserve? In the United States in 2003, chief executives made twenty-four times as much as the average production worker (with production workers being among our most highly paid laborers). In Germany, chief executives made eight times as much as the average production worker.[5]

Pope John Paul II, in his 1987 encyclical *Solicitudo Rei Socialis*, criticized what he perceived to be dangerous ideologies: *communism* (as Americans would expect) and *capitalism* (which upset lots of Americans). It is worth reading his clear, personalist, and pithy account of the failings of both. It helps us to understand both the communist and capitalist worldviews, both of which base themselves solely upon an *economic* understanding of the person.

Ideologies

Key ideas of an era are based on the economic and social conditions of industry, and are the ideas of those in power promoting their own selfish interests over the interests of others. Those with less power and influence accept these assumptions without questioning them adequately. For example, the ideas of God and rewards in heaven keep the poor from complaining about their misery in the present since their future reward will be great. Marx himself did not entirely blame the poor for taking this attitude: when he wrote that "religion is the opiate of the people," he meant both that people are being drugged by the powerful and that they drug themselves so as to hide from themselves the extent of their misery.

Marx called concepts such as God, heaven, and hell *ideologies*. (Note that "ideology" is a negative term here.) He, and many other thinkers, considered religion to be the worst deception, but not the only one. In fact, Marx's writings, especially *The German Ideology*, support the notion of a "hierarchy of ideologies" which people need to see through. Thus, religious ideology is only one ideology among others. There is a hierarchy of ideologies (distorted representations of reality in human consciousness). In order of increasing "density," they are: science, art, politics, law, morality, philosophy, and religion.

Dialectical Stages of History

The stages of history produced by dialectic are necessary. We can't proceed from one to another without passing through the intermediate stages. Thus, capitalism cannot be avoided; it has to be passed through. It produces the economic efficiencies that alone make an abundant material product possible. This abundant product offers the material basis for communism, or the ideal state, in which everything is based on equality. Moreover, the tensions in dialectic expose the falsity of many of the ideologies that Marx lists above, especially by revealing the way they are used to alienate the worker.

Thus, Marx reversed Hegel's belief that Spirit is the most important thing in reality. Rather, Marx claimed that material things are the basis of all reality. Everything is determined by the state of economic production of a particular period. These are the five key stages that Marx thought society had passed through or was in the process of passing through: Primitive Communism, Ancient Slavery, Feudalism, Capitalism, Socialism. The fifth stage — socialism — had not yet been reached, but society was on the verge of reaching it through inevitable historical development from modern modes of production. Eventually, socialism would give way to communism, which would be the final synthesis. After communism, there would be no more need for dialectic, since there would be no more structural tension. Within these stages, the prevailing mode of production produced characteristic results in seven areas. (See table 7.1 for details.)

SOCIAL AND INSTITUTIONAL DIMENSION

Marxist Societies and Applications

Other than control by the working class, Karl Marx laid out no plans for the structuring of a communist society or of the society that the working class would build on the way to communism. He assumed the working class could do that for themselves, and that it would be a productive society able to meet the needs of the people and much more. The political parties that adopted his theories followed Marx in his optimistic approach, so detailed plans for the structuring of socialist society were not put forth or developed.

Historically, Marx was claimed by many different revolutionary movements. The best known was his appropriation by Russian revolutionaries, led by Vladimir Lenin.

Leninism

Lenin modified Marx substantially in several ways. He insisted that the movement of history, though inexorable, was too slow — power had to be taken through revolution by those who knew what needed to be done. He explained this idea by coining the phrase "dictatorship of the proletariat." A small group would lead the revolution of the masses, organize and educate

Table 7.1.[6]

	Primitive Communism	Ancient Slavery	Feudalism	Capitalism	Socialism
Prevailing mode of production	Hunting, gathering, and fishing	Slave labor to increase private property [growth of agriculture and irrigation]	Peasant labor and use of animals for farming	Commerce and small-scale manufacturing	Mass production
Measure of wealth	Group welfare	Number of slaves and amount of land	Amount of land	Amount of money	Satisfaction of human needs
Ruling class	None	Slave-owners and emperor	Landholders and king	Entrepreneurs and capitalists (bourgeoisie)	Workers (proletariat)
Oppressed class	None	Slaves	Peasants	Factory workers and unemployed persons	None
Government	Communal rule	Emperor and open coercion	King and court of lords with personal loyalty to immediate superior	Capitalistic democracy or fascism	People's state governed by workers' party
Prevailing philosophy	Collectivism (what is good for the group?)	Pragmatic obedience to those with power (what is commanded?)	Loyalty to immediate superior in exchange for protections (what is expected by my overseer?)	Individualism or totalitarianism (what is good for me?)	Collectivism (what is good for the group?)
Prevailing religion	Tribal gods and personified natural forces	Worship of God, who is powerful and demanding	God works through the church, His intermediary (Catholicism)	God deals directly with individuals (Protestantism)	No divine master (atheism)
Prevailing art form	Decoration of everyday objects	Palaces and monuments for emperors	Art for worship and for the pleasure of the king and court	Snobbish art for those with money and leisure	Art to advance collectivist attitudes and for edifying the life of the masses

them, and eventually become obsolete as socialism and then communism were fully realized.

There were many flaws in this theory. First of all, Lenin and his companions were trying to bring revolution to a feudal society. As we have seen above, Marx insisted that you cannot "skip" a phase of history. Further, Lenin had to explain why the economic collapse that Marx expected had been delayed. He concluded that England and other European countries had been enabled to offer decent wages at home by exploiting their colonies overseas. They just exported their exploitation. (Marxist jargon called this "imperialism.") Thus they bought the cooperation of their workers at home by bribing them at the expense of foreign workers. If you are stealing millions, you can afford to use thousands to buy a few lieutenants!

The modern Norwegian peace theoretician Johan Galtung explains that every country has a "center" and a "periphery." Further, some countries are "center" countries and others are "periphery" countries. Thus, the elites at the "center" of a "central" country, say Britain, strike a deal with the elites at the "center" of a "peripheral" country, say India, to exploit the common Indians (the "periphery of the periphery") for the benefit of the British elites. Indian elites get permission to skim off some of the wealth as it leaves India for Britain, and Britain promises to provide the local elites with military support so they can stay in power. (This works really well when you prop up local leaders who couldn't maintain power without your support.) The British elites then convince the British workers that this arrangement is in their interest by bribing them with better wages. Of course, they also expect British commoners to fight in wars designed to maintain this arrangement. Indian common people—the "periphery of the periphery"—are just out of luck.

The whole system begins to unravel when the common people in the central country (Britain) realize that they have more in common with the common people in the peripheral country (India) than with their own elites. British textile workers came to this conclusion when Gandhi visited England. Many American citizens came to this conclusion when President Reagan seemed poised to invade Nicaragua in the mid-1980s.

Attitudes toward Religion

Lenin was actively hostile to religion because it supported his adversaries in Tsarist Russia. Marx did not plan to attack churches: he believed that, as the workers realized their power and took over, religion would no longer be needed because there would be no more misery to explain through religion. But in fact, since the Russian society of the time was not yet "ripe" for socialism (according to Marx's thought), when its new revolutionary leaders forced it into communism, they attacked the Orthodox Church and other churches for resisting this move. Severe persecution followed.

The results would be disastrous. Lenin and his comrade Leon Trotsky believed in *worldwide* revolution and movement toward socialism. Later in his
life, Lenin would come to prefer a *one-state* socialism—since the rest of the
world wasn't coming around, we'd better work with what we have. This
change led ultimately to the totalitarian government of Stalin, who executed
or exiled many of his opponents and finally assassinated Trotsky in Mexico
because he dared to oppose Stalin's rise to power.

Stalin

When most people think of Marxism, they think first of what was called the
"Bolshevik" civil war in Russia that led to the establishment of the Soviet Union.
It is important to question whether Stalin and his followers were, in fact, actually "Marxists"—many would say there was little difference between Stalin and
the fascist dictators of his time other than the rhetoric they used. Stalin carried
out merciless purges of any and all who opposed him in leadership or policy—
until World War II moderated his savagery. Once the war started and German
troops were threatening Moscow, he needed all the help he could get.

The Cold War

After World War II, Russia double-crossed Eastern Europe and took over
many countries by treachery. This experience made many people suspicious
of Russian intentions in other cases. From the Russian standpoint, the satel-
lite countries were protection against a new invasion from the West.

Nikita Khrushchev was "liberal" in many areas. It was he who publicly admitted Stalin's crimes. He also worked for peaceful coexistence with Western
democracies. But he *increased* attacks on churches. When he pressed Cuba to
accept nuclear-armed Russian missiles, leading to the Cuban Missile Crisis
and a humiliating defeat for Russia, he was eased out of office. The world can
be grateful that he accepted his own demotion rather than insisting on a devastating nuclear war.

Mikhail Gorbachev had the courage to say publicly what many Russian
people believed privately: that the system wasn't working well and could not
continue without radical changes. He hoped to make the changes gradually
and maintain a communist government, but once he opened the possibility of
change he couldn't hold it back.

Ironically, the collapse of the Soviet Union does echo one of the key predictions of Marxism-Leninism—that the state would gradually "wither
away." Even in the capitalist West, the traditional institutions of 19th- and
20th-century republican government have been declining in importance—in
favor of multinational corporations! Thus, in a new dialectic, the decline of

the traditional state institutions has tended to increase the power of capitalists and decrease the democratic power of common people.

In addition, the political repression and economic problems of several historical communist states have done much to destroy Marx's reputation in the Western world, particularly following the fall of the Berlin Wall and the collapse of the Soviet Union, as the Soviet bureaucracy often invoked Marx in their propaganda. Yet the changes have not brought the prosperity that many in Russia hoped for, at least not yet. Those who held power in the old system have found ways to hold power in the new system.

In China, Mao Zedong appropriated Marxism in many ways quite differently than did the Bolsheviks in the Soviet Union, which caused tensions between the two countries. Without idealizing Chinese communism, it did move somewhat closer to Marxist ideals. There had been some burgeoning capitalism in China prior to the communist takeover, although not much. What may have been a key difference was the attitude of the population. First, a society influenced by Confucian ideas tended toward the practical. This fit Marxist concerns better. Second, it is often overlooked that, before communists took control in China, "workers" or peasants had no real standing at all as members of society. They were not even regarded as people, let alone as workers. Membership in the Party gave many of them an identity and a common cause that they had been lacking. Paradoxically, this new worker/peasant identity and dignity caused problems for Mao's government. He wanted a communist society, but on his terms, and not too fast! China has weathered many changes in the post-socialist world because it appropriated Lenin's openness to markets. Many question whether the Marxist Party in China today is truly a Marxist Party and a party of the people.

North Korea stands as a powerful, ideological form of Marxism patterned in many ways after Stalinism. It has even spawned a religion of its own called *Juche,* which reveres absolute loyalty to the leader of North Korea and the party. It also emphasizes Korean military and economic *self-reliance.* Although Westerners may consider this a *cult* of the leader, those who follow it closely claim that it is not religious at all, but the embodiment of the spirit of North Koreans. It does, however, follow the pattern of a "one-state" socialism and is highly intolerant of outsiders.

MARXIST THEORY TODAY

Euro-communism was different in many ways from Russian and Eastern European communism. Antonio Gramsci in Italy was an important Marxist thinker and anti-fascist activist. What is going on in Europe now that the Eastern European communist governments have collapsed?

There is still today a very active interest in both socialism and Marxism, although it is necessarily modified for the current socioeconomic climate and realities of the 21st century. Many countries practice a modified form of socialism in terms of benefits for the poor and the elderly. Some question how effective and sustainable these programs are, but they have for many years been a success story supporting a socialist outlook, if not a Marxist one. For example, Europe and Scandinavia have adopted more moderate forms of Marx's views leading to a socialist state, although they have rejected Lenin's dictatorship of the proletariat.

Criticisms of Marxism

Critics from capitalist societies and from elites who dominate the global market reject any form of socialism, whether liberal democratic, socialist, or Marxist. These criticisms come from the Right, and most often from those with power and privilege. Some aspects of Marxism have also been criticized from the Left. Most especially, democratic socialists and social democrats reject the idea that socialism can be accomplished only through class conflict and violent revolution.

Some today question the theoretical and historical validity of "class" as an analytic construct or as a political actor. Similarly, the Marxist stages of history and theory of social evolution have been criticized. Some argue that class is not the most fundamental inequality in history and call attention to patriarchy or race. Marxists respond that these inequalities are linked to class and therefore will largely cease to exist after the formation of a classless society. Political "realists" retort that, since human nature is naturally self-seeking, it will reproduce a class society no matter how thoroughgoing a revolution has been. The best we can do is manage conflict with the society and the human nature that we have.

Not Dead Yet

A lot of Latin Americans still believe Marxism's criticisms of capitalism. A new wave of resistance to U.S.-controlled capitalism and "free trade" has led socialist-style leaders to power through elections in Brazil, Bolivia, Nicaragua, and Venezuela—a movement that Hugo Chávez of Venezuela calls a "Bolivarian Revolution."

Those who support free-market capitalism with as few controls as possible claim that the collapse of old-style communism has proved that capitalism is "right." But the world economic system shows major signs of strain. The cheap hydrocarbons, especially petroleum and natural gas, which have fueled an unprecedented expansion of human power, are at or near their peak production, while global industrialization is rapidly increasing demand.[7] Pollution from their use along with unsustainable depletion of other resources including forests, soils, fresh water, and natural food stocks, threaten major, potentially disastrous global changes in climate and habitat which could lead to major social collapse.[8] Competition for the control of energy resources has already spawned war between the United States and Iraq, and generated intense hatred leading to terrorist attacks. The U.S. economy and the international financial system depend on foreign countries enabling huge U.S. deficits in its balance of payments by buying U.S. Treasury Bonds—a sort of Ponzi or pyramid scheme. American consumers have been financing their spending spree by withdrawing equity from an inflated housing bubble under the lure of low interest rates. Many of these loans have been short-term; refinancing at much higher interest rates could bring down the house of cards. As cheap, exploited global labor and widespread technology multiply product and weaken markets, the "boom and bust" cycle that Marx saw as the Achilles heel of capitalism looks increasingly dangerous. Only time will tell whether one of the two old systems was "right," or whether they both contained fatal flaws.

ISSUES FOR JUSTICE AND PEACE

Exploitation, Oppression, Violence, and War

Traditionally, Marxists believed that war was necessary for workers to gain power from the owner class. "You can't make an omelet without breaking eggs," they said. But some see war now as too dangerous in a nuclear world, which gives them second thoughts.

In the early 1980s, the Solidarity labor union movement in Poland used nonviolence successfully until the government cracked down with martial law. Then, many people said that nonviolence was impractical: the Poles had tried it and it "didn't work." As it turned out, they spoke too soon. By 1991, Polish—and East European—communism was overcome.

Afghanistan resisted Soviet communist control violently, with support from outsiders including the United States, which secretly supplied Osama bin Laden and other resistance fighters. Soviet violence and technology proved inadequate to maintain control. After the Soviets left, the Afghans continued fighting each other, until order was restored by Islamic extremists called Taliban. When the Taliban asked too high a price for an oil pipeline from the Caspian Sea to the Persian Gulf, the United States planned an attack. Conveniently, Osama bin Laden, still active in Afghanistan, orchestrated the

September 11, 2001, attacks on the World Trade Center and the Pentagon. (Some would add, "with help from the Bush administration.") When the Taliban asked to see evidence that bin Laden was responsible for the attacks before turning him over to the United States for trial, George Bush refused to provide any. Their hesitation gave Bush the pretext he needed to bomb and invade Afghanistan and overthrow the Taliban. At present, it is not clear whether the United States is doing any better than the Soviets did in controlling Afghanistan. The Taliban seem to be making a comeback. Once violence has been started, it is hard to stop.

U.S. pressure in Nicaragua, especially terrorist attacks by U.S.-financed "Contras," led to an electoral defeat for the Marxist Sandinista Party in 1990. But the Sandinista Party remained a major political force in Nicaragua just as the Democratic Party is in the United States, despite the fact that Sandinistas held a minority of seats in the legislature and lost several presidential elections. In 2007, as a result of a split between conservative parties, Daniel Ortega, the former president of communist Nicaragua, was re-elected president.

In Latin America, wealthy elites tend to call anyone who threatens their privileges a "communist" or "Marxist." Working with the poor is considered threatening. But Christian liberation theologies are very different from Marxism. Sometimes liberation theologians and Marxists appreciate each others' passion for justice. Sometimes in Latin America, communists undermine the work of liberation theology because it challenges them for power. They also argue that partial alleviation of misery prevents people from carrying out the full revolution that is necessary to bring in a socialist government and society.

The United States has been trying to isolate Fidel Castro's government in Cuba by maintaining an economic boycott of Cuba that has been in place since the time of President Kennedy (1960). The boycott is not supported by other countries, however, which resent what they consider interference in their foreign affairs. The boycott is strongly supported by several groups of Cuban refugees, but other Cuban refugees believe that it is time for the United States to accept Cuba's right to decide its own form of government. Pope John Paul II visited Cuba against the desires of the U.S. government, seeking to promote a Catholic religious revival on the island.

A number of groups in the United States challenge the Cuba boycott, notably the Pastors for Peace, who have been organizing and leading illegal trips to Cuba by pastors and other interested people bringing supplies and labor to help Cuba cope with the effects of the U.S. boycott. Pastors for Peace publicize the boycott so that Americans understand its impact and pressure their government to end it. The U.S. government is indicting a number of those who have made these trips, and is threatening to punish with large fines and up to ten years in prison those who have traveled to Cuba bringing relief supplies, including medicines.

As globalization and structural adjustment policies of the International Monetary Fund have put pressure on Third World governments, many Latin Americans have been electing socialist leaders and governments. Hugo Chavez has been using Venezuelan oil money to build housing for the poor. He has brought in teams from Cuba for a major literacy campaign. When the United States helped sponsor a coup to overthrow his rule, a massive demonstration by Venezuelans brought him back to power. When the United States and Venezuelan elites forced a vote seeking to end his term in office, Chávez triumphed easily. He has been forming networks with other socialist-leaning leaders in Argentina, Brazil, Chile, Cuba, and Bolivia.

There is growing suspicion that American interventions have been designed to counter socialist economies and governments. U.S. sanctions on Cuba are a prime example. Our relations with North Korea are another. During the Cold War, Yugoslavia had one of the most successful economies of Eastern Europe. When the Berlin Wall fell, the United States cancelled its foreign aid to Yugoslavia. U.S. policies helped to destabilize the Yugoslav society and then supported "democratic" leaders, which in practice meant secessionist leaders, leading to the country's dismemberment. The bombing of Serbia continued the destruction.

The U.S. invasion of Iraq has in practice been a huge experiment in dismantling a socialist economy. The first American appointed to administer the occupation, General Jay Garner, was dismissed the night he arrived, by his own account "because he wanted free elections and rejected an imposed program of privatization."[9] His successor, Paul Bremer, put up nearly all the government-owned businesses for sale. Iraq's economy, before Saddam Hussein was incited to invade Iran in 1980, had been one of the most successful Arab economies, with widespread high-quality health care, education, affordable housing, and food. Ten years of war with Iran and ten years of crippling sanctions left the country devastated. The 2003 U.S. invasion and subsequent occupation have been even more disastrous.

In addition to military coercion, modern forms of imperialism make use of economic pressures. John Perkins introduces us to the "Economic Hit Man":

Economic hit men (EHMs) are highly paid professionals who cheat countries around the globe out of trillions of dollars. They funnel money from the World Bank, the U.S. Agency for International Development (USAID), and other foreign "aid" organizations into the coffers of huge corporations and the pockets of a few wealthy families who control the planet's natural resources. Their tools include fraudulent financial reports, rigged elections, payoffs, extortion, sex, and murder. They play a game as old as empire, but one that has taken on new and terrifying dimensions during this time of globalization.

I should know; I was an EHM.[10]

There were two primary objectives of my work. First, I was to justify huge international loans that would funnel money back to MAIN and other U.S. companies (such as Bechtel, Halliburton, Stone & Webster, and Brown & Root) through massive engineering and construction projects. Second, I would work to bankrupt the countries that received those loans (after they had paid MAIN and the other U.S. contractors, of course) so that they would be forever beholden to their creditors, and so they would present easy targets when we needed favors, including military bases, UN votes, or access to oil and other natural resources.[11]

A condition of such loans is that engineering and construction companies from our own country must build all these projects.[12]

According to Perkins, when Economic Hit Men failed to convince local elites to cooperate, "jackals" came behind to assassinate the troublesome leaders. He mentions specifically Jaime Roldós of Ecuador and Omar Torrijos of Panama. When the troublesome leaders proved impossible to assassinate, as did Saddam Hussein with his multiple doubles, U.S. elites found pretexts to send in the Marines, as in Panama, or the entire military, as in Iraq. The most spectacular failure has been Cuba. But Cuba has been neutralized by sanctions.

SUMMARY

Outraged at the sufferings caused by 19th-century industrial capitalism, Karl Marx identified its problems, especially the alienation of workers from themselves, their product or service, and their fellow workers, together with the instability of the system's anarchic planning, which leads to periodic crises and the eventual pauperization of all but a few mega-industrialists. He predicted that the system was unsustainable and would collapse, leading to a new stage of society directed by workers.

Marxism as it was *practiced* in the Soviet Union and Eastern Europe proved to be an inadequate answer to the problems Marx raised. Whether global capitalism as practiced under the leadership of the United States will be more successful in the long run remains to be seen. But Marx's *criticisms* retain their force for many people in the world. In the chapters on Christian Social Teaching and Liberation Theologies, we will consider additional criticisms of global capitalism for comparison and alternative suggestions for solutions.

KEY TERMS

alienation	boom-bust cycle
antithesis	capitalism
Berlin Wall	capitalization

class struggle	ideology
communism	imperialism
Communist Manifesto	juche
Cultural Revolution	*Das Kapital*
dialectic	oppression
dialectical materialism	socialism
dictatorship of the proletariat	state capitalism
economic hit men	synthesis
exploitation	theory of value
Great Leap Forward	thesis

DISCUSSION QUESTIONS

1. Which of the figures in this chapter would you describe as a spokesperson or actor for justice and peace? On what grounds?
2. Is Marxism still a significant force in the world? What is bad about Marxism and socialism? What is good about them?
3. Do you think that worldwide capitalism is facing serious trouble, or can it overcome its problems and prosper in the long term? Can it do so in a way which increases justice and reduces poverty?

NOTES

1. Marx, *The Communist Manifesto,* 69–70. Used by permission of W. W. Norton.

2. "Die Philosophen haben die Welt nur verschieden *interpretiert,* es kömmt drauf an, sie zu *verändern,*" www.marxists.org/deutsch/archiv/marx-engels/1845/thesen/thesfeue-or.htm (accessed June 13, 2006).

3. For very extensive documentation, see "Marxists' Internet Archive," www.marxists.org/ and www.marx.org/ (accessed January 25, 2007). Note that this site has been under periodic hostile attack in 2006 and 2007.

4. For a description of how a "power elite" consisting of perhaps a half of one percent of Americans effectively controls American politics, economy, and media, see Domhoff, *Who Rules America?*

5. Domhoff, *Changing the Powers That Be: How the Left Can Stop Losing and Win.*

6. From *Confronting War: An Examination of Humanity's Most Pressing Problem,* 4th ed. © 2001 Ronald J. Glossop by permission of McFarland & Company, Inc., Box 611, Jefferson, N.C. 28640. www.mcfarlandpub.com.

7. See Heinberg, *The Party's Over* and *Power Down.*

8. See Diamond, *Collapse.*

9. Leigh, "General Sacked by Bush Says He Wanted Early Elections."

10. Perkins, *Confessions of an Economic Hit Man.* See also Hiatt, ed., *A Game As Old As Empire.* Reprinted with permission of the publisher. All rights reserved. www.bkconnection.com.

11. Perkins, *Hit Man,* 6. Reprinted with permission.
12. Perkins, *Hit Man,* xvii. Reprinted with permission.

SUGGESTIONS FOR FURTHER READING

A Marx Bibliography, www.sussex.ac.uk/Users/sefd0/bib/marx.htm (accessed July 10, 2006). *There is an enormous and reliable set of documents on the World Wide Web about all forms of Marxism (as long as you stick to the original thinkers!). This website has everything you could want online, and then refers you to the other academic Marx sites. It is helpful in its diversity, its use of online materials (though one should check the translators), and its listing of contemporary debates and issues.*
Bottomore, ed. *A Dictionary of Marxist Thought.*
Brecht. *The Caucasian Chalk Circle.*
Clark and Holquist. *Mikhail Bakhtin.*
Domhoff. *Changing the Powers That Be: How the Left Can Stop Losing and Win.*
———. *Who Rules America?*
Kropotkin. *Memoirs of a Revolutionist.*
Lash. *A Matter of Hope: A Theologian's Reflections on the Thought of Karl Marx.*
Leigh. "General Sacked by Bush Says He Wanted Early Elections."
Lenin. *The Lenin Anthology.*
———. *What Is to Be Done?*
Luxemburg. *Reflections and Writings.*
Marx and Engels. *The Communist Manifesto.*
———. *Karl Marx: Selected Writings.*
———. *Karl Marx, Frederick Engels: Collected Works.*
———. *The Marx-Engels Reader.* Ed. Tucker.
McLellan. *Karl Marx: His Life and Thought.*
———. *Marx before Marxism.*
Perkins. *Confessions of an Economic Hit Man.*
Solzhenitsyn. *One Day in the Life of Ivan Denisovich.*
Solzhenitsyn. *The Gulag Archipelago 1918–1956.*
Trotsky. *The Revolution Betrayed.*

Chapter Eight

The Israeli-Palestinian Conflict

"Then Moses went up from the plains of Moab to Mount Nebo, the headland of Pisgah which faces Jericho, and the LORD showed him all the land ... The LORD then said to him, 'This is the land which I swore to Abraham, Isaac and Jacob that I would give to their descendants.'"

—Deuteronomy 34:1–4

"Glory to (Allah) Who did take His servant for a Journey by night from the Sacred Mosque to the farthest Mosque [Masjid Al-Aqsa], whose precincts We did bless."[1]

—Quran 17:11

"Our ancestors worshiped on this mountain; but you people say that the place to worship is in Jerusalem." Jesus said to her, "Believe me, woman, the hour is coming when you will worship the Father neither on this mountain nor in Jerusalem. . . . The hour is coming, and is now here, when true worshipers will worship the Father in Spirit and truth . . . God is Spirit, and those who worship him must worship in Spirit and truth."

—John 4:20–24

PURPOSE OF THIS CHAPTER

Now that we have looked at Muslim, Jewish, Christian, and Marxist worldviews, we can consider a current dispute involving all four: the Israeli-Palestinian conflict. This chapter is a case study to determine whether understanding various worldviews helps us to understand and resolve conflicts. As

189

you read the following account, consider which of the points would be most significant to each of the following:

1. A *Political Zionist Jew* whose main concern is to create a Jewish state, with the support of foreign world powers, where the Jews of the world can be separate and safe;
2. A *Socialist Zionist Jew* whose main concern is to create a Marxist-style classless society where Jews can labor together, as on a kibbutz, until eventually they form the critical mass needed to establish a worker-controlled Jewish state;
3. A *Cultural Zionist Jew* who doesn't care who runs the state so long as they can live their Jewish life fully in the land where it originated;
4. A *Religious Zionist Jew* who believes that G-d wants Jews to "redeem" every square inch of the land that G-d gave them, moving off of the land non-Jews, who shouldn't be there anyway;
5. A *Religious Non-Zionist Jew* who believes that forming a Jewish state before the Messiah comes is an act of rebellion against G-d;
6. A *Reform Jewish peace activist* who fears that Judaism is losing its soul and violating its prophetic heritage by occupying Palestinian land and oppressing Palestinian non-Jews;
7. An *uncommitted Israeli Jew* who just wants to raise a family in peace;
8. A *Palestinian Muslim supporter of the Palestinian Authority* or a *Christian Palestinian* who would prefer a secular, bi-national state offering full citizenship and freedom to Muslims, Jews, and Christians, but who would accept a two-state solution if Israel would allow a Palestinian state in the pre-1967 Palestinian areas;
9. A *Palestinian Muslim supporter of Hamas* who believes that Palestine is an Islamic Waqf (religious endowment) which no human can "give away" to "infidels" and which, by rights, ought to have an Islamic government based on Islamic law;
10. An *uncommitted Palestinian* who grieves the loss of ancestral land and home, but above all just wants to raise a family in peace;
11. An *American Christian Zionist* who is eager to create the circumstances required for the return of Jesus, and who either doesn't notice the Palestinians or considers them an obstacle to the fulfillment of that dream;
12. An *American peace activist* who feels outraged by Israeli oppression of Palestinians;
13. An *average American* who has Jewish friends but no Palestinian friends and who knows little about the situation;
14. An *American politician* who wants the United States to control the oil-rich Middle East and, wanting to be elected, fears the political power of the American Israel Public Affairs Committee;

15. An *Israeli politician* who seeks election in a society marked by deep fears for survival and safety with a broad range of contradictory, deeply held convictions, with numerous settlements in occupied Palestinian territory that are heavily populated by religious Zionists;
16. A *Palestinian politician* who, with deep divisions between Hamas and the Palestinian Authority, has had almost nothing positive to offer his people in return for their support.

Despite the basic *scholarly* agreement on the main historical facts, there is *popular* ignorance or confusion about those same facts. The American mainstream media have not reported the facts accurately or completely. There is wide disagreement on which facts are *significant* for understanding the problem and *why* they are significant. And we often don't know the *motivation* of the actors: *why* they did what they did. Since the issue makes a great deal of difference for the people involved, there is a strong temptation to lie, exaggerate, or leave out evidence. Even eyewitness accounts, documents, and memoirs of leaders can be misleading. In addition to *deliberate* distortion, people's *unconscious* presuppositions lead them to notice, remember, and emphasize certain realities and ignore, forget, or discount others. People *trust* reports that favor their interests and disbelieve reports that threaten their interests.

History is a mystery puzzle inviting us to test whether the data are true, whether they adequately represent the whole reality, and whether the conclusions drawn from the data are justified. Since some speakers and writers lie, some omit or obscure inconvenient facts, and some are poorly informed or confused, it may be hard to understand what is actually going on and what one should do about it. Understanding the actors' major worldviews helps us to discover their motivations and to anticipate their actions.

PALESTINE-ISRAEL GEOGRAPHY AND HISTORY

Humans have lived in Israel-Palestine for about one hundred thousand years. In the 2nd millennium BCE, wandering Hebrew tribes and, a half-millennium later, their Israelite descendants, occupied the areas between strong Canaanite city-states.

For about four and a half centuries, from about 1,000 BCE, the Israelites exercised primary political control over the highlands to the west of the Jordan River, while contesting the highlands to the east of the Jordan with other tribal groups. Then they came under the rule of foreign empires. At the beginning of the Common Era, they were living under Roman rule and hoping for a leader to be anointed by God—a "Messiah"—who would destroy foreign rule and restore their independence. Romans called these people "Jews" after Judea, their main province.

A Galilean Jew named Jesus made a deep impact by his teaching and healing. After the Roman occupiers crucified him, his followers claimed that they had seen him risen from the dead and that he was the awaited "Messiah," but that destroying Roman rule and restoring Jewish independence was not his role. Their energetic preaching and growth produced a new religion, Christianity. Their descendants in Palestine form one of the three main groups in the current struggle.

When the Jewish community revolted against Roman rule in 66 CE and again in 132 CE, even their limited political power was destroyed, they were forbidden to live in their capital, Jerusalem, and most of them were scattered outside their homeland. Small communities of Jews remained in Palestine along with pagans, Samaritans, and Christians. When the Roman Empire embraced Christianity, Palestine came under Christian control centered in Constantinople—the "Byzantine" Empire—and much of the population became Christian.

When the Arab Muslims took political control in the 7th century, many inhabitants converted to Islam. From the end of the 7th century until the 20th century, the people and culture of the country were predominantly Arab and Islamic. From 1516 until the end of the First World War, Palestine was a province of the Muslim Ottoman Empire centered in Istanbul, Turkey. By 1900, most of the inhabitants of modern Palestine (Palestinians) were Muslim Arabs, a minority of about 6% were Christian Arabs, and a smaller group were Jewish Palestinians. After the formation of the state of Israel in 1948, Jews—even those who would earlier have been called "Palestinians"—generally preferred to be called "Israelis." In this chapter the term "Palestinian" will refer to the indigenous *non-Jewish* Arab inhabitants of the land—Muslim and Christian. Palestinian *Muslims* form the second main group in the current struggle.

The Jews of the Diaspora (outside Palestine) centered their lives around study of the Torah and observance of its laws, developing the way of life we call "Jewish." A strong community sense helped maintain their distinct way of life. They were frequently persecuted because they refused to accept the customs, habits, and religions of their neighbors. Some Jews dreamed of returning to the land of their origins, rejoining the few who had never left and re-establishing their former glory, but few made serious attempts to do so. Most believed that God did not want them to until the Messiah returned.[2]

Christian and Jewish Zionism: Historical Overview to 1930

As we saw in chapter 4, around the 1840s some Christians began to believe that Jesus would soon return to a Jewish Jerusalem with a functioning Jewish temple. But this could not happen until the Jewish community and temple were restored. Some of these Christians moved to Jerusalem and worked to encourage a Jewish restoration.

A few decades later, as we saw in chapter 3, some Jews also began thinking of an expanded Jewish presence in Palestine. Baron Edmond de Rothschild financed two agricultural settlements in (Ottoman) Palestine in 1882–1891 for about twenty-five thousand mostly Eastern European Jews. These Zionist Jews were not coming to a "land without a people"—the indigenous Arab population of Palestine in the 1880s (Muslim and Christian) was about half a million people.³ A modern revived form of Hebrew was beginning to be spoken and used in schools by the Jewish immigrants. These Zionist Jews who were moving to Palestine, with their successors, form the third main group in the current struggle.

Renewed persecution in Europe accelerated Jewish efforts to colonize Palestine. The question arises whether Jewish Zionist leaders were simply looking for a safe place for Jews to live (a Jewish "home"), or whether they intended from the beginning to gain Jewish political control with a majority Jewish population (a Jewish "state"). Intentions varied and leaders did not always express their aims clearly—even to their supporters. In 1899, Theodor Herzl wrote to the Arab mayor of Jerusalem: "You see another difficulty, Excellency, in the existence of the non-Jewish population in Palestine. But who would think of sending them away? It is their well-being, their individual wealth which we increase by bringing in our own."⁴ But he was freer to consider other plans in his diary. There, Herzl proposed to form a company or association which suddenly, within a week, would purchase massive amounts of land in Palestine through intermediate agents not known to be Jews, then help European Jews sell their property in Europe, move them to Palestine, organize their life there, and act as the precursor to an eventual Jewish state. In an entry for 1895, he wrote:

> We shall try to spirit the penniless [indigenous] population across the border by procuring employment for it in the transit countries whilst denying it any employment in our own country. The property-owners [many of whom were absentee landowners] will come over to our side. Both the process of expropriation and the removal of the poor must be carried out discreetly and circumspectly. Let the owners of immovable property believe that they are cheating us, selling us things for more than they are worth. But we are not going to sell them anything back. . . .

For Palestinian property owners who might not want to sell out and move away, he added an extra inducement: "[Those reluctant to part with their properties for sentimental reasons] will be offered a complete transportation to any place they wish, . . . This offer will be made only when all others have been rejected."[5] This offer was a subsidized relocation plan. Zionist leaders occasionally considered subsidizing Palestinian relocation, but they never put such plans into practice. If even this offer failed, Herzl proposed leaving the recalcitrant locals in place and organizing Jewish life and commerce without them.[6] Although early Jewish properties in Palestine were purchased by wealthy European Jews, often from absentee landowners, most displaced Palestinians lost their homes and property after 1947 unwillingly and without compensation. The one consistent feature was this: once property came into Jewish ownership, it did not return to non-Jewish ownership.[7]

From 1904 to the start of the First World War, about forty thousand Russian Jewish immigrants came to Palestine, but only about half stayed. Many were socialists or communists disappointed by the failure of the 1905 Russian Revolution. They came as laborers in the *moshavim* or as *urban* laborers, formed strong labor unions and political parties, founded the first *kibbutz*, founded the new city of Tel Aviv, formed the first Jewish self-defense organization, and expanded the use of modern Hebrew.[8]

Except for a brief period of European Christian control during the Crusades (barely over one hundred years for Jerusalem; another hundred years for parts of the seacoast), Palestine had been under Muslim control from 638 CE until the First World War—a period of nearly 1,300 years. The Muslims had been mostly tolerant of other faiths; the Crusaders, in contrast, slaughtered Jews and Muslims when they captured Jerusalem in 1099.

At the time of the First World War, many peoples in the world, including Arab Muslims and Christians under the Turkish Ottoman empire, sought national self-determination. Arab independence conflicted with the secular Zionist movement to build a Jewish homeland in Palestine.

Germany and Turkey were allies in the First World War. England wanted to protect its access to India through the Suez Canal, to gain control of the territory along its access routes, to assure access to Middle Eastern oil, and to limit German control in the Middle East, so it courted Arab leaders. The war was not going well for England in 1915. So when Sharif Husayn ibn Ali, the ruler of Mecca and Medina (in Arabia) and descendant of Muhammad (but not a Palestinian), asked the British whether Britain would support him if he declared himself to be "King of the Arabs" and independent from the Ottomans, the British agreed with qualifications. Husayn specified for his Arab state everything from the Mediterranean Sea to Iran and from southern Turkey to the Persian Gulf.[9] The British tried to avoid specifying borders. When Husayn objected, they agreed to his area with certain exceptions along the Mediterranean coast which they left vague. Arabs insisted that Palestine was to be part of Husayn's state; Zionists insisted that it was excluded by the vague British qualifications. In June 1916, reassured by Britain's ambiguous promises and aided by the British General T. E. Lawrence ("Lawrence of Arabia"), Husayn revolted against Turkey. The following year, Britain also attacked, moving from Egypt to capture Palestine.

Meanwhile, other British negotiators had been talking with the French. In May 1916, in the Sykes-Picot Agreement, the British had offered to give Syria and Lebanon to France and to put Palestine under international control.[10]

The war continued to go badly. By 1917, Britain feared that Russia, whose tsar had just been overthrown by the Bolshevik revolution, might withdraw from combat against Germany. Russian Jewish socialists and communists were prominent in the new government. Britain also wanted the United States, which had a large Jewish community, to declare war on Germany. To avoid Russian withdrawal from the war and to achieve American entry into the war, in November 1917 Arthur James Balfour of the British Foreign Office sent to Lord Rothschild, a leader of the Jewish community, a declaration approved by the British Cabinet (the "Balfour Declaration"), which read in part:

> His Majesty's Government view with favour the establishment in Palestine of a national home for the Jewish people, and will use their best endeavours to facilitate the achievement of this object, it being clearly understood that nothing shall be done which may prejudice the civil and religious rights of existing non-Jewish communities in Palestine, or the rights and political status enjoyed by Jews in any other country.[11]

Note that nothing was said about the *political* rights of non-Jewish communities in Palestine.

Unfortunately, these British promises to Sharif Husayn, to the French, and to Lord Rothschild, were incompatible. After the war, the French and British ignored the Sharif's claims. Britain assumed sole control of Palestine, freezing out "internationals"—specifically the French—against the terms of the Sykes-Picot Agreement. The League of Nations granted "mandates" to govern the former Ottoman territories. Britain was given mandates over Palestine, Transjordan, and Iraq, and France was given mandates over Lebanon and Syria. Meanwhile, the Saud family had chased Sharif Husayn out of Mecca and Medina and set up their kingdom of "Saudi Arabia." Britain installed one of the Sharif's sons, Amir Abdullah, as king of (Trans) Jordan, which they separated from their mandate for Palestine, to the annoyance of the Zionists, who wanted Transjordan included in their Jewish homeland. The Arabs elected Husayn's other son, Faysal, to be king of Syria (including Palestine), but the French drove him out of Damascus, so Britain installed Faysal as king of Iraq—minus Kuwait, which they established as a separate kingdom, denying Iraq its natural seaport. All of these countries were newly carved out of the Arab areas of the former Ottoman Empire—the territory promised to the Sharif—with the European powers determining the lines of division.

England's mandate for Palestine included the following provisions:

> ART. 2. The Mandatory shall be responsible for placing the country under such political, administrative and economic conditions as will secure the establishment of the Jewish national home, . . . and also for safeguarding the civil and religious [*not political*] rights of all the inhabitants of Palestine, irrespective of race and religion. . . . ART. 6. The Administration of Palestine, while ensuring that the rights and position of other sections of the population are not prejudiced, shall facilitate Jewish immigration under suitable conditions and shall encourage . . . close settlement by Jews on the land.[12]

After the First World War, about thirty-five thousand committed Zionist Jews immigrated, mostly from Russia and Eastern Europe. New kibbutzim and moshavim were established, mostly secular and socialist in orientation, although there were a few religious kibbutzim. The *Histadrut* labor organization was founded in 1920 with the following resolution:

> It is the aim of the United Federation of all the [*implied* Jewish] workers and laborers of Palestine who live by the sweat of their brows without exploiting the toil of others [meaning, without sharing the work with Arabs], to promote land settlement, to involve itself in all economic and cultural issues effecting [*sic*] labor in Palestine, and to build a Jewish workers society there.[13]

Arabs objected vigorously to the British mandate, insisting that, since the British had promised them self-government, they should be able to control immigration into their own country. Instead, the British allowed open immigration and land sales to Jews. In 1920 and 1921, when Arab demonstrations led to riots, Ze'ev Jabotinsky created an armed Jewish defense force. The local British administration convicted him of creating an unauthorized police force and sentenced him to fifteen years in prison, but he was soon released on orders from London. He went on to organize the *Haganah*—an unofficial (illegal) Jewish army.

The Arabs sent a delegation to London in late 1921 demanding that the British repudiate the Balfour Declaration and support a democratic government elected by all the inhabitants of Palestine: Muslim, Christian, and Jewish. A British White Paper declared that Britain did "not contemplate that Palestine *as a whole* should be converted into a Jewish National Home, but that such a Home should be founded *in* Palestine" (emphases added).[14]

Britain also promised to limit immigration to what the country's economy could absorb, and to work toward setting up a "legislative council." Palestinians responded that immigration quotas should be a political decision, not an economic one, and should be set democratically by the population affected. The 1922 census showed that the Jewish community had grown to be 11% of the population of Palestine.

In place of traditional family and tribal leaders, the British appointed weak Palestinian leaders who would depend on the British for their power. As Grand Mufti of Jerusalem, they appointed Hajj Amin al Husayni, who was hostile to Zionism and had supported the riots of 1920, naming him head of the newly-created Supreme Muslim Council (SMC), which provided him substantial money from various fees and religious endowments to distribute to his favorites. The British encouraged Jews and Arabs to develop modern political organizations connected to the British administration. The Jews took advantage of this offer; the Arabs boycotted the organizations to avoid validating the British mandate. The organizations designed for the Arabs were, in any case, markedly less effective than those designed for the Jews.[15]

In 1924, persecution of middle-class Jews in Poland brought a new wave of shopkeepers, artisans, and small industrialists to Palestinian cities. The new settlers were attracted to the Revisionist Zionism promoted by Ze'ev Jabotinsky, who preferred liberal capitalism to the earlier labor union socialism. He rejected the dominant Zionist view that the Jewish community should quietly build up its population, along with its economic and political strength, until it had a majority before proposing a Jewish state. Believing that the British were committed to Jewish colonization, he urged the Jewish community to capture Palestine and Jordan by force of arms, maintain control by means of a political and military "iron wall," and declare a Jewish state on both sides of the Jordan River.

In 1929, Arabs complained that Jewish worship at the Western Wall was interfering with Muslim worship at the al-Aqsa Mosque. Muslims feared that Jews would destroy the Dome of the Rock to rebuild the temple, a position advocated by some right-wing Revisionist Jews although, according to mainstream Jewish tradition, the temple should not be rebuilt until the Messiah comes. Tensions and provocations mounted on both sides. False rumors of a Jewish attack on the al-Aqsa Mosque circulated. Arabs burned Jewish prayer books at the Western Wall, pillaged Jewish neighborhoods, and killed seventeen Jews in Jerusalem. Some Arab families protected their Jewish neighbors by hiding them. Rioters from Jerusalem traveled to Hebron, site of the tomb of Abraham and Sarah, revered ancestors of Jews, Christians, and Muslims. Within a few hours, riots had killed sixty-seven Jews and wounded hundreds. Britain evacuated Jewish survivors from Hebron to Jerusalem. Overall, the riots killed 133 Jews and 116 Arabs. Most of the Jews were killed by rioters, most of the Arabs by British police. The armed Jewish settlers in Hebron today, who moved into the city center illegally after 1967, refer to this riot to justify their demand for special protection by the Israel Defense Forces.

An official study by the British Shaw Commission reported in 1930 that 30% of the Palestinian population, which had been mostly farmers, had lost their land, so that there was not enough land left to the Arabs for their children to inherit. They were not necessarily unemployed, since industrial development directed by the British was creating many new jobs and the Arab population was actually increasing. The Passfield White Paper (also 1930) recommended that Jewish immigration be stopped and land sales be restricted. The British Parliament repudiated the White Paper, and the League of Nations pointed out that stopping Jewish immigration would violate terms of the mandate. This exchange was characteristic: local British administrators tended to sympathize with Arab complaints, while the government in London tended to favor the Jewish community, often reversing decisions made locally.

Beginning in 1929 and increasing rapidly as Nazis gained power, Jewish professionals from Germany and Austria flooded into Palestine. Jewish land purchases drove up prices, tempting absentee Arab landholders to sell for profit, just as Herzl had predicted. The purchaser was the Jewish National Fund,[16] which held the land for Jewish use and leased it to Jews, displacing its former Arab laborers. In addition, during the depression of the 1930s, many small Arab farmers lost their land when they couldn't pay taxes to the government or rent to the landowner.

The Arab Revolt of 1936–1939

In 1935, alarmed by the growing Zionist community, the Arabs demanded an end to Jewish immigration, an end to land sales to Jews, and the creation of a Palestinian national government. The local British administration offered to form a legislative council on which Arabs, though not proportionally represented, would have a majority. The Jewish community strongly objected, fearing that the council would cripple development of their national home, and London killed the proposal. A full-scale Arab revolt (1936–1939) resulted. The "Arab High Command," led by the Grand Mufti, called a general strike of Arab workers and a boycott of Jewish products. England was approaching war with Germany. She needed Middle Eastern oil. In 1937, the British Peel Commission recommended that Palestine be divided between Arabs and Jews. About 20% would go to the Jews; Britain would retain control of Jerusalem, Bethlehem, and Nazareth. Jews would be moved out of the

Arab section and Arabs out of the Jewish section, preferably by agreement with compensation, but by compulsion if necessary.[17] As precedent, the commission pointed to the forced transfer of Greek and Turkish populations after the First World War.[18] Although they objected to the proposed boundaries, Jewish leaders considered the project seriously, arguing among themselves that it was only a first step which could later be expanded, eventually giving them control of the whole of Palestine. They discussed how to transfer Arabs to Jordan or Iraq.[19]

The Arabs rejected the plan and declared that, if the British did not limit Jewish immigration, the Arabs would side with their enemies in the impending European war. A new commission trashed the Peel proposal, proposing a much smaller Jewish state; now the plan was unacceptable to *both* sides. The Arab revolt resumed. The British suppressed it harshly, exiling many of its leaders. They also allowed the Jews to arm the *Haganah*, and they trained its *Special Night Squads*, which attacked Arab villages. Jabotinsky broke away from the *Haganah* to form the *Irgun*. Two years later, another breakaway group formed the *Stern Gang*, also known as *Lehi*. Believing that the *Haganah* was too restrained, these two groups committed themselves to attack Arab civilians:

> The Irgun established the pattern of terrorism adopted 30 years later by [the Palestinian party] Al-Fatah. Among its actions were the wheeling of a vegetable barrow containing a bomb into an Arab market in Jerusalem, firing at a bus and throwing bombs into market places (Jerusalem, Haifa). The perpetrators of these acts were declared national heroes and martyrs.[20]

Overall, the Arab revolt of 1936–1939 killed 415 Jews and about 5,000 Arabs. The Arabs also suffered 15,000 wounded, 5,600 imprisoned, and most of their leadership exiled. Putting down the revolt required 20,000 British troops. The failure of the revolt crippled Arab political and military strength, which would be sorely needed in 1947–1948. In contrast, the *Jewish* military posture was enhanced, since Britain had armed many Jews to help put down the revolt. In addition, the Arab boycott encouraged the Jewish economy to become more self-sufficient.

Although Britain had suppressed the Arab revolt, she understood Arab grievances. A 1939 White Paper seriously limited Jewish immigration: no more than seventy-five thousand to be admitted over the next five years, thereafter immigration subject to Arab approval, and the promise of a Palestinian state within ten years.

As Nazi persecution of Jews intensified and Jews urgently needed to emigrate, most countries severely restricted their immigration. In 1938, the World Zionist Organization boycotted a multinational conference in France convened to deal with the resettlement of Jewish refugees from Nazism *in countries other than Palestine*, fearing it would reduce immigration to Palestine.[21] A poll taken in November 1938, immediately after the destructive German anti-Jewish riots called Kristallnacht ("Night of Broken Glass"), showed that 94% of Americans opposed the Nazi treatment of Jews, but 72% opposed letting more German Jews immigrate to the United States, and two-thirds even opposed accepting twenty thousand German Jewish *children* as emergency refugees.[22] With nearly all countries closed to their immigration by restrictive quotas, many European Jews headed for Palestine. Some managed to enter illegally; others were arrested or deported. Zionist groups organized illegal shipments of refugees on whatever rickety ships they could acquire; many were turned back by the British or sank.

The Biltmore Program

In 1942, a conference declaration signed at the Biltmore Hotel in New York City signaled a major shift in the Zionist position. The British White Paper of 1939 had effectively ended British support for the Balfour Declaration. The Biltmore Declaration condemned the White Paper, promised Jewish military participation in the war against Nazism, and implicitly demanded a Jewish *state* covering *all* of Palestine: "The Conference calls for the fulfillment of the original purpose of the Balfour Declaration and the Mandate which recognizing the historical connection of the Jewish people with Palestine, was to afford them the opportunity, . . . that *Palestine* be established as a Jewish Commonwealth integrated in the structure of the new democratic world" (emphasis added).[23] Note that "commonwealth" has a very different connotation than "national home," and that it was not the *original purpose* of Balfour to transform *the whole of Palestine* into a Jewish state.

While the Haganah, the largest Jewish underground army, chose to support Britain's war effort against Nazi Germany, the Irgun and the Stern Gang (Lehi) attacked the British occupation. In Cairo in 1944, two Lehi members murdered Lord Moyne, the British Minister of State for the Middle East. He had been a personal friend of Winston Churchill, and his assassination turned Churchill against the Zionists. The Haganah began to see the Irgun and Lehi as liabilities and acted to reduce their influence, even helping British police to capture their members.

As the Second World War ended and it became clear that the British would not support a Jewish state, both the Irgun and Lehi launched terrorist attacks against British forces in Palestine, bombing trains, railroad stations, and the British government headquarters at the King David Hotel in Jerusalem, killing ninety-one. A weakened and exhausted Britain decided to withdraw from both India and Palestine.

The United Nations Plan: The War of 1948

England announced its withdrawal date and asked the United Nations to work out a settlement. In November 1947, the United Nations recommended that the land be divided into a Jewish area and an Arab area based on the majority population in each area. After more than a half century of Jewish land purchases, Jews or the Jewish Agency owned about 7% of Palestine, Arab individuals owned slightly less than half, and the state claimed slightly less than half.[24] Much of the state-owned land was desert or unproductive. Under the UN plan, the Arab city of Jaffa, assigned to the Arab state, was completely surrounded by the Jewish state. The Jerusalem-Bethlehem district, split almost equally between Jewish and Arab inhabitants, was wholly contained within the Arab area with no Jewish land access; it was to be an international area controlled by neither group.[25] The UN intended the two states to form an economic union with open borders.

The partition plan heavily favored the Jews. Although Jews represented only 33% of the population, the Jewish state was allotted 55% of the land area, the Arab state 42%. The final 3% — mainly Jerusalem and Bethlehem — would be under international control. *Within* the proposed Jewish area, Jews made up a slim majority of 55%. If wandering Bedouin herders were included in the count, the population of the Jewish area was almost evenly split between Jews and Arabs. The proposed *Arab* area was 99% Arab![26] The lines as drawn gave the Jewish area as much land as possible — supporters said the extra territory would provide space to settle Jewish refugees — but as a result the Jewish majority was very fragile.

The majority of the Jewish community accepted the recommendation, although it had reservations and intended to expand the territory allotted to itself. The Arab community rejected it and promised to resist by force of arms. Violence from both sides started almost at once, as a natural intensification of the agitation and terrorism which had induced the British to end their occupation. Realizing that the plan was unworkable, the United Nations withdrew it. Fighting between Zionists and Palestinians was well underway by January 1948.

Based on recently released archives, Israeli Jewish historian Benny Morris shows that Jewish attacks on Arab villages in 1948 were much more extensive and deliberate than previously thought.[27] Although the attacks were designed at first to defend Jewish settlements and their supply lines, the distribution of settlements meant that few Arab villages were unaffected. As the struggle in April 1948 produced an unexpected flood of Palestinian refugees, Zionist leaders recognized the advantage of reducing the Arab population in what would become the Jewish state and began to provoke the flight deliberately.[28] "Ultimately, the atmosphere of transfer . . . prevailed through April—June: Most communities attacked were evacuated and where no spontaneous evacuation occurred, communities more often than not were expelled. Throughout, Arabs who had fled were prevented from returning to their homes."[29] Morris judges that those attacks were *necessary* to assure Jewish control of the new state. "Ben-Gurion was a transferist. He understood that there could be no Jewish state with a large and hostile Arab minority in its midst. . . . Without the uprooting of the Palestinians, a Jewish state would not have arisen here."[30]

Zionist spokespersons have claimed that Arab radio broadcasts encouraged the Arab flight so that civilian Arabs would be out of the way when Arab armies pushed the Jews into the sea. This claim is not supported by records of radio broadcasts, and Arab historians have long denied it. Morris shows there was no such generalized appeal: changing situations and local leaders produced contradictory orders which more often than not the Palestinians ignored. He concludes: "In the main, what the [various Arab leaders] and the various [Arab] militias did or did not do during April–June to promote or stifle the exodus was only of secondary importance; the prime movers throughout were the Yishuv [the Jewish community] and its military organizations. It was their operations that were to prove the major precipitants to flight."[31]

A prime example was an Irgun attack on the village of *Deir Yassin*, just outside Jerusalem near the highway from Tel Aviv.[32] Deir Yassin had negotiated nonbelligerency status with the Jewish leaders and had resisted infiltration by Arab fighters. In their attack on the village, the Irgun killed over one hundred Palestinians, all of them civilians. Early reports numbered the dead at 254. A careful study in the 1980s by the Palestinian Bir Zeit University reduced the number to 110–120.[33] Both sides knew at the time that the number was exaggerated but found it convenient to accept it: Palestinians hoped to induce neighboring Arab nations to send troops to their support; Jews realized that the story was causing Arabs from other villages to flee in panic. The Jewish Agency, which controlled the Haganah, publicly denounced the attack, but other leading Jews helped spread the panic. Menachem Begin (leader of the Irgun and, later, prime minister of Israel) wrote in his memoirs that the flight of the Arabs was a welcome result of the attack.[34]

The State of Israel

The Jewish community declared the state of Israel on May 14, 1948. U.S. President Harry Truman, concerned about Jewish war refugees, impressed by recent Jewish advances in the war, annoyed by Zionist lobbying but grateful for crucial Jewish financial and political support in a desperate election campaign, recognized the new state eleven minutes after its declaration;[35] the Soviet Union followed almost at once. Britain withdrew the next day. Jordan's Arab Legion and armies from Egypt, Syria, and Iraq entered Palestine. The invading armies were crippled by conflicting objectives: King Abdullah of Jordan wanted to annex to Jordan the area of Palestine along his border (the West Bank), President Quwatly of Syria feared that Abdullah intended to grab part of his territory to create and control a "Greater Syria," and King Farouq of Egypt sought control over southern Palestine and as much of the West Bank as he could capture, in order to limit Abdullah's power. None of the invaders wanted a new Arab state in Palestine ruled by Haj Amin. There was little coordination and no central control.

The Zionists had better arms, motivation, organization, and leadership than the Arabs, along with significant numbers of veteran soldiers from the World War. Israel ended up controlling 42% more territory than had been allotted to them in the original plan—from 55% of the territory to 78%—including all of Galilee, most of which had been allotted to the Palestinian state. An ancient Jewish dream, long thought impractical, seemed on the verge of fulfillment. For the Palestinians, the war was disastrous; they named it *al-Nakhba*—"The Catastrophe."

When the fighting ended with an armistice, Palestinians who had been driven out of their homes or had fled to save their lives tried to come home, but the Israeli army blocked their way. Israel argued that the returning refugees might be spies or subversive. It is more likely that Israel sealed the borders to guarantee an overwhelming Jewish majority in the new state. The Israeli decision not to let the refugees go home is a key turning point in Israeli-Palestinian relations. In December 1948, UN General Assembly Resolution 194 declared: "The General Assembly . . . resolves that the refugees wishing to return to their homes and live at peace with their neighbours should be permitted to do so at the earliest practicable date, and that compensation should be paid for the property of those choosing not to return and for loss of or damage to property."[36]

Other Arab countries did not want 750,000 instant immigrants. Palestinians wanted to return to their homes, orchards, and fields. Caught in between, they struggled to survive near the borders, occasionally sneaking across to harvest crops or rescue items from their homes. Not until late 1949 did the United Nations begin to administer refugee camps with tents for the refugees to live in. After a short time, Israel confiscated the lands and homes of the Palestinians whose reentry they were blocking and either gave them to new Jewish immigrants, who were flooding into the new state of Israel, or bulldozed the Arab villages and planted new villages or forests in their place. Israel argued that it was resettling thousands of Jews—the neighboring Arab countries could resettle the refugee Arabs. The Arab League urged Arab countries not to grant citizenship to the refugees; except for Jordan, most complied. Several million, including their descendants, are still unsettled today; many of these have no citizenship in any country.

The 1956 Suez War

The surrounding Arab nations were shaken by their defeats in 1948—within four years, Abdullah of Jordan was assassinated and the governments of both Syria and Egypt fell to revolutions. In 1952, Gamal Abdel Nasser seized control of Egypt from King Farouq. In 1956 he nationalized the Suez Canal Company's assets. Supported by an Israeli attack across the Sinai Desert, English and French military forces captured the Canal. But U.S. President Eisenhower, angry that he had not been consulted, pressed the United Nations to condemn the attack, and the armies retreated.

The 1967 Six-Day War

In 1967 Israel and Syria were in conflict over Israeli military patrols and land cultivation in the demilitarized zone between them, and over use of water from the sources of the Jordan River. Moshe Dayan claims that Israel deliberately provoked Syrian shelling from the Golan Heights so that Israel could seize more Syrian land.[37] Egypt moved about 100,000 troops and 600–700 tanks into defensive positions facing the Israeli border in the Sinai, ordered the UN to withdraw its observers, and blockaded shipping lanes to the Israeli port of Eilat. Nasser probably hoped this threat alone, without war, would make Israel ease up on Syria and deal fairly with Palestinian refugees, since Israel's reserve army could not remain mobilized for very long without devastating its economy. But Israel brought matters to a head by attacking Egyptian airfields in a move widely portrayed in the West as defensive. In a surprisingly short time Israel captured the rest of the areas of Palestine allotted to the Arabs by the 1947 UN Partition Plan—Gaza, the West Bank, and East Jerusalem—plus the entire Sinai peninsula between Israel and Egypt and the strategic Golan Heights of Syria. About 350,000 Palestinian refugees were forced to move again. UN Security Council Resolution 242[38] declared that the acquisition of territory by war was invalid. Israel's continued military control over the conquered territories is known as "the occupation" and is illegal under international law.

Impressed by the Israeli military power demonstrated in the war and seeking a counter-force to Soviet influence in the Middle East, the United States greatly increased its financial and military support to Israel.

Shortly after the 1967 war, Israel began building Jewish-only settlements inside the newly captured territories—a policy which Israeli leaders called *"creating facts on the ground"*: promise whatever you like, but create physical realities which make those promises impossible to keep, thus consolidating Israeli control. Over time, Israel reserved half of the West Bank and nearly a third of the Gaza Strip either for military use or for Jewish-only colonies—about two hundred Jewish-only settlements which monopolized the productive land and water rights around them. The occupied territories were also cut into isolated blocks by "access roads" which only Jews were allowed to use. Israel closes off those isolated blocks arbitrarily, not allowing Palestinians to cross the access roads. As of early 2007, throughout the West Bank there were at least five hundred checkpoints impeding Palestinian movement. *Palestinians* (but not Israelis) in the occupied territories were governed not by Israeli civil law but by Israeli military decrees. They have experienced frequent arrest, detention without trial, torture (85% of Palestinian prisoners are tortured), deportation, severe injury, destruction of homes (since 1967, Israel has demolished twelve thousand Palestinian homes in the occupied territories),[39] loss of land and livelihood, and death. They are treated as stateless noncitizens without rights.

Under international law, an occupying power is not allowed to move its own population into the occupied area. Israel argued that the territories should not be considered "occupied" because they had not been independent before Israel captured them but had been governed by Jordan and Egypt. The United Nations and the International Court of Justice rejected those arguments and ordered Israel not to settle the territories.[40]

Palestinians felt betrayed by their Arab neighbors, who had failed to defend their rights. Some decided to take matters into their own hands. In 1968, Yasser Arafat assumed leadership of the Palestine Liberation Organization (PLO), which had been founded four years earlier in Egypt. In addition to its administrative, social service, and diplomatic functions, the PLO began to use terrorist attacks against civilian targets to harass the Israeli leadership and gain world attention. Some Palestinian exiles turned to *international* terrorism, killing Jewish athletes at the 1972 Olympic Games in Munich and seizing airliners and a cruise ship for hostages.

The 1973 Yom Kippur or Ramadan War

In 1973, Egypt and Syria, supplied with Soviet weapons, simultaneously attacked Israeli forces in the occupied territories on their high holy day of Yom Kippur. Egypt especially had surprising success at first. Israeli casualties were very high, both in soldiers and equipment. But in desperate fighting, aided by a U.S. resupply of weapons to replace those destroyed, Israel regained much of the invaded territory though not the Suez Canal. After a UN cease-fire that had been accepted by Israel and Egypt went into effect (UN Resolution 338),[41] Israeli General Ariel Sharon broke the cease-fire to cut off the Egyptian Third Army in the desert and threatened to starve it out, giving Israel a bargaining advantage and the appearance of victory in the war. But Israel had lost confidence and the Arabs regained their dignity.

Furious at the U.S. resupply of weapons to Israel, the Arab states mounted an oil boycott that escalated fuel prices in the United States, causing a price inflation and an economic recession. When Jimmy Carter was elected president, he pursued a comprehensive settlement resulting in the 1978 Camp David Accords,[42] which mandated the return of the Sinai to Egypt; a self-governing authority in the West Bank and Gaza; the withdrawal of Israeli forces from those areas; and normalized relations between Israel, Egypt, and Jordan within five years, based on UN resolutions 242 and 338. Withdrawing from the Sinai in accordance with the agreement, Israel contravened the rest of the agreement by annexing the Golan Heights and continuing to expand settlements in the West Bank and Gaza. With Egypt no longer a threat, Israel felt less constrained in its military occupation of the West Bank. Religious Zionists founded the group *Gush Emunim* ("Block of the Faithful") to promote the settlement and "redemption" of Gazan and West Bank land. Jordan and the other Arab states, accusing Egypt of weakening the Arab position, refused to negotiate with Israel.[43]

The 1982 Lebanon Invasion

In 1982, the Israeli army invaded Lebanon. Although Israel claimed it was trying to eliminate guerrilla attacks launched from Lebanon, its invasion violated a truce negotiated by the United States that had eliminated such attacks throughout the previous year. Israel provoked a minor violation by an anti-PLO Palestinian splinter group to justify their pre-planned attack. After the invasion killed an estimated seventeen thousand civilians, the PLO leadership agreed to abandon Lebanon and move to Tunisia. Still, Israeli success was limited: the invasion took much longer than expected, costs were high, and many Israeli politicians, generals, and soldiers began to resist government policies. Especially damaging to Israel's reputation was the massacre of Palestinians in the *Sabra* and *Shatila* refugee camps in Beirut. The Israeli army surrounding the camps allowed soldiers of the Lebanese Phalange (a Christian Fascist political group) to enter the camps and massacre from one thousand to three thousand refugees.[44] An Israeli investigation blamed the Israeli commanding officer, Ariel Sharon, for failing to prevent the massacre when he could and should have done so.

The First "Intifada"

In the fall of 1987, a spontaneous uprising began in a refugee camp in Gaza and continued until 1993. The Arabic term for uprising is *intifada*—literally "shaking off." The intifada utilized many nonviolent tactics, although their effectiveness was weakened (see chapter 11) by Palestinian demonstrators who threw rocks, burned tires, and murdered unrepentant collaborators. Gene Sharp, a scholar of nonviolent movements, has estimated that the intifada was 85% nonviolent; the 15% violence was mostly youth throwing stones. But perception is often as important as reality, and the U.S. media concentrated attention on *Palestinian* violence—the Israeli Defense Forces were far more violent—giving a distorted impression which muted the impact of Palestinian nonviolence. Still, the sight of violent Israeli military responses to Palestinian nonviolence began to change world opinion.

Palestinians within the occupied territories began the intifada to express their frustration both with the illegal Israeli occupation and with the failure of the exiled PLO leadership in Tunisia to end it. Arab leaders quickly adjusted to this new movement and supported it.

Hamas

The Muslim Brotherhood has been active in Palestine since 1948, when they provided fighters to oppose Zionist forces fighting to establish the new state of Israel. More recently, in Gaza, they have provided schools, libraries, health facilities, and youth activities. In 1987, Shaikh Ahmed Yassin, a Gazan member of the Brotherhood, created a local chapter which he named Hamas. Their 1988 covenant refused to accept the state of Israel: "'Israel will exist . . . until Islam will obliterate it, just as it obliterated others before it' (The Martyr, Imam Hassan al-Banna, of blessed memory)."[45] Yet, before his assassination by Israel in 2004, Sheikh Yassin stated publicly that he would "consider a long-term ceasefire" in exchange for Israel's withdrawal from the occupied territories.[46]

Palestine National Congress Recognizes Israel

Early in the first intifada, in 1988, the Palestine National Congress voted to accept Israel's right to exist within internationally recognized secure borders *if Israel accepted the right of a Palestinian state to exist*. Israel refused to accept the offer, arguing that the written constitution of the Palestine Liberation Organization (PLO) still called for the destruction of Israel. Palestinians felt that neither Israel nor the United States responded fairly to the PNC vote, which involved a major concession on their side—they relinquished any claim to sovereignty over 78% of Palestinian land, including areas conquered by Israel in 1948 that the UN had allotted to the Palestinian state. In return they asked Israel to recognize that Palestinians had an equal right to a state and a normal life with self-determination and justice.

The Israeli government at first thought it could squash the intifada quickly. Brutal responses included arbitrary arrest, beating, destruction of houses of suspects and their relatives, and the use of "rubber bullets" (rubber-coated metal) for crowd control—sometimes at point-blank range resulting in serious injury and death. An Israeli colonel, on trial for ordering soldiers to break the arm and leg bones of Arab children and teenagers, swore under oath that the tactic had been ordered by Yitzhak Rabin, the defense minister.[47]

After the First Gulf War in 1991, renewed pressures from the United States, including restrictions on financial aid, pushed Israel toward negotiations. When Yitzhak Rabin of the Labor Party defeated the incumbent Likud president Yitzhak Shamir in 1992, voters anticipated sincere efforts to come to an agreement with the Palestinians.

The Oslo Accords

Hope was high in September 1993 as Yitzhak Rabin and Yasser Arafat signed a preliminary peace agreement called the "Declaration of Principles" (DOP) or "Oslo Accords" on the White House lawn under the eye of President Bill Clinton.[48] The agreement established "a Palestinian Interim Self-Government Authority . . . in the West Bank and the Gaza Strip, for a transitional period not exceeding five years, leading to a permanent settlement based on Security Council Resolutions 242 and 338."[49] Yasser Arafat returned triumphantly from Tunisia to inaugurate the Palestinian Authority. The most difficult questions still needed to be decided: Israeli withdrawal from the rest of the West Bank, arrangements to share land and water resources, the status of Jerusalem, final borders, Israeli settlements in the occupied territories, and the rights of refugees from those parts of pre-1948 Palestine which had become the state of Israel.

Many *Palestinians* considered the agreement to be too little. *Israeli* settlers in the West Bank wished to maintain control of all the occupied territories; they harassed Palestinians and attacked whatever they thought threatened the permanence of their settlements. In 1994, a Jewish settler physician entered the Ibrahim Mosque in Hebron on the Jewish feast of Purim and killed twenty-nine Muslim worshipers with a hand grenade and automatic rifle; thirty more people died in the riots that ensued. Settlers inscribed his gravestone as follows: "Here lies the saint, Dr. Baruch Kappel Goldstein, blessed be the memory of the righteous and holy man, may the Lord avenge his blood, who devoted his soul to the Jews, Jewish religion and Jewish land. His hands are innocent and his heart is pure. He was killed as a martyr of God. . . ." After the massacre, Palestinians began to attack Jewish civilians with suicide bombers.[50] In 1995, Yitzhak Rabin was assassinated by a right-wing Jewish law student. In 1996, the Israeli secret service assassinated Yahya Ayyash, a Hamas bomb-maker, with an exploding telephone. Five Palestinian suicide bombings followed, killing seventy-two Israelis in two months. Rabin's successor, Shimon Peres, then lost the elections to the right-wing Binyamin Netanyahu in a wave of fear.

Netanyahu had promised to continue the "peace process" but never to allow a Palestinian state—an impossible combination that repudiated the Oslo Accords. He stalled Israeli withdrawals for six months, using suicide attacks as justification, finally withdrawing from about 80% of Hebron in January 1997 but continuing to occupy its central market with about 450 extremist Jewish settlers protected by several thousand Israeli soldiers in a city of over 100,000 Palestinians.[51] Arafat wanted Netanyahu to withdraw further from rural areas, but Netanyahu's political base expected him to stop or even reverse the withdrawals.

Israeli leaders complained that they had traded land for peace but terrorism continued. Furthermore, their agreements were signed with the *Palestine Liberation Organization* (PLO) headed by Yasser Arafat, but the rival organization *Hamas*, which had been gaining support did not recognize the agreement or the state of Israel. *Palestinian* leaders complained that Israeli attacks and expansion of settlements continued, and the isolated Palestinian areas left them worse off under Oslo than before.

Wye River Memorandum

In 1998, U.S. President Bill Clinton convened another peace conference at the Wye River plantation in Maryland. Israel agreed to withdraw from more of the West Bank, to allow the Gaza Airport to open, to develop an industrial park on the Israel-Gaza border, to arrange a safe-passage route for Palestinians between Gaza and the West Bank, and to develop an eventual Gaza seaport. Arafat agreed to demobilize terrorist groups. Both sides agreed to work toward a final settlement in 1999. Criticized by right-wing Israelis, Netanyahu explained that Israel wouldn't have to carry out the agreements because Arafat wouldn't be able to end all terrorism. He began the withdrawals, but suspended them partway through, and left most of the other points of the agreement unfulfilled.[52]

The process of regaining land for a Palestinian state stalled. The Palestinian economy grew worse as Israel periodically closed the borders to trade, ostensibly in retaliation for terrorist attacks. Only individual cities of the West Bank without their surrounding rural areas had been granted to Palestinian control, producing a series of isolated pockets that made travel difficult—travelers had to pass through multiple checkpoints that were frequently closed. Furthermore, as Yasser Arafat tried to rein in terrorist groups, some Palestinians alleged that he had "sold out" to Israel in return for power—that Arafat was simply executing Israeli oppression under the guise of a Palestinian authority. Finally a vote of "no confidence" in the Israeli legislature, the Knesset, forced an early election in which the Labor Party won back power from the right-wing Likud.

Ehud Barak

The new premier, Ehud Barak, promised to restore the movement toward peace. Barak withdrew the Israeli army from southern Lebanon, which it had been occupying since 1982. But he also accelerated the illegal construction of Jewish settlements in occupied Palestinian territory.

Barak's "Offer"

In the summer of 2000, under pressure from U.S. President Bill Clinton, Barak is said to have extended to the Palestinians a "generous offer" which would have given them possession of 95% of the West Bank, but 10% of that total was to remain under "temporary" Israeli control—duration unspecified—as was a network of access roads that only settlers could use; 80% of the Israeli settlers in the West Bank were to remain; and there would be no sharing of Jerusalem, no right of return for Palestinian refugees, and no viable water policy.[53] Arafat rejected the proposal.

Ariel Sharon's Temple Mount Visit

In late September 2000 Barak allowed Ariel Sharon to visit the Muslim *al-Haram al-Sharif* (the Noble Sanctuary) in Jerusalem accompanied by over one thousand armed Israeli police. The Temple Mount carries special religious significance for both groups, and sovereignty over it was one of the issues that Barak and Arafat had contested. Sharon had designed the 1982 Israeli invasion of Lebanon and had colluded in the Sabra and Shatila massacre. His visit triggered a riot followed by Israeli suppression. The next day, a Friday, crowds of Muslims gathered at the al-Aqsa Mosque to demonstrate their displeasure. As they left the mosque, some threw stones at Israeli police, who responded with "withering fire": four Palestinians were killed and hundreds were injured.[54] Thus began the second intifada (see below).

Figure 8.1. Palestinian home dynamited by Israel to clear area through Rafah near wall dividing Gaza from Egypt. Courtesy David Whitten Smith, July 2005.

Taba Talks

Threatened with a vote of no confidence, Barak called early elections. At Taba, an Egyptian resort town, U.S. President Bill Clinton made one last effort in January 2001 to negotiate peace. These discussions significantly narrowed the gaps between the parties,[55] but Barak ended the talks without making any offers, claiming that the Israeli elections were too close.[56] He lost the elections to Ariel Sharon.

The Second (Al-Aqsa) Intifada

The second intifada had a more violent character than the first. Palestinian suicide bombings increased greatly. Israel regularly fired on Palestinian homes from helicopter gunships and tanks, dropped bombs, and launched rockets into Palestinian neighborhoods.

Ariel Sharon as Prime Minister

If Israelis expected Sharon to re-establish peace with a show of force, they got half of what they had voted for: shows of force, but no peace. As the situation spiraled downward, Palestinian violence continued and Israel assassinated selected Palestinian leaders—especially, but not exclusively, leaders of Hamas and of guerrilla groups that had carried out terrorist attacks; such extrajudicial murder violates international law. Early in 2002, Israel re-invaded Palestinian areas, killing more than two hundred Palestinians, wounding more than four hundred, and detaining more than four thousand; in addition, Israeli forces bulldozed more homes and buildings, cut trenches across highways, and uprooted fruit trees for what they claimed were security reasons. They closed down major areas of the West Bank and Gaza with twenty-three- or twenty-four-hour "curfews," forcing inhabitants to stay indoors for days at a time unable to buy food or medicines, and destroying the Palestinian economy.

Israel's Separation Barrier/Wall

In June 2002, Israel began to build a "separation barrier" allegedly to separate the West Bank from Israel as protection against terrorist infiltration. It consists of a wall or fence sandwiched between patrol roads, trenches, raked gravel, and electronic sensors, and guarded by watchtowers and firing posts every two hundred meters. In rural areas, the main "fence" is chain link and razor wire. In urban areas, it is a concrete wall eight meters high. It is constructed almost entirely within the West Bank (as much as twelve miles inside) in order to locate major Jewish settlements on the Israeli side of the barrier. About 10% of the West Bank, where over five thousand Palestinians live, lies on the Israeli side of the barrier. In 2003, these areas to the west of the barrier were declared "closed military zones." Palestinians need special permits to enter, exit, or live in them; Israeli settlers do not require these permits.[57] The main barrier with its subsidiary barriers and checkpoints to its east (inside the West Bank) cuts off Palestinian villages from their fields and often from their water supplies, schools, hospitals, and resources in other Palestinian villages. Construction of the wall has destroyed significant amounts of Palestinian farmland and uprooted thousands of productive olive trees. The Israeli government says it is protecting Israel from terrorists. Palestinians and international observers say it is confiscating West Bank land and water. They call it Israel's apartheid wall.

International Law on the Barrier

In July 2004, the International Court of Justice ruled overwhelmingly that the Israeli separation barrier was illegal by international law wherever it intruded on Palestinian land, including East Jerusalem, which Israel claims to have incorporated — a claim which the Court and the UN reject. The barrier would be legal if it were built on the Israeli side of the 1948 cease-fire line between Israel and the occupied territories. The court ordered Israel to cease building the intrusive sections, dismantle them where they exist, and make reparation for the damage caused; it also ordered other UN member countries to ensure that Israel complies with the ruling.[58]

The Geneva Accord

In late 2003 and early 2004 an unofficial group of Israeli and Palestinian leaders engaged in a "Geneva Initiative" leading to a "Geneva Accord," which proposed a detailed solution to the conflict and distributed it widely to both populations. The document follows closely the understandings reached at the Taba negotiations. For the first time, a publicly available document offers concrete solutions to most of the outstanding issues, although its proposals for refugees (to re-settle them in Israel, in Palestine, in the countries where they currently reside, or in other countries willing to accept them) depend on preferences of the refugees themselves and on the willingness of various countries to absorb them (with compensation). Also it says nothing about Palestinian citizens of the state of Israel. Hard-liners on both sides denounced the document and its signers, but it showed that there are partners on both sides willing to make compromises for peace. It also provided a benchmark against which other proposals can be measured.[59]

Gaza Redeployment

Also in 2004, Prime Minister Sharon announced his intention to close the Jewish settlements in Gaza and move out all Israelis—settlers and soldiers—relocating the settlers primarily in West Bank settlements. Religious Zionist settler groups strongly protested Israel's abandonment of any occupied territory. Israeli public opinion surveys showed a majority even of Israeli *settlers* supporting the plan, but Sharon's *Likud Party* was opposed, so he formed a new coalition government less dependent on Likud. A leading advisor to Sharon declared publicly that the purpose of the Gaza withdrawal was to kill the "peace process," providing "just enough formaldehyde" to prevent the formation of a Palestinian state. Sharon disavowed the statement.[60]

New Leadership in Palestine

In late 2004, Chairman Arafat died of an unexplained, and suspicious, illness. Mahmoud Abbas (Abu Mazen), elected to succeed him, had campaigned to use only nonviolent resistance to Israeli occupation. He convinced militant groups to cease their rocket and bomb attacks, sending Palestinian police to patrol the areas from which such attacks had most often been launched. Israel then ended proactive assassinations of militants and relaxed some major checkpoint controls.

In August 2005, the Israeli army moved all the Jewish settlers and soldiers out of Gaza. Gazans were concerned whether Israel would supply them with electricity and allow them to use their own water resources, to cross their border for travel and trade, to open and operate their airport, and to construct a seaport. Their fears were well placed. Israel continued to control the border of Gaza, its water, and its airspace. Claiming danger from terrorists, Israel kept the border closed for most of the harvest season, causing the Gazan export crop to spoil.

Palestinian Elections

Israel's hard line in Gaza came just as the Palestinians were campaigning for elections to their parliament, leaving Mahmoud Abbas with no success to show for his policy of nonviolence and conciliation. In democratic elections held in January 2006, Hamas captured a majority of the seats in Parliament and the right to create the new Palestinian government. Israel attempted to cripple the Hamas government by refusing to turn over the border duties which it collects on behalf of the Palestinian Authority. The U.S. Congress and the European Union also cut off funding to the Palestinians. As a result, Palestinian public school teachers and thousands of other civil servants went for months without salaries. In addition, Israel closed the crossings into Gaza for extended periods, causing severe shortages of food and medicine.

Israeli Elections

After the Gaza disengagement, Prime Minister Ariel Sharon proposed withdrawing from a few West Bank settlements, while strengthening the major settlements and the separation barrier. When his Likud Party objected, he formed a new party, *Kadima* (the Hebrew word means "Forward"—it also means "Eastward"). Then Sharon suffered a massive stroke and was succeeded by Ehud Olmert. In the elections of 2006, Kadima gained the largest number of seats in the Knesset and formed a government. Sharon had insisted that the separation barrier would not constitute the border with Palestine and could be moved or removed, but Olmert announced that the barrier would become the border; this policy is called "convergence." Palestinians maintain that borders cannot be set unilaterally.

In 2006, Gazans fired Qassam rockets into Israel and Israel attacked Gaza with shells, bombs, and helicopter gunships. When Gazan militants captured an Israeli soldier, Israel re-invaded Gaza, destroying the electric-generation plant on which its water and sewage systems depend. Soon after, Hezbollah fighters in Lebanon captured two more Israeli soldiers, triggering an Israeli re-invasion of Lebanon that had been long planned. The operation went badly—although Israel caused massive damage by bombing and invasion, it suffered heavy casualties, failed to defeat Hezbollah, and withdrew.

Hard-Line Religious Positions

The Israeli government refuses to negotiate with the Hamas government because Hamas does not recognize the legitimacy of the state of Israel. But neither does the Israeli government recognize as legitimate a Palestinian state in the pre-1967 territories nor internationally recognized borders. Here are some quotations from the Hamas Charter:

> The Islamic Resistance Movement is a distinguished Palestinian movement, whose allegiance is to Allah, and whose way of life is Islam. It strives to raise the banner of Allah over every inch of Palestine, for under the wing of Islam followers of all religions can coexist in security and safety where their lives, possessions and rights are concerned." (Article 6)

"The Islamic Resistance Movement believes that the land of Palestine is an Islamic Waqf [religious endowment] consecrated for future Moslem generations until Judgement Day. It, or any part of it, . . . should not be given up. Neither a single Arab country nor all Arab countries, neither any king or president, . . . neither any organization . . . possess the right to do that." (Article 11).[61]

Compare these statements with the platform (as of February 2007) of the Israeli Likud Party:

The Jewish communities in Judea, Samaria [that is, the West Bank] and Gaza are the realization of Zionist values. Settlement of the land is a clear expression of the unassailable right of the Jewish people to the Land of Israel and constitutes an important asset in the defense of the vital interests of the State of Israel. The Likud will continue to strengthen and develop these communities and will prevent their uprooting. . . . The Government of Israel flatly rejects the establishment of a Palestinian Arab state west of the Jordan river. . . . The Palestinians can run their lives freely in the framework of self-rule, but not as an independent and sovereign state. . . . The Jordan Valley and the territories that dominate it shall be under Israeli sovereignty. The Jordan river will be the permanent eastern border of the State of Israel.[62]

The new Kadima Party sees that claiming the whole of the West Bank and Gaza for Israel will lead to an Arab majority and produce a state which will be either non-Jewish or nondemocratic:

The Israeli nation has a national and historic right to the whole of Israel. However, in order to maintain a Jewish majority, part of the Land of Israel must be given up to maintain a Jewish and democratic state. Israel shall remain a Jewish state and homeland. Jewish majority in Israel will be preserved by territorial concessions to Palestinians. Jerusalem and large settlement blocks in the West Bank will be kept under Israeli control.[63]

SPOKESPERSONS FOR JUSTICE AND PEACE

Refuseniks

Israeli Defense Force officers and troops who in conscience refused their assignment to fight in Lebanon formed the group *Yesh Gevul,* which means "There is a border [limit]." That is, there is a border with Lebanon (or the occupied territories) that should be respected, and there is a limit to what Israel may do. Once the first intifada started, the movement also resisted assignment to the occupied territories. Recently, high-school age draft resisters (the

Shministim) have formed *Ometz Le'sarev* (Courage to Refuse) and New Profile.[64] As of this writing (February 26, 2007) there have been 1,673 public resisters to serving in the territories or Lebanon.[65] Resisters can be imprisoned for up to twelve months, then released, re-assigned to the occupied territories, and re-imprisoned—effectively being kept in jail without limit.[66] More commonly, resisters are given punitive assignments, sent home after a brief jail term, or reassigned outside the problem areas—the government does not want to draw attention to the issue. One refusenik, applying for conscientious objection status, said: "When I try to consider in what kind of a world I would like to live, I know that such a world does not include violence. . . . My refusal is one expression of my belief in . . . the power of nonviolent resistance."[67]

"Combatants for Peace" consists of former *Israeli and Palestinian* fighters who, having renounced their former violence, now cooperate nonviolently for a just and peaceful two-state settlement. They say, "Only by joining forces, will we be able to end the cycle of violence, the bloodshed and the occupation and oppression of the Palestinian people."[68]

Uri Avnery

Uri Avnery, a former member of the Knesset and author of the book *My Friend, the Enemy*, risked his life and reputation by traveling to Beirut to meet with Yasser Arafat when such contacts were illegal and considered treasonous. He founded the Israeli Council for Israeli-Palestinian Peace with the newsletter *The Other Israel*, and helped found *Gush Shalom*, which carries out nonviolent resistance to Israeli settlements in the occupied territories.[69]

International Peace Teams

Inspired by Gandhi's dream of nonviolent peace teams, several groups have organized teams of Israeli, Palestinian, and international nonviolence activists. From a largely secular perspective, the *International Solidarity Movement* (ISM)[70] was founded by Palestinians. Their website explains: "Internationals with the ISM are not in Palestine to teach nonviolent resistance. Palestinians resist nonviolently every day. The ISM lends support to the Palestinian resistance to the occupation and their demand for freedom through Direct Action . . . Emergency Mobilization . . . [and] Documentation."[71] The U.S. college student Rachel Corrie was serving as an ISM volunteer when she was killed in March 2003 by an Israeli bulldozer demolishing a home in Rafah (Gaza Strip) that she was trying to protect. Similar groups active in Israel-Palestine include, from a Protestant Peace Churches perspective, the *Christian Peacemaker Teams* (CPT: their website asks, "What would happen if Christians devoted the same discipline and self-sacrifice to nonviolent peacemaking that armies devote to war?")[72] and, from a largely Roman Catholic perspective, the *Michigan Peace Team* (MPT).[73]

Abuna Elias Chacour

Many Jews, Muslims, and Christians—religious, political, and educational leaders—have cooperated with the Palestinian Arab Christian priest Elias Chacour, who built an interfaith Christian-Muslim-Jewish grade school, high school, and college in Ibillin, Galilee.[74] In February 2006 he was elected Bishop of Akko, Haifa, Nazareth, and All of Galilee (whose territory includes all of Palestine and Israel) for the Melkite (Greek Catholic) Church.[75] He is the first Israeli citizen to be named a Catholic bishop. See his fascinating, moving, and mind-expanding books *Blood Brothers* and *We Belong to This Land*.

SUMMARY

After two millennia of Diaspora, the Jewish world community split between those who recommended assimilation or patience in exile and those who wished to establish an explicitly Jewish nation in Palestine despite the fact that another people were living there. The Holocaust tilted the scale decisively toward a Jewish state, although the majority of Jews still live outside Israel. The Zionist dream has been to establish (a) an explicitly Jewish state, (b) which is a Western-style democracy, (c) in the territory once controlled by the ancient kingdoms of Judah and Israel. Some Jews believe that this territory was promised to them by God, so they have an obligation to "redeem" it by settling there and dominating it—the dream requires major dispossession of its non-Jewish inhabitants. Even today, a border encompassing (c) would result in a Jewish minority, allowing at best either (a) a Jewish state, or (b) a democratic state, but not both. All three could be realized only by further dispossession.

Some Muslim Palestinians believe that the area is an Islamic Waqf—religious endowment given them by God—which they are required to preserve. Most Palestinians have not traditionally been committed to an Islamic government; they seek a secular state with freedom and justice for all faiths. All Palestinians suffer under the injustice of dispossession and illegal occupation. Efforts by Israel to encourage Palestinian emigration by making life in Palestine unlivable and by preventing refugees from exercising their right to return have failed to solve the problem. Israeli leaders dispute whether to accept less territory, at least temporarily, or to "transfer" the remaining Palestinians by force. To date, no Israeli government has been willing to propose a sovereign Palestinian state in all of the West Bank, including East Jerusalem, and Gaza, although the Palestinian Authority has said that it would accept such a solution.

Within Israeli society attitudes vary greatly, from settlers determined to retain control over all the land to peace activists nonviolently resisting their government's illegal military occupation of the West Bank and Gaza. Some Muslims and some Jews believe that religion requires them to exercise political control over all the land—incompatible positions that cannot both succeed. Others appeal to religious prophets who spoke for justice and compassion—suggesting some kind of sharing. Similar splits divide Christians between Zionists who support complete Jewish control and others who seek religiously based justice and compassionate nonviolence for all parties to the conflict.

Local and international political leaders have various reasons for supporting one party or another, combining religious convictions, compassion, and self-interest. Currently, the United States massively supports the state of Israel. How long Israel can count on support from a declining imperial power is a serious question.

FOR MORE INFORMATION

Check the reading list below and at the end of this book for works by Ateek, Avnery, Chacour, Ellis, and Ruether. For up-to-date references to many more groups and individuals, see the website for this book at www.stthomas.edu/justpeace/Rowman/ (under construction in February 2007).

KEY TERMS

access roads	"facts on the ground"
al-Aqsa Mosque	Al Fatah
apartheid wall	Gaza withdrawal
Balfour Declaration	Golan Heights
checkpoints	Gush Emunim
closed military zone	Gush Shalom
Deir Yassin	Haganah
Diaspora	Hamas

Hezbollah
Histadrut
International Solidarity Movement
intifada
Irgun
Israel Defense Forces
Jewish home
Jewish settlements
Jewish state
Judea
Kadima Party
Knesset
Kristallnacht
Labor Party
League of Nations mandate
Lebanese Phalange
Lehi
Likud Party
al-Nakhba
Noble Sanctuary
Oslo Accords
Ottoman Empire
Palestine Liberation Organization
Palestine National Congress

peace teams
PLO
Qassam rockets
redemption of land
refugees
Refuseniks
Revisionist Zionism
Sabra and Shatila
Samaria
security/separation barrier/wall
Special Night Squads
Stern Gang
Sykes-Picot Agreement
Temple Mount
terrorism
transfer
waqf
Western Wall
Women in Black
Women in Green
Yesh Gevul
Yishuv
Zionism

DISCUSSION QUESTIONS

1. Which of the fifteen character-types mentioned at the beginning of the chapter would be closest to representing your own approach to this conflict?

2. How much of the history presented here were you aware of from previous reading and from the media? How much of what you were *not* aware of is important for understanding the conflict?

3. Let each student role-play one of the character types or actual persons mentioned in the chapter by entering into conversation with other students over the history presented here: its accuracy and completeness, its biases, the significance of the various events, and appropriate responses.

4. Within the context of the conflict, discuss the appropriateness of the following terms and of the controversial realities they signify: apartheid, collective punishment, colonization, ethnic cleansing, facts on the ground, Holocaust, international law, intifada, martyrs, military necessity, nonvio-

lent action, occupation, occupied territories, racism, redeeming the land, self-defense, state terrorism, suicide bombing, targeted assassination, terrorism, transfer, Zionism.
5. How would you resolve the Israel-Palestinian conflict? What steps would you take to bring about justice and peace for both peoples?

NOTES

1. *The Holy Qur'ân*, trans. Yusuf Ali [1938; 1952], www.sacred-texts.com/isl/quran/index.htm (accessed March 2, 2007).
2. See Shahak and Mezvinsky, *Jewish Fundamentalism*, 18–19.
3. Population estimates are very difficult. See www.mideastweb.org/palpop.htm (accessed July 2, 2006).
4. Quoted in "Theodor Herzl," www.geocities.com/CapitolHill/Senate/7854/transfer03.html (accessed January 23, 2006), a section of Rabbi Dr. Chaim Simons, *A Historical Survey of Proposals to Transfer Arabs from Palestine, 1895–1947*. See footnote 55 in that work, "Theodor Herzl to Youssuf Zia Al-Khalidi, 19 March 1899 (CZA H iii D 13); Walid Khalidi, ed., *From Haven to Conquest* (Beirut, 1971), p. 92." This article helped identify the following quotations as well.
5. All quotations are from Herzl, *The Complete Diaries of Theodor Herzl*, 90. Used by permission of Herzl Press.
6. Herzl, *The Complete Diaries*, 90.
7. The most influential of Herzl's writings, while going into great detail on the character of the "Jewish State" he envisioned, scarcely mentioned the indigenous population at all. See Herzl, *The Jewish State*.
8. www.jafi.org.il/education/100/concepts/aliyah3.html (accessed January 22, 2006); www.jewishvirtuallibrary.org/jsource/Immigration/Second_Aliyah.html (accessed January 22, 2006).
9. www.jewishvirtuallibrary.org/jsource/History/hussmac1.html#1 (accessed January 22, 2006).
10. www.lib.byu.edu/~rdh/wwi/1916/sykespicot.html (accessed January 22, 2006).
11. www.lib.byu.edu/~rdh/wwi/1917/balfour.html (accessed January 22, 2006).
12. www.mideastweb.org/mandate.htm (accessed March 2, 2007).
13. Quoted in "The Histadrut," in "A History of Israel: From Dream to Reality" at www.historycentral.com/Israel/1920HistadrutFounded.html (accessed June 1, 2006).
14. Quoted in "Palestine," *Encyclopædia Britannica*, from Encyclopædia Britannica 2006 Ultimate Reference Suite DVD (accessed June 8, 2006).
15. www.wnyc.org/news/articles/898 (accessed June 1, 2006).
16. www.jnf.org/site/PageServer?pagename=history (accessed March 3, 2007).
17. Morris, *Righteous Victims*, 139.
18. The commission report is available at www.jewishvirtuallibrary.org/jsource/History/peel1.html (accessed June 11, 2006). See especially Section 10, "Exchange of Land and Population."

19. Morris, *Righteous Victims*, 139–44.

20. Flapan, *Zionism*, 116. He refers to Katz, *Days of Fire*, 31–37.

21. Quigley, *Palestine and Israel: A Challenge to Justice*, 26–27.

22. Quoted from the United States Holocaust Memorial Museum, www.ushmm .org/museum/exhibit/online/stlouis//teach/supread2.htm (accessed July 2, 2006).

23. www.mideastweb.org/biltmore_ program.htm (accessed July 2, 2006).

24. MidEast Web, www.mideastweb.org/briefhistory.htm (accessed June 12, 2006). Most sources put Jewish ownership at 7%, not 8% as quoted here.

25. This is UN Resolution 181, available at www.yale.edu/lawweb/avalon/un/ res181.htm (accessed June 11, 2006).

26. Report of UNSCOP—September 1, 1947. Available on MidEast Web at www.mideastweb.org/unscop1947.htm (accessed June 12, 2006).

27. Morris, *Birth of the Palestinian Refugee Problem Revisited*. See especially chapter 4: "The Second Wave: The Mass Exodus, April–June 1948," 163–308.

28. Morris, *Birth of the Palestinian Refugee Problem Revisited*, 163–308.

29. Morris, *Birth of the Palestinian Refugee Problem Revisited*, 171.

30. Morris, quoted in "Survival of the Fittest," by Ari Shavit, *Haaretz*, January 26, 2004, www.haaretz.com/hasen/pages/ShArt.jhtml?itemNo=380986&contrassID= (accessed January 26, 2004).

31. Morris, *Birth of the Palestinian Refugee Problem Revisited*, 181. See the whole of chap. 4, pp. 163–308.

32. Morris, *Birth of the Palestinian Refugee Problem Revisited*, 237–40.

33. Morris, *Birth of the Palestinian Refugee Problem Revisited*, 238 and n 566.

34. Begin, *The Revolt*, 164–65.

35. Truman's motives are highly controverted. See Cohen, *Truman and Israel*.

36. MidEast Web Historical Documents, United Nations General Assembly Resolution 194 (III), 11 December 1948. www.mideastweb.org/194.htm (accessed June 12, 2006).

37. Jews for Justice in the Middle East, *The Origin of the Palestine-Israel Conflict*, 14.

38. Available as appendix 1 (217–18) in Carter, *Palestine: Peace Not Apartheid*.

39. "The Israeli Committee against House Demolitions," www.icahd.org/eng/faq .asp?menu=9&submenu=1 (accessed February 10, 2007).

40. See, for example, the 1980 UN Resolution 465, available as appendix 5 (pp. 235–36) in Carter, *Palestine: Peace Not Apartheid*.

41. Available as appendix 2 (219) in Carter, *Palestine: Peace Not Apartheid*.

42. Available as appendix 3 (221–30) in Carter, *Palestine: Peace Not Apartheid*.

43. Carter, *Palestine: Peace Not Apartheid*, ch. 3 (37–53).

44. Bennis, *Palestinian-Israeli Conflict*, 63. Israel Defense Forces estimate 700; Bayan Nuwayhed al-Hout names 1,300 victims; Robert Fisk and the Palestinian Red Cross estimate 2,000; Amnon Kapeliouk of *Le Monde Diplomatique* estimates 3,000–3,500. See "Sabra and Shatila Massacre" at *Wikipedia*, en.wikipedia.org/wiki/ Sabra_and_Shatila_massacre (accessed July 3, 2006).

45. www.yale.edu/lawweb/avalon/mideast/hamas.htm (accessed July 2, 2006).

46. Interview with Khaled Mashaal in *Der Spiegel*, February 6, 2006.

47. Brilliant, "'Rabin Ordered Beatings', Meir Tells Military Court," and "Officer Tells Court Villagers Were Bound, Gagged and Beaten. Not Guilty Plea at 'Break Bones' Trial." See also "General Assembly Security Council A/43/166 S/19537 25 February 1988 DOCUMENT S/19537* Letter dated 24 February 1988 from the representative of Jordan to the Secretary-General," domino.un.org/UNISPAL.NSF/3822b5e39951876a85256b6e0058a478/cb4d8c6c519240ef852564050072199d!Open Document (accessed February 4, 2007).

48. Text available at www.yale.edu/lawweb/avalon/mideast/isrplo.htm (accessed July 2, 2006).

49. www.yale.edu/lawweb/avalon/mideast/isrplo.htm (accessed July 2, 2006).

50. A list of Hamas suicide bombings is available at en.wikipedia.org/wiki/List_of_Hamas_suicide_attacks; Palestinian Islamic Jihad bombings at en.wikipedia.org/wiki/List_of_Palestinian_Islamic_Jihad_suicide_attacks; and Al-Aqsa Martyrs' Brigades bombings at en.wikipedia.org/wiki/List_of_Al-Aqsa_Martyrs%27_Brigades_suicide_attacks (accessed February 10, 2007).

51. See www.jewishvirtuallibrary.org/jsource/Peace/tiph5.html (accessed February 10, 2007).

52. Morris, *Righteous Victims*, 646–49.

53. Bennis, *Palestinian-Israeli Conflict*, 53–54. For a projection of the Final Status Map showing what Barak was offering, see www.fmep.org/maps/map_data/redeployment/projection_final_status_map.gif (accessed July 2, 2006), and for maps in general on Israel-Palestine, "Report on Israeli Settlement in the Occupied Territories," www.fmep.org/maps/overview.html (accessed July 2006).

54. Bennis, *Palestinian-Israeli Conflict*, 42. See also Morris, *Righteous Victims*, 660.

55. The following notes taken by Miguel Moratinos, the European representative to the talks, were leaked to the press. Israel said they were not accurate, and Israel was not bound to these views. www.jewishvirtuallibrary.org/jsource/Peace/Taba.html (accessed July 2, 2006).

56. Carter, *Palestine: Peace Not Apartheid*, 152.

57. "Israel's 'Separation Barrier' in the Occupied West Bank: Human Rights and International Humanitarian Law Consequences—A Human Rights Watch Briefing Paper," February 2004. hrw.org/english/docs/2004/02/20/isrlpa7581.htm (accessed June 18, 2006).

58. electronicintifada.net/cgi-bin/artman/exec/view.cgi/10/2890 (accessed July 2, 2006).

59. The official English-language website of the Geneva Initiative is www.geneva-accord.org/HomePage.aspx?FolderID=11&lang=en (accessed June 18, 2006). The full text of the Accord is at www.genevaaccord.org/Accord.aspx?FolderID=33&lang=en (accessed June 18, 2006). For results of a 2003 poll of Israeli and Palestinian attitudes toward this proposal in general and in detail, see www.ccmep.org/2003_articles/Palestine/122003_survey_of_palestinian.htm (accessed June 18, 2006).

60. Mike Whitney, "Embalming the Peace Process," *Z-net,* October 15, 2004, www.zmag.org/content/showarticle.cfm?ItemID=6428 (accessed July 2, 2006).

61. www.yale.edu/lawweb/avalon/mideast/hamas.htm (accessed July 2, 2006).

62. Excerpts from the 'Peace & Security' chapter of the Likud Party platform, www.knesset.gov.il/elections/knesset15/elikud_m.htm (accessed February 5, 2007).

63. en.wikipedia.org/wiki/Kadima (accessed February 5, 2007). See also the official Kadima website at www.kadimasharon.co.il/11-en/index.aspx (accessed February 25, 2007).

64. See their combined website (Refuser Solidarity Network) at www.refuser solidarity.net/default.asp (accessed July 2, 2006).

65. www.refusersolidarity.net/default.asp (accessed February 26, 2007).

66. Update June 1, 2006, at www.refusersolidarity.net/default.asp?content_new= prison_update_1_06 (accessed June 19, 2006).

67. www.refusersolidarity.net/default.asp?content_new=prison_update_1_06 (accessed June 19, 2006).

68. www.combatantsforpeace.org/. For the quotation, click on "About Us" (accessed February 25, 2007).

69. zope.gushshalom.org/home/en (accessed July 2, 2006).

70. www.palsolidarity.org/ (accessed July 5, 2006).

71. www.palsolidarity.org/main/about-ism/ (accessed July 5, 2006).

72. www.cpt.org/ (accessed July 5, 2006).

73. michiganpeaceteam.org/mpt/ (accessed July 5, 2006).

74. His Mar Elias Educational Institutions have a website at www.meei.org/ (accessed September 10, 2007).

75. See the website of the Melkite Greek Catholic Church Information Center at www.mliles.com/melkite/abounaeliaschacour.shtml (accessed July 5, 2006).

SUGGESTIONS FOR FURTHER READING

Ateek. *Justice, and Only Justice.*
Ateek, ed. *Faith and the Intifada.*
Avishai. *The Tragedy of Zionism.*
Avnery. *Israel and the Palestinians.*
———. *My Friend, the Enemy.*
Begin. *The Revolt: Story of the Irgun.*
Beit-Hallahmi. *The Israeli Connection.*
———. *Original Sins.*
Bennis. *Understanding the Palestinian-Israeli Conflict.*
Carter. *Palestine: Peace Not Apartheid.*
Chacour. *Blood Brothers.*
Chomsky and Herman. *Middle East Illusions.*
Ellis. *Beyond Innocence and Redemption.*
Farber. *Radicals, Rabbis and Peacemakers.*
Flapan. *The Birth of Israel: Myths and Realities.*
———. *Zionism and the Palestinians.*
Herzl. *The Complete Diaries of Theodor Herzl.*

Jews for Justice in the Middle East. *The Origin of the Palestine-Israel Conflict*.
Katz. *Days of Fire.*
Khalidi, ed. *From Haven to Conquest.*
London Sunday Times. The Yom Kippur War.
Lucas. *The Modern History of Israel.*
Morris. *The Birth of the Palestinian Refugee Problem Revisited.*
———. *Righteous Victims.*
Ruether and Ruether. *The Wrath of Jonah.*
Ruether and Ellis, eds. *Beyond Occupation.*
Schiff and Ya'ari. *Intifada.*
Shahak. *Jewish History, Jewish Religion.*
Shahak and Mezvinsky. *Jewish Fundamentalism in Israel.*
Tessler. *A History of the Israeli-Palestinian Conflict.*

Chapter Nine

Christian Social Teachings

"Towards the end of the last century the Church found herself facing . . . a critical point. A traditional society was passing away and another was beginning to be formed—one which brought the hope of new freedoms but also the threat of new forms of injustice and servitude. . .

"In the sphere of economics, . . . new structures for the production of consumer goods had progressively taken shape. A new form of property had appeared—capital; and a new form of labor—labor for wages, characterized by high rates of production which lacked due regard for sex, age or family situation, and were determined solely by efficiency, with a view to increasing profits.

"Labor became a commodity to be freely bought and sold on the market, its price determined by the law of supply and demand, without taking into account the bare minimum required for the support of the individual and his family. Moreover, the worker was not even sure of being able to sell 'his own commodity,' continually threatened as he was by unemployment, which, in the absence of any kind of social security, meant the specter of death by starvation.

"The result . . . was a society 'divided into two classes, separated by a deep chasm'. . .

"At the height of this clash, when people finally began to realize fully the very grave injustice of social realities . . . and the danger of a revolution . . . Pope Leo XIII . . . dealt in a systematic way with the 'condition of the workers.'"

—Pope John Paul II, *Centesimus Annus*, par. 4[1]

HIGHLIGHTS OF CHRISTIAN
SOCIAL CONCERN THROUGH HISTORY

Jesus' teaching and practice of wealth sharing is reflected in the history of Christianity, as these instances illustrate:

Jesus himself associated with sinners and the poor: nobodies. The early community in Jerusalem "shared all things in common" (Acts 2:44). Christian communities had deacons to share community alms with the poor. Christian preachers insisted that Christians had a responsibility toward the poor, whether Christian or non-Christian. They attacked ill-gained riches and the selfishness of the rich. John Chrysostom, especially noted for such attacks, was exiled by the Empress Eudoxia.

After the persecutions ended, many Christians went into the desert and became hermits, renouncing possessions in favor of prayer. From about the 4th century in the Eastern Roman Empire, hermits began to come together and form communities called monasteries, typically in the rural areas.

In the early Middle Ages in Europe, Francis of Assisi and Dominic formed new orders of friars (from the Latin word for "brother") who owned nothing but lived in the cities, challenging contemporary ideas about riches. These orders were called *mendicant*—"begging" in Latin. Nursing orders provided much-needed social service and medical care, anticipating modern Christian hospitals.

The Papal States

When barbarian invaders destroyed political power in Rome, the popes offered the only effective civil leadership. Constantine had moved the capital of the Roman Empire to Constantinople in the 4th century, leaving little effective authority behind in Rome. This civil leadership of the popes gradually developed into the "Papal States" in (central) Italy—states in which the pope was the civil ruler and many administrative functions were carried on by priests. For some centuries the popes were involved in civil power struggles and intrigues. The Papal States were only abolished in 1870, when Giuseppe Garibaldi marched on Rome as part of his campaign to unify Italy. As Garibaldi approached Rome, the pope directed his army and police not to resist the invader, and moved into the Vatican in a self-imposed exile. Shortly before the Second World War, Mussolini recognized the Vatican City State as a civil territory, thus settling the uncertain situation of the papacy that had existed since 1870.

Settlement of the New World

When they first encountered the "New World," many Europeans enslaved the indigenous inhabitants. Some of the religious leaders who accompanied the conquerors accepted this situation, believing that they could make converts more easily if the Europeans were dominant. Others, like Bartholomé de Las Casas, the first bishop of Chiapas, Mexico, strongly and courageously resisted the injustices. In *North* America, in contrast to Latin America, rather than enslaving the natives, settlers tended to appropriate the land and just push the native people away.

ROMAN CATHOLIC SOCIAL TEACHING

In the 19th century, industrialization was radically altering society in Europe and North America, creating great tensions.

Pope Leo XIII (1810–1903; pope from 1878)

Leo XIII published as an *encyclical* the first of the modern papal documents on social teaching. An encyclical is a papal circular letter sent to all bishops of the world dealing with some problem of common interest to the church. Leo's encyclical, *Rerum Novarum* (1891), dealt with the problems raised by recent social changes. He listed injustices connected with the changes, some matching those earlier attacked by Karl Marx, but he rejected Marx's analysis and proposals. Leo challenged the rich to accept responsibility for the common good, and proposed a new system of *guilds* to organize workers and managers. He wanted workers and managers to cooperate for the common good rather than fight each other in class struggle.

Private Property

Leo supported *private ownership* of property, but what his *arguments* actually supported was *widely distributed* ownership of *modest amounts* of property. He did not want a few people to own so much property that most people could own nothing. He argued that people care for property better when they own it, they have more incentive to work well, and they have the security of being able to pass something on to their children. Notice that he is talking primarily about *workers* owning property.

> If a workman's wages be sufficient to enable him comfortably to support himself, his wife, and his children, he will find it easy . . . to practice thrift, and he

will not fail, by cutting down expenses, to put by some little savings and thus secure a modest source of income. . . . The law, therefore, should . . . induce as many as possible of the people to become owners. (par. 46)

Many excellent results will follow from this; and, first of all, property will certainly become more equitably divided. (par. 47)

Leo encouraged employers and workers to cooperate: a fair day's work for a fair wage. He suggested new social forms for such cooperation, proposing a *corporative state* where worker-management cooperation would be promoted by the political and economic structures of the society itself. The idea was to develop political and economic structures by which different classes in society could be represented as classes and thus feel that they were part of a cooperative venture. "The great mistake is to [think] that class is naturally hostile to class. . . . The direct contrary is the truth. . . . Capital cannot do without labor, nor labor without capital." (par. 19)

Pope Pius XI (1857–1939; pope from 1922)

In 1931, Pope Pius XI wrote the encyclical *Quadragesimo Anno* (Forty Years Ago) confirming and bringing up to date Leo's ideas. Fascist and Nazi thinkers had claimed to be developing Leo's idea of a corporative state. Rather than having the legislature represent *territorial districts*, as is the case in most democracies (local precincts and wards drawn without regard to what type of people lived in them), they designed it to represent different *economic groups*: industrialists, labor unions, farmers, universities, etc. Their system sounded good in theory, but in practice the government ended up controlling all the institutions of society. Pius responded that their system was not what Leo had in mind.

Subsidiarity

Pius XI introduced the principle of *subsidiarity*: "It is an injustice and . . . a grave evil and disturbance of right order to assign to a greater and higher association what lesser and subordinate organizations can do. For every social activity ought of its very nature to furnish *help* to the members of the body social, and never *destroy and absorb* them." (par. 79, emphases added)

Note the *two* characteristics of subsidiarity: (1) higher levels of political (and economic) organization should not take over responsibilities that lower levels can accomplish (that is, we should push control and decision-making to the lowest level at which it can be effectively done), but (2) higher levels should give aid (Latin: *subsidium*) to the lower levels to enable them to do what they can. The aid (subsidium) is what gives subsidiarity its name. Notice its relation to our word "subsidy," although we tend to connect subsidies solely with money, whereas the word *subsidium* actually refers to any kind of aid.

Example: (1) local school boards control the schools, but (2) they get state and federal *subsidies* to help even out inequality between wealthy neighborhoods and poor ones. State and federal departments of education also provide *expert advice* and programs to local schools.

Pius objected to injustices against workers even more strongly than Leo had. Leo had proposed workers' organizations, but he had in mind something like the ancient guilds. Pius more clearly supported the new *manufacturing unions* that were coming into being: "Dead matter comes forth from the factory ennobled, while men[2] there are corrupted and degraded" (par. 135). Given the mixed record of communism in Russia, Pius warned Christians against the kind of *socialism* that had developed there. Note also that the Nazi Party in Germany called itself the *National Socialist* Party.

Then the Second World War claimed everyone's attention.

Pope John XXIII (1881–1963; pope from 1958)

Shortly before the Second Vatican Council opened, on the 70th anniversary of *Rerum Novarum*, Pope John XXIII published the encyclical *Mater et Magistra* (Mother and Teacher). To the previous concerns, he added agriculture and aid to developing countries. He was much more open to socialist ideas than earlier popes had been, leading some elite Catholics to respond, "Mater, si; Magistra, no." In his encyclical the pope wrote:

> Probably the most difficult problem today concerns the relationship between political communities that are economically advanced and those in the process of development. . . . The solidarity which binds all men together as members of a common family makes it impossible for wealthy nations to look with indifference upon the hunger, misery and poverty of other nations whose citizens are unable to enjoy even elementary human rights. (par. 157)

Two years later Pope John published *Pacem in Terris* (1963). This was the first papal encyclical addressed not just to Catholics through their bishops but to "all people of good will." Published shortly after the Cuban Missile Crisis and the building of the Berlin Wall, it dealt mainly with human rights and a better organization of international society. Among the new topics was the right of people to emigrate from one country to another:

> Every human being has the right to freedom of movement and of residence within the confines of his own State. When there are just reasons in favor of it,

he must be permitted to emigrate to other countries and take up residence there.
[22] The fact that he is a citizen of a particular State does not deprive him of
membership in the human family, nor of citizenship in that universal society, the
common, worldwide fellowship of men. (par. 25)

Second Vatican Council (1962–1965)

The Second Vatican Council produced the document *Gaudium et Spes* (Pastoral Constitution on the Church in the Modern World), which speaks of recognizing the "signs of the times"—the special circumstances, opportunities,
and responsibilities of each historical period. There has been much contro-
versy over what these signs are and what they mean:

> The Church has always had the duty of scrutinizing the signs of the times and
> of interpreting them in the light of the Gospel. Thus, in language intelligible to
> each generation, she can respond to the perennial questions which men ask
> about this present life and the life to come, and about the relationship of the one
> to the other. We must therefore recognize and understand the world in which we
> live, its explanations, its longings, and its often dramatic characteristics. (par. 4)

**Figure 9.1. American Catholic preist, Charlie
Hardy, with neighbors in Nueva Taagua,
Venezuela, a *barrio* outside Caracas,
Venezuela. Courtesy David Whitten Smith,
October 1988.**

Pope Paul VI (1897–1978; Pope from 1963)

In 1967 Pope Paul published *Populorum Progressio*, moving from the struggle between rich and poor *classes* to that between rich and poor *nations*. The letter came out during the "decade of development" that was supposed to bring the developing countries closer to the rich countries. (See the following chapter on liberation theologies.) Paul VI challenged the church (dioceses and religious orders) to share 10% of their resources—both money and personnel—with Latin America. He proposed a world fund financed by money saved by reducing the arms race. He criticized major aspects of capitalism:

> Certain concepts have somehow arisen out of these new conditions and insinuated themselves into the fabric of human society: . . . profit as the chief spur to economic progress, free competition as the guiding norm of economics, and private ownership of the means of production as an absolute right, having no limits nor concomitant social obligations. This unbridled liberalism paves the way for a particular type of tyranny . . . the 'international imperialism of money.' . . . But if it is true that a type of capitalism . . . has given rise to hardships, unjust practices, and fratricidal conflicts that persist to this day, it would be a mistake to attribute these evils to the rise of industrialization itself, for they really derive from the pernicious economic concepts that grew up along with it. We must . . . acknowledge the vital role played by labor systemization and industrial organization in the task of development. (par. 26)

Paul VI observed the 80th anniversary of *Rerum Novarum* by writing *Octogesima Adveniens* (1971)—not an encyclical but an "apostolic letter" to the president of the Pontifical Commission on Justice and Peace. In it he discussed the problems of urbanization and considered how Christians and local churches could respond to injustice: "Man is experiencing a new loneliness; it is not in the face of a hostile nature which it has taken him centuries to subdue, but in an anonymous crowd which surrounds him and in which he feels himself a stranger. Urbanization, undoubtedly an irreversible stage in the development of human societies, confronts man with difficult problems" (par. 10).

The 1971 worldwide synod of Catholic bishops produced a document on world justice:[3]

> We have . . . been able to perceive the serious injustices which are building around the world of men a network of domination, oppression and abuses which stifle freedom and which keep the greater part of humanity from sharing in the building up and enjoyment of a more just and more fraternal world. [par. 3] . . . Action on behalf of justice and participation in the transformation of the world fully appear to us as *a constitutive dimension of the preaching of the gospel*, or,

in other words, of the Church's mission for the redemption of the human race and its liberation from every oppressive situation. (par. 6, emphasis added)

Paul VI also published the apostolic exhortation *Evangelii Nuntiandi* on "evangelization in the modern world"—sharing the good news of the Gospel—in which he claimed that you can't preach the Gospel without combating injustice:

> Evangelization would not be complete if it did not take account of the unceasing interplay of the Gospel and of man's concrete life, both personal and social. This is why evangelization involves an explicit message . . . about the rights and duties of every human being, about family life without which personal growth and development is hardly possible, about life in society, about international life, peace, justice and development—a message especially energetic today about liberation. (par. 29)

Pope John Paul II (1920–2005; pope from 1978)

Pope John Paul II commemorated the 90th anniversary of *Rerum Novarum* with the encyclical *Laborem Exercens* (On Human Work). It presented a powerful and novel treatment of human work, criticized both capitalism and Marxism, and emphasized that human work is always more important than capital. The following paragraph illustrates the Church's support for labor unions:

> There is a need for ever new *movements of solidarity of* the workers and *with* the workers. . . . whenever it is called for by the social degrading of the subject of work, by exploitation of the workers, and by the growing areas of poverty and even hunger. The Church is firmly committed to this cause, for she considers it her mission, her service, a proof of her fidelity to Christ, so that she can truly be the "Church of the poor." (par. 8; emphases are in original)

The encyclical emphasized how important work is for humans. It enables them to (a) express themselves in a creative way, (b) support their own families, and (c) make a contribution to the larger society.

It also defined capital and labor in a new way. For John Paul, management is not capital. All human activity is labor. Capital is the tools of production that humans make and use. Managers are doing one form of labor; workers on the line are doing another. The assembly line itself is one form of capital; the books in the manager's library are another. In this sense, labor always has priority over capital because people have priority over things:

> [W]e must first of all recall . . . *the priority of labour over capital* . . . labour is always a primary *efficient cause,* while capital, the whole collection of means of

production, remains a mere *instrument* or instrumental cause. . . . Everything that comes from man throughout the whole process of economic production, whether labour or the whole collection of means of production and the technology connected with these means (meaning the capability to use them in work), presupposes these riches and resources of the visible world, riches and resources *that man finds* and does not create. . . . At the beginning of man's work is the mystery of creation. . . . All the means of production . . . *everything that is at the service of work*, everything that in the present state of technology constitutes its ever more highly perfected 'instrument,' *is the result of work.* . . . Everything contained in the concept of capital . . . is only a collection of things. Man, as the subject of work, and independently of the work that he does—man alone is a person. (par. 12, emphases in original)

In 1988, on the twentieth anniversary of *Populorum Progressio,* John Paul II published *Sollicitudo Rei Socialis* (On Social Concern). This letter is noteworthy for its strong emphasis on the reality of *structural sin.*

Structural Sin

"Structural sin" refers to unjust laws, customs, situations, and habitual ways of doing things. Slavery is an example of structural sin—it was held in place by laws, but also by custom and habit. Racial segregation is a structural sin. Gender injustice is a structural sin. So is U.S. urban homelessness, although in that case the structures that hold it in place are less obvious.

In *Sollicitudo Rei Socialis* Pope John Paul points out the relationship between personal sin and structural sin: those who cause, intensify, protect, or share in the unjust fruits of—or fail to combat—unjust political, economic, and other structures are guilty of personal sin. We may fail to combat these structures because we or our friends are benefiting from them, because we are too apathetic to be bothered, or because we are afraid we may get hurt or lose friends if we object:

It is not out of place to speak of "structures of sin," which . . . are rooted in personal sin, and thus always linked to the concrete acts of individuals who introduce these structures, consolidate them and make them difficult to remove.[65] And thus they grow stronger, spread, and become the source of other sins, and so influence people's behavior. (par. 36)

Here is the "[note] 65" referred to in par. 36 above:

Whenever the Church speaks of situations of sin, or when she condemns as social sins certain situations or the collective behavior of certain social groups . . . she knows . . . that such cases of social sin are the result of the accumulation and concentration of many personal sins . . . of those who cause or support evil or who exploit it; of those who are in a position to avoid, eliminate or at least limit certain social evils but who fail to do so out of laziness, fear or the conspiracy of silence, through secret complicity or indifference; of those who take refuge in the supposed impossibility of changing the world, and also of those who side-step the effort and sacrifice required. . . . The real responsibility, then, lies with individuals. A situation—or likewise an institution, a structure, society itself— is not in itself the subject of moral acts.

The Hundredth Year

Finally in 1991, John Paul published the encyclical *Centesimus Annus*. In it he "re-read" *Rerum Novarum* in the light of the human person as uniquely valuable—made in God's image and destined to spend eternity with God. He re-emphasized the importance of human solidarity, both affirmed and criti-cized key concepts of capitalism, and called for a new economic system now that communism had collapsed and capitalism in its current forms had proved inadequate. He affirmed the value of free markets, but only when wealth is well enough distributed to give all humans significant buying power to "vote" in the market:

> It would appear that . . . the *free market* is the most efficient instrument for uti-lizing resources and effectively responding to needs. But this is true only for those needs which are "solvent," insofar as they are endowed with purchasing power, and for those resources which are "marketable," insofar as they are ca-pable of obtaining a satisfactory price. But there are many human needs which find no place on the market. It is a strict duty of justice and truth not to allow fundamental human needs to remain unsatisfied, and not to allow those bur-dened by such needs to perish. It is also necessary to help these needy people to acquire expertise, to enter the circle of exchange, and to develop their skills in order to make the best use of their capacities and resources. (par. 34)
>   [I]t is right to speak of a struggle against an economic system, if the latter is understood as a method of upholding the absolute predominance of capital, the possession of the means of production and of the land, in contrast to the free and personal nature of human work.[73] In the struggle against such a system, what is being proposed as an alternative is not the socialist system, which in fact turns out to be State capitalism, but rather *a society of free work, of enterprise and of participation*. Such a society is not directed against the market, but demands that the market be appropriately controlled by the forces of society and by the State, so as to guarantee that the basic needs of the whole of society are satisfied . . . profitability is not the only indicator of a firm's condition. It is possible for the financial accounts to be in order, and yet for the people—who make up the firm's most valuable asset—to be humiliated and their dignity offended. . . . The purpose of a business firm is not simply to make a profit, but is to be found in its very existence as a *community of persons* who in various ways are endeav-ouring to satisfy their basic needs, and who form a particular group at the ser-

vice of the whole of society. Profit is a regulator of the life of a business, but it is not the only one; *other human and moral factors* must also be considered which, in the long term, are at least equally important for the life of a business. (par. 35, emphases in original)

It is not wrong to want to live better; what is wrong is a style of life which is presumed to be better when it is directed towards "having" rather than "being," and which wants to have more, not in order to be more but in order to spend life in enjoyment as an end in itself.[75] It is therefore necessary to create life-styles in which the quest for truth, beauty, goodness and communion with others for the sake of common growth are the factors which determine consumer choices, savings and investments. . . . *Even the decision to invest in one place rather than another, in one productive sector rather than another, is always a moral and cultural choice.* . . . The decision to invest, that is, to offer people an opportunity to make good use of their own labour, is also determined by an attitude of human sympathy and trust in Providence, *which reveal the human quality of the person making such decisions.* (par. 36, last two emphases added)

Centesimus Annus also gives significant new attention to problems of the environment.

Social Teaching of Groups of Catholic Bishops

National and regional groups of Catholic bishops were also studying social justice. The United States Catholic bishops produced pastoral letters on nuclear war (1983) and on economic issues (1986). Here are some key passages from the bishops' pastoral letter on nuclear war, *The Challenge of Peace: God's Promise and Our Response*:[4]

Under no circumstances may nuclear weapons or other instruments of mass slaughter be used for the purpose of destroying population centers or other predominantly civilian targets. (par. 147)

Retaliatory action whether nuclear or conventional which would indiscriminately take many wholly innocent lives, lives of people who are in no way responsible for reckless actions of their government, must also be condemned. This condemnation, on our judgment, applies even to the retaliatory use of weapons striking enemy cities after our own have already been struck. *No Christian can rightfully carry out orders or policies deliberately aimed at killing noncombatants.* (par. 148, emphasis added)

We do not perceive any situation in which the deliberate initiation of nuclear warfare, on however restricted a scale, can be morally justified. (par. 150)

These considerations . . . lead us to a strictly conditioned moral acceptance of nuclear deterrence. We cannot consider it adequate as a long-term basis for peace. (par. 186)

And from *Economic Justice for All: Pastoral Letter on Catholic Social Teaching and the U.S. Economy*:[5]

> Every perspective on economic life that is human, moral, and Christian must be shaped by three questions: What does the economy do *for* people? What does it do *to* people? And how do people *participate* in it? (par. 1, emphases in original)
>   The dignity of the human person, realized in community with others, is the criterion against which all aspects of economic life must be measured. (par. 28)
>   The obligation to provide justice for all means that the poor have the single most urgent economic claim on the conscience of the nation. (par. 86)
>   (a) The fulfillment of the basic needs of the poor is of the highest priority . . . (b) Increasing active participation in economic life by those who are presently excluded or vulnerable is a high social priority . . . (c) The investment of wealth, talent, and human energy should be specially directed to benefit those who are poor or economically insecure . . . (d) Economic and social policies as well as the organization of the work world should be continually evaluated in light of their impact on the strength and stability of family life. (par. 90–93)

Perhaps the most important feature of these two letters is the process by which they were written. They were published in three drafts, with comments invited on the first two drafts from anyone who cared to offer them. This process gave rise to extensive comments, so that the final product was the result of much more democratic sharing than is usual for church documents. For this reason among others, the documents have had a much wider influence than is usual for bishops' pastoral letters.

Latin American Bishops

In Latin America, after the Second Vatican Council, the bishops moved quickly to establish the Conferencia Episcopal Latino-Americana, abbreviated CELAM. Their second and third meetings, in *Medellin,* Colombia, and in *Puebla,* Mexico, were most significant. In Medellin the bishops committed themselves to a "preferential option for the poor"—meaning that, when resources are limited, the poor deserve help first. They applied the principle quite radically:

> A business, in an authentically human economy, does not identify itself with the owners of capital, because it is fundamentally a community of persons and a unit of work, which is in need of capital to produce goods. A person or a group of persons cannot be the property of an individual, or a society, or of the state.
>   The system of liberal capitalism and the temptation of the Marxist system would appear to exhaust the possibilities of transforming the economic structures of our continent. Both systems militate against the dignity of the human

person. One takes for granted the primacy of capital . . . in the function of profit-making. The other, although it ideologically supports a kind of humanism, is more concerned with collective man, and in practice becomes a totalitarian concentration of state power. We must denounce the fact that Latin America sees itself caught between these two options and remains dependent on one or other of the [foreign] centers of power which control its economy. (Document on Justice, par. 10)[6]

Summary of Catholic Social Teaching

The great wealth of Catholic social teaching is frequently summarized in the following nine principles:[7]

1. *Dignity of the human person.* Every human person is sacred because God makes humans in God's own image and likeness and gives them an eternal destiny. People do not lose dignity because of their race, sex, nationality, age, disability, poverty, or lack of success. People are more important than things; what we *are* is more important than what we *have*.[8]
2. *Realized in community.* This "human dignity can be realized and protected only in community."[9] The human person is both sacred and social.
3. *Involving rights, responsibilities, and the common good.* This dignity in community implies that people have rights (civil, political, and economic) and responsibilities. People have a fundamental right to "life, food, clothing, shelter, rest, medical care, education and employment."[10] Society as a whole has the responsibility to organize itself in such a way that these rights will be provided for all.[11] Corresponding to these rights are duties and responsibilities to respect the rights of others and to work for the common good.
4. *Not just given, but participated in.* All people also have a right to *participate* in economic life and in the decisions and activities that affect their lives.[12]
5. *Through dignified and productive work.* The right to participate in society includes the right to meaningful work which enables people (a) to express themselves through their talents and initiative, (b) to support their families through fair wages, and (c) to contribute to the larger society.[13]
6. *Marked by subsidiarity.* Humans carry on their work in association with other people. As we saw above, subsidiarity involves two principles:
   a. What individuals can accomplish by their own initiative and industry should not be taken from them and given to the community; what lesser and subordinate organizations can accomplish should not be taken over by larger or higher associations.

  b. If individuals or lesser organizations need help (financial, technical, or-
     ganizational) to accomplish these tasks, the higher associations should
     provide that aid (*subsidium*).[14]
7. *Solidarity and the universal destination of the earth's goods.* We are all related as members of one human family that is only superficially divided
   by race, sex, nation, ideology, and class. The riches of the earth are intended for all humans. We may or may not be responsible for *causing* injustice, but we are all responsible to work to *end* it.[15]
8. *With special attention to the poor.* Because we are all related, and because
   much poverty is a result of injustice, not simply of misfortune, the poor
   have the most urgent moral claim on the conscience of the nation. A society is judged on how it treats its most vulnerable members. Decisions on
   public policy should be judged especially in terms of how they affect the
   poor.[16]
9. *Maintaining care for God's creation.* The goods of the earth are gifts from
   God. We have a responsibility to care for these goods as stewards and
   trustees, not as mere consumers and users, both because we recognize our
   solidarity with future generations and because we revere God's creation
   for its own sake.[17]

   In their document *Economic Justice for All*, the U.S. Catholic bishops explain how its treatment of justice differs from philosophical treatments of justice that deal with individual human rights: "Biblical justice is more comprehensive than subsequent philosophical definitions. It is not concerned with a
strict definition of rights and duties, but with the rightness of the human condition before God and within society. Nor is justice opposed to love; rather, it
is both a manifestation of love and a condition for love to grow."[18]

Five Key Concepts (The Five S's)

Five concepts can encapsulate and help us remember key points of Catholic
social teaching: solidarity, sharing fairly, subsidiarity, structural and cultural
change, and simple living. The numbers in parentheses refer to the nine principles explained above.

Solidarity. "Love your neighbor as yourself" (including even "love your
enemy") presumes that our neighbor, whether now alive or yet to be born
(principle 9), is, like us, a human being with an eternal destiny (1) with needs
like our own, dependent on the goods of God's creation (7). So our brother or
sister should be treated with dignity (1), in community with ourselves (2),
with rights as well as responsibilities (3) that require him or her to be accepted
as a participant (4). Each one needs dignified and productive work (5) which

calls on all of her or his skills, including skills of planning and decision-making (6). No one is to be left out, so the poor need special help (7).

Sharing Fairly. If we truly love our brother and sister as ourselves, we will share goods and burdens fairly with each other. Goods include created resources (7), the fruits of human labor (5), and access to basic human institutions (2) such as health care and education. Goods also include the opportunity to participate in decisions that affect one's life (4, 6). Burdens include work (4), compromise for the sake of common effort (2), and risks such as crime and pollution (9). Positive externalities of economic life, such as the human development that comes from having responsibility and making decisions (4–6), need to be shared fairly, as do negative externalities such as depletion and pollution (9).

Subsidiarity. Community (2) involves division of labor, but in such a way that work challenges the full humanity of the worker and allows workers to express themselves (5), and in such a way that decision-making is shared as widely and democratically as possible (6).

Structural and Cultural Change. Solidarity and fair sharing of both resources and decision-making (subsidiarity) require changes in the structures which organize our society. An example would be unfair laws and rules for international trade. We also need to change the cultural practices and explanations that attempt to justify unjust structures. (Johan Galtung calls such explanations "cultural violence.") An example would be arguments in favor of "free trade" that fail to point out how current trade rules maintain U.S. agricultural subsidies while insisting that Third World countries eliminate food subsidies. Such changes require courage (because those who benefit from the status quo will attack those who try to change the structures) and commitment of resources (time and money).

Simple Living. Sharing fairly (7, 8) presupposes that we have something to share. The consumer society, driven by advertising, threatens to devour all our resources, leaving us nothing to share. So an authentic Christian life includes resistance to the lure of possession, and choice of a simple life that will leave us with resources to share. Such a life may leave us poorer in material goods but richer in relationships with our brothers and sisters—and with God. Indeed, surrender to the consumer society can leave us constantly dissatisfied, since no one is able to buy all the goods one sees advertised. Choice of a simple life with abundant human relationships may be both more peaceful and more satisfying.

Johan Galtung observes that, in the modern capitalistic world economy, "the major conditions for economic growth are hard work, saving/investment, greed, and inconsiderateness."[19] He is thinking of inconsiderateness toward nature (9), toward national and international labor (5, and 2: how wide is our community?), and even toward oneself (1: one's noneconomic needs). Inconsiderateness implies exploitation of these factors without reflecting on what they need to be sustainable, to reproduce themselves, and to maintain a dignified existence according to their own natures.

PROTESTANT SOCIAL TEACHING

Protestant Christianity has also contributed significantly to Christian social teachings. In this section we focus particularly on the issues of (a) economic justice and (b) war and peace. The Protestant denominations surveyed below periodically issue statements on these and various other social issues, such as the environment, health care, politics, gender, race, and more.

The Evangelical Lutheran Church in America (ELCA)

Economics

The ELCA's recent "Social Statement on Economic Life"[20] begins by questioning whether Christian identity is compatible with economic success:

> The power, scope, and influence of economic thinking and practices in our day can feel god-like in how they rule over our lives. This raises central theological questions which this social statement addresses: In what or whom do we place our trust? . . . How is Christian identity, freedom, and hope rooted in Jesus Christ, rather than in economic success or failure? . . . We are called to seek changes in economic life in light of the biblically grounded imperative of "sufficient, sustainable livelihood for all."

Noting that "outrage over the plight of people living in poverty is a theme throughout the Bible," it stresses the human dignity of workers and the imperative to provide adequate compensation (a living wage) for their labor, to defend their rights, and to enhance their well-being.

> "Sufficiency" highlights the sharp contrast between those who do not have enough, and those who have too much. This statement commits us as a church to respond to and address why so many in our midst continue to live in poverty. God calls us to a life of mutual generosity toward all who are our neighbors. Government also is expected to promote the common good and provide assistance for those unable to provide for their livelihood. Many of us have far more than we need, and fall into bondage to what we have. Consumerism and endless accumulation become ends in themselves. Enormous disparities in income and wealth become scandalous. Large transnational corporations continue to grow in financial power and influence. These disparities need to be lessened, and large corporate interests held more accountable to the whole human community.

The statement also supports environmental preservation, maintaining agriculture as a "viable means of livelihood" for farmers, and developing low-income communities in a sustainable way.

War and Peace

The statement "Peace in God's World," adopted by a church-wide ELCA assembly in 1995, recommends that the church be a "disturbing presence" during times of apparent peace "when there is no peace" (Jeremiah 6:14) by refusing "to be silent and instead speak[ing] the truth." The "just war" criteria must be met if a military action is to be legitimate: "We begin with a strong presumption against all war; support for and participation in a war to restore peace is a tragic concession to a sinful world." Just war principles may obligate Christians to "say 'no' to wars in which their nation participates." Nuclear war is absolutely rejected, and "selective conscientious objection" is upheld. Just war principles must also be used to evaluate coercive political activities such as the imposition of sanctions.

In support of pacifism, the document states:

> This church today needs the witness of its members who in the name of Jesus Christ refuse all participation in war, who commit themselves to establish peace and justice on earth by nonviolent power alone, and who may suffer and die in their discipleship. We support members who conscientiously object to bearing arms in military service. . . . We must continue the perennial discussion in the Church universal about whether Christian love and discipleship prohibit participation in war in all circumstances, or whether they may permit it in some circumstances.

The United Methodist Church[21]

Economics

In its statement on "the economic community," the United Methodist Church requires governments to create and support policies that promote individual and corporate economic well-being, including "full employment" and minimal inflation. Businesses are accountable for the "social costs" they incur, for example, damage to the environment. Governments should take action to equalize wealth distribution, including real tax reform and laws against "corporate welfare" (tax-supported subsidies to corporations).

War and Peace

War is accepted "only as a last resort in the prevention of such evils as genocide, brutal suppression of human rights, and unprovoked international aggression." "Military claims" should be subordinated to "human values"; "the militarization of society must be . . . stopped"; and the making, selling, and use of conventional weapons must be "reduced and controlled." Nuclear weapons are banned. "We endorse general and complete disarmament under strict and effective international control."[22]

The Episcopal Church[23]

Economics

Similar to the ELCA and UMC teachings above, Episcopal Church teaching on the economy argues for the priority of human well-being over profit, for the "empowerment and liberation of the poor," and for the right of labor to unionize. Also, social justice and economics are inseparable; "work and labor are God-given means intended for furthering God's creation and his kingdom"; and "social responsibility and action to advance social justice for all, protection of workers and economically dislocated communities, and protection of the environment are to be priorities of modern corporate management along with strategies for making money." Christian stockholders share the "moral responsibility" for corporate practices.

War and Peace

Episcopal teachings on war and peace have varied over the past seven or so decades. A pastoral letter in 1934 defined war as mass murder, and a 1937 pastoral letter declared that "modern war could no longer be justified," but by 1962 not only were "limited wars" considered acceptable under certain conditions, so was *nuclear deterrence*—though *not* "massive nuclear retaliation." A 1982 pastoral letter ruled out a policy of "nuclear first-strike deterrence." The 1982 General Convention recommended that Christians use nonviolent civil disobedience against government "military and defense policies," and called (*before* the collapse of the Soviet Union) for a bilateral freeze on the production of nuclear weapons.[24]

National Association of Evangelicals[25]

The NAE statement "For the Health of the Nation" (passed unanimously on October 7, 2004)[26] claims that Evangelicals should be able to influence America . . . since they make up one-quarter of all Americans. They show quite explicitly the biblical roots of their teaching. The document justifies Christian social action as follows:

> We engage in public life because God created our first parents in his image and gave them dominion over the earth (Gen. 1:27–28). The responsibilities that

emerge from that mandate are many, and in a modern society those responsibilities rightly flow to many different institutions, including governments, families, churches, schools, businesses, and labor unions. Just governance is part of our calling in creation.

We also engage in public life because Jesus is Lord over every area of life. Through him all things were created (Col. 1:16–17), and by him all things will be brought to fullness (Rom. 8:19–21). To restrict our stewardship to the private sphere would be to deny an important part of his dominion and to functionally abandon it to the Evil One . . . to deny the all-encompassing Lordship of Jesus (Rev. 19:16).

Regarding just government and fundamental liberty, it reads:

As followers of Jesus, we obey government authorities when they act in accord with God's justice and his laws (Titus 3:1). But we also resist government when it exercises its power in an unjust manner (Acts 5:27–32) or tries to dominate other institutions in society. A good government preserves the God-ordained responsibilities of society's other institutions, such as churches, other faith-centered organizations, schools, families, labor unions, and businesses.

On religious freedom and liberty of conscience:

God has ordained the two co-existing institutions of church and state as distinct and independent of each other with each having its own areas of responsibility (Rom. 13:1–7; Mark 12:13–17; Eph. 4:15–16, 5:23–32). We affirm the principles of religious freedom and liberty of conscience, . . . As God allows the wheat and tares to grow together until the harvest, and as God sends the rain on the just and on the unjust, so those who obey and those who disobey God coexist in society and share in its blessings (Matt. 5:45, 13:24–30). . . . Participating in the public square does not require people to put aside their beliefs or suspend the practice of their religion. All persons should have equal access to public forums, regardless of the religious content or viewpoint of their speech.

On family life and children:

From Genesis onward, the Bible tells us that the family is central to God's vision for human society. God has revealed himself to us in the language of family, adopting us as his children (Rom. 8:23, Gal. 4:5) and teaching us by the Holy Spirit to call him *Abba Father* (Rom. 8:15, Gal. 4:6). Marriage, which is a lifetime relationship between one man and one woman, is the predominant biblical icon of God's relationship with his people (Isa. 54:5; Jer. 3:20, 31:32; Ezek. 16:32; Eph. 5:23, 31–32). In turn, family life reveals something to us about God, as human families mirror, however faintly, the inner life of the Trinity. . . . Many social evils—such as alcohol, drugs, gambling, or credit-card abuse, pornography, sexual libertinism, spousal or child sexual abuse, easy divorce, abortion on demand—represent the abandonment of responsibility or the violation of trust by family members, and they seriously impair the ability of family members to function in society. These evils must be viewed not only as matters of individual sin and dysfunction, but also as violations of family integrity. Because the family is so important to society, violations of its integrity threaten public order. Similarly, employment, labor, housing, health care, and educational policies concern not only individuals but seriously affect families. In order to strengthen the family, we must promote biblical moral principles, responsible personal choices, and good public policies on marriage and divorce law, shelter, food, health care, education, and a family wage (Jas. 5:1–6).

On the "sanctity of human life":

Abortion, euthanasia, and unethical human experimentation violate the God-given dignity of human beings.

On *economic justice* both domestic and in relation to foreign policy:

Care for the vulnerable should extend beyond our national borders. American foreign policy and trade policies often have an impact on the poor. We should try to persuade our leaders to change patterns of trade that harm the poor and to make the reduction of global poverty a central concern of American foreign policy. We must support policies that encourage honesty in government, correct unfair socioeconomic structures, generously support effective programs that empower the poor, and foster economic development and prosperity.

On human rights:

As recipients of God's gift of embodied life, people need food, nurture, shelter, and care. In order to fulfill their God-given tasks, all people have a right to private property. God's design for human existence also implies a right to marry, enjoy family life, and raise and educate children. While it is not the primary role of government to provide everything that humans need for their well-being, governments are obligated to ensure that people are not unjustly deprived of them and to strengthen families, schools, businesses, hospitals, social-service organizations, and other institutions so they can contribute to human welfare . . . American foreign policy should reward those countries that respect human rights and should not reward (and prudently employ certain sanctions against) those countries that abuse or deny such rights. We urge the United States to increase its commitments to developing democracy and civil society in former colonial lands, Muslim nations, and countries emerging from Communism.

On *peace and restraining violence*:

Jesus and the prophets looked forward to the time when God's reign would bring about just and peaceful societies. . . . But from the beginning, Christians have recognized that God did not call them to bring in God's kingdom by force. . . . We have long differed on when governments may use force and whether we may participate in government-authorized force to defend our homelands, rescue others from attack, or liberate other people from oppression. . . . We urge governments to pursue thoroughly nonviolent paths to peace before resorting to military force. We believe that if governments are going to use military force, they must use it in the service of peace and not merely in their national interest. Military force must be guided by the classical just-war principles. . . . In an age of nuclear and biological terrorism, such principles are more important than ever.

And finally on the environment:

We affirm that God-given dominion is a sacred responsibility to steward the earth and not a license to abuse the creation of which we are a part. We are not the owners of creation, but its stewards, summoned by God to "watch over and care for it" (Gen. 2:15). This implies the principle of sustainability: our uses of the Earth must be designed to conserve and renew the Earth rather than to deplete or destroy it. . . . The Bible teaches us that God is not only redeeming his people, but is also restoring the whole creation (Rom. 8:18–23). . . . We show our love for the Creator by caring for his creation. . . . Because clean air, pure water, and adequate resources are crucial to public health and civic order, government has an obligation to protect its citizens from the effects of environmental degradation. . . . Because natural systems are extremely complex, human actions can have unexpected side effects. We must therefore approach our stewardship of creation with humility and caution. . . . We urge Christians to shape their personal lives in creation-friendly ways: practicing effective recycling, conserving resources, and experiencing the joy of contact with nature. We urge government to encourage fuel efficiency, reduce pollution, encourage sustainable use of natural resources, and provide for the proper care of wildlife and their natural habitats.

Progressive Presbyterians

For progressive Presbyterian "news and views," go to www.witherspoonsociety .org. On the home page sidebar (leftmost column) under "social and global concerns" are listed, for example: the Middle East conflict, the war in Iraq, Israel and "anti-Semitism," U.S. politics, economic justice, sexual justice, peacemaking and international concerns, caring for the environment, racial concerns, the death penalty, etc. There is also an archive section among other features.

Peace Churches: The Quakers

The "Friends General Conference" of the Religious Society of Friends (Quakers) is explicitly pacifist, with links on its website to centers for conscientious objection.[27] The website posts a March 19, 2003, letter from Bruce Birchard, general secretary, which says in part:

> As I write today, it appears that a United States-led war against Iraq is imminent. I am appalled and deeply dismayed by the terrible and tragic decisions made by U.S. political leaders. Nevertheless, I believe that Friends are still being called to witness and work for peace and nonviolent responses that fully reflect our understanding of how God's love is active in the world. As Chuck Fager explained in a message I received today, in the midst of the shrill voices of war and the many lies and half-truths that are generated, Quaker meetings are "places of refuge from the spirit of war." . . . I am reminded of George Fox's explanation of why, in 1651, he refused to join Oliver Cromwell's army in order to get out of prison: "I told them I lived in the virtue of that life and power that took away the occasion of all wars and I knew from whence all wars did rise. . . . I told them I was come into the covenant of peace which was before wars and strife were."[28]

Peace Churches: The Mennonites

The Mennonite Central Committee[29] published a speech titled, "The Peace Making Commitment of MCC" (by the Argentinean 1980 Nobel Peace Prize laureate and liberation theologian Adolfo Pérez Esquivel).[30] In that speech, Esquivel gives the following example of Mennonite commitment to loving one's enemy:

> In 1569 Dirk Willems, an early Dutch Anabaptist, translated the theology of "loving the enemy" and "overcoming evil with good" into harsh reality when he turned back to rescue his government pursuer who had fallen through the ice. Willems was later burned at the stake. Anabaptists responded to intense persecution by debating, hiding and migrating. Those who were tortured and killed often sang hymns as they suffered. Where possible, Anabaptists built strong, caring communities whose members ministered to each other's needs and reached out to help people beyond their own communities.[31]

PRELUDE TO LIBERATION THEOLOGIES

Most Christian social teaching, Catholic and Protestant, is optimistic that commitment to Gospel values will inspire participants in the American free-market system tempered by democratic politics to empower the poor and engage all levels of society in social justice. Some Christian thinkers are more doubtful that a system using power politics and self-interest as its basic motivating forces is capable of promoting justice.

The next chapter will deal with liberation theologies, which represent above all a new way of doing theology, characterized by the "circle of praxis" described in that chapter. Because liberation theologians are less likely to trust elite leaders to accept the social teachings expressed in this chapter and to adopt its prescriptions, they seek more radical ways to influence public life.

SUMMARY

The various Christian denominations have developed social teachings to help guide public life. The Roman Catholic Church, especially over the past century, has developed the most extensive body of teaching, and perhaps holds the greatest confidence that its teaching can affect public policy through political, business, and other leaders of good will. Mainline Protestant churches like the Lutherans, Methodists, Episcopalians, and Presbyterians hold positions similar to Catholic ones. The historic peace churches have differed radically on questions of war and the extent to which Christians should be involved in public life. More recently, some Evangelical churches, forming a "Moral Majority," have offered their own distinctive policy positions.

Key issues have included poverty and wealth, private property, labor unions, socialism and capitalism, war and peace, and—most recently—the environmental carrying capacity of the planet. Important principles for judgment have included human rights and dignity, solidarity, subsidiarity, and a preferential option for the poor. Some churches have seriously considered major structural changes that could help to achieve a better society. The tension between prosperity and an evangelical poverty has been a point of difference.

KEY TERMS

CELAM	solidarity
corporative state	structural sin
decade of development	subsidiarity
encyclical	sufficiency
mendicant orders	universal destination of the earth's goods
Papal States	

DISCUSSION QUESTIONS

1. Did any of the social principles of the various Christian churches surprise you? If so, which ones and why?

2. Which of the social principles of the various Christian churches do you agree with? Which do you disagree with? On what grounds?
3. Could a fully committed member of one of these churches follow its principles and still be a successful Chief Executive Officer (CEO) of a major multinational corporation?
4. Could a fully committed member of one of these churches follow its principles and still be a successful President of the United States? Could he or she get elected?

NOTES

1. The translations of papal and council documents are from the Vatican website at www.vatican.va. For individual documents, see the bibliography under the names of the popes (for encyclicals, apostolic exhortations, or apostolic letters) or "Second Vatican Council," followed by the name of the document.

2. Most official Vatican documents use "man" in the generic sense of man and woman. The U.S. Catholic bishops have urged the Vatican to introduce nonsexist language, but to date with no success. Rather than inserting a multitude of "corrections" in square brackets or [*sic*], we invite the reader to make the appropriate adjustments.

3. Roman Synod of Catholic Bishops, *Justice in the World*.

4. National Conference of Catholic Bishops, *The Challenge of Peace*.

5. National Conference of Catholic Bishops, *Economic Justice for All*.

6. Gremillion, ed., *The Gospel of Peace and Justice*, 449.

7. Material from Galtung, and from *Principles of Catholic Social Teaching,* (electronic document) in OSJ Catholic Social Teaching (Office for Social Justice; Archdiocese of St. Paul and Minneapolis), www.osjspm.org/cst/themes.htm (accessed July 10, 2006). See also the links in woodstock.georgetown.edu/links/links_ethics.htm (accessed July 10, 2006).

8. *Economic Justice for All*, intro. par. 13; body par. 25, 28, 32.

9. *Economic Justice for All*, intro. par. 14.

10. *Economic Justice for All*, intro. par. 17.

11. *Economic Justice for All,* intro. par. 18.

12. *Economic Justice for All*, intro. par. 15; body par. 15.

13. *Economic Justice for All*, intro. par. 15.

14. *Economic Justice for All*, body par. 99.

15. *Economic Justice for All*, body par. 12, 13, 28, 34, 40.

16. *Economic Justice for All*, body par. 16, 19, 35, 36, 38–40.

17. *Economic Justice for All*, body par. 25, 31.

18. *Economic Justice for All*, body par. 39.

19. Galtung, *Peace by Peaceful Means*, 131.

20. www.elca.org/socialstatements/economiclife/synopsis/ (accessed July 10, 2006). For ELCA's statements on peace, see www.elca.org/socialstatements/peace/ (accessed July 10, 2006).

21. The United Methodist Church's Social Principles can be found at archives.umc.org/interior.asp?ptid=1&mid=1686 (accessed July 10, 2006) and the links and sublinks it provides (Preamble | The Natural World | The Nurturing Community | The Social Community | The Economic Community | The Political Community | The World Community | Our Social Creed) (accessed June 15, 2006).

22. archives.umc.org/interior.asp?mid=1736 (accessed June 15, 2006).

23. See www.episcopalchurch.org/atoz.htm (accessed July 10, 2006). It is an A to Z directory. See especially the entries for economic justice, peace ministries, peace and justice ministries.

24. Hood, "Chapter 4: Pictures of an Exhibition: Episcopal Social Teachings I."

25. Under "Resolutions and Documents," the website for the "National Association of Evangelicals, Office of Governmental Affairs," www.nae.net/index.cfm? 1FUSEACTION=nae.oga (accessed June 16, 2006), links to "Policy Resolutions," "Policy Documents," and "For the Health of the Nation: An Evangelical Call to Civic Responsibility." Used by permission.

26. www.nae.net/images/civic_responsibility2.pdf (accessed June 16, 2006).

27. www.fgcquaker.org (accessed July 10, 2006). Under "Quaker Library" in the left-hand column are listed, e.g., peace, racial equality, and economics.

28. www.fgcquaker.org/library/peace/friendswitness.html (accessed June 16, 2006).

29. www.mcc.org/ (accessed June 16, 2006).

30. See www.mcc.org/about/peacecommitment/ (accessed July 10, 2006).

31. www.mcc.org/about/peacecommitment/beliefs.html (accessed June 16, 2006).

SUGGESTIONS FOR FURTHER READING

Curran. *Catholic Social Teaching, 1891–Present.*

Dwyer, ed. *The Catholic Bishops and Nuclear War: A Critique and Analysis of the Pastoral, The Challenge of Peace.*

Dwyer, ed. *The New Dictionary of Catholic Social Thought.*

Fernando and Sullivan. *Launching the Second Century: Catholic Social Thought in Asia.*

Flannery, ed. *Vatican Council II: More Postconciliar Documents.*

Galtung. *Peace by Peaceful Means.*

———. "A Structural Theory of Imperialism."

Hiatt, ed. *A Game As Old As Empire.*

Hood. *Social Teachings in the Episcopal Church.*

Lebacqz. *Justice in an Unjust World.*

———. *Six Theories of Justice.*

Maas Weigert and Kelley, eds. *Living the Catholic Social Tradition.*

Massaro. *Living Justice: Catholic Social Teaching in Action.*

Maurin. *Easy Essays.*

Mich. *Catholic Social Teaching and Movements.*

National Conference of Catholic Bishops. *The Challenge of Peace: God's Promise and Our Response*.

National Conference of Catholic Bishops. *Economic Justice for All.*

Palackapilly and Felix. *Religion and Economics: A Worldview*.

Perkins. *Confessions of an Economic Hit Man*.

Pontifical Council for Justice and Peace. *Compendium of the Social Doctrine of the Church*.

Pope John XXIII. *Mater et Magistra*.

——. *Pacem in Terris*.

Pope John Paul II. *Centesimus Annus*.

——. *Laborem Exercens*.

Pope Leo XIII. *Rerum Novarum*.

Pope Paul VI. *Evangelii Nuntiandi*.

——. *Octogesima Adveniens*.

——. *Populorum Progressio*.

Pope Pius XI. *Quadragesimo Anno*.

Roman Synod of Catholic Bishops. *Justice in the World*.

Second Vatican Council. *Gaudium et Spes*.

——. *Lumen Gentium*.

——. *Nostra Aetate*.

Strain, ed. *Prophetic Visions and Economic Realities: Protestants, Jews, and Catholics Confront the Bishops' Letter on the Economy*.

Walsh Davies, ed. *Proclaiming Justice and Peace: Papal Documents from Rerum Novarum through Centesimus Annus*.

Wink. *Unmasking the Powers*.

Chapter Ten

Liberation Theologies

"The evil inequities and oppression of every kind which afflict millions of men and women today openly contradict Christ's Gospel and cannot leave the conscience of any Christian indifferent."

— Vatican Instruction on Christian Freedom and Liberation[1]

"A broad and deep aspiration for liberation inflames the history of humankind in our day, liberation from all that limits or keeps human beings from self-fulfillment, liberation from all impediments to the exercise of freedom. Proof of this is the awareness of new and subtle forms of oppression in the heart of advanced industrial societies, which often offer themselves as models to the underdeveloped countries. . . . We must beware of all kinds of imitations as well as new forms of imperialism— revolutionary this time—of the rich countries, which consider themselves central to the history of humankind."

— Gustavo Gutiérrez[2]

Christian liberation theologians share much with the social teachings of Christian churches described in the previous chapter. They also share with Marxists a sense of outrage over socioeconomic injustice and a suspicious attitude toward status quo structures. They illustrate how important it is to share the experience of oppressed people. This experience makes the existence of injustice so palpable that elaborate theories are not necessary to prove that it exists. Oppression turns people into "nonpersons." Their poverty is not just unfortunate; it is caused by the dominant structures themselves. As a result, it will not be resolved by "development" within the current world structures. Liberation theologians, therefore, do not seek a formula for distribution or exchange; they seek a restoration of right relationships in a fractured community.

If they are Christians or Jews, they seek this restoration because they observe that this is what God sought in the Exodus from Egypt, in the denunciations of social injustice by the prophets, and (for Christians) in the ministry of Jesus of Nazareth. If they are Muslims, they seek it because they believe it is mandated by God in the Quran.

HISTORICAL BACKGROUND

Liberation theologies first developed in Latin America, so it is helpful to know some Latin American history.

European Colonization of the Americas

Spanish warriors, fresh from successful wars against Muslims, came to "newly discovered" lands to win kingdoms for themselves. Their mentality was feudal. In contrast, *North* America was not colonized for another hundred years or more, so the colonization of the North took place in the post-feudal era of developing trade and industry. A number of religious leaders, like *Bartholomé de Las Casas* (one of Gustavo Gutierrez's heroes), were sincerely interested in sharing their faith with the natives on an equal footing, and resisted Spanish oppression. But the main goal of the "conquistadores," or conquerors, was to enrich themselves by exploiting natural and human resources in the "new" lands.

This pattern has continued to the present day in important ways. Many of the Latin American elites are not interested in developing their countries for the benefit of their fellow citizens. They establish industries to sell goods to the First World, invest much of their wealth in First World enterprises (buying stock in General Motors and Nestlé rather than investing in local companies), do their shopping in Miami and their vacationing in Nice, see themselves primarily as world citizens, and use their own country primarily as a resource for their own wealth and power.

For a sense of how separate the elites feel from the common people, the film *Romero* (1989) is especially revealing. It dramatizes the situation in El Salvador in the 1970s. A remarkable example of the early struggle between honest evangelization and selfish oppression is dramatized in the film *The Mission* (1986). This film deals with the Jesuit utopian communities, or "reductions" for indigenous people in Paraguay. Striking and provocative, the film also raises interesting historical questions. You should be aware that the reductions were also criticized as being too patriarchal, treating natives as children. (Perhaps it is better to be treated as children than to be treated as slaves.)

Independence

"Independence" from Spain was not so much a social revolution as it was a coup d'état by local elites against their absentee Spanish lords. It did not change local power realities significantly. There was no real social change. One result of postcolonial independence in many places was to exile Spanish priests because of their loyalty to the crown. The result was to leave the people for as long as a century with virtually no priests. This did not improve Christian life and practice.

In the late 19th and early 20th century, church leaders had a reputation for supporting corrupt political leaders. Recently there has been a change: many elites feel that the church has abandoned them, or at least that certain elements in the church have done so. The process of change in church leadership is very well dramatized in the film *Romero*. Archbishop Romero was a conservative priest who enjoyed good relations with the elites in El Salvador when he was named archbishop. The film shows how he came to a deep conversion.

Catholic Action

In the 1930s, Cardinal Cardijn in Belgium promoted a movement called the Young Christian Workers (in French abbreviated JOC, in English YCW). The same movement developed Young Christian Students. Collectively, these movements were called "Catholic Action." Members of these movements met in small groups to carry out a three-part process: *observe, judge, act.* These JOCists were very influential in both North and South America.

The Decade of Development

In the 1960s, President John Kennedy and the United Nations launched a "decade of development" for industrialized nations to help poor ones. There was a lot of hope at this time. (John Kennedy is still widely regarded in Latin America as their favorite U.S. president.) But at the end of the decade, the gap was worse than before. Developing nations had much higher debt and, because of the oil crisis brought on by the OPEC oil embargo, the United States and other industrial nations allowed interest rates to increase enormously. Thinkers asked, is it really a question of underdevelopment, or of oppression by the stronger nations? They began to think it was the latter.

With "development" falling apart in the 1970s, some began to expand the JOCist idea. Theologians said, the dominant reality of our world is oppression. Theology needs to have something to say to the situation. But as theologians we are not experiencing oppression directly. Therefore, if we are to follow the pattern observe, judge, act, we first have to get into the situation we are concerned about. We have to experience oppression along with our brothers and sisters. So they added a fourth step at the beginning of the process, and went deeper into the other three, coming up with the "circle of praxis":

The Circle of Praxis in Four Steps

1. *Insert* yourself into the situation. Share it in real *experiences*.
2. *Analyze* the situation carefully with the help of sociological, economic, historical, and cultural studies. Find out *what is* and *why* things are that way. This is a *descriptive* analysis: it does not yet evaluate the situation.
3. *Theologize* about the situation. What *should be* according to the Gospels and church teaching? What practical alternatives are there? This is a *normative* analysis: it asks what is good about the current situation, what is bad about it, and what might be a better situation.
4. Make a *pastoral plan* that will help us to move from what *is* toward what *should be*. This is an *action step*.

Insertion, or step 1, usually involved sharing the life of small groups of poor Christians formed in the immense parishes of Latin America where the poor were often left to their own devices. As an outgrowth of the discussion groups previously encouraged by the JOCist movement, these small groups of ten to thirty people were the church in miniature. They were a place for discussion, mutual support, and common action. They were called *Base Christian Communities—Communidades Ecclesiales de Base*, abbreviated *CEB*.

In many areas where priests were scarce, the CEBs provided most of the effective ministry. More traditional clergy were sometimes alarmed by this development, both because they feared a transfer of power from clergy to laity and because these small local groups often raised embarrassing political questions and engaged in activities that threatened the status quo. Laity, empowered by small-scale local action, began to form larger associations and networks and to hold regional and national meetings.

In Brazil, the bishops quickly approved of the Base Christian Communities, providing yearly discussion guides and protecting them from hostile political pressures. Some of the other hierarchies have been less encouraging or even positively hostile to the CEBs.

This four-step process of analysis is called a *circle* because, once you put step 4 into operation, you will change the situation. For example, the poor may have new means to organize their economic life, certain elites may feel threatened and retaliate, you may end up in jail or dead. So then you will need to start the analysis over again (if you are still alive). Specifically, it is called a circle of *praxis*. Praxis is activity that is reflected upon and consciously chosen to produce a particular effect, a transformation of society. The activity and the reflection go together and influence each other.

Three Power Questions

Three questions useful in this analysis are the following:

1. Who is *making the effective decisions* in this situation?
2. Who is *benefiting* from the decisions made?
3. Who is *paying the cost* of those decisions?

If you are a student, you might ask those questions about your own school. Who decides, for example, about grades, classes, teachers, major field requirements, what field you major in, what courses you take, what you read and do in a given course, and how much tuition you pay? What effect does your cooperation or lack of cooperation have on those decisions?

Where is this kind of analysis done? Here are a few places:

1. Some Latin American universities, but not many. Most Latin American universities cater to the elites and promote the status quo. (Would that be true of your school?)
2. "Think tanks" (study centers), especially those in contact with the poor and with pastoral action.
3. Groups of church workers, ministers, priests, and sisters.
4. Base Christian Communities, usually on a fairly simple level.

Conscientization

This kind of analysis makes people aware of the power relations in their world, who is controlling them, and what they might do about it. It brings them into a new consciousness of reality and empowers them to make decisions consciously rather than just following the path laid out for them by power brokers. This process of coming to awareness is called *conscientization*—you become "conscious" of the way things are and the causes that have made them that way. Conscientization involves learning how to ask questions and find answers. Most people have come to believe the way of seeing things promoted by the elites, and this is usually a way of seeing things that maintains the privileges of the elites. (Even the elites are often not aware of how much this is true. It is largely an unconscious process.)

Gustavo Gutiérrez

In 1968, a Peruvian diocesan priest and theologian put into writing the new ideas that were developing in Latin America and titled his book *A Theology of Liberation*. It is from the title of that book that the movement took its name. *Gustavo Gutiérrez* has been one of the key thinkers in its development. He lives with the poor in Lima, Peru, and works at a study center for pastoral action.

Gutiérrez was also a key consultant for the second general meeting of the Latin American Bishops' Conference. This conference, abbreviated in Spanish as CELAM, was organized as a result of the Second Vatican Council. The second meeting of the conference was held at *Medellín* in Colombia. At that conference CELAM announced a *"fundamental option for the poor,"* meaning that the poor deserve help first.

Some more conservative leaders hoped that the third meeting, held about ten years later, would reverse the direction that Medellin had set. But it didn't. The meeting held at *Puebla* in Mexico confirmed the earlier meeting and carried it further. Pope John Paul II also attended Puebla and approved the general direction of the conference. Both the Medellin and Puebla conferences produced documents that are very important for justice and peace.

An Example: CEBs in Brazil

In the 1980s, Brazil probably had the largest number of CEBs and the most support from the bishops for this movement. The bishops distributed study questions for the CEBs each Advent and Lent. There were about eighty thousand CEBs in Brazil. But if you counted up all the members of these eighty thousand groups, the total still represented only between 1 and 3% of Brazilian Christians. (Another 1 to 3% of the Brazilian Christian population were evangelical Protestant Christians who tended to support the status quo power structures.) It is important to realize that percentages do not have to be large to have a major social effect. We are used to thinking in terms of electoral majorities, but a group of truly committed people amounting to 1 to 3% of a society can have a major effect on that society.

Most CEB members are simple people who depend on theologians and other experts to get them started. Still they need to trust their own understanding and not just accept the views of the experts. In terms of their own experiences they know much more than the experts do.

The Question of Violence

A key concept of liberation theology is *structural violence*. If the laws and the way they are carried out result in half of the children in a country dying before age five, as is true in many Latin American countries, then the people who develop, support, and defend those laws and ways are guilty of violence against the poor, for example, by preventing adequate nutrition, even if they don't physically attack the person.

The question, then, is whether violent revolution is justified in response to unjust laws and structural violence. Most liberation theologians are unwilling to renounce the validity of just war theory—as is even Pope Benedict XVI, who was head of the Vatican Congregation for the Teaching of the Faith at the time that liberation theology was developing. While just war theory, following the specific teaching of St. Thomas Aquinas, allows for just revolution in extreme cases, most of the poor in Latin America prefer nonviolent approaches and choose them whenever they can. This is especially true of indigenous peoples. A great deal of active nonviolence is being practiced there, with great courage and at high cost.

Some of the liberation theologians I talked with in Latin America explained that, although they preferred nonviolent approaches, they were unwilling to condemn just war or just rebellion. They were afraid that unjust elites would use their condemnation to attack those who were resisting injustice by means of armed force. They didn't want their words, for example, to be used against their friends in Nicaragua.

Michael Novak and José Miguez-Bonino

The North American thinker Michael Novak wrote the book *Will It Liberate?* in which he raised critical questions about liberation theologies. When I was in Argentina, I attended a small seminar at a Protestant seminary discussing the book under the leadership of *José Miguez-Bonino*, a leading liberation theologian and a Methodist. (Most Latin American liberation theologians are Catholics because most Latin Americans are Catholics.) He has written some of the best books for students, because his writing is especially clear and simple.

Miguez-Bonino found some good points in Novak's book, for example, the idea that a democratic-capitalistic society should have a mixture of economic, political, and moral forces; the importance of inventiveness; the need for small-scale enterprise; and the conviction that U.S. prosperity is not essentially dependent on Latin American oppression. The United States would still be a prosperous country even if Latin America sank into the sea. Bananas would be more expensive, but even with its level of affluence considerably reduced, the U.S. standard of living would remain well above the current level in Latin America. And most U.S. industry produces for an internal market: we use what we produce.

But Novak's weakness is that he doesn't take seriously enough the power question and the extent of corruption; to follow his suggestions in Latin America can get you murdered. If Latin America sank into the sea, *its elites* would not continue to prosper. And some key North American elites would lose a large part of their economic power base.

When liberation theology was beginning in the late 1960s, its writers spoke of the United States oppressing Latin America. By 1988, they were speaking of Latin American *elites* in collusion with North American *elites* against the interests of the common people in both places.[3]

Juan Luis Segundo

When I spoke with the Uruguayan Jesuit *Juan Luis Segundo,* he reflected on how he had come to appreciate the apostle Paul. Earlier, he had preferred Matthew's Gospel and thought that Paul had sold out to the establishment. But then his experience of how resistant the establishment is, and how difficult it is to bring about change, made him appreciate Paul more.

Vatican Reactions

Many people have heard that "the Vatican is opposed to liberation theology." The reality is more complex. People who really are opposed to liberation theology will find little support from the Vatican's position. The Vatican Congregation for the Teaching of the Faith (directed at the time by Cardinal Ratzinger) published two documents on Liberation Theology. The first expressed caution, especially with regard to Marxist methods of analysis. The second pointed out what was positive in the movement.

The First Vatican Document

In the 1984 *Instruction on Certain Aspects of the "Theology of Liberation,"* the Congregation warned that Marxist principles may be dangerous bases for a theology—especially if they draw our attention away from human sin to concentrate exclusively on earthly liberation. Yet it insisted that the struggle for justice, freedom, and human dignity is an important aspect of Christian faith and life:

> Faced with the urgency of certain problems, some are tempted to emphasize, unilaterally, the liberation from servitude of an earthly and temporal kind . . . they seem to put liberation from sin in second place, and so fail to give it the primary importance it is due. Others . . . make use of different concepts without sufficient critical caution. It is difficult, and perhaps impossible, to purify these

borrowed concepts of an ideological inspiration which is incompatible with Christian faith and the ethical requirements which flow from it. . . .

The present Instruction has a . . . limited and precise purpose: to draw the attention of pastors, theologians, and all the faithful to the deviations, and risks of deviation, damaging to the faith and to Christian living, that are brought about by certain forms of liberation theology which use, in an insufficiently critical manner, concepts borrowed from various currents of Marxist thought.

This warning should in no way be interpreted as a disavowal of all those who want to respond generously and with an authentic evangelical spirit to the "preferential option for the poor". It should not at all serve as an excuse for those who maintain an attitude of neutrality and indifference in the face of the tragic and pressing problems of human misery and injustice. It is, on the contrary, dictated by the certitude that the serious ideological deviations which it points out tends [*sic*] inevitably to betray the cause of the poor. More than ever, it is important that numerous Christians, whose faith is clear and who are committed to live the Christian life in its fullness, become involved in the struggle for justice, freedom and human dignity because of their love for their disinherited, oppressed and persecuted brothers and sisters. More than ever, the Church intends to condemn abuses, injustices and attacks against freedom, wherever they occur and whoever commits them. She intends to struggle, by her own means, for the defense and advancement of the rights of mankind, especially of the poor. (Introduction)

The following passage of the document makes it clear that the Congregation is not speaking in a detached, "spiritualizing" sense, but is addressing concrete social problems of our day:

In certain parts of Latin America, the seizure of the vast majority of the wealth by an oligarchy of owners bereft of social consciousness, the practical absence or the shortcomings of a rule of law, military dictators making a mockery of elementary human rights, the corruption of certain powerful officials, the savage practices of some foreign capital interests constitute factors which nourish a passion for revolt among those who thus consider themselves the powerless victims of a new colonialism in the technological, financial, monetary or economic order. The recognition of injustice is accompanied by a pathos which borrows its language from Marxism, wrongly presented as though it were scientific language. (VII,12)[4]

The Second Vatican Document

Here are some passages from the second, 1986 document, the *Instruction on Christian Freedom and Liberation*:

New relationships of inequality and oppression have been established between the nations endowed with power and those without it. The pursuit of one's own interest seems to be the rule for international relations, without the common good of humanity being taken into consideration. (par. 16)

Figure 10.1. Children living in a dump; their homes are in the background, near Du-maguete City, Philippines. Courtesy David Whitten Smith, 7 February 1998.

When man [*sic*] wishes to free himself from the moral law and become independent of God, far from gaining his freedom he destroys it. Escaping the measuring rod of truth, he falls prey to the arbitrary; fraternal relations between people are abolished and give place to terror, hatred and fear. Because it has been contaminated by deadly errors about man's condition and his freedom, the deeply-rooted modern liberation movement remains ambiguous. It is laden both with promises of true freedom and threats of deadly forms of bondage. (par. 19)

Man's sin, that is to say his breaking away from God, is the radical reason for the tragedies which mark the history of freedom. In order to understand this, many of our contemporaries must first rediscover a sense of sin. In man's desire for freedom there is hidden the temptation to deny his own nature. Insofar as he wishes to desire everything and to be able to do everything and thus forget that he is finite and a created being, he claims to be a god. (par. 37)

Having become his own centre, sinful man tends to assert himself and to satisfy his desire for the infinite by the use of things: wealth, power and pleasure, despising other people and robbing them unjustly and treating them as objects or instruments. Thus he makes his own contribution to the creation of those very structures of exploitation and slavery which he claims to condemn. (par. 42)

For the Beatitudes, by teaching trust which relies on God, hope of eternal life, love of justice, and mercy which goes as far as pardon and reconciliation, enable us to situate the temporal order in relation to a transcendent order which gives the temporal order its true measure but without taking away its own nature. . . .

The Beatitudes prevent us from worshipping earthly goods and from committing the injustices which their unbridled pursuit involves.[90] They also divert us from an unrealistic and ruinous search for a perfect world. (par. 62)

Man is worth more for what he is than for what he has. [The Church] bears witness to the fact that this dignity cannot be destroyed, whatever the situation of poverty, scorn, rejection or powerlessness to which a human being has been reduced. She shows her solidarity with those who do not count in a society by which they are rejected spiritually and sometimes even physically. (par. 68)

The recognized priority of freedom and of conversion of heart in no way eliminates the need for unjust structures to be changed. It is therefore perfectly legitimate that those who suffer oppression on the part of the wealthy or the politically powerful should take action, through morally licit means, in order to secure structures and institutions in which their rights will be truly respected. It remains true however that structures established for people's good are of themselves incapable of securing and guaranteeing that good. The corruption which in certain countries affects the leaders and the State bureaucracy, and which destroys all honest social life, is a proof of this. Moral integrity is a necessary condition for the health of society. It is therefore necessary to work simultaneously for the conversion of hearts and for the improvement of structures. (par. 75)[5]

One person I talked with on my Latin America trip emphasized that there is little or no Marxism in liberation theology. He said, "Most students and practitioners of liberation theology couldn't do Marxist analysis if you held their head under water."

Leonardo Boff

In 1985, the Vatican Congregation also condemned *Leonardo Boff*, a Franciscan priest, university professor, and leading Brazilian liberation theologian, to a period of reconsideration and prayer. He was "condemned to 'obsequious silence' and was removed from his editorial functions and suspended from religious duties."[6] Fr. Boff cooperated with the discipline. The Brazilian bishops went to Rome in a body and spent a week talking with Pope John Paul II. They explained to the pope what Fr. Boff and others were trying to do, and how important for Brazil their efforts were. After the meeting, Fr. Boff was released from the discipline early by the Vatican Congregation. And Pope John Paul II wrote a letter to the Brazilian bishops in response to the meeting, affirming that liberation theology is *essential to the Church*. In 1992, faced with a new censure, Boff left the priesthood. He described his treatment as "cruel harassment."

It is useful to note that Pope John Paul II was especially concerned about Marxism because of his experience in Poland. He felt that many people had been betrayed by Marxist visions, and he didn't want other parts of the world to fall into the same problems. Some Americans criticize this viewpoint as if the pope's experience made him hypercritical and unfit to judge. But we should recognize the importance of respecting each other's insights, especially in those areas where they have more experience than we do. Out of a certain tension and dynamic of discussion comes a better understanding than any one person could have alone. Also, just as the pope was influenced by his environment and early experience, so were we by ours. Of course, it takes a lot of courage to present your experience and insight in dynamic tension with a pope! But that is what the Brazilian bishops did.

Appointments of Bishops

Appointments of bishops in Latin America from the 1980s through 2005 caused much concern to people who esteem liberation theologies. The character of the bishops in a particular area has a major effect on what is allowed, encouraged, and supported. The bishops appointed by Pope John Paul II tended to be people who agreed with him on such questions as women's ordination and birth control, but who supported the elites against liberation theologies—something which John Paul II didn't do: he was a strong advocate for social justice.

But it seemed that when he had to make a choice, the doctrinal questions of women's ordination and birth control were more important to the pope than the social justice questions were. So the effect of many (not all) of his bishops' appointments has been to slow down support for liberation theologies, and the pope must take some responsibility for that effect even if it was not directly intended. On the other hand, liberation theologians must take some responsibility for the unintended side effects of *their* choices and actions, too.

Examples of Pope John Paul's concern for social questions are his 1987 encyclical letter *Sollicitudo Rei Socialis*[7] and his 1991 letter *Centesimus Annus*.[8] A very important feature of those letters is their explicit support for the concept of "structures of sin" that become the source of other sins and influence people's behavior.[9] For a discussion of those documents, see chapter 9 on Christian Social Teaching.

Pentecostals and Charismatics

When I spent four months on sabbatical in Latin America in 1988, I paid special attention to how four groups or movements interacted: liberation theologies, active nonviolence, charismatic renewal, and Christian missions. I had personal experience with and commitment to all four of these groups. As I had expected, there was a fair amount of mutual misunderstanding and some antagonism among them. (If all my heroes ever got together in one room, a terrible fight would break out.)

Charismatic Christians—Pentecostal, mainline Protestant, and Roman Catholic—were gaining strength. Often charismatics emphasized evangelism and personal spirituality with less attention to social context, but not always. I found charismatic communities that were both serving the poor and empowering them in El Paso, Texas, and Juarez, Mexico (Fr. Rick Thomas, a Jesuit, at "Our Lady's Youth Center" and "The Lord's Ranch"),[10] Mexico City (Fr. Don Hassler, Maryknoll), Trinidad, West Indies (Rhonda Maingot and Rose Jackman, female founders of the "Living Water Charismatic Community"),[11] Cochabamba, Bolivia (Fr. Patricio Rearden, a Dominican), and Bogotá, Colombia (Fr. Rafael Garcia Herreros, "El Minuto de Dios" community, parish, radio and TV, grade schools, high school, university).[12] They did tend to do less social analysis and to be less critical of economic and political structures, but most of them would still make a U.S. parish look conservative by comparison and would agitate typical North American elites.

The missions I visited also tended to raise social issues and to have a real "option for the poor"—for example, Parroquia San Lucas Toliman, Guatemala.[13] That's probably because I searched for contacts at Maryknoll, New York. Active nonviolence was less often well understood, but Fr. Don Hassler in Mexico City was an exception. No one I contacted voiced support for violent revolution.

Recent Developments

Responding to the Vatican censure, younger priests in Brazil have taken traditional liberation theology in several new directions, focusing on environmental, racial, and gender issues, among others. Nevertheless, it is probably an exaggeration to say that Latin American liberation theology is dead. Two examples of liberation theologians in action are Dorothy Stang, an American nun, martyred in 2005, who struggled to help landless peasants gain land in rural Brazil;[14] and a priest named Julio Lancelotti who operates a homeless shelter for children suffering from AIDS in São Paulo. Recently, when receiving a reward, Lancelotti claimed that "the city is applying a 'cleanup' policy against those considered undesirable . . . [it] accuses the Churches of turning misery into a Cult and tries to hide the poor from the eyes of the elite who cannot stand to see the results of the economic concentration. 'São Paulo belongs to its residents,' he said."[15] Another ray of hope—in his youth, Pope Benedict XVI was known as a progressive.

OTHER FORMS OF LIBERATION THEOLOGY

Palestinian Liberation Theology

Naim Ateek (1937–), a Palestinian Anglican priest, inspired the founding in 1990 of the Palestinian liberation theology organization and peacemaking center known as *Sabeel*, which is based in Jerusalem and Nazareth. As a child in 1948, Ateek experienced dispossession when he and his family were forced to leave their hometown, Beisan, and move to Nazareth. Ateek did his ministerial training at San Francisco Theological Seminary, returning to Palestine to work as a priest. In 1989 he published *Justice and Only Justice: A Palestinian Theology of Liberation*, which includes a chapter on political-historical background. Most people forget that about 150,000 Palestinian Arabs were left in the territory bordered by the "green line" (the cease-fire line). That territory became the state of Israel in May 1948. Ateek outlines three stages through which these Palestinians have gone between 1948 and 1988: shock, resignation, and awakening. The stage of "awakening" included the Palestinians in the Occupied Territories (East Jerusalem, the West Bank, and the Gaza Strip); it produced the first intifada (1987–1993).

Ateek notes that the Palestinian churches were relatively silent for about twenty years (from the late 1960s to the late 1980s). He encourages them to speak out, following the courageous examples of people like the Christian theologian *Rosemary Radford Ruether*, who investigated and publicized chemical warfare by Israel in 1988, and the Jewish theologian *Marc Ellis,* who has led the way in creating a Jewish liberation theology, including confrontation with Israeli anti-Semitism. The churches must pursue both justice and peace, Ateek insists. Shifting from a war mentality to a peace mentality takes work—it doesn't happen automatically.

Ateek himself had to struggle to accept Israel's existence. He came to believe that the land of Israel/Palestine is intended for both peoples. Two states are necessary because Israel will not accept one bi-national state. Palestinian self-determination and Israeli security go together. Reconciliation requires two equal states. New attitudes are needed on both sides: Palestinians must acknowledge the Holocaust, and Israelis must acknowledge the catastrophe they have inflicted on the Palestinians. Israel must abolish its nuclear weapons, a shared Jerusalem is essential for peace, and the final solution is to love our enemies while insisting on justice.

Jewish Theology of Liberation

Rosemary Radford Ruether[16] promotes a new theology of Jewish-Christian solidarity encouraging a relationship between "peer communities." Both

communities (a) have power and have been oppressive, (b) must work to recover a "prophetic consciousness" along with their "prophetic traditions" so
that they can practice mutual solidarity with the poor and oppressed, including Palestinians, and (c) need to help Israel normalize itself as a pluralistic
country with equal rights for non-Jewish citizens. She notes that only 20% of
Jews worldwide are Israelis while 80% are citizens of other nations.

Marc Ellis[17] is the leading representative of Jewish liberation theology. An
American Jew, Ellis remembers "growing up in 1950s America" before the
Holocaust had been named and learning "little of contemporary Jewish history."[18] American Jews joined the Black struggle for civil rights, but mostly
ignored Israel's repressive treatment of Palestinians. His first two visits to Israel, in 1973 and 1984, brought him into contact with Palestinians as well as
Israelis.

Focusing on the Palestine issue as a Jew, Ellis has become the foremost
voice of Jewish liberation theology. He rejects a "Holocaust theology" that
denies the (ongoing) injustice done to the Palestinians by the state of Israel.
Rather he seeks a theology that would embrace *both* Jewish empowerment
and Jewish solidarity with all suffering humans—especially the victims of
modern Israel. Only in this way will Jews re-embrace their ethical, prophetic
traditions. Jews of conscience must confront "Constantinian Judaism," and
"Jews, Christians, and Muslims of conscience must come together." Christian
Zionists he condemns as "participants in [the] crime against the Palestinian
people . . . I cannot embrace my own history or religion," Ellis writes, "without embracing the Palestinian people"[19]

Ellis maintains that (a) with Jews, Christians must change their mutual dialogue which began with the Second Vatican Council, by helping Jews repent
for the way they have treated the Palestinians, (b) so that Jews no longer demand that Christians support the policies of the state of Israel as a condition
for continuing the dialogue, which Ellis terms an "ecumenical deal." (c) Instead, Christians must demand that Jews criticize their own oppression of the
Palestinians, just as Christians have criticized their own anti-Semitism, and
(d) religious communities who work to liberate the poor and oppressed must
also resist the all-powerful state. Some Jewish thinkers have tended to regard
Third World liberation struggles as anti-Jewish. Gutiérrez (see above) by contrast links liberation theology and the Holocaust, emphasizing that for Latin
Americans the Holocaust is *now* and there is no contradiction between them.

Islamic, or Quranic, Theology of Liberation[20]

Farid Esack (1958– , South Africa) grew up very poor in South Africa. For
ten years in his youth, he belonged to the Muslim movement *Tablighi Ja-
ma'at*, which seeks spiritual renewal through group pilgrimages.[21] For eight

years he studied Islam in Pakistan, where he was influenced by Christian organizations working against poverty as he imagined "a radical Islam which is committed to social justice, personal freedom, and the search for the transcendent. . . ."[22] Back in South Africa, he founded "Call of Islam" in 1984, seeking "liberation from apartheid," gender equality, environmental preservation, and religious pluralism. Regarded as the foremost Muslim liberation theologian in the world today, Esack opposes silence in the face of injustice and personal morality divorced from any social context; the individual must be socially responsible. To maintain our individual integrity while expressing solidarity with each other, it is necessary to renew our inner capacity to heal in solitude with God.[23]

Islamic liberation theology differs from both traditional and modern Islamic theology yet, like them, draws directly on the Quran and Hadith. Esack proposes a "hermeneutic of liberation" with attention to *taqwa, tawhid, al-nas*, the oppressed, balance and justice, and *jihad*.

Taqwa means *responsibility to God and to humans*. Its consequences include taking care (a) to remain in the conscious presence of Allah, to whom one has surrendered, so that one's interpretation of the Quran will not be biased by one's ideologies or popular enthusiasms, (b) to maintain aesthetic and spiritual balance when overwhelmed by one political crisis after another, and (c) to be aware that struggle for justice has to change *oneself* as well as *society* if the activist is not to become a tyrant.[24]

Tawhid refers to God's *oneness*. It opposes the dualism of sacred and secular, religion and politics, and insists that religion—theology and social analysis done together—is an appropriate means of struggling for justice. Similar to the Christian concept of "solidarity," it opposes racial, ethnic, and class divisions, especially when "money worship" leads one group to oppress others, regarding apartheid as apostasy or heresy.[25]

Al-nas signifies the *people* in contrast to the apartheid *state*: the people are sovereign because Allah has entrusted creation to *them* as stewards. The Quran sides with the marginalized and against the powerful elites, refusing to take a "neutral" position (see Quran 107:1–3, 104, and 22:45). The Quran echoes the Christian "option for the poor" in that Allah identifies with the *oppressed*: the prophets (whose message is revolutionary) were peasants and shepherds; Muhammad was well received by common people—the "weak and destitute"—and opposed by the powerful rich. The Quran teaches social equality and upholds "the principle of distributive justice," and in Mecca Muhammad challenged not only *shirk* (faithlessness) but also economic injustice (see Quran 28:4–8).[26]

Justice is a crucial theme in the Quran. For example, "God created the heavens and earth for a true purpose: to reward each soul according to its deeds" (see Quran 45:22 on justice and creation). For Muslim liberation theologians, the Quran is a "force for justice" that is more than socioeconomic, and Islam is a religion of justice. Drawing on both the Quran and Islamic tradition, Esack defines *jihad* as the "struggle to transform both oneself and society."[27] Jihad is the Muslim's liberation "struggle and praxis" to achieve justice—not to impose "Islam as a religious system"—within a historical-social context.[28] Jihad means resistance in solidarity with the oppressed against the systems that dehumanize them.

Black Liberation Theology[29]

James Cone, author of *A Black Theology of Liberation,* among other works, is the foremost American black theologian. He maintains that black theology has always been a theology of liberation, and that gender and class are now part of its subject matter. (Notice the parallelism with Womanist theology.) Black theology refers back to the original black American experience of enslavement by white, self-identified Christians. Having salvaged Christianity from a racist misrepresentation, black theology operates between two polar realizations: that the world does not reflect God's will, and that the world does not have to remain as it is. For black theologians, Christ is identified with the black experience of oppression, and human nature is fulfilled only in liberation. "Jesus is the oppressed man *par excellence* and the liberator of all who suffer and are exploited."[30]

Feminist Liberation Theology

Feminist theologians seek justice for women and social transformation. Elizabeth Johnson (1941–) is an American feminist theologian, a Sister of St. Joseph, and past president of the Catholic Theological Society of America. Her most famous book is *She Who Is: The Mystery of God in Feminist Theological Discourse,* published in 1992. She has edited a collection of essays entitled, *The Church Women Want: Catholic Women in Dialogue.* Her own essay in that collection, "Imaging God, Embodying Christ: Women as a Sign of the Times," traces support for gender inequality in the Christian theological tradition, contrasting it with the gender equality expressed in such biblical passages as Genesis 1:26–28 and Galatians 3:27–28. Scrutinizing two ambiguities in recent papal teaching, she discusses the fallacy of determining social roles on the basis of gender, and being the image of Christ nonliterally.[31]

U.S. feminism has an equal rights agenda and is especially concerned to rectify the exclusion of women from power. "Romantic" feminists regard gender from an "essentialist" perspective, seeing gender as shaped primarily by nature (genetic determination). "Radical" feminists focus on oppressive patriarchy. "Socialist" feminists consider class as well as gender in their analysis: they highlight ways that gender is shaped by nurture or culture.

Feminist theologians work to expose unjust (sexist) theologies and practices and to create a feminist liberation theology.[32] The Second Vatican Council was a major (positive) turning point for Roman Catholic feminist theologians. For Protestant feminist theologians, the World Council of Churches, established in 1948, served as a beacon of hope in their pursuit of women's ordination and global justice for women.[33]

Today feminist theology is found in Europe, the global south, the Muslim world, and elsewhere. *Womanist* theology is black feminist theology done by black women, who include race and class as well as gender in their analysis. Hispanic feminist theology is called *Mujerista* theology. The *Women Church Movement* began in the United States in 1983 with a membership of 1,400 Catholic women; now it is interfaith and global.[34]

Asian Liberation Theology[35]

Although much less prevalent in Asia than it is in Latin America, liberation theology is notable in India, Sri Lanka, South Korea, Taiwan, and the Philippines.[36] Two main sources of this theology are the Ecumenical Association of Third World Theologians (EATWOT) and the Conference of Churches in Asia (CCA). Asian liberation theology differs from Latin American in that most of Asia's poor are non-Christian, and so it is strongly interfaith. Because most repressive Asian governments do not use Christianity to justify their repression, the "establishment ideologies" that most Asian liberation theologians critique tend to be non-Christian.

Asian liberation theologians confront widespread poverty; the reality of suffering is recognized in Buddhism's first noble truth (see chapter 2). They also confront state sponsorship of global capitalism, which threatens democratic rights; the negative role of religion, for example, in relation to women; and ecological concerns in response to which the "little tradition" may correct and perfect the "great tradition." Some Asian liberation theologians draw on Shamanism and Messianic (Maitreya) Buddhism as they turn grief and rage into revolutionary energy for justice, embodying the power of the resurrection.[37]

A Taiwanese liberation theologian named Choan-Seng Song talks about the meeting of the cross and the lotus, and about the suffering that must be faced by those who struggle for liberation. In India and South Korea the crucified Christ symbolizes God's identification with suffering humans. Indian liberation theology draws on the egalitarian heritage of the Dalits and their experience of Christ as liberator (see chapter 1 for more on the Dalits). "Dalit theology" expresses the Dalits' outrage at their oppression and their yearning for equal status. Fr. Sebastian Kappen (d. 1993) saw Jesus as a counter-cultural prophet modeling a "praxis of subversion" that was relevant to the Indian struggle between oppressive theologies (e.g., the Vedas, Manu) and liberative theologies (Buddhism, Hindu Bhakti). In his view, Indian society needs to be liberated from "both orthodox Hinduism and modern capitalism."[38]

Korean Minjung theology is an outgrowth of the suffering of the Korean "common people" (translation of Minjung). In the late 19th century, Protestant missionaries in Korea connected with poor people by translating the Bible into Korean instead of Chinese, giving them access to biblical symbols and stories that they found meaningful in their quest for liberation from poverty. Note that when Japan ruled Korea from 1905 to 1945 they banned the Exodus story: God rescuing slaves from Egypt![39]

The Sri Lankan Jesuit Alois Pieris has a doctorate in Buddhist studies which he has used to engage in dialogue with the Buddhist community. He identifies two Asian forms of religious socialism: *monastic* and *peasant*—the simple, voluntarily shared cooperative life chosen and lived by monks and members of ashrams, and the dehumanizing, grinding, hopelessly shared poverty that peasants are forced to live. He calls *involuntary* poverty "*enslaving* religion" and *voluntary* poverty "*liberating* religion."[40]

Philippine liberation theology[41] arose in the midst of armed struggle by the Muslim community on the southern island of Mindanao against the central (Christian) government in Manila. Public perceptions of political power were transformed when a popular movement (trained by the Goss-Mayers of the Netherlands and supported by the Roman Catholic Cardinal Sin) used techniques of active nonviolence to install Corazon Aquino as president after she had defeated Ferdinand Marcos in an election but was being denied her victory. Filipinos began to speak of "people power."

THE VISION OF KAREN LEBACQZ

Theologian and ethicist Karen Lebacqz, ordained in the United Church of Christ, offers a compelling vision of justice, incorporating elements from Christian social teaching enriched by liberation theology:

1. Justice is not primarily a philosophical determination of rights. It is right relationships in community among humans who understand their need for each other, and between humans and God.

2. For this reason, it deals primarily with the duties necessary to create and maintain human community—duties appropriate to humans who care for each other. It is not dominated by individual human beings asserting their rights.
3. The primary injustice is exploitation, domination, and oppression, which break the community's covenant, violating the human dignity of the victim and destroying the humanity of the oppressor. Both the victim and the oppressor need to be liberated.
4. The move toward justice is then a move toward restoration of what has been damaged by injustice. This move involves God and humans acting together to *rescue* the oppressed, who themselves have engaged in *resistance,* refusing to accept their degradation. It also involves God and humans acting together to *rebuke* oppressors and to challenge them to make *reparations* to set things right. This move toward reparation involves both ending the oppression itself and acting to undo the damage caused by past injustice. In particular, those who benefit from the effects of past injustice, even if they were not responsible for the injustice in the first place, should be challenged to share those benefits with those who suffered from the effects of the injustice. The biblical concept of a periodic jubilee of redistribution is appropriate in this context.
5. All of these actions should be expected to be incomplete. One must continually return to the beginning in the circle of praxis to assess, from the standpoint of the most oppressed, what the actual effects have been of the actions taken. Then one must seek again to approximate the ideal. Work for justice is unending, and celebration of the jubilee redistribution of resources must recur time after time.[42]

SUMMARY

Beginning in Latin America, liberation theology felt impelled to ask what God had to say about situations of injustice—glaring disparities between wealth and poverty. They applied a "circle of praxis" (insertion, descriptive analysis, normative analysis, and action plans) and a series of power questions (who is making the effective decisions, who gains from the decisions, and who loses?). Because the analysis challenged status-quo structures and power relations—trying to rescue the oppressed, resist the oppression, rebuke oppressors, and demand reparations to restore Christian community—it became very controversial. While accepting much of the social criticism, Catholic Church leadership warned against secular aspects of Marxist analysis; wealthy elites simply labeled the whole process "communist," attacking its theologians and their communities with police, military, and paramilitary violence.

The Christian Latin American movement gave rise to similar liberation movements in Judaism and Islam, among blacks and feminists, and in Asia and Palestine.

KEY TERMS

action possibilities	al-nas
Base Christian Communities	normative analysis
CELAM	pastoral plan
circle of praxis	praxis
conscientization	reductions
Dalit theology	shirk
descriptive analysis	structural violence
insertion	taqwa
JOCists	tawhid
Minjung theology	Womanist theology
Mujerista theology	

DISCUSSION QUESTIONS

1. This chapter has discussed several types of liberation theology. What type is most likely to deal with situations that are important to you? Which of its insights caught your attention?
2. How might the circle of praxis apply to some situation that you think needs to be changed? What would you need to do to fulfill each of its four parts?
3. Apply the three power questions to a particular situation to help judge whether or not it is a situation of oppression. For example, how might the three power questions apply to a college or university system of grading? That is, who decided that your university would adopt its current system of grading (e.g., A–F; number rankings; pass-fail for certain courses or for all courses; no grades, but faculty-written evaluations of students; no grades at all)? What groups gain something from that system (faculty, staff, administration, students, boards of directors, employers, accrediting agencies, corporations producing standardized tests, the overall society)? What do they gain? What groups lose something from that system, and what do they lose? Did the groups that made the decision get all the gains, and did someone else pay all the costs?

NOTES

1. Ratzinger, *Instruction on Christian Freedom and Liberation*, par. 57.
2. Gutiérrez, *A Theology of Liberation*, rev. ed., 17–18. Used by permission.
3. The new understanding is well explained in Galtung, "A Structural Theory of Imperialism." See also Domhoff, *Who Rules America?*
4. Ratzinger, *Instruction on Certain Aspects of the Theology of Liberation.*
5. Ratzinger, *Instruction on Christian Freedom and Liberation.*
6. "Personal Information" link at Leonardo Boff's home page, www.leonardoboff .com/ (accessed July 6, 2006).
7. www.vatican.va/holy_father/john_paul_ii/encyclicals/documents/hf_jp-ii_ enc_30121987_sollicitudo-rei-socialis_en.html (accessed July 6, 2006).
8. www.vatican.va/holy_father/john_paul_ii/encyclicals/documents/hf_jp-ii_enc_ 01051991_centesimusannus_en.html (accessed July 6, 2006).
9. See Pope John Paul II, *Sollicitudo Rei Socialis*, par. 36.
10. www.network935.org/models/stories/mcalpine/ladys.html (accessed July 6, 2006).
11. community.wow.net/lwc/ (accessed July 6, 2006).
12. Main link: www.minutodedios.org/; radio: www.radiominutodedios.com/web/ 107bogota/omd.htm; university: www.uniminuto.edu/; "Build me a home": www.dameunacasa.com/index2.html (accessed July 6, 2006).
13. www.dnu.org/service/sanlucas.html (accessed July 6, 2006).
14. www.guardian.co.uk/brazil/story/0,1419087,00.html#article_continue and www.sndohio.org/dotstang.htm (accessed July 6, 2006).
15. wfn.org/2005/12/msg00102.html. See also www.phillyblog.com/philly/ showthread.php?t=7478 and www.washingtonpost.com/wp-dyn/articles/A51511-2005 Apr13.html (accessed July 6, 2006).
16. Ruether, "False Messianism."
17. Ellis, "Jews, Christians, and Liberation Theology." See also Ellis, *Jewish Theology of Liberation.*
18. Farber, *Radicals, Rabbis and Peacemakers*, 213.
19. Farber, *Radicals, Rabbis and Peacemakers*, 217–20.
20. Esack, *Quran, Liberation, & Pluralism*, 82–113.
21. See en.wikipedia.org/wiki/Tablighi_Jamaat (accessed July 10, 2006).
22. Berndt, *Non-Violence in the World Religions.*
23. Berndt, *Non-Violence in the World Religions*, 60–63.
24. Esack, *Quran, Liberation, & Pluralism*, 87–90.
25. Esack, *Quran, Liberation, & Pluralism*, 90–94.
26. Esack, *Quran, Liberation, & Pluralism*, 97, 101.
27. Esack, *Quran, Liberation, & Pluralism*, 107.
28. Esack, *Quran, Liberation, & Pluralism*, 107.
29. Antonio, "Black Theology," 63–88.
30. Antonio, "Black Theology," 82.
31. Johnson, "Imaging God, Embodying Christ: Women as a Sign of the Times."
32. Grey, "Feminist Theology: A Critical Theology of Liberation," 90–91.

33. Grey, "Feminist Theology: A Critical Theology of Liberation," 92.
34. Grey, "Feminist Theology: A Critical Theology of Liberation," 94, 100–101.
35. Wielenga, "Liberation Theology in Asia," 39–62.
36. Wielenga, "Liberation Theology in Asia," 39.
37. Wielenga, "Liberation Theology in Asia," 40–44, 49.
38. Wielenga, "Liberation Theology in Asia," 46–47, 51–53.
39. Wielenga, "Liberation Theology in Asia," 47–48.
40. Wielenga, "Liberation Theology in Asia," 53–54.
41. Gorospe, *Filipino Social Conscience.*
42. Lebacqz, *Justice in an Unjust World,* 155–56.

SUGGESTIONS FOR FURTHER READING

Antonio. "Black Theology."
Ateek. *Justice, and Only Justice: A Palestinian Theology of Liberation.*
Berndt. *Non-Violence in the World Religions.*
Berryman. *Liberation Theology.*
Domhoff. *Who Rules America?*
Ellis. *Toward a Jewish Theology of Liberation.*
Esack. *Quran, Liberation & Pluralism.*
Farber. *Radicals, Rabbis and Peacemakers.*
Fernandes, ed. *The Emerging Dalit Identity.*
Galtung. "A Structural Theory of Imperialism."
Gorospe. *Forming the Filipino Social Conscience.*
Grey. "Feminist Theology: A Critical Theology of Liberation."
Gutierrez. *A Theology of Liberation.*
Johnson. "Imaging God, Embodying Christ: Women as a Sign of the Times."
Lebacqz. *Justice in an Unjust World.*
———. *Six Theories of Justice.*
Maduro, ed. *Judaism, Christianity, and Liberation: An Agenda for Dialogue.*
McGovern. *Liberation Theology and Its Critics: Towards an Assessment.*
Nelson Pallmeyer. *Harvest of Cain.*
Pieris. *An Asian Theology of Liberation.*
Pope John Paul II. *Centesimus Annus.*
———. *Sollicitudo Rei Socialis.*
Ratzinger. *Instruction on Certain Aspects of the "Theology of Liberation."*
———. *Instruction on Christian Freedom and Liberation.*
Rowland, ed. *The Cambridge Companion to Liberation Theology.*
Topel. *The Way to Peace: Liberation through the Bible.*
Wielenga. "Liberation Theology in Asia."
Wink. *Engaging the Powers.*

Chapter Eleven

Active Nonviolence

"Pursuit of truth [does] not admit of violence being inflicted on one's opponent but . . . he must be weaned from error by patience and sympathy. For, what appears to be truth to the one may appear to be error to another."[1]

"If you want something really important to be done you must not merely satisfy the reason, you must move the heart also. The appeal of reason is more to the head but the penetration of the heart comes from suffering. It opens up the inner understanding in [humans]. Suffering is the badge of the human race, not the sword."[2]

"It is the acid test of nonviolence that in a nonviolent conflict there is no rancor left behind, and in the end the enemies are converted into friends. That was my experience in South Africa with General Smuts. He started with being my bitterest opponent and critic. Today he is my warmest friend."[3]

"Nonviolence is a power which can be wielded equally by all— children, young men and women or grown up people—provided they have a living faith in the God of Love and have therefore equal love for all [humanity]."[4]

—sayings of Mohandas K. Gandhi

WHAT IT IS AND HOW IT WORKS

Active nonviolence is an exercise of power for social and political change that courageously refuses to support evil but also refuses to cause harm to its opponents. The power exercised is spiritual, moral, and persuasive.

Unspiritual, immoral, and unpersuaded people experience this power when they discover that other people on whom they depend for their power no longer support them or their goals. Thus Ferdinand Marcos experienced the power of active nonviolence when he discovered that his army was no longer following his orders.

Many people quit supporting their leaders when they see those leaders unjustly attacking people who are causing no harm. When Chinese tanks ran over unarmed students and Chinese soldiers shot unarmed students in Tianamen Square, Beijing, bystanders lost their confidence in their army and government. They may still go along with the government for a while, but they will do so inefficiently and without enthusiasm. And if an opportunity arises to shift their support to a different government or to different leaders, they will be inclined to do so.

Power Depends on Cooperation

A key insight of active nonviolence is that power depends on widespread cooperation. The more powerful a leader is, the more people she depends on to produce that power. An Amazon tribal chief may depend only on twenty picked warriors, but he has only modest power. The president of the United States has much more power, but that power depends on the cooperation of many more people. When a significant number of those people lost confidence in President Johnson's prosecution of the Vietnam War and began to cooperate halfheartedly, seek primarily their own safety, do no more than they absolutely had to, protest the war, or actively interfere with it, the president found that his power was seriously weakened.

Modern leaders depend on generals, sergeants, privates, police, jailers, cabinet members, senators, congresspersons, judges, lawyers, editors, newspaper reporters, union leaders, industrial workers, transportation workers, farmers, construction workers, schoolteachers, janitors, garbage collectors, and many other people. Senators who refuse to vote "right" can interfere with a president's power, but so can garbage collectors who deliver their gatherings to the front door of the White House just as a foreign diplomat arrives.

Why People Obey Authority[5]

Some people feel morally obliged to obey authority. The rule of law seems fairer than naked personal power. Laws may be seen as God's will, or legitimate, reasonable, and essential for a good society. But laws can also be arbitrary—enriching and protecting elites rather than common people.

Some obey because they identify themselves with the ruler or government. Rulers encourage this identification by appealing to common nationality, tribe, religion, or other deeply held identities.

Some obey out of habit—they don't realize they have a choice. Anyone who "empowers" common people to think for themselves and make choices threatens the power of authoritarian rulers.

Some obey because unjust laws benefit them personally. They support the corrupt system which has enriched them. They may not be conscious of the injustice their privilege is based on. When poverty is widespread, the privileged fear that any change of the power structure will throw *them* into poverty.

Some obey because they fear punishment. Half the governments of the world torture prisoners routinely, not primarily to gain information but to intimidate the population, make people mistrust each other, and destroy any group that might challenge the government's authority.

Some are just too timid to challenge authorities. When their self-confidence increases, authoritarian rulers lose power over them.

Finally, many don't care about a particular law, especially if it doesn't affect *them*. We can't give serious attention to everything. We may just want to live our everyday lives without thinking about the needs of *strangers*.

Give or Withdraw Cooperation

The starting point for a campaign of active nonviolence is the conviction of injustice. Usually it is a relatively small group that first notices the injustice and draws attention to it, or that comes to believe it is possible to do something about it. The *circle of praxis* described by liberation theologians is a process for clarifying the suspicion of injustice. *Insertion* puts one into the experience where injustice is suspected, *social analysis* clarifies its causes, *theological reflection* shows how things could and should be, and *pastoral action* moves the situation toward justice. If the injustice is deep, those who profit from it will usually resist the pastoral action and attack the campaigners. At that point, the hidden violence which held the injustice in place will become visible through the resistance and attacks.

Three Types of Nonviolent Action

Theorist Gene Sharp has identified 198 forms of nonviolent action, arranged into three main types:[6]

1. *Protest and persuasion* involves moral appeals to those in power, and includes letters to political leaders and editors, public appeals and marches, and other attempts to influence public opinion.

Figure 11.1. Nonviolent demonstration seeking to close the School of the Americas, also known as the Western Hemisphere Institute for Security Cooperation, at Fort Benning, Georgia. Each cross bears the name of someone killed by graduates of the school. Courtesy David Whitten Smith, November 2002.

2. *Noncooperation* involves refusing to do what one is normally expected to do. It includes strikes, boycotts, and other refusals to follow orders. Bulgarians who refused to hand over Jews to Nazis were practicing noncooperation. So were the politicians who refused to serve in General Kapp's cabinet after his 1920 putsch in Germany,[7] and the Catholic bishops in Chile who refused to give Pinochet's government the legitimation it expected.[8]
3. *Intervention* involves "getting in the way" of injustice by doing what one is normally forbidden to do. Czechs intervened in 1968 by taking down all the street signs in Prague so that the invaders couldn't find those they wanted to arrest.[9] Philippine civilians intervened in 1986 by standing between two factions of Marcos's army.

Strategy and tactics require careful planning. Both nonviolence and war can be effective or ineffective. Some nonviolent campaigns have been unsuccessful; so have many wars—which is why modern nations support war colleges. If we spent as much energy studying nonviolent action as we devote to war, our modern world would be revolutionized.

Find Symbolic Action and Bring the Injustice into the Open

Nonviolent actions must symbolize the injustice being resisted. A few protesters at the government center don't carry much weight—they look like extremists. We need a more powerfully symbolic action. When Gandhi marched to the sea in India to make salt in violation of British tax laws, the British government of India couldn't ignore the action, nor could they resist it effectively. It symbolized the issue too clearly. In a hot climate like India, people die without salt. The poor could make salt for themselves, but the colonial government wouldn't let them because it taxed the government-monopolized salt.[10]

In Sicily, Danilo Dolci led villagers to repair for free the road leading into the village. The government objected because repair of roads was *their* responsibility. The villagers were dramatizing government inaction in the face of severe unemployment. When Dolci and a number of villagers were arrested, the well-publicized trial made the government look ridiculous.[11]

In Brazil in the 1970s and early 1980s, two lawyers preparing a routine case were astonished to find that the legal archives of the oppressive military government held trial transcripts in which prisoners described their tortures in detail. Cardinal Arns of São Paulo helped the lawyers copy thousands of pages of testimony, analyze and record the data, and publish a single-volume account of the information. Published with no advance publicity, with only the Archdiocese of São Paulo identified on the title page, the book was delivered to bookstores all across Brazil on a single day. Realizing it had been widely distributed already, the military government decided to ignore it. A few months later, the diocesan newspaper printed lists of the torturers with the number of times each had been named by defendants.[12]

Active Nonviolence Is Not Passive

Nonviolent leaders choose *provocative actions* which publicly reveal their *opponents'* violence. In Chile, when Pinochet was torturing citizens in secret, nonviolent activists unfurled banners which read, "People are being tortured here." They did so during rush hour when a lot of people could see them. Those people also saw police clubbing and hosing the nonviolent demonstrators. They came to realize that Pinochet felt threatened because he had something to hide. They also felt respect for the demonstrators, who were willing to be beaten without retaliating.[13]

In the 1990s, the American organization Voices in the Wilderness,[14] founded by Kathy Kelly, dramatized the results of U.S. sanctions against Iraq by delivering medicines and toys to Iraq. In 1998, the group and its leaders were given a "pre-penalty notice" by the Office of Foreign Assets Control

(OFAC) of the U.S. Department of the Treasury that they could be fined $160,000 for delivering these donated medicines and toys without prior authorization. In response, they delivered to the Treasury Department, OFAC, and U.S. Attorney General Janet Reno declarations signed by numerous people stating that they supported and had taken part in the campaign to end the UN/U.S. sanctions against Iraq. Those who had traveled to Iraq offered to assist investigators by bringing samples of the medical supplies and toys in question, along with enlarged photographs of Iraqi children they had met, most of whom had since died for lack of medicines to treat curable diseases. On January 15, 1999, the birthday of Martin Luther King and eight years since the first Gulf War began, Witness for Peace members began an eighteen-day walk from the Pentagon to the United Nations in New York City. Along the way, they campaigned for an end to the UN/U.S. sanctions against Iraq and called on the United Nations to "walk away from the Pentagon": to stop allowing the U.S. policy to pervert the UN into an instrument of warfare that brutalizes children.[15]

Imperative That Action Remain Nonviolent

Active nonviolence works to keep its followers nonviolent and to help the public see that they are nonviolent. If some of the activists begin to throw bombs or to burn tanks, then the soldiers will feel that they are only defending themselves, and bystanders will be sympathetic to that view. But if the activists can maintain the discipline of nonviolence, then the more the ruler orders a violent response the more he or she will lose public respect and support.

At the same time that they maintain their own nonviolence, nonviolent leaders choose *provocative actions* that bring out into the open their *opponents'* violence, which is otherwise hidden. Some examples of such nonviolent public actions have just been given. Similarly, if a leader is supporting unjust wage laws that cause half of the laborers' children to die from malnutrition before the age of five, then the activists will seek a means of making that connection visible. For example, they might hold massive public children's funerals with long processions around the government center to keep the problem before the eyes of the general public. Or workers in luxury industries could strike and offer their services to meet the basic needs of the poor, and then march in a body to city hall to present a bill for their labor.

Expect Violent Repression

It is a misunderstanding to think that the campaign of active nonviolence has failed if violence breaks out against the campaigners. The first response of unjust governments is *usually* violent repression. If the injustice is deep and the nonviolence effective, those who profit from the injustice will attack the campaigners. Activist leaders will be arrested and perhaps tortured. Or they will be beaten up by thugs, as were opposition leaders in Panama. Or they will be murdered or made to disappear, as frequently happens in Central America. This repression brings out into the open the violence which was previously only threatened but which has held the unjust situation in place through fear.

If the activists overcome their fear of pain and death and remain firm, the repression will further weaken the government's support. A kind of moral *ju-jitsu* begins to operate: instead of defending themselves from the opponent's violence by responding with violence of their own, the activists use that violence to throw the opponent off balance and to raise hesitations in his supporters' minds. The more repression the opponent uses, the worse he looks to his supporters and the weaker he becomes. When enough supporters become hesitant, inefficient, or obstructive, the opponent's power dissolves.

Three Forms of Success

As the process of nonviolent resistance proceeds, success can come to the resisters in one of three ways. The opponent's leadership may actually be *converted* to see the justice of the resisters. This result is not so rare as is normally believed, but it tends to occur years *after* the issue has been resolved by the second form of success: *accommodation.*

In *accommodation,* leaders decide that maintaining their position is not worth what it is costing them. For example, the Southern white establishment in the United States *first* accepted integration as an *accommodation.* Much *later* they came to *conversion*—to see that segregation had been unjust.

The third possible form of success is by *coercion.* In this case, the leader desires to continue the status quo, but finds that the army, police, lawyers, judges, and others he depends on refuse to carry out his orders. Ferdinand Marcos lost power in the Philippines through coercion when both his army and the U.S. government refused to support his administration.

Not Just for Nice Guys

Active nonviolence can work even against the most oppressive governments if the activists are persistent and courageous enough. If enough people overcome their fear of death and pain, the process is very powerful. But it is a serious question whether a community is courageous enough to make it work.

Remember that these activities produce their effects from the bottom up, by influencing first, not the main leader, but those on whom the leader depends for support. It isn't Hitler who has to be convinced, but rather those who support him. The contrast between the activists' nonviolence and the oppressors' violence affects various people in various ways. Uncommitted third parties are repelled by the violence. Members of the opponents' group begin to have doubts. And the grievance group gains encouragement and support.

Among Gene Sharp's vast array of historical examples (198 different types of active nonviolence)[16] are several successful actions taken against Hitler's "final solution" and against communist governments. The nonviolent actions all had a significant effect. They did not necessarily solve the problems being faced, but neither did the violent efforts made to solve the same problems.

For example, in Berlin in 1943 the Gestapo arrested the Jewish husbands of Gentile wives. The wives responded, some six thousand of them, by demonstrating at the gates of the center where their husbands were being detained. Although security police kept trying to disperse the crowd, they kept reassembling. Despite the fact that Gestapo headquarters were a short distance away, the authorities negotiated with the women and eventually released their husbands.

In Norway under Nazi occupation, the Norwegian leader installed by the Germans, Vidkun Quisling, attempted to promote fascist education with a new teachers' organization. Ten thousand of the twelve thousand Norwegian teachers wrote letters, personally signed, refusing to have anything to do with fascist teaching or Quisling's organization. When the government closed the schools, teachers taught in homes. When Quisling arrested a thousand teachers and shipped them to concentration camps, schoolchildren gathered at the railroad stations the trains passed through singing songs of support. The teachers who remained still refused to give in. Quisling raged at the teachers, "You teachers have destroyed everything for me!" Eight months after the original arrests, all the arrested teachers were sent home to heroes' welcomes.

The 1989–1991 collapse of communism in Eastern Europe and the Soviet Union shows how much power active nonviolence can have when the situation is right. But even under earlier, harsher Soviet rule, there were nonviolent campaigns that had significant effect. Among these earlier campaigns were strikes in the slave labor camps, especially at Vorkuta after Stalin died. That strike involved thirty thousand prisoners. Some of the leaders were shot during the three-month strike, and the strike ended without an official victory, but considerable material improvements in the conditions of the prisoners did follow.

Better known is the resistance to Russia's 1968 invasion of Czechoslovakia. Russian leaders expected that the invasion of over a half million troops would eliminate resistance within a few days and allow them to replace President Alexander Dubcek with a conservative president who would follow the Moscow line. Instead the invaders were met with massive noncooperation and concealed disruption. Czechs climbed onto tanks to ask their invaders why they had come. "No, we didn't ask for your help. We were doing fine." The night before massive arrests were to be made, citizens of Prague took down the street signs and piled them in large heaps so that the invading police couldn't find the addresses they had been given. Engineers and mechanics cheerfully went out of their way to carry out long repairs on equipment that somehow broke down anew as soon as the repairs were completed. Secret radio transmitters broadcast new ideas for resistance and information on Soviet moves. Political leaders refused to cooperate with the invaders despite the invaders' overwhelming military power. Invading troops hadn't brought food for such a long campaign—it was eight months before the Soviets were finally able to gain some of their objectives. And their final gains were a compromise, which is unusual given such overwhelming force—defeated countries aren't supposed to have bargaining power.

The Czech experience influenced the Poles, who founded an independent labor union, *Solidarinose* (Solidarity), rival to the official communist union. That move seemed at first to be too weak to affect Poland; later events showed just how powerful it actually was. The Polish experience then paved the way for the stunning "house of cards" collapse of communist rule in Eastern Europe and the Soviet Union. When active nonviolence surfaced again in Czechoslovakia and led to full independence, who reappeared but Alexander Dubcek!

These examples are incomplete in the sense that the gains they achieved were limited. Still, they were mostly ad hoc efforts without planning in advance. A campaign that did enjoy planning in advance was the 1986 Philippine resistance to Ferdinand Marcos. A year before the election that led to his downfall, the Philippine Catholic Church under Cardinal Sin invited a Dutch couple noted for their nonviolence training programs, the Goss-Mayers, to run training sessions for the people. During the height of the crisis, the Goss-Mayers met daily with Cardinal Sin to plan what they would do under various potential situations. They had worked out in advance that, if the army divided and seemed about to engage in civil war, they would ask civilians to turn out in force and crowd in between the two army units, making it difficult for them to attack each other. The situation occurred just as they had imagined it might, and their pre-planned strategy succeeded brilliantly.

This example illustrates that active nonviolence can be a lot more effective if it is carefully planned and prepared in advance. Gandhi's success in India and Martin Luther King Jr.'s in the United States are other illustrations of the value of such planning.

All of these examples, and many which could be added, show that even the most brutal governments are vulnerable to campaigns of active nonviolence if the population is courageous enough to persist in the face of repression. Of course the population may not be courageous enough. But it may not be courageous and committed enough to make a *violent* campaign such as a revolution or armed resistance work, either. The United States was either not committed enough, not courageous enough, or not powerful enough to "win" in Vietnam. Most critics conclude that it was not committed enough, in part because American opponents of the war convinced enough people that the damage being caused was out of proportion to the possible good that could be gained. It is probably also true that most Americans were unwilling to lose their lives and fortunes in the war.

Overcoming Fear of Death

Attackers or oppressors expect their victims to fight or to run. They are prepared for either of those reactions. They are not prepared to face people who offer them no threat, but who also refuse to cower or shrink in fear. This unexpected reaction derails their attack and substitutes a human relationship for a master-victim relationship. Gordon Fellman speaks of "opening the frame of adversarialism."[17] James Aho studies how adversaries constitute each other as enemies and how that enemy-formation can be reversed, using the example of a Jewish cantor who converted a Ku Klux Klan grand dragon who was threatening him and his family.[18]

Because willingness to suffer and die is so important for successful social change to promote justice, either through war or through active nonviolence, activists would do well to call on the deepest energies and commitments available to humans. These energies and commitments usually flow from the deepest elements of a person's worldview. For religious people, their religious convictions give them the most courage. For secular people, we should consider what aspects of their worldview carry a similar energy.

Fr. Emmanuel Charles McCarthy says, "For the Christian, survival is not a problem. For the Christian, survival is guaranteed." The same could be said of, at least, Hinduism and Islam. Aleksandr Solzhenitsyn points out how concentrating on survival leads to disaster:

> And the conclusion is: . . . 'Survive! At any price!' . . . And whoever takes that vow, whoever does not blink before its crimson burst—allows his own misfortune to overshadow both the entire common misfortune and the whole world. This is the great fork of camp life. . . . If you go to the right—you lose your life, and if you go to the left—you lose your conscience. . . . 'At any price' means: at the price of someone else.[19]

SOME NONVIOLENT ACTIVISTS

Many proponents of active nonviolence have been deeply religious persons. See chapter 1 for discussion of Vinoba Bhave and Mohandas Gandhi; chapter 2 for A.T. Ariyaratne, Aung San Suu Kyi, the Dalai Lama, Nagarjuna, and Thich Nhat Hanh; chapter 3 for Martin Buber, Ahad Haam, and Etty Hillesum; chapter 4 for Jane Addams, Dorothy Day, and Dr. Martin Luther King Jr.; chapter 5 for Khan Abdul Ghaffar Khan, Giasuddin Ahmed, Fatima Mernissi, and Chandra Muzaffar; chapter 6 for Bartholomé de Las Casas and Winona LaDuke; chapter 8 for Uri Avnery, Abuna Elias Chacour, the Israel Defense Force Refuseniks, and various local and international peace teams; and chapter 10 for Marc Ellis, Farid Esack, and Rosemary Radford Ruether.

Here are ten more examples from the last two centuries:

Adin Ballou (1803–1890, United States, Protestant minister) was an active member of the New England Non-Resistance Society, which promoted radical social change without violence, and a friend of William Lloyd Garrison, who campaigned against slavery. Ballou developed the principles of pacifism and nonviolence, influencing Thoreau, Tolstoy (with whom he corresponded), and Gandhi. His 1846 book *Christian Non-Resistance* exercises our imaginations with numerous accounts of creative, compassionate, and effective nonviolence. Tolstoy translated Ballou's writings into Russian and circulated them there.

Henry David Thoreau (1817–1862, United States, Transcendentalist) was jailed overnight in 1846 when he refused to pay the Massachusetts poll tax because it was in support of the war with Mexico, which he believed was designed to extend slavery. When his friend Emerson saw him in prison, he said, "What are you doing in there?" Thoreau responded, "What are you doing out there?" As a result of this experience, Thoreau wrote the famous essay "On Civil Disobedience."

Count Leo von Tolstoy (1828–1910, Russia, disaffected Orthodox Christian). A renowned Russian novelist, author of *War and Peace,* Tolstoy was converted to radical pacifism late in his life, arguing that there would be no wars if soldiers would simply refuse to fight. His writings were very influential in the late 1880s, giving rise to numerous Tolstoy Clubs for the study of his ideas. Strongly influenced by Ballou and Thoreau, he himself influenced Jane Addams (see chapter 4) and Mohandas K. Gandhi.

Eleanor Roosevelt (1884–1962, United States, Christian).[20] Probably the best known first lady (1933–1945) in the history of the United States, she was a feminist, a supporter of the civil rights movement (in contrast to her husband, who was president), and a human rights advocate. She and her fifth cousin once removed, Franklin Delano Roosevelt, were married in 1905 and had six children. When the Daughters of the American Revolution (DAR), to which Eleanor belonged, would not allow the great black opera singer Marian Anderson to perform in their Constitution Hall in Washington, D.C., Eleanor dropped her membership in the organization and organized a performance by Anderson at the Lincoln Memorial before an audience of about seventy thousand people; the concert was broadcast live by radio to millions more. During World War II, Eleanor disagreed with Executive Order 9066, which authorized the confinement of 110,000 Japanese and Japanese-American citizens of the United States in internment camps. Among her most important achievements was her work as chair of the committee that wrote the United Nations Universal Declaration of Human Rights, approved by the UN General Assembly in December 1948.

Corrie Ten Boom (1892–1983, Netherlands, Dutch Reformed Christian). Working as a Dutch watchmaker in her family's jewelry store, Ten Boom was forty-eight when the Nazis occupied Holland. Once when a visiting pastor turned down her request to help a Jewish mother and her baby on the grounds that he and his family might die as a result, her father took the baby in his arms and said to the pastor, "You say we could lose our lives for this child. I would consider that the greatest honor that could come to my family."[21] Like her father, Ten Boom joined the Dutch underground (resistance), finding or offering shelter to homeless Jews and helping to feed them. She hid seven Jews in a secret room behind a false wall in her bedroom. After an informer betrayed her family to the Gestapo and they had been arrested, her father died. She and her sister were sent to various prisons and camps, the last being Ravensbruck in Germany, where her sister died. Two of her sister's visions came true: a home for recovering former detainees and a camp for survivors of the Third Reich. After giving a talk about forgiveness in a Munich church in 1947, Ten Boom was approached by a former guard from Ravensbruck whom she recognized. He thanked her for her talk and extended his hand. She found herself unable to move her arm; she had to ask God to share with her *God's* forgiveness of this guard. "As I took his hand, the most incredible thing happened. From my shoulder along my arm and through my hand a current seemed to pass from me to him, while into my heart sprang a love for this stranger that almost overwhelmed me. And so I discovered that it is not on our forgiveness any more than on our love that the world's healing hinges, but on His."[22]

Rosa Parks (1913–2005, United States, Baptist Christian). Rosa Parks is best known for her refusal to give up her seat on a Montgomery, Alabama, city bus in December 1955. Parks had lived in Alabama all of her life, but in 1957 she and her husband moved first to Virginia and then to Detroit, Michi-

gan. As a child in Pine Level, Alabama, Parks walked to and from school because there was no school bus for black children there or anywhere else in the
South with its Jim Crow segregation laws. She remembered seeing the white
bus go by every day: "The bus was among the first ways I realized there was
a black world and a white world."[23] She graduated from high school in 1933
with her husband's support, one of only 7% of African Americans to do so.
After two failed attempts, she registered to vote, and she became a member
of the local NAACP chapter in 1943. Her activism was furthered by the
friendship of a white couple named Durr, for whom she worked.

Before the famous 1955 incident, Parks had encountered the same hostile
bus driver in 1943 when she sat in a "white" bus seat momentarily on her way
out of the bus in order to retrieve her purse. The driver drove away before she
could reenter the bus at the back, and she faced a rainy five-mile walk home.
On December 1, 1955, the same driver asked her and three other black riders
to move back to make room for more whites entering the bus. Parks was the
only one of the four who would not stand up; committing civil disobedience,
she said to the driver, "I don't think I should have to stand up." When he told
her he would call the police and have her arrested, she responded, "You may
do that." Later she commented that her reason was neither ordinary fatigue
nor old age (she was forty-two), but rather that she was "tired of giving in."
During her arrest, she realized, "It was the very last time that I would ever
ride in humiliation of this kind." Parks' arrest and her subsequent trial pre-
cipitated the Montgomery bus boycott, which lasted for 382 days, forcing the
bus system to desegregate. Parks wrote two books: *Rosa Parks: My Story*
(1992) and *Quiet Strength* (1995). Martin Luther King Jr., praised Parks as
"one of the finest citizens of Montgomery."

Gene Sharp (1928– , United States, Christian promoting a universal active
nonviolence). Sharp wrote *The Politics of Nonviolent Action* (1973) and numerous other books promoting the thesis that governments and nations can defend themselves from their enemies with exclusively nonviolent means if they
educate and train their people appropriately. Such defense has the advantage
that one's enemies do not feel threatened by it, so it does not lead to an arms
race. It also has the advantage that the things people learn from it encourage
them to act nonviolently in their everyday relations with others, whereas emphasizing armed resistance can easily encourage domestic violence.

Mubarak Awad (1943– , Palestinian born in Jerusalem, U.S. citizen, Greek
Arab Christian) founded the Center for the Study of Nonviolence in
Jerusalem, which began to develop nonviolent strategies and tactics for the
Israeli-Palestinian dispute. He has promoted Gandhi's methods of resistance
effectively among Arabs in Israel and the Occupied Territories (the West
Bank, Gaza, and East Jerusalem). In 1988, the Israeli government refused to

renew his visa, although he was born in Jerusalem and holds U.S. citizenship, suggesting that they find promotion of nonviolence to be particularly dangerous. When he was expelled from Jerusalem, Awad founded Nonviolence International in the United States.[24] Inspired by Awad's ideas, the Arab village of Beit Sahour, near Bethlehem, carried on a tax revolt against Israel for several years. They took as their motto "No taxation without representation," pointing out that they received no services for their taxes. In retaliation, the Israeli army entered the village and confiscated automobiles as well as appliances, furniture, clothing, and machinery used for small manufacturing such as sewing machines from people's homes.[25]

Shirin Ebadi (1947– , Iran, Muslim).[26] Winner of the 2003 Nobel Peace Prize, Shirin Ebadi is an Iranian lawyer, who served in the Iranian Justice Department, in particular as a judge, until the revolution of 1979, when all women judges were demoted to clerical positions. After protests, they were promoted to the level of "expert." She retired early and was not able to engage in the practice of law again until 1992. While unemployed, she wrote articles and books. Her cases have involved the assassination of liberal dissidents, child abuse, banned periodicals, etc. Her dedication to human rights and to democracy has become internationally known. After receiving the Nobel Peace Prize, she stated her opposition to foreign interference in Iranian affairs, including the Iranian struggle for human rights.

Chaiwat Satha-Anand (1955– , Thailand, Muslim). In his essay "The Nonviolent Crescent," the Thai scholar-activist Chaiwat Satha-Anand concludes with "eight theses on Muslim nonviolent action." Note that these theses begin from principles of *just war*. Since those principles prove incapable of being satisfied (1–4), he is led to principles of *nonviolent action* (5–8).

1. For Islam, the problem of violence is an integral part of the Islamic moral sphere.
2. Violence, if any, used by Muslims must be governed by rules prescribed in the Quran and Hadith.
3. If the violence used cannot discriminate between combatants and noncombatants, then it is unacceptable in Islam.
4. [The] modern technology of destruction renders discrimination virtually impossible at present.
5. In the modern world, Muslims cannot use violence.
6. Islam teaches Muslims to fight for justice with the understanding that human lives—as all parts of God's creation—are purposive and sacred.
7. In order to be true to Islam, Muslims must utilize nonviolent action as a new mode of struggle.
8. Islam itself is fertile soil for nonviolence because of its potential for disobedience, strong discipline, sharing and social responsibility, perseverance and self-sacrifice, and the belief in the unity of the Muslim community and the oneness of [human]kind.[27]

WOMEN'S GROUPS

Much of the peace work carried on by women has been carried on in groups where no single woman stands out. Because of social attitudes toward women, groups of women are harder for repressive governments to attack than are individual men or groups of men. We have already noted the Gentile wives of Jewish husbands who faced down the Gestapo in Berlin in 1943. Here are some other famous groups of peacemaking women courageously confronting repressive situations and governments:

Women Abolitionists against Slavery

In the 1860s in the United States, no blacks (male or female) and no white women had any legal rights. The Northern black women who began organizing usually had jobs; they tended to form mutual aid societies and established orphanages, settlement houses, schools, and cultural (e.g., literary) societies. A landmark event was the public lecture by a black woman named Maria Stewart in Boston; she was the first woman to give a public speech in the United States.[28]

Black and white women abolitionists attended the Antislavery Convention of American Women in New York City in 1837; attendees at the convention supported a women's abolitionist movement independent of the men's abolitionist movement. The Grimké sisters associated the issue of women's rights with abolitionism (the issue of slavery). There was widespread Northern opposition to the women's abolitionist movement and to any interracial women's (anti-slavery) movement; one incident showing this opposition was the burning of the convention hall—Pennsylvania Hall—in Philadelphia in 1838.[29] Among the actions of abolitionist women was the rescue of runaway slaves about to be sent back to the South.

Women used the practice of political petitioning frequently, since they could not vote. The homes of black and white women served as stations along the Underground Railroad (by which southern slaves traveled north to freedom), despite a law passed in 1850 making this illegal.

Greenham Common (Britain)

In 1981 the Greenham Women's Peace Camp was established on Greenham Common in southern England as a protest site next to a military base where the United States had stationed some of its cruise missiles. Protest actions by the women peaked in 1983, with the participation of thirty thousand women. Partly as a result of this campaign, the United States and the Soviet Union ratified the INF (Intermediate-Range Nuclear Forces) Treaty in 1988. By 1991 the base had been emptied of all missiles.

The women who struggled nonviolently against these nuclear weapons were seen as unconventional by the British society around them; often they were banned from local businesses and subjected to police brutality. Yet they steadfastly adhered to the fundamentals of nonviolent resistance, refusing to retaliate or to be verbally abusive. "Hundreds of women learned the principles and practice of nonviolence at Greenham. It changed from a tactic to a way of life, a sustainable system of recognition of the other not based on religion or rules," writes Di McDonald in an article entitled "A Way of Life."[30]

A key action by the Greenham women was their piecemeal destruction, using wire cutters, of the barbed wire fence erected around the base, resulting in hundreds of arrests leading to charges and fines; many chose to serve prison terms rather than pay the fines. Developing legal expertise, the women were able to demonstrate the illegality of the base in that it had been constructed on "common land," which could not be occupied by any military.

Mothers of the Disappeared (Guatemala [GAM], Argentina, Chile)

On April 13, 1977, fourteen mothers of "disappeared" children demonstrated for the first time at the Plaza de Mayo in Buenos Aires, Argentina. They continued demonstrating there every Thursday afternoon by walking around in a circle and holding pictures of their disappeared loved ones. Eventually they numbered between two hundred and three hundred. On October 5, 1977, they placed an advertisement in *La Prensa* showing pictures of 237 of the disappeared together with their mothers' names and the words, "We do not ask for anything more than the truth." On October 15, the women went to the congress building with a petition signed by twenty-four thousand Argentineans and demanded a government investigation into the disappearances.

Government repression followed, and the group was infiltrated by a young man whose activity led to the kidnapping and disappearance of twelve of the women. The demonstrations at the Plaza de Mayo died out for a while, but the women met silently in churches instead. In 1979 they formed a legal association with elections and a bank account, and in 1980 they began to rent office space and publish a bulletin; as a result, their membership increased from hundreds to thousands. They resumed demonstrations in the Plaza, despite police repression, gaining more popular support. In December 1983 the military regime was replaced with a democratic government.[31]

Women in Black

Women in Black is an international peace movement founded in 1988 by a group of Israeli women. Its name was taken from the practice of wearing black at a weekly hour-long vigil held on Friday in cities and towns across Israel. At the vigils the women hold up signs reading "Stop the Occupation," meaning the Israeli military occupation of the Palestinian West Bank and Gaza Strip. Among major actions organized by the Israeli Women in Black was a march of about five thousand Israeli and Palestinian women and men from Israeli West Jerusalem to Palestinian East Jerusalem in December 2001. Two banners leading the procession read, "The Occupation is Killing Us All" and "We Refuse to be Enemies."[32]

Women in Black exist around the world—in Italy, Germany, India, the former Yugoslavia, and many other countries. They seek justice and a world without violence. In Israel, Women in Black is a member organization of the Coalition of Women for a Just Peace. A film entitled "Stuck with the Truth," made in 2003 by the Canadian Friends of Sabeel (a Palestinian nonviolent liberation theology organization), shows these Women in Black at a vigil in Jerusalem. One of them talks about praying for peace so that the next generation will not live in fear as her generation has. Another woman affirms that "there is a peaceful way out of this conflict . . . we can live together" in two nations side by side.

The international organization and the Israeli Women in Black have won various peace prizes; the movement was nominated for the Nobel Peace Prize in 2001. At the end of her address to the UN Security Council on October 23, 2002, Israeli peace activist Gila Svirsky asked, "Is it not preposterous that not a single Israeli woman, and only one Palestinian woman, have held leadership roles at a Middle East peace summit? . . . Is it any wonder that we are still locked in combat?" She concluded, "What we need now is leadership committed to swiftly concluding this era awash in blood. . . . What we need now is women."[33]

NONVIOLENCE AS A TACTIC, OR AS A WAY OF LIFE

Some advocates, like Gene Sharp, promote active nonviolence as a *tactic* suited to the 20th-21st century nuclear stalemate: if we can just teach people how to *fight differently*, we may be able to prevent nuclear devastation. To insist that people commit to nonviolence in *every situation* would weaken its power by reducing the number of people who would use it.

Others, like Gandhi, promote it as a *way of life* to be used in all situations and independent of its success in achieving our goals. Gandhi distinguishes the *satyagraha* ("truth force"—his word for active nonviolence that emphasizes its spiritual power) of the *strong* from that of the *weak*. *The weak* choose satyagraha when they feel they don't have the power to use force. If later they get the power, they prefer to use force. *The strong* choose satyagraha even when they have the power and opportunity to use force. They do so because they are committed to it as a way of life.

Satyagraha as a way of life implies that no human being can be sure that she is right. Therefore she should struggle in a way which respects the opponent, who sees things differently. She accepts suffering at the opponent's hands because she believes that innocent suffering has the power to touch and transform hearts. She trusts that most humans cannot long attack those who do not threaten them with harm. Those who can continue to attack the nonviolent will find themselves more and more isolated.

Each of the worldviews presented in chapters 1–7 seeks to foster the courage and energy that a person needs in order to realize satyagraha. Here are some comments on how they do this:

Hinduism. The pleasures and attractions of this visible world are impermanent and disappointing, but by a disciplined life we can escape from the dreary round of rebirth and come to union with the divine ground of all reality. Part of this self-discipline involves ahimsa, the refusal to harm living things. If we harm living things, we produce bad karma, which will draw us away from the salvation we seek. But compassion and love will produce good karma, which will move us toward this eventual salvation. When we reach union with the divine reality, we will realize through experience the truth that my self and your self are in fact the same, and identical with the divine Self which is the divine reality. Then we will realize how we have harmed ourselves when we have harmed others. Gandhi added the insight that undeserved suffering lovingly accepted has spiritual power to touch the deep heart of our opponent and lead her to conversion.

Buddhism. The emphasis on bad karma is even stronger than in Hinduism. It is very difficult to exercise political power without developing bad karma, because political power so often involves corruption and keeps us attached to the visible world. The Buddhist need not fear death, because the "self" is only an accidental concatenation of forces that dissolves in death. If the Buddhist has reached enlightenment, he will pass into nirvana. If not, he will return in another birth (perhaps after some time in the spirit world) to resume progress toward enlightenment. The use of force is likely to indicate that the Buddhist is not yet detached. By speaking the truth courageously, the Buddhist will be showing that she is not attached to this life. She will also be calling her opponent to detachment from the selfishness that is at the base of his injustice, thus helping him forward toward enlightenment.

Judaism. God has called the Jewish community into being and made a covenant with it. All Jews are brothers and sisters, and the common inheritance of the community is a gift from God. God will protect the community if his people trust him rather than their own strength. He leads them into situations where everyone can see that they do not have the power to save themselves, so that all will know that it is God who has saved them. Jews are called to be just to each other, to be fair to foreigners, and to be an example (a "light") to Gentiles of God's love and justice. Some Jews believe that their race is also called, in some mysterious way, to suffer for the world.

Christianity. God has created all humans as brothers and sisters to share the goods of creation and the burdens of work. God is just and calls humans to be just. God knows the secrets of hearts and will reward the just and punish the guilty after this life. Sin has set humans on a selfish path, but the self-sacrificing love of Jesus of Nazareth, who in some mysterious way is God and human, has destroyed the power of sin to destroy humans. Jesus invites us to surrender to the pain and suffering caused by human injustice as he did, by confronting that injustice courageously but without violence and trusting God to raise us from the death that injustice will threaten. By accepting pain and suffering in this way, we will come to a closer union with Jesus and discover by experience that we are all members of his body, dependent on him and on each other. When we refuse to fear death, refuse to cooperate with injustice and evil, and confront evil with goodness and truth, the power of Jesus' surrender to the cross works through us, touching the deep hearts of sinners and calling them to repentance. This repentance of sinners is worth the suffering and death with which we are threatened.

Islam. God has created this world, and we are all brothers and sisters. God calls us to be just and loving, and after this life God will reward the good and punish the wicked. Most of all, God has called us to trust him and to surrender to his will. We should trust him to be our protection. If we die at the hands of wicked humans, we need not fear, because God will vindicate and reward us. God calls us into the *ummah*, a community of caring and sharing where all are equals.

Native American Worldviews. All aspects of the world are filled with spirit and are thus related to us. Animals are people like us. Plants, too, and even minerals and the earth itself share the spirit. The earth belongs to God—it cannot be monopolized by a few humans and denied to others. Powerful people draw their power from the spirit world. Perhaps certain animals could share with us their nonviolent power if we were to seek it in a quest.

Marxism. Humans overcome their sense of alienation by committing themselves to work for the revolution which will seize power from the bourgeois elite and put it in the hands of the proletariat, that is, all the people. When this process is complete, oppression will be at an end because the abundant product of modern industry will be fairly distributed and everyone will have what they really need. We all will then enjoy good relations with each other, freed from the isolation caused by selfishness. While the revolution is not yet a success throughout the world, and there are difficulties so long as it is not worldwide, those who sacrifice themselves for the future will have the satisfaction of knowing that they are helping to create the new human in a just world.

WALTER WINK, *ENGAGING THE POWERS*

To illuminate the specific Christian view of active nonviolence developed by the American biblical scholar Walter Wink, Jack Nelson-Pallmeyer explains some of the insights contained in Walter Wink's three-volume study of the New Testament language for "principalities and powers," titled *Engaging the Powers* (1984–1992).

"ACTIVE NONVIOLENCE: JESUS' THIRD WAY," BY JACK NELSON-PALLMEYER (MAY 1994)

The persistence of evil and the pervasiveness of violence serve to legitimate violence and make it difficult for Christians and others to take nonviolence seriously, including the nonviolence of Jesus. Television shows and movies, nightly news programs, and daily living surround us with images of violence. From battered women, crime, urban riots, and Bosnia we are nearly overwhelmed with violence.

In most instances the solution to the problem of pervasive evil and violence is projected to be the exercise of more creative, and oftentimes more lethal, forms of violence. Violence saves, or in the words of New Testament scholar Walter Wink, we believe in "the myth of redemptive violence." According to Wink, in his provocative book *Engaging the Powers*,[34] violence and not Christianity is the real religion of America. The myth of redemptive violence "undergirds American popular culture, civil religion, nationalism, and foreign policy" (p. 13). Wink writes that "one of the most pressing questions facing the world today is, How can we oppose evil without creating new evils and being made evil ourselves?" The answer, he says, involves taking the nonviolence of Jesus seriously.

Wink describes the traditional responses to danger and evil as flight or fight:

- Flight = submission; passivity; withdrawal; surrender.
- Fight = armed revolt; violent rebellion; direct retaliation; revenge.

Wink says Jesus offers a third alternative or way: creative, active nonviolence. Drawing out the wisdom and tactics of Jesus as described in the Matthew text (turn the other cheek, give your cloak, walk an extra mile), Wink shows how Jesus' Third Way empowers oppressed people to take the initiative and respond with dignity to a situation of oppression, to put the oppressor in an awkward position while offering the possibility of repentance and transformation.

Wink summarizes Jesus' Third Way as follows:[35]

- Seize the moral initiative.
- Find a creative alternative to violence.
- Assert your own humanity and dignity as a person.
- Meet force with ridicule or humor.
- Break the cycle of humiliation.
- Refuse to submit to or to accept the inferior position.
- Expose the injustice of the system.
- Take control of the power dynamic.
- Shame the oppressor into repentance.
- Stand your ground.
- Make the Powers make decisions for which they are not prepared.
- Recognize your own power.
- Be willing to suffer rather than retaliate.
- Force the oppressor to see you in a new light.
- Deprive the oppressor of a situation where a show of force is effective.
- Be willing to undergo the penalty of breaking unjust laws.
- Die to the fear of the old order and its rules.
- Seek the oppressor's transformation.

Wink notes that in the Matthew passage we see Jesus as a tactician of nonviolence and that these tactics need to be adapted to our own time. However, Jesus' commitment to nonviolence goes beyond tactics. It is reflected in his death on a cross. Jesus was committed to nonviolent resistance because nonviolence reflects and reveals the character of God.

Before dismissing the nonviolence of Jesus as somehow utopian, we would do well to remember that Jesus also lived during very violent times. Rome routinely crucified those it considered agitators, and it sent in its legions to destroy entire cities when necessary; some Jewish groups assassinated Jews who collaborated with Rome, and eventually there was an armed rebellion against Rome, led by the Zealots. There were also many Jews waiting for a violent coming of God, a messiah who would come and throw out the hated Romans, cleanse the temple, and re-establish Israel as an independent nation ruled by a Davidic-type king. In other words, Jesus' nonviolence was as strikingly counter-cultural in his time as active nonviolence is in our own.

SUMMARY

Active nonviolence is based on the observation that political power depends on the cooperation of the ruled. When they withdraw consent—by protesting, refusing to cooperate, or even getting in the way—an oppressive leader's power can collapse. Oppressive leaders can be expected to respond with violent repression, which brings into the open the threatened violence that has maintained the unjust situation. If the nonviolent campaigners can overcome fear and maintain their resistance in the face of suffering and death, they can destroy the political power even of tyrants. This is because the effect works from the bottom up, not by making the tyrant change his or her mind, but by causing those the tyrant depends on to change their minds. Occasionally an oppressor is led to see the injustice. More commonly, the oppressor gives in because maintaining the unjust situation costs more than it is worth. At its extreme, an oppressor may lose political control entirely, despite every effort to maintain the unjust situation. Numerous examples show that active nonviolence has been effective even against Nazi Germany and Soviet Communism. If it were studied as intently as military force is studied, it could be even more effective.

KEY TERMS

accommodation	ju-jitsu
ahimsa	noncooperation
coercion	nonviolence of the strong
conversion	nonviolence of the weak
dilemma	persuasion
dispute	protest
intervention	satyagraha

DISCUSSION QUESTIONS

1. This chapter refers back to over thirty leaders of active nonviolence discussed in previous chapters and introduces thirteen more plus several women's groups. Which of them would you be most interested in reading about further? What caught your attention and interest? Which of their ideas did you particularly agree or disagree with?
2. Do you believe that active nonviolence can be a practical and effective way to struggle for justice and peace? If so, would you be committed to it as a tactic to be used in particular circumstances, or as a way of life to be used in all circumstances? If as a tactic, under what circumstances would you set nonviolence aside in favor of violence or war? (This leads to the next chapter. But first, see the special study questions proposed below by Jack Nelson-Pallmeyer.)

SPECIAL STUDY QUESTIONS

3. Watch several Saturday morning cartoons. In what ways is the message of redemptive violence conveyed to children?
4. Read Matthew 5:38–42. You might also want to read pp. 175–82 in *Engaging the Powers*. Why do you think the nonviolence of Jesus is often not taken seriously? What are some examples from recent history of people and movements that have rooted their commitment to nonviolence in the example of Jesus?
5. Choose a recent or current situation where violence is/was pervasive—for example, Bosnia, Darfur, Iraq, Israel-Palestine, Rwanda, or the U.S. urban crisis. What might a strategy of nonviolent action based on Jesus' third way look like in one of these situations?

NOTES

1. Gandhi, *Young India*, November 1919, quoted in *All Men Are Brothers*, 88; also in Fahey and Armstrong, *A Peace Reader*, 173. Reprinted by permission of UNESCO, © 1958.

2. Gandhi, *Young India*, November 4, 1931, quoted in *All Men Are Brothers*, 91; also in Fahey and Armstrong, *A Peace Reader*, 174. Reprinted by permission of UNESCO, © 1958.

3. Gandhi, quoted in *All Men Are Brothers*, 97. Reprinted by permission of UNESCO, © 1958.

4. Gandhi, *Harijan*, September 5, 1936, quoted in *All Men Are Brothers*, 91; also in Fahey and Armstrong, *A Peace Reader*, 174. Reprinted by permission of UNESCO, © 1958.

5. Sharp, *The Politics of Nonviolent Action*, 16–23.

6. Sharp, *The Politics of Nonviolent Action*, xii–xvi.

7. Sharp, *The Politics of Nonviolent Action*, 79–81.

8. Cavanaugh, *Torture and Eucharist*, 1998.

9. Sharp, *The Politics of Nonviolent Action*, 300–301.

10. Bondurant, *Conquest of Violence*, 88–102.

11. Sharp, *The Politics of Nonviolent Action*, 402.

12. Archdiocese of São Paulo, *Torture in Brazil*, 1986.

13. I am describing the Sebastian Acevedo Movement Against Torture. See Cavanaugh, *Torture and Eucharist*, 273–77.

14. vitw.org/ (accessed June 25, 2006). The site says that it is no longer maintained, but will be left available "for archival and research purposes."

15. "Voices in the Wilderness: A Brief History (1996–2005)," compiled by Heidi Holliday and Tess Kleinhaus, vitw.org/archives/317 (accessed July 12, 2006).

16. Sharp, *The Politics of Nonviolent Action;—Gandhi as a Political Strategist;—Waging Nonviolent Struggle: 20th Century Practice and 21st Century Potential*.

17. Fellman, *Violence to Nonviolence*, 220–23.

18. Aho, *This Thing of Darkness*. The Larry Trapp case is also mentioned in Fellman, *Violence to Nonviolence*, 222–23, where he refers to a book-length study of the case: Watterson, *Not by the Sword*.

19. Solzhenitsyn, *The Gulag Archipelago*, 602–3. Reprinted by permission of HarperCollins Publishers.

20. "Eleanor Roosevelt," en.wikipedia.org/wiki/Eleanor_Roosevelt (accessed May 20, 2006).

21. Ten Boom et al., *The Hiding Place*, 99. Used by permission.

22. Ten Boom et al., *The Hiding Place*, 238. Used by permission.

23. Quoted from her autobiography in "Rosa Parks, Civil Rights Figure," at www.answers.com/topic/rosaparks (accessed July 6, 2006).

24. www.nonviolenceinternational.net/who.htm (accessed July 6, 2006).

25. For a comparison of violent and nonviolent strategies in the Israel-Palestine dispute, with special attention to Mubarak Awad and Beit Sahour, see Baker, "How to Fight Back."

26. "Shirin Ebadi," en.wikipedia.org/wiki/Shirin_Ebadi (accessed July 12, 2006).

27. Quoted from Paige and Satha-Anand, eds., *Islam and Nonviolence*, 23–24. Used by permission. See also Satha-Anand, "Three Prophets' Nonviolent Actions: Case Stories from the Lives of the Buddha, Jesus, and Muhammad," in *The Frontiers of Nonviolence*, ed. Satha-Anand, et al.

28. Olson, *Freedom's Daughters*, 27.

29. Olson, *Freedom's Daughters*, 29.

30. McDonald, "A Way of Life."

31. McAllister, *You Can't Kill the Spirit*.

32. coalitionofwomen.org/home/english/organizations/women_in_black (accessed July 6, 2006).

33. "'What we need now is women': Woman in Black Gila Svirsky addresses UN Security Council," at www.awakenedwoman.com/svirsky_talk.htm (accessed July 6, 2006).

34. Wink, *Engaging the Powers*.

35. Wink, *Engaging the Powers*, 186–87. Copyright 1992. Used by permission of Augsburg Fortress.

SUGGESTIONS FOR FURTHER READING

Ackerman. *A Force More Powerful.*

Aho. *This Thing of Darkness.*

Ballou. *Christian Non-Resistance.*

Berndt. *Non-Violence in the World Religions.*

Bhave. *Shanti Sena.*

Bondurant. *Conquest of Violence.*

Burrowes. *The Strategy of Nonviolent Defense.*

Catholic Church, Archdiocese of São Paulo (Brazil). *Torture in Brazil.*

Cavanaugh. *Torture and Eucharist: Theology, Politics, and the Body of Christ.*

Cooney & Michalowsk, eds. *The Power of the People: Active Nonviolence in the United States.*

Dolci. *A New World in the Making.*

———. *Outlaws.*

Fellman. *Rambo and the Dalai Lama.*

Gandhi. *All Men are Brothers: Life and Thoughts of Mahatma Gandhi.*

Gandhi. *Non-Violent Resistance (Satyagraha).*

Gregg. *The Power of Nonviolence.*

Hallie. *Lest Innocent Blood Be Shed.*

Hasek. *The Good Soldier Schweik.*

Holmes and Gan. *Nonviolence in Theory and Practice.*

King. *A Testament of Hope: The Essential Writings and Speeches of Martin Luther King Jr.*

McAllister. *You Can't Kill the Spirit.*

McDonald. "A Way of Life."

McManus and Schlabach, eds. *Relentless Persistence: Nonviolent Action in Latin America.*

Olson. *Freedom's Daughters: The Unsung Heroines of the Civil Rights Movement from 1830 to 1970.*

Paige, Satha-Anand, and Gilliatt, eds. *Islam and Nonviolence.*

Rosenberg. *Nonviolent Communication: A Language of Compassion.*

Samuel. *Safe Passage on City Streets.*

Satha-Anand et al., eds. *The Frontiers of Nonviolence.*

Sharp. *Gandhi as a Political Strategist.*

———. *The Politics of Nonviolent Action.*

———. *Waging Nonviolent Struggle: 20th Century Practice and 21st Century Potential.*

Suttner. *Lay Down Your Arms: The Autobiography of Martha von Tilling.*

Ten Boom, Sherrill, and Sherrill. *The Hiding Place.*

Tolstoy. *Writings on Civil Disobedience and Nonviolence.*

Watterson. *Not by the Sword: How the Love of a Cantor and His Family Transformed a Klansman.*

Wink. *Engaging the Powers: Discernment and Resistance in a World of Domination.*

Yoder. *What Would You Do?: A Serious Answer to a Standard Question.*

Zahn. *In Solitary Witness: The Life and Death of Franz Jägerstätter.*

Zunes, Kurtz, and Asher, eds. *Nonviolent Social Movements: A Geographical Perspective.*

Chapter Twelve

Just War Theory

"What is the evil in war? Is it the death of some who will soon die in any case, that others may live in peaceful subjection? This is mere cowardly dislike, not any religious feeling. The real evils in war are love of violence, revengeful cruelty, fierce and implacable enmity, wild resistance, and the lust of power, and such like; and it is generally to punish these things, when force is required to inflict the punishment, that, in obedience to God or some lawful authority, good men undertake wars."[1]

—Augustine of Hippo

"In order for a war to be just, three things are necessary. First, the authority of the sovereign by whose command the war is to be waged. . . . Secondly, a just cause . . . namely that those who are attacked should be attacked because they deserve it on account of some fault. . . . Thirdly, it is necessary that the belligerents should have a rightful intention, so that they intend the advancement of good, or the avoidance of evil."[2]

—Thomas Aquinas

"A tyrannical government is not just, because it is directed, not to the common good, but to the private good of the ruler. . . . Consequently there is no sedition in disturbing a government of this kind, unless indeed the tyrant's rule be disturbed so inordinately, that his subjects suffer greater harm from the consequent disturbance than from the tyrant's government. Indeed it is the tyrant rather that is guilty of sedition."[3]

—Thomas Aquinas

GENERAL POINTS[4]

For the first three centuries, the Christian church refused to engage in warfare, although it occasionally accepted soldier converts without requiring them to renounce their profession. Soon after Constantine (280–337 CE) was converted in the early 4th century and Christianity was established as the official religion of the Roman Empire in the late 4th century, the bishop Augustine of Hippo (354–430 CE) developed a Christian justification for the use of armed force in limited circumstances. Thomas Aquinas, Martin Luther, Franciscus de Vitoria, and the legal scholar Hugo Grotius made important contributions to Christian just war theory.[5] In this chapter, we concentrate on the moral questions, not the legal ones. Christian just war theory is based on two key principles: the presumption against war and violence, and the duty to resist evil.

Presumption against War and Violence

As the just war principles are usually presented *academically*, the presumption is against violence and killing. It requires a strong case to override that presumption and to justify violence and killing in a particular instance.

As the just war principles are often argued *in an actual case,* the presumption seems to be in favor of one's own government. Thus, in the 1991 Gulf War, the U.S. Catholic bishops concluded that war in the Persian Gulf "might well" violate just war principles, but that they did not have sufficient certitude in the matter to ask Catholics to disobey their government and *refuse* to go to war. If the bishops had intended the presumption to be against war and violence, they could have concluded rather that they did not have sufficient certitude in the matter to *allow* Catholics to obey their government and go to war.

Duty to Resist Evil

In tension with the presumption against violence is the duty to resist evil. Individuals have a duty to resist evil. Governments have a duty to protect people in their charge. Note that this duty does *not necessarily imply a duty to use lethal or damaging force,* though the use of lethal force is not in principle excluded. If individuals can resist evil and governments can protect people in their charge by nonviolent means, the duty would be adequately fulfilled.

Possible Choices

In the face of injustice, humans have several choices, not all good. (a) They can cooperate with the injustice or benefit from it. (b) They can do nothing, avoiding trouble. (c) They can resist with lethal violence. (d) They can resist with provocative nonviolence. Gandhi used to say that the fourth choice was the best, and the third was the second best. Doing nothing or cooperating were not acceptable choices to him.

The just war principles can help a *sincere* person judge when to resist with lethal violence. Basic to this judgment is the presumption that an unjust attacker forfeits his or her right to have his or her life protected. But note that one should threaten another's life only to stop an unjust attack.

How can we tell whether one is sincere in their use of these principles? They can, after all, be appealed to in an insincere way. The best judge of sincerity is *consistent use of the principles across a range of situations*. If a leader uses the principles one way when discussing his own interventions and differently when discussing interventions of others, we have reason to presume insincerity. Other criteria of sincerity include the character of the leader, the character of the government the leader heads, the circumstances, and the leader's actions before, during, and after war.

Demonstrations

Do public demonstrations against government policy and discussions questioning the direction being taken by government leadership weaken a nation? For example, did demonstrations against the Vietnam War weaken the United States and encourage the communists to continue their resistance?

Demonstrations tend to suggest to an adversary that we are not united in our position. They may, then, encourage the adversary to continue their fight (or their actions which threaten war), and discourage our own soldiers from fighting. But this only weakens a nation if it is certain that war is the right choice. If war is the wrong choice, then denying or restricting discussions and demonstrations of concern weakens the nation by making a bad choice more likely. Unfortunately, we can't know which one is the true situation unless there is a genuine public discussion. So in general, *restricting* debate *weakens* a nation.

Universality of Just War Discussion

The "just war principles" that we will be discussing have roots in varied traditions: pagan, Christian, chivalric, crusader, and so forth. Everyone who chooses or considers war makes use of *some* principles to judge whether or not war is appropriate.[6] No one would be upset by atrocities if they really thought that "all's fair in love and war."

Just war principles in general act to the advantage of warriors. While they may make some aspects of war more difficult or more dangerous, they also protect soldiers from especially cruel or inhumane practices. An example would be principles for the treatment of prisoners of war.

Wider Application of Principles

The moral principles that are appealed to for or against war actually have wider application. They can be used with modest change for almost any act of communal force that harms or inconveniences people in some way. Examples would include boycotts, strikes, and third-party electoral politics. That is why the principles are titled as they are here.

The mnemonic (*C-Can*, *Ah*, *I*, *Lawfully-Like*, *Attack Dose People Dere?*) is just an easy way to remember the ten principles. You will seldom find all ten of these principles listed. When a number is given, it is most often seven—but different authors include different principles in their list of seven. Thomas Aquinas listed three, the Catechism of the Catholic Church four, the U.S. Catholic bishops seven in their 1983 pastoral letter. I have simply assembled and arranged all the principles which I have found people using and which seem to me to be appropriate. The principles are listed in table 12.1, which follows our discussion of the Principle of Double Effect.

Principle of Double Effect

When an action has several foreseen effects, not all of which are willed by the actor, action can be morally chosen *if* (a) the agent *intends only* the effects that are morally good or indifferent, *not* those that are morally evil, *and* (b) the good effects are *not the result* of the evil effects (that is, the good does not come about *because of the evil*; if, for example, the evil effects do not happen, the good can still be attained), *and* (c) the good effects *outweigh* the evil effects, since *all are foreseen,* even if the evil is *not willed or wanted. Note that all three conditions must be met.*

Example: Bomb a factory that is manufacturing tanks. Some of the workers may be injured or killed. If it turns out that the workers are all off on a picnic, the raid is still a success since the factory can no longer make tanks.

Example: A police sharpshooter fires into a room where a terrorist is holding captives and threatening to kill them all. The sharpshooter aims carefully at the terrorist, although the bullet may also injure one or more of the hostages. The terrorist (by just war principles) has forfeited his right to life by his unjust intention to kill the hostages. If a hostage is injured by a wayward bullet or ricocheting fragment, the injury is not intended, and it is worth the risk. If no hostages are killed, the mission is even more of a success.

Example: Bomb the residential area of a city in which a tank factory is located, hoping that the deaths will move the survivors to pressure the government to end the war. The raid is *not* considered just, because the good effect (the end of the war) comes about through the terror caused by the deaths of uninvolved civilians. This is an example of state-sponsored terrorism.

Example: Blow up the room where a terrorist is holding captives so that future terrorists will know that they had better not fool around with us. While the aim would still be attained even if all the captives miraculously escaped, the action would still be immoral because the *likely result clearly foreseen* would be damage (deaths of innocent captives) disproportionate to the good attained.

Example: A guest caught in a burning hotel jumps from the ninth story window as the flames surround her. She is terribly afraid of death by fire, but knows that the fall will probably kill her anyway. Her action is justified because, although she is moving from one deadly risk to another, it is not her death from the fall that would save her from death by fire: if by some chance she landed on a new shipment of marshmallows and survived the fall, she would be delighted. On the other hand, she endangers pedestrians she might land on.

Example: Another guest in a nearby hotel jumps from the ninth story window because life has become too much for her. Her action is not justified because it is the death itself that she seeks: if she by chance was caught by a protruding awning and softly deposited on the terrace, she would be disappointed.

PRINCIPLES OF JUST WAR

To illustrate the principles, we will consider the 1991 Gulf War between United Nations forces (principally the United States) and Iraq, the sanctions which followed, and the 2003 U.S. invasion and occupation.

Classical discussions on just war distinguish two sets of questions: *jus ad bellum*—whether it is justified to *begin* a war [or to *continue* one]; and *jus in bello*—how a war, once begun, can be justly carried out. This distinction does not clearly divide the principles of just war, which generally must be satisfied for both situations. So we will not make use of this distinction.

PRINCIPLE 1: *JUST* CAUSE

Note that the key justification is "defense against *unjust* aggression: a real and certain danger." Defense of the Auschwitz extermination camp in World War II would fail to be justified by this principle because the aggression which was trying to close the camp down was not unjust. A pre-emptive nuclear

Table 12.1. Principles for a Just Use of Communal Force (War, Revolution, Strike, Boycott)
Mnemonic: C-Can Ah, I, Lawfully, Like, Attack Dose People Dere?

Principle	OK	Disputed	No Good
1. Just Cause	Defense against unjust aggression: a real and certain danger. Protect innocent in our own charge. "The damage inflicted by the aggressor on the nation or community of nations must be lasting, grave, and certain." (Catholic Catechism 2309)	Protect innocent in someone else's charge. Correct injustice other authority ignores. (Re)-establish order necessary for decent human existence, basic human rights. Other side crossed border first. Punish evildoers. Correct wrong ideology.	Empire building, glory, selfish advantage.
2. Comparative Cause	Compare grievances on both sides. No one has absolute justice, but the war is justified only if there is a preponderance of justice on one side over the other.		No effort made to consider justice of other side. Major injustice on both sides, no clear preponderance. Values at stake not significant enough to justify damage/killing.
3. Attitude	Love weak, enemy. Sorrow and regret for damage and killing caused. See opponent as human like oneself.		Revenge, cruelty, love of violence, wild resistance, the lust of power, delight in killing and destruction, pride and self-seeking.

Criterion			
4. Intention	Establish justice and peace. Incapacitate combatant: (a) capture, (b) wound, (c) kill.	Help rebuild conquered enemy. "Convert" enemy.	Unreasonable demands, e.g., unconditional surrender.
5. Last Resort	Tried all other steps had reasonable time for.	Pre-emptive strike in face of imminent unjust threat.	Other options not seriously considered.
6. Likely Success	Reasonably likely to achieve goals.	Defend key values against great odds as proportionate witness.	Lost cause: no hope of winning. Destroy what one is fighting for. Both sides perhaps annihilated.
7. Authority	Those responsible for common good really supported by those they represent.	Revolutionary movements.	Unrepresentative despot or rebel seeking own advantage. Private citizen.
8. Declared	Publish reasons, including conditions for settlement, before attack.	Undeclared but not unexpected in broad sense.	"Sneak attack."
9. Proportionality	More good gained than damage caused for war as a whole, and for each strategy/step/weapon. Include all affected, especially poor, helpless.	Include spiritual dimensions in calculation.	More damage caused than good gained. Destroy all life to preserve some principle ("we had no choice").
10. Discrimination	Immune: noncombatants, prisoners, future citizens. Long-term effects.	"Defense workers"—how broadly conceived? Guerrilla war.	Harm hostages, uninvolved; guerrillas "hugging the people."

attack by the United States against the Soviet Union in, say, 1983 would fail to be justified by this principle because there was not a real and certain danger of invasion or attack by the Soviet Union.

"Protect the innocent in your own charge" refers primarily to the innocent in your own country. The United States has an obligation to preserve innocent Americans, but not a clear obligation to preserve innocent Kuwaitis or Iraqis. The morality of protecting the innocent in someone else's charge (so-called "humanitarian intervention") is disputed because it has so often been used as an excuse for heinous actions. Mussolini used it to justify his invasion of Ethiopia, and Hitler used it to justify his invasion of Czechoslovakia.

Few would dispute that someone should have done something about the slaughter of Jews in Germany's charge in World War II. What *is* disputed is whether the Allies in the Second World War were very much motivated by that slaughter. They didn't prosecute the war in a way designed to rescue the Jews quickly.

Many believed that someone should have done something about the slaughter of Muslims in Bosnia-Herzegovina in the 1990s. Just what one *could effectively* have done is another question. The use of foreign troops to keep the two sides apart and to enforce the Dayton Accords depended on the warring factions being willing to stop the fighting.

Most Americans feel that something should have been done about the slaughter in 1975–1979 of about two million Cambodians—about a quarter of the population—by Pol Pot's government, which leaves us wondering why our government continued to support that government after it was forced out of power by a Vietnamese invasion.

For many years, most Americans were not aware of the slaughter in East Timor by Indonesian troops—a slaughter long ignored by the United States government and press. Perhaps "ignored" is not the right word. President Ford and Henry Kissinger visited the Indonesian president in Jakarta twenty-four hours before Indonesia invaded East Timor.

As you can see, the just war principles have been inconsistently applied in these examples.

In the Gulf Wars

Before the 1991 Gulf War, U.S. Catholic bishops, in testimony before Congress, commented that too many reasons were given for the war: Iraq's invasion of Kuwait, protection of oil supplies, jobs in the U.S. economy, the regional threat of a strong Iraq, and the threat of a nuclear-armed Iraq.

Inconsistent application of principles suggested that the U.S. administration was not sincere. President George H. W. Bush said that the invasion of a sovereign nation could not go unchallenged, yet the United States under his leadership had invaded Panama, and the United States had done little to challenge the Israeli invasion of the Palestinian territories from 1967 (Palestinians would go back to the "catastrophe" of 1948) to the present time.

The 2003 Gulf War was even less clearly justified. President George W. Bush says he went to war to prevent Hussein from developing weapons of mass destruction and to fight the terrorism responsible for the attacks on the World Trade Center and the Pentagon. There is no credible evidence that Hussein was connected with the attacks or with Al-Qaida, and no weapons of mass destruction have been found in Iraq. The war seems rather to have *increased* terrorist attacks on Americans: the U.S. soldiers in Iraq. The U.S. occupation force has acted to dismantle Iraqi socialism and sell off its state assets to foreign private investors. U.S. construction companies have received lucrative construction contracts in Iraq, but hundreds of millions of dollars are unaccounted for.

On February 26, 2003, before the invasion, Bishop Wilton Gregory released a statement on behalf of the U.S. Catholic bishops that said, in part, "With the Holy See and many religious leaders throughout the world, we believe that resort to war would not meet the strict conditions in Catholic teaching for the use of military force." The Vatican's permanent observer at the United Nations, to the Security Council, said in part, "The Holy See is convinced that in the efforts to draw strength from the wealth of peaceful tools provided by international law, to resort to force would not be a just one [*sic*]." Earlier, the bishops had written to the president, "We conclude, based on the facts that are known to us, that a preemptive, unilateral use of force is difficult to justify at this time. We fear that resort to force, under these circumstances, would not meet the strict conditions in Catholic teaching for overriding the strong presumption against the use of military force." They challenged the President with these questions:

> Is there clear and adequate evidence of a direct connection between Iraq and the attacks of September 11th or clear and adequate evidence of an imminent attack of a grave nature? Is it wise to dramatically expand traditional moral and legal limits on just cause to include preventive or preemptive uses of military force to overthrow threatening regimes or to deal with the proliferation of weapons of mass destruction? Should not a distinction be made between efforts to change unacceptable behavior of a government and efforts to end that government's existence?

PRINCIPLE 2: *COMPARATIVE* CAUSE[7]

It is not enough to show that an opponent has hurt us. We also need to investigate whether we have hurt the opponent, and then compare the two grievances to see whether there is a clear preponderance of cause on one side or the other. "He hit me back first" is not a good justification for a fight.

In their 1983 pastoral letter, the U.S. Catholic bishops wrote, "No state should act on the basis that it has 'absolute justice' on its side. Every party to a conflict should acknowledge the limits of its 'just cause' and the consequent requirement to use only limited means in pursuit of its objectives." And in the following paragraph:

> Given techniques of propaganda and the ease with which nations and individuals either assume or delude themselves into believing that God or right is clearly on their side, the test of comparative justice may be extremely difficult to apply. Clearly, however, this is not the case in every instance of war. Blatant aggression from without and subversion from within are often enough readily identifiable by all reasonably fair-minded people.[8]

After September 11, 2001, George Bush said that Osama bin Laden attacked the United States because he hated our freedoms. Before our 2003 invasion of Iraq, bin Laden himself said that Al-Qaida attacked the United States because (a) the United States supported Israeli oppression of Palestinians; (b) the United States maintained sanctions against Iraq that have resulted in the deaths of over five hundred thousand Iraqi children, not to mention elderly and others; (c) the United States maintained troops in Saudi Arabia near the holy sites of Mecca and Medina; and (d) the United States propped up repressive Arab governments that deny Arabs the freedoms which Americans enjoy.

In the Gulf Wars

The Iraqi invasion of Kuwait was generally judged unjust but not unprovoked. That is, Iraq was not justified in invading Kuwait, but there is suspicion that Kuwait and the United States, knowing Saddam Hussein's character, goaded him into taking rash action that would justify a harsh response. At least, Kuwait took dangerous chances that would have been foolhardy if it had not been sure of American support. Both Kuwait and the United States may have been surprised by the *extent* of Hussein's action. Here are some of the actions that provoked Iraq: (a) Kuwait used American experts in oil drilling to slant wells from their side of the border with Iraq into oil fields under the Iraqi side of the border. (b) Kuwait had lent Iraq much money to help finance its war against Iran. In 1991, they were demanding that it be repaid *at once.* Iraq objected that it had fought for *all* modern Arabs, including Kuwait, against Iranian Islamic fundamentalism, so the loans should be forgiven. (c) Iraq and Kuwait were arguing over the location of their border. Iraq wanted OPEC to limit oil production to keep prices up and let it repay its loans, but Kuwait *increased* its production to drive prices down and give it leverage over Iraq in its border dispute. (d) Historically, Kuwait had been separated from Iraq and defended by the British, cutting Iraq off from its natural harbor on the Persian Gulf.

Iraqi human rights violations in Kuwait were probably real but exaggerated (we now know that infants were not dumped out of incubators), and they were not unlike others in the region (for example, in Syria—or U.S. violations in Iraq today) that go unchallenged by our government.

There are challenges to American sincerity in the case of Kuwait. The United States had helped to arm Iraq right up to the invasion itself; President Bush overrode efforts by Congress to cut off arms shipments. America called for Iraqis to rebel against Hussein after the United States booted him out of Kuwait, but it apparently wanted some Sunni army general to lead the rebellion. When the Kurds and southern Shi'ites responded to the call, the United States allowed Hussein to use his helicopter gunships to slaughter the rebels. *After* the rebellion had been crushed, we instituted the "no-fly zones."

By 2003, Iraq had even more grievances against the United States. Ten years of economic sanctions had resulted in the death of some million and a half Iraqis, including a half million children. Theoretically, medical supplies and food were not included in the sanctions, but they did require explicit permission for each shipment, and permission was frequently denied. Doctors were unable to give consistent treatment, since medications were inconsistently available. More important, the sanctions prevented Iraq from importing the machine parts it needed to repair the damage that U.S. bombing had caused to their electric grid, water purification, and sewage disposal systems—especially critical, since Iraq is basically a desert watered by two rivers. Sanctions also severely limited supplies of chlorine needed to purify the water. Finally, the 1991 war had littered Iraq with depleted uranium shells, which were causing major cancers especially to children, and also to U.S. servicepeople.

PRINCIPLE 3: ATTITUDE

You won't find this principle appealed to very often, although it is one of Augustine's main principles. Augustine was highly influential in developing Christian principles of just war. He insisted that an army at war should love the weak and the enemy, and fight with sorrow and regret for the damage and killing that it caused.

Soldiers and their leaders may well object that it is impossible to sustain a war with these attitudes. Some will claim that this principle is unrealistic, so we should conclude that just war principles have been discredited. An alternative response is to agree that this principle is unrealistic, but to conclude that it is *war,* not the principles, that has been discredited.

Two quotations from Augustine may be helpful:

> But, say they, the wise man will wage just wars. As if he would not all the rather lament the necessity of just wars, if he remembers that he is a human. . . . Let everyone, then, who thinks with pain on all these great evils, so horrible, so ruthless, acknowledge that this is misery. *And if anyone either endures or thinks of them without mental pain, this is a more miserable plight still, for he thinks himself happy because he has lost human feeling.*[9]

> *What is the evil in war? Is it the death of some who will soon die in any case, that others may live in peaceful subjection? This is mere cowardly dislike, not any religious feeling. The real evils in war are love of violence, revengeful cruelty, fierce and implacable enmity, wild resistance, and the lust of power, and such like; and it is generally to punish these things, when force is required to inflict the punishment, that, in obedience to God or some lawful authority, good men undertake wars.*[10]

The peace theoretician Johan Galtung makes *attitude* one of the three key dynamics in conflict. The other two are *behavior* and *contradiction.* Contradiction is caused either by a *dilemma* (one actor wants two incompatible goals) or by a *dispute* (two or more actors want the same one goal, which is in scarce supply and can't be shared). Frustrating contradiction leads to dangerous attitudes (emphasizing one's own humanity and importance while dehumanizing the opponent), which lead to destructive behaviors. His proposal for resolution is *creative, compassionate nonviolence* to search out innovative proposals that benefit all the combatants.[11]

In the Gulf Wars

Hatred and racism were encouraged. The enemy was demonized. Disrespectful language was used of Saddam Hussein (a "Hitler-type character") and of Iraq (part of an "Axis of Evil," thus playing on the World War II "Axis" of Nazi Germany, Fascist Italy, and Imperial Japan). Atrocity stories were invented or exaggerated. Connections with terrorism, most famously with the September 11 attacks, were implied but carefully not alleged.

PRINCIPLE 4: INTENTION

A just intention for war is to establish justice and peace. It is reasonable to wish to stop or prevent unjust invasion or violence. But one should use the

Figure 12.1.   Children in Baghdad, January 2003, shortly before the U.S. invasion, outside the Al-Amariya Shelter, which was destroyed by U.S. bombing in 1991. Courtesy David Whitten Smith.

lowest level of force that can be reasonably expected to accomplish that goal. If one can stop the injustice by capturing the enemy, that should be the first choice. If capture is not possible, then capture or destruction of the enemy's weapons or wounding the soldiers so that they cannot fight is the second choice. Only if these are insufficient is it reasonable to kill the attacker.

In the actual heat of combat, such distinctions are extremely difficult to make, since combat is characterized by limited information and deliberately induced uncertainty. Dennis Carroll, an experienced Army officer wrote, "I have been in combat and in heavy jungle and when the shooting starts it is next to impossible to decide if you are going to just wound someone, capture him or kill him."[12]

The intention to "convert" the enemy, for example from communism to capitalism (or vice versa), is a disputed intention because it is very likely to promote or continue a war that otherwise could be settled.

The intention to help rebuild an enemy's country after the war is admirable (if it is sincere) but not generally considered to be essential, particularly if the conflict was the enemy's fault in the first place. Americans remember the Marshall Plan after the Second World War without understanding that U.S.

elites decided it was urgent to rebuild West Germany and Japan as bulwarks against communist Eastern Europe and the Soviet Union. It was also urgent to limit the appeal of communism in Western Europe.

Unconditional surrender is widely held to be an unreasonable demand except in very special circumstances, because it normally lengthens the war. Few people are willing to surrender with no conditions; most would give up much sooner if they knew the conditions would be tolerable. Because of the special nature of the Nazi government in Germany, some would support the Allied demand for unconditional German surrender in World War II. In particular, the demand for unconditional surrender signaled to German leaders that the Allied forces were committed to a unified position and prevented Germany from trying to negotiate with their enemies one at a time to split the alliance.

Most moralists conclude that the demand for unconditional *Japanese* surrender was unjustified. Some argue that it lengthened the war with Japan and resulted in the unnecessary and tragic use of atomic bombs on Hiroshima and Nagasaki.

In the Gulf Wars

In 1991, George Bush emphasized that all he wanted Iraq to do was to "get out of Kuwait," but when it was in fact doing so, the UN forces destroyed the fleeing column. Other possible intentions for United States participation in the 1991 war have been suggested and have enough plausibility to be investigated or discussed. None of these would be justifiable intentions under just war principles: test new weapons, new strategies, and personnel untried in battle; control the Middle East region; control oil supplies; weaken the Iraqi army so that it will be less of a factor in the region; and intimidate other possible opponents of the United States by displaying frightening power: "Don't tread on me. Mess with us and you will be in trouble."

Likely intentions for the 2003 war include: reassure Americans frightened by the attacks of September 11, 2001; control oil supplies and the Middle East region for leverage over other leading industrialized nations; build permanent military bases in Iraq to replace threatened bases in Saudi Arabia; weaken the Iraqi army so that it will not threaten the state of Israel; destroy a successful Middle Eastern socialist economy and replace it with an extreme free-market capitalist economy; help George W. Bush win election for a second term; and provide lucrative construction contracts for major U.S. corporations.

The intensity of bombing in 1991, for example, the bombing of the electric power stations, water purification system, and sewage disposal system, seemed to go beyond military necessity and to have other intentions—probably to weaken Iraq for the future.

In 1991, a demand for unconditional surrender was considered. There does not seem to have been justification for it. In fact, the United States appeared to resist negotiations.

The demand to depose an established leader (Saddam Hussein) is generally considered unjustified. Countries should determine their own leadership. At the same time, they are not free to follow or support that leadership in attacking their neighbors. If they do so, they carry much of the responsibility if their neighbors force them to change that leadership.

PRINCIPLE 5: LAST RESORT

This principle presumes that one has tried all other practical steps one *reasonably had time for*. It does not demand rigidly that everything else be tried. The principle "justice delayed is justice denied" means that a prudential judgment has to be made about what is reasonable and practical.

If a threat is grave and imminent, some moralists would justify a preemptive strike to resist it. This is the new principle the United States is proposing, but without the qualifier "imminent."

It is not clear that the United States would be willing to accept this justification if other countries were to claim it. An example often given is the Israeli attack on Egyptian and Syrian airfields in 1967. Historians dispute whether Egypt intended to attack, or simply to "bleed" Israel by forcing an extended period of mobilization for war and consequent slowdown of the civilian economy. Israel, on the other hand, welcomed the opportunity to extend its borders, to control more territory, and to move its enemies farther away from its main population centers.

The principle of last resort is especially relevant now that we have concrete experience of how effective active nonviolence can be—it is the "other practical option" that is rarely considered seriously. Within the past hundred years, it has affected probably a third of humanity: Mohandas Gandhi in India and South Africa, Martin Luther King Jr. in the United States, Nelson Mandela in South Africa, Corazon Aquino in the Philippines, "Solidarity" in Poland, and similar movements elsewhere in Eastern Europe and Russia.

In the Gulf Wars

This principle received extensive discussion in both Gulf Wars. Economic sanctions were imposed early in the 1990–1991 crisis. Many people argued that they were having effect and should be continued without military attack. The U.S. government argued that the boycott would not be effective. Sincerity was damaged by the awareness that previous U.S. support of Saddam Hussein despite his bad human rights record had helped to "set up" the crisis, as had long inattention to the Palestinian problem. Published estimates that the boycott had reduced Iraqi GNP by 50% suggested that the economic sanctions were working. The insistence of the U.S. government that such sanctions are ineffective seems inconsistent with their continuing use of such sanctions against South Africa, Nicaragua, and Cuba. In fact, the United States continued sanctions against Iraq for ten years *after* the war—sanctions that have caused major damage to civilian health and survival.

Officially the 1991–2003 boycott did not include food and drugs, but there was good evidence that in practice it did. Such a boycott is morally questionable. The FOR (Fellowship of Reconciliation) reported in its newsletter for 18 January 1991 that a shipment of medicines which they had collected for Iraq was being held up by regulation 31 CFR 575 of the U.S. Treasury Department—a regulation that required a license to ship medicines to Iraq. Penalties that the FOR was threatened with included $250,000 in civil fines, $1 million in criminal fines, and twelve years in prison. The FOR challenged the regulation by shipping the medicines anyway, but the U.S. government seized them in the warehouse and prevented their shipment. The FOR then publicized the situation in newspapers and on television, and within a few days the government reversed its position and granted the license.

In the 2003 war, George W. Bush argued that we "couldn't afford to wait for a mushroom cloud." There is much evidence that war planners suppressed contrary evidence and exaggerated supporting evidence for their position. The UN inspection teams insisted that Iraq had ended its nuclear program. Evidence since the invasion supports that conclusion.

PRINCIPLE 6: LIKELY SUCCESS

One should not go to war unless one is reasonably likely to achieve one's goals. In almost every case, at least one side in a conflict fails to apply this principle correctly. Often both sides fail. In exceptional circumstances one might be justified in fighting to defend key values against great odds as a witness to justice. But such a witness could be given in other ways without lethal resistance. It is never justified to go to war when the result is to destroy what one is fighting for, much less when the result is to destroy human life on the planet. Yet nuclear deterrence may well threaten exactly that result. The study of "nuclear winter" in the mid-1980s finally made this danger salient to world leaders.

John Chrysostom, in the late 4th century CE, said, "War is the plaything of the rich." Aleksandr Solzhenitsyn, in *The Gulag Archipelago*, said that *governments* need victories, but *people* need defeats. Victories strengthen governments and tend to launch them onto new adventures—adventures which eventually lead to disaster. Defeats weaken governments and enable people to insist on—and usually achieve—peace.

An example of Solzhenitsyn's principle would be the Falklands-Malvinas war between Argentina and England. After the war, the Argentine military government was so discredited that it resigned and the country was restored to democracy. The 2003 Iraq war may produce a similar result—but in the United States rather than in Iraq.

In the Gulf Wars

There are precedents. England occupied Iraq after the First World War, attempting to establish a pro-British Iraqi government. "Ultimately, the British-created monarchy suffered from a chronic legitimacy crisis. . . . The continuing inability of the government to gain the confidence of the people fueled political instability well into the 1970s."[13]

The U.S. Catholic bishops testified before Congress that the effects of the 1991 war in the whole Middle East were likely to be more negative than positive. At that time, objections to likely success included the following points: War will continue Western colonial control in the Middle East. It will isolate Arab government leaders who supported the war from their populations that didn't. There may still be popular uprisings against unpopular leadership. The rise in "fundamentalist Islam" in the area suggests that we do not yet see the final results of these policies. War poisoned U.S. relations with Iraq and with most Arab societies for a long time into the future.

What was gained overall by the 1991 war? Iraq was expelled from Kuwait. Iraq was weakened. Its nuclear program was dismantled. But the war left Saddam Hussein in power. Kuwait is still not a very free society. The Middle East is increasingly unstable. Admittedly, for a time, the United States tried, unsuccessfully, to follow up on the Palestinian problem, which it refused to "link" with Iraq-Kuwait at the time of the war.

Success in the 2003 war is even less likely, despite the execution of Saddam Hussein on December 30, 2006. The U.S. Catholic bishops warned Bush before the war:

> War against Iraq could have unpredictable consequences not only for Iraq but for peace and stability elsewhere in the Middle East. Would preventive or preemptive force succeed in thwarting serious threats or, instead, provoke the very kind of attacks that it is intended to prevent? Would the use of military force lead to wider conflict and instability? Would war against Iraq detract from our responsibility to help build a just and stable order in Afghanistan and undermine the broader coalition against terrorism?[14]

U.S. troops are mired down in a costly, unpopular and probably un-winnable invasion and occupation. Western-oriented Iraq lost power in con-trast to conservative Islamic Iran. Terrorists are attracting recruits and gain-ing valuable experience against U.S. soldiers. Iran and North Korea have concluded that only nuclear weapons can protect them from U.S. invasion. The United States has lost the sympathy it gained from the terrorist attacks of September 11, 2001. In Abu Ghraib and Guantanamo, the United States has begun torturing and "disappearing" opponents—something that we thought only Third World governments did.

PRINCIPLE 7: AUTHORITY

War should be undertaken under the authority of leaders who are responsible for the common good and are really supported by those they represent. Un-acceptable would be war ordered by unrepresentative despots or by rebels seeking only their own advantage. A special problem arises in the case of a popular revolutionary uprising against a despotic government. The revolu-tionary leader is not legally recognized, but the "legally recognized" leader is not seeking the common good. Thomas Aquinas says that in such a case the legally constituted despot, who is seeking private advantage rather than the common good, is responsible for the outbreak of revolution. His or her lead-ership is not morally justified, whatever the law says.

> A tyrannical government is not just, because it is directed, not to the common good, but to the private good of the ruler. . . . Consequently there is no sedition in disturbing a government of this kind, unless indeed the tyrant's rule be dis-turbed so inordinately, that his subjects suffer greater harm from the consequent disturbance than from the tyrant's government. Indeed it is the tyrant rather that is guilty of sedition.[15]

In such a case, we need to ask to what extent the leaders of the revolutionary movement truly represent the common good and the aspirations of most of the population.

In a democratic system, the leaders are supposed to seek out and reflect the common judgment. To the extent that they manipulate public opinion, they are interfering with the normal functioning of a healthy democracy and plac-ing in question the extent to which they are really supported by those they represent. Good public discussion requires that honest and adequate informa-tion be provided to the citizens. Various forms of media control prevent peo-ple from knowing relevant facts, varied points of view, and possible options to consider. It is important to involve the entire population in vital decisions through open public discussion, and to define "proper authority" broadly for purposes of just war.

In the Gulf Wars

The question of authority was more widely discussed in the 1991 and the 2003 disputes than is usually the case. Although Congress was consulted both times, the U.S. Constitution is not satisfied with *consultation*—war is supposed to require a *declaration* by Congress. Congress *chose* to avoid responsibility for a declaration, and to allow the president to initiate both wars. In the case of the 2003 war, President Bush argued that earlier UN declarations gave him authority to attack. But he refused to let the UN decide the issue, and the secretary general complained that the attack was not authorized. As signatory to the UN Charter, the United States yields authority to authorize war to the UN except in the case of defense against invasion. International treaties carry constitutional authority in the United States. Unauthorized war making is considered a war crime.

PRINCIPLE 8: DECLARED

The purpose of requiring a clear declaration of war is to let an opponent know how the war can be avoided or ended. Opponents are more willing to avoid or end a war if they can do so without public humiliation. Demands should be clear and unchanging, as much as possible. "Creeping demands" are especially unfortunate, since they give the impression that the adversary is playing on sheer power rather than justice, and is interested in getting away with whatever he can. They convince the other side that it would be dangerous to appear weak or to give in.

It is worth noting that very few of the wars in which the United States has been involved in the 20th century have been declared. There is a lack of consistency in United States attitudes toward declaration. While we repeat often that it was Japan's sneak attack on Pearl Harbor that justified our war with them, and we refer to that attack as a "day of infamy," many of our own wars have started with similar undeclared attacks. This would be true of our attacks on Libya, on Grenada, and on Panama.

In the Gulf Wars

The actions that both Presidents Bush took and the public statements that they made seemed designed to humiliate Saddam Hussein rather than to give him a "face-saving" honorable way to retreat. Such an approach increased the likelihood of war and reduced the likelihood that the war would end quickly once it had begun.

The United States employed creeping demands in the 1991 war. Stages in the escalation that were publicly discussed included: get out of Kuwait; surrender unconditionally; change your government; face a war crimes trial. In the 2003 war, when Hussein suggested at the last minute that he was willing to leave Iraq, the United States declared that it would invade anyway.

PRINCIPLE 9: PROPORTIONALITY

More good should be gained than damage caused for (a) the war as a whole, and for (b) each strategy, step, and weapon employed along the way. When measuring damage caused, one should include everyone who is affected, especially the poor and helpless, future citizens, and the environment we will have to live in.

Including spiritual dimensions may change the balance of judgment. For example, how valuable is freedom of speech, of the press, of worship, of a decent economic life? Is God calling us to respond beyond our own self-interest (often verbalized as "vital national interests")? Of what value to a country is integrity? (The United States "won" in its wars with Native American tribes, but what did that victory "cost" in terms of the character that we developed in the process?)

The phrase "we had no choice" usually indicates failure of thought, of imagination, or of honesty. There are always choices. What the phrase usually means is, "We didn't want to consider any other choices" or, "We didn't like the cost of other choices." (The relative costs of various choices are rarely thought through adequately.)

This principle appears in several different forms, which we might call the gold medal, silver medal, bronze medal, and lead medal form. (a) The *gold medal form* is as stated above: more good must be gained than damage caused by the war. (b) The *silver medal form* is weaker: no more damage should be caused than necessary to achieve our objective. I have often seen the principle presented this way in discussions of just war. The weakness here is that one might need to cause much more damage than good gained in order to achieve our objective—but *we* gain the good and *someone else* receives the damage. In *this* form, the principle would not prevent war unless *my side* stood to lose more than it gained; in the *gold medal* form, war is unjustified if the *sum total of damage on both sides* exceeds the sum total of good gained. (c) The *bronze medal form* states that we should cause no more evil than we ourselves have suffered. This might also be called the "eye for an eye" or the "Hatfield and McCoy form" — it tends to produce permanent war. Gandhi said that it leaves the whole world blind. (d) The *lead medal form,* which could be called "shock and awe," recommends that we cause much more evil than we have suffered in hopes of so shocking our opponent that they will just give up. This fourth appears to be the form preferred by the U.S. leadership, as exemplified in Hiroshima, Nagasaki, and — explicitly — in Iraq.

In the Gulf Wars

The U.S. Catholic bishops testified before Congress that war against an industrial and populous society like Iraq is likely to produce unacceptably high costs. They doubted that this war would be proportionate to the issues involved.

It is hard to determine just what the costs were in 1991. Estimates of Iraqi casualties vary wildly from a low of about 1,500 to highs in the range of 250,000 to 300,000. The most common figures range between one hundred thousand and two hundred thousand. Part of the problem with determining casualties is deciding whose deaths count. Those of soldiers? Civilians? What about deaths after the war caused by unexploded landmines or cluster bombs, by depleted uranium, or by the destruction of the electric net, of sewage disposal, of medical care?

Many interpreters conclude that there was excessive civilian destruction in Iraq, beyond what was necessary to achieve the publicly declared purposes of the war. The after-war report of the United Nations said that Iraq was returned to a pre-industrial state. (Note that Iraq does not possess the pre-industrial social structures that are common in pre-industrial states. It is one thing to lose air conditioning in an Amazon hut, quite another to lose it in a high-rise building with windows that don't open — and summer temperatures in the range of 110–140 degrees Fahrenheit.)

Extensive destruction of Iraq's electric generation and distribution net eliminated refrigeration of medicines and vaccines, and water and sewage purification. Without water and sewage purification, cholera and other diseases become dangerous. Destruction of roads and bridges interfered with food transport. Many of these transportation links were far from Kuwait.

Ecological damage was extensive. The damage caused by burning oil wells could have reasonably been foreseen.

The 1991 death and destruction of columns retreating from Kuwait seem excessive to many. While soldiers are not required to gamble their lives that enemy soldiers who are not surrendering are truly out of the war (soldiers driven out by military action rather than by their own free will are liable to regroup and return once the pressure is off), American soldiers and fliers who described the situation as a "turkey shoot" suggest that the use of force was excessive.

In the 2003 war, the U.S. bishops warned Bush:

> War against Iraq could have unpredictable consequences not only for Iraq but for peace and stability elsewhere in the Middle East. How would another war in Iraq impact the civilian population, in the short- and long-term? How many more innocent people would suffer and die, or be left without homes, without basic necessities, without work? Would the United States and the international community commit to the arduous, long-term task of ensuring a just peace or would a post-Saddam Iraq continue to be plagued by civil conflict and repression, and continue to serve as a destabilizing force in the region?[16]

Finally, one should include in the calculations the psychological damage to one's own soldiers. Dave Grossman explains what militaries have to do to human beings to induce them to kill other humans.[17] J. Glenn Gray shares rare philosophical reflections on his experiences in World War II.[18] Rachel Mac-Nair explains psychological research showing that by far the strongest cause of post-traumatic stress is not danger of *being* killed, but rather *killing* another human being.[19] And Daniel Hallock has collected searing descriptions of combat veterans struggling with their psychological pain:

> In the military, everyone is expendable. . . . They will bring the primal beast out from everyone, and they will train you how to kill another human being. What they don't teach you, though, is how to deal with the emotions afterward. They just spit you out and find someone else to take your place. . . . My experience has left me a very lonely person. . . . The true hell of war doesn't start until you come home.[20]

In the end, it seems, U.S. success in overcoming its soldiers' natural resistance to killing assures that our combat veterans will suffer far more than they used to and our society will carry part of the damage.

PRINCIPLE 10: DISCRIMINATION

This principle requires that lethal violence be directed only at those who are threatening to do violence. Excluded are noncombatants, prisoners of war, children, and the unborn. Ecological damage affects the unborn as future citizens. While it is sometimes claimed that lethal violence is *directed* only at combatants, *excessive damage to noncombatants that can reasonably be anticipated* is also excluded by this principle. Damage that can be anticipated but which is undesired, when honest attempts are made to avoid it, falls under the principle of double effect that was described above. Several problems have been made acute by modern warfare: nuclear war, defense workers, guerrilla warfare, and future populations after the war.

Nuclear weapons, because of their wide range of destruction, are by nature indiscriminate on most foreseeable land targets. (Presumably one could isolate from civilian targets an aircraft carrier task force at sea.) In 1983, the U.S. Catholic bishops gave nuclear weapons a "strictly limited" temporary justification as deterrents in the face of a hostile enemy similarly armed, so long as serious efforts were made to seek disarmament. Now that there is no credible hostile enemy similarly armed, it is difficult to justify maintaining nuclear weapons, especially in the numbers the United States currently holds. There seems to be a fleeting window of opportunity to reduce actual nuclear forces to zero (recognizing that humans will not "forget" how to make them), as a result making it much less likely that they would ever be used. They are much more likely to be used if they are in place, armed, and "combat ready" than if they have been dismantled and would have to be re-manufactured first.

The dependence of armies on complex arms has raised the question whether to consider defense workers as valid targets in war. Are workers in a factory making fighter aircraft or tanks truly noncombatants? Is it true to say that they are not threatening violence to us? What about Caterpillar employees making armored bulldozers which are destroying Palestinian homes? What about steelworkers? What about railroad workers, if *part* of what they ship is ammunition? The tendency in this century has been toward "total war," arguing that *everyone* in a modern industrial society is participating in the war. Just war theorists consider these justifications to be exaggerated.

In guerrilla warfare, soldiers try to hide among the civilian population "as fish swim in the sea." Such activity makes it very difficult for their opponents to discriminate between combatants and civilians. Anyone might pick up a gun or explode a mine. In such a war, who is to blame for civilian deaths? Guerrilla warfare often catches those who truly are noncombatants in the middle. Both sides in the war try to enlist peasants on their side; guerrilla fighters hide deliberately in civilian areas in order to put the other side in a bad light if it attacks. It becomes difficult for civilians to remain neutral, and one may be killed by one side or the other in any case.

Anti-personnel land mines are a prime example of weapons that kill long after the war has ended, that kill more civilians than military, and that are much more expensive to remove than they are to place. If armies cleaned up properly after themselves, they would remove the mines they had laid after the war was over. But they rarely do. Poor people and their children are the chief victims of the mines that remain active for decades afterward. Some areas in Europe are still unsafe from World War I mines. Large areas in Indochina are unsafe or unusable; the same is true of southern Lebanon. Since mines were invented that use little or no metal, it has become much more difficult to detect and remove them. The most effective method is still to probe the soil diagonally with a rod while lying on one's stomach. Currently there is an international treaty to ban the production and use of land mines. The United States joins a few other states, such as Iraq, Israel, and North Korea, in refusing to sign the treaty. The ban is likely to be only partially successful, since mines are low-tech, cheap, and much more useful to poor armies than to wealthy ones: wealthy countries can afford tanks, and they like their tanks to be able to move around without being blown up by a $35 mine. One of the world's largest producers of land mines is Bosnia.

High-tech American companies, like Alliant Techsystems in Minnesota, argue that their mines are designed to disarm themselves after a certain number of weeks or months. But this does not mean that they are "safe" afterward. Machines are never 100% effective, as you may have noticed if you have used computers or automobiles. The most dangerous minefields are often those that one thinks are safe. And it is only the fuse or trigger that disarms; the mine is still full of explosive.

In the Gulf Wars

In 1991, the U.S. Catholic bishops warned Congress that there were many military targets in civilian areas of Iraq, so that discrimination would be difficult. Initial reports suggested that U.S. bombs were "smart," very well directed, and successful in discriminating between civilian and military targets. After the war, it was admitted that most bombs used were not "smart" but old-fashioned gravity bombs that cannot be accurately aimed. It was also admitted that the targets that the "smart" bombs were aimed at were not always what the targeters thought they were. It doesn't do much good to discriminate if the target you are aiming at is not a poison gas factory, as you thought, but a baby milk factory. So targeting depends on accurate information.

In the 2003 war, the U.S. Catholic bishops warned Bush: "While we recognize improved capability and serious efforts to avoid directly targeting civilians in war, the use of massive military force to remove the current government of Iraq could have incalculable consequences for a civilian population that has suffered so much from war, repression, and a debilitating embargo."

OVERALL APPLICATION OF THE PRINCIPLES TO THE GULF WARS BETWEEN THE UNITED STATES AND IRAQ

Here is an outline schema of comments with regard to the various criteria.

Table 12.2. The 2003 Persian Gulf War and Following Occupation in Relation to Just War Principles

The War and Occupation Are Just	The War and Occupation Are Not Just
1. (a) Iraq has weapons of mass destruction (WMD) or soon will. Iraq could give those weapons to terrorists like Al-Qaida. Iraq supported Al-Qaida in its attack on the United States. (b) Hussein destroyed weapons or moved them to Syria; he had capacity to produce them. Regime change was the main point: Hussein is captured.	1. (a) No evidence Iraq has WMD, inspections guarantee it won't. Unlikely he would give such weapons to people who hate him and whom he does not control. No evidence that Iraq supported Al-Qaida in its attack on the United States. (b) No weapons of mass destruction found. No evidence they were moved or destroyed. Capacity was not the original argument. Regime change was not the original argument, nor is it legal by international law.
2. Hussein oppressed his own people and used poison gas on them. So he might well use it on others, including us. Sanctions were necessary to keep Hussein from developing nuclear weapons.	2. The U.S. CIA helped Hussein overthrow the previous government, and helped keep him in power. U.S. companies provided chemicals and seed germs for WMD, and the U.S. administration refused to condemn his use of poison gas. After Iraq had eliminated its WMD, the United States and UN continued sanctions that killed a million and a half Iraqi civilians.
3. Principle not considered.	3. Hatred was evoked toward Iraq. Iraqis are daily dishonored and humiliated. Iraqi civilians are killed and arbitrarily arrested.
4. (a) Iraq must eliminate weapons of mass destruction, change regime. (b) Iraq must eliminate Ba'ath Party and disempower its former members, democratize, and renounce weapons of mass destruction.	4. (a) Regime change not acceptable intention by international law. (b) Protection of oil ministry while all else looted indicates that oil and regional control are intended; sale of state-owned enterprises indicates that privatization of socialized economy and foreign control of Iraq are intended.
5. Iraq did not cooperate with inspections. Hussein destroyed weapons or moved them to Syria; he had capacity to produce them.	5. Inspections and weapons control have contained Iraq. There were no WMDs, no evidence they were moved, no active program to produce them.

Table 12.2. (*Continued*)

The War and Occupation Are Just	The War and Occupation Are Not Just
6. (a) There is little doubt the United States can defeat Iraq. Iraqis will welcome us and welcome democracy. (b) The United States defeated Iraq easily. ManyIraqis refused to fight; others welcomed the United States with open arms—except for a small minority of Hussein supporters.	6. The U.S. has stepped into a quagmire that looks like Lebanon in the 1980s, involving guerrilla warfare that is impossible to control. Establishing a stable democratic government is very unlikely. Puppet government will be rejected by Iraqis. Our actions promote Al-Qaida volunteers.
7. Bush is legally our president; was re-elected. Congress gave Bush authority to act. The UN gave implicit authority in the fall of 2002. The UN has become an irrelevant debating society.	7. There was little real debate. Information was incomplete or false. Congress wimped out. When the United States realized that the UN would refuse authority, it chose not to ask. The attack violated the UN charter to which the United States is signatory, making the invasion a violation of U.S. law as well.
8. (a) Demands for disarmament and regime change were clear. (b) Hussein hid his program so effectively that we have not yet found it, but we will. Regime change was worth it in any case.	8. (a) Absolute disarmament is probably impossible ever to confirm. (b) It now appears there was nothing to disarm. Regime change is an unacceptable condition by international law.
9. Terrorist use of weapons of mass destruction is so horrible that almost any means is appropriate to prevent it. We can't wait for a mushroom cloud.	9. There is no absolute security. Attempts to secure it by sanctions themselves caused mass death of Iraqis. Our invasion and occupation feed the very terrorism we seek to prevent.
10. (a) We made every effort, with use of smart bombs and missiles, to prevent civilian casualties. (b) Predictions of massive civilian deaths in the attack proved wrong. We are working to rebuild Iraqi civil society as a model of democracy for the region.	10. (a) Sanctions before the attack killed a million and a half civilians. "Shock and awe" leaving "no safe place to hide in Baghdad" (as announced beforehand) would not have been safe for civilians. The UN projected massive civilian deaths in an attack. (b) The initial attack did avoid civilian deaths, but partly because the Iraqi army did not resist very vigorously—it was saving its resistance for later. Our response to later armed resistance (e.g., in Fallujah) has caused massive death, injury, and destruction. Our record in Afghanistan (and the Philippines in 1898), where we also promised democratization, is not encouraging. We seem more intent on privatizing than on democratizing.

Note: (a) before the invasion, (b) after.

SUMMARY

From its pre-Christian beginnings, just war theory has been shaped first through religious moral reflection and then through secular legal reflection. Love for an innocent victim justifies a violent response to violence. Ten principles have been put forward to limit when and how a war can be morally undertaken and carried on: just cause, comparative cause, attitude, intention, last resort, likely success, authority, declaration, proportionality, and discrimination. The last principle allows for "collateral" damage or injury to people who are not involved in the dispute when the "principle of double effect" is satisfied. These principles can be appealed to sincerely or insincerely, leaving moralists undecided as to whether the principles are helpful or merely a justification for leaders to engage in power politics that are driven in reality by very different principles. The overwhelming destructiveness of modern warfare, together with the recent development of active nonviolence, prompts the question whether war should continue to be acceptable under any circumstances.

KEY TERMS

attitude	jus in bello
authority	just cause
comparative cause	last resort
declared	likely success
discrimination	noncombatant immunity
intention	principle of double effect
jus ad bellum	proportionality

DISCUSSION QUESTIONS

1. How would you apply the ten principles of just war to a war that you know something about? How would you apply them to a nonviolent communal struggle with which you are familiar?
2. Do you think a presumption against violence is realistic and desirable? In other words, should a war be considered unjust unless a strong case is made to the contrary?
3. Would you allow the government of your own country to determine when a war is just, and presume that it is judging rightly unless you had strong evidence to the contrary? Would you do the same for the government of Iran, of Israel, of the former Soviet Union, or of Nazi Germany?

4. Do you respect individuals who have chosen to become conscientious objectors either to war in general or to particular wars, or do you think they are just unpatriotic cowards?

5. Do you think that the principles of just war are appropriate and practical in the real world? If not, is there something wrong with the principles, or is there something wrong with the real world?

NOTES

1. Augustine of Hippo, *Reply to Faustus the Manichean*, 22; quoted in Holmes, ed., *War and Christian Ethics*, 64.

2. Aquinas, *Summa Theologica*, 2-2 Q 40, trans. Fathers of English Dominican Province; quoted in Holmes, ed., *War and Christian Ethics*, 107f.

3. Aquinas, *Summa Theologica*, 2-2 Q 42 A 2, reply to 3rd objection; quoted in Holmes, ed., *War and Christian Ethics*, 117.

4. Walzer, *Just and Unjust Wars*, gives an excellent overview. James Turner Johnson has written prolifically on historical and modern developments of the principles. Ramsey, *The Just War*, is a classic 20th-century study. In *The Challenge of Peace*, the U.S. Catholic bishops applied the principles to nuclear deterrence and introduced a new principle, *comparative* cause.

5. A convenient collection of texts is available in Holmes, ed., *War and Christian Ethics*.

6. Our local Air Science detachment (U.S. Air Force) lent me a copy of Wakin, ed., *War, Morality, and the Military Profession*, written from a military point of view.

7. I first saw this principle in National Conference of Catholic Bishops, *The Challenge of Peace: God's Promise and Our Response*.

8. National Conference of Catholic Bishops, *The Challenge of Peace*, par. 93–94.

9. Augustine, *City of God* 19:7; emphasis added.

10. Augustine, *Reply to Faustus the Manichean*, book XXII.

11. Galtung, *Peace by Peaceful Means*, 70–76.

12. Dennis Carroll, personal letter to David Smith.

13. "A Country Study: Iraq—Chapter 1—Historical Setting (Mark Lewis)—World War I and the British Mandate" (Library of Congress Country Study on Iraq), lcweb2 .loc.gov/frd/cs/iqtoc.html (accessed July 11, 2006). They *also* have posted (as of July 11, 2006) a revised study which abbreviates this section and omits this judgment.

14. Gregory, "Letter to President Bush on Iraq."

15. Aquinas, *Summa Theologica*, 2-2 Q A 2, reply to 3rd objection.

16. Gregory, "Letter to President Bush on Iraq."

17. Grossman, *On Killing*.

18. Gray, *The Warriors: Reflections on Men in Battle*.

19. MacNair, *Psychology of Peace*.

20. Hallock, *Hell, Healing, and Resistance*, 90.

SUGGESTIONS FOR FURTHER READING

Cromartie. *Religion, Culture, and International Conflict.*

Dwyer, ed. *The Catholic Bishops and Nuclear War: A Critique and Analysis of the Pastoral Challenge of Peace.*

Galtung. *Peace by Peaceful Means.*

Gray. *The Warriors: Reflections on Men in Battle.*

Gregory. "Letter to President Bush on Iraq."

Grossman. *On Killing: The Psychological Cost of Learning to Kill in War and Society.*

Hallock. *Hell, Healing, and Resistance: Veterans Speak.*

Holmes. *On War and Morality.*

Holmes, ed. *War and Christian Ethics.*

Johnson. *The Holy War Idea in Western and Islamic Traditions.*

———. *Just War Tradition and the Restraint of War.*

Kelsay. *Islam and War: A Study in Comparative Ethics.*

MacNair. *The Psychology of Peace.*

National Conference of Catholic Bishops. *The Challenge of Peace: God's Promise and Our Response.*

Ramsey. *The Just War.*

Wakin. *War, Morality, and the Military Profession.*

Walzer. *Just and Unjust Wars.*

Glossary

access roads   Roads connecting Jewish-only settlements in the occupied territories of the West Bank (and formerly of Gaza) to each other and to the state of Israel. Palestinians are not allowed to use the roads.

accommodation   One of the possible outcomes of a nonviolent campaign. Opponents "accommodate" activists' demands when they remain convinced that they are right and just (and the activists are wrong) but decide that maintaining their position is costing them more than it is worth.

action possibilities   The final step in the circle of praxis outlined by liberation theologians. *See also* pastoral plan

adl   Justice as *maintaining* equal balance proportionate to a person's potential and situation. In Islam, *adl* is to *ihsan* more or less as justice is to charity in Christianity.

Advaita Vedanta   The nondual final meaning of the Hindu scriptures: My Atman is Brahman. That is, there is no real distinction between the Atman of an individual human and Brahman. It represents one interpretation in opposition to others.

ahimsa   Nonharm to all living beings in Hinduism.

al-Aqsa Mosque   The mosque located on the Southern side of the Haram al-Sharif (Noble Sanctuary) in Jerusalem. Muslim tradition connects it with the "farthest mosque" mentioned in the Quran and identifies it as the site from which Muhammad ascended to heaven on the "night journey."

al-nas   An Islamic (Arabic) term denoting "the people" as contrasted with "the (apartheid) state." They are sovereign, because Allah has entrusted creation to them as stewards.

Aleuts   The indigenous people of the Aleutian Islands that lie between Alaska and Russia. They are one of the far northern or circumpolar tribes.

Al-Fatah   A Palestinian political party; the largest component of the Palestine Liberation Organization. "Fatah" is a reverse acronym based on the Arabic phrase for "Palestine National Liberation Movement."

alienation   The state of being separated from someone or something that one should be closely related to. In Marxist thought, industrial capitalism alienates workers from nature, the productive activity of their work, their product, themselves, and other workers.

Allah   [The One] God, creator and judge of the universe, who has sent the prophets, including those also recognized by Jews and Christians.

Allah (hu) akbar   A common Islamic exclamation, meaning "God is greater [than anything or anyone else]."

al-Nakhba   "The catastrophe"; Palestinian term for the 1947–1948 war between the Jewish and Palestinian inhabitants of British Palestine that resulted in the forced displacement of more than 750,000 Palestinians and the destruction of more than 500 of their villages, both in the area allotted to the state of Israel by the UN partition plan and in additional areas conquered by Israel in 1948.

Amalek   An ancient desert tribe that opposed the Israelites as they fled from Egypt through the desert toward the "promised land" (Exodus 17: 8–16). Two centuries later, God ordered Saul to utterly destroy them—man, woman, and child—in punishment for this opposition (1 Samuel 15). Some militant modern Jews compare opponents of the state of Israel to Amalek and support radical policies of attack or expulsion. *See also* herem.

American Indian Movement (AIM)   A modern North American Native movement advocating Native rights and compensation by the U.S. government for broken treaties and other historic injustices. It was targeted by COINTELPRO.

Anabaptists   Christians who, in the Protestant Reformation, held that infant baptism is invalid, and so insisted on re-baptizing adults who had been baptized in infancy.

anatman   Buddhist belief that there is no "atman" or eternal spiritual reality (in the Hindu sense) which could be the subject of the experiences of an individual human being.

animism   The belief that all natural material things—humans, animals, plants, rocks, lakes and rivers—have souls, or a conscious, underlying spiritual reality.

Anishinaabeg   The name that Ojibwa or Chippewa Natives of North America use of themselves. It means "original people."

Anno Hegirae (A.H.)   The calendric year counting from Muhammad's "Hegira," or flight from Mecca to Medina in 622 CE. Because the Muslim year consists of twelve lunar months, and thus is ten or eleven days shorter than a solar year, one cannot match AH to the Common Era (CE) or a year expressed in Anno Domini (AD) by adding 621 or 622 to a year expressed in AH.

antithesis   The second stage of Marx's dialectical theory of history. As society begins to change under the influence of new forms of production, new forces and ideas challenge the status-quo *thesis*.

Apache   Group of native tribes of the southwest United States, including the Navajo, with a large reservation in Nevada and New Mexico, noted for their warrior skills exemplified by their famous leaders Geronimo and Cochise. Navajo speaking their native language were used by the U.S. Marines in World War II in place of code for secret messages.

apartheid wall   Palestinian designation for what Israelis call the "security barrier" or "separation barrier."

Armageddon   The anticipated final battle between Jesus and his forces against Satan and his forces, described in the New Testament Book of the Apocalypse (The Revelation of John).

Aryan   "Noble People"—the word that light-skinned Indians (who invaded from the Northwest and took control in India) used to refer to themselves.

Ashkenazic   Adjective describing Jews (and their culture) who were strongly influenced by Germanic and Eastern European cultures.

Atman   The Self, the imperishable part of each human.

attitude   The just war principle relating to one's beliefs about and images of one's enemies or opponents: one should love one's enemies, seek to do them good, and regret the damage and suffering one is causing them.

authority   The just war principle regarding who is a legitimate leader to declare and lead a just war.

avidya   The ignorance or delusion that (in Hinduism) keeps us from realizing the true nature of reality: the unity of all things; and (in Buddhism) keeps us from realizing the four noble truths.

Aztec   Central American native tribe leading an empire centered around what became Mexico City. They captured neighbors so that on a daily basis they could tear beating hearts out of living humans to keep the sun rising.

Baal Shem Tov   (Abbreviated Besht) "Master of the Good Name"—the honorary title of Israel Ben Eliezer, the Polish founder (died 1760) of 18th century Hasidism. In a time of persecution and despair, he taught that personal piety, as expressed in prayer and joyful, ecstatic worship of God, is more important than intellectual study of the Torah and literal Torah obedience.

Balfour Declaration   Official letter from Arthur James Balfour of the British Foreign Office to Lord Rothschild in November 1917 declaring that "His Majesty's Government view with favour the establishment in Palestine of a national home for the Jewish people . . . [providing that] nothing shall be done which may prejudice the civil and religious rights of existing non-Jewish communities in Palestine . . ."

Base Christian Communities   Small groups of people within a large parish, originally in Latin America, who discuss how the church and Christian faith should influence current situations, offer mutual support, and promote common action.

Berlin Wall   Fortified barrier separating East Berlin from West Berlin—part of the "Iron Curtain"—designed to prevent East Berliners from fleeing to the West. Begun in 1961, it was demolished in 1989.

Besht   Abbreviation of the Baal Shem Tov. *See also* Baal Shem Tov.

Bhagavad-Gita   Story of the god Krishna and warrior Arjuna on the eve of an epic battle; part of the epic poem the *Mahabharata.*

bhakti   In Hinduism, devotion or faith expressed in the fervent worship of a personal god.

Bhoodan   A land redistribution program, promoted by Vinoba Bhave, involving voluntary donations of land to heal the wealthy of their slavery to money and to help the poor stand on their own feet with productive resources of their own.

bi-national state   A modern nation-state embracing two "nations," preferably providing members of both nations with equal rights and responsibilities of citizenship. Palestinians have largely preferred a bi-national state in Palestine, giving equal rights to Jews, Muslims, and Christians, but many Palestinians have come to accept two unitary states dividing Palestine, since Israeli Jews have largely insisted on their state being Jewish.

bodhi   Enlightenment. Applied to the "bodhi tree" under which Siddhartha Gautama attained enlightenment, and to "bodhisattvas" who delay entry into nirvana so that they can help others to attain enlightenment; also related to the Buddha—the "enlightened one."

Bodhisattva   A person destined to become a Buddha but who delays his or her own progress toward Buddhahood out of compassion for other living beings.

boom-bust cycle   Alternation between economic growth and economic crisis caused by the over-production resulting from a lack of central planning.

Brahma (capital B)   Creator god, early period of Hinduism.

Brahman (capital B)   Power (capital P); the one source or ground of being in the universe—unborn, uncreated, eternal, unchanging—that manifests itself in all the many gods of Hindu tradition.

brahman (lowercase b)   Spiritual power (lowercase p); for example, the ability of a Brahmin to make sacrifices and prayers that would effectively control spiritual reality on behalf of those who ask for his help.

Brahmana   (1) Brahmin, a Hindu priest; (2) part of the Shruti, inspired traditions used by the Brahmins to regulate their ritual.

Brahmin   A Hindu priest; a Western form for the term Brahmana in its first meaning, and an attempt by Westerners to avoid confusion. In the Hindu caste system, Brahmins constitute the first (twice-born) caste.

Buddha   "Enlightened One." The most famous Enlightened One was Siddhartha Gautama.

caliph   Successor to Muhammad as leader of the *ummah.*

capitalism   An economic system characterized by private ownership and control of the means of industrial production.

capitalization   Gathering enough resources to build machines and factories.

caste   A Western term reflecting two overlapping Indian systems that distinguish humans by birth into categories of work and social standing that affect who one can marry, associate with, and eat with. The system of *varnas*, or "colors," divides society into four major categories (*brahman, kshatriya, vaishya, shudra*); that of *jatis* divides society into hundreds of occupational groups. The"outcastes" are outside the system and marginalized from society.

categorical imperative   According to Kant, moral principles for decision making that avoid religious doctrine: treat other humans as ends, never as means; and act so that what you do could be a general law.

CELAM   Conference of Latin American Bishops.

checkpoints   In the Israeli-occupied Palestinian territories, barriers to travel staffed by Israeli police or military personnel that restrict passage based on a traveler's documents or other characteristics. Palestinians complain that the principles used are often arbitrary.

Cherokee   Native American tribe that adopted European dress and created a syllabary with which it published a newspaper. When gold was discovered in its territories in Georgia, members were forced to relocate to Oklahoma in violation of a ruling of the U.S. Supreme Court that upheld their rights.

Chiapas   Largely Mayan city and rural region in southern Mexico. Bartholomé de las Casas was its bishop in colonial times. When the North American Free Trade Agreement went into effect in January 1994, a movement called Zapatista began to resist the agreement.

Chilam Balam   A sacred book of the Maya.

Christian Zionism   The conviction that, for Jesus to return as promised, the Jewish community must first return to the historic holy land, reestablish its rule there, rebuild the temple, and resume offering sacrifices. When Jesus returns, he will convert a large portion of the Jewish population. The rest will be annihilated in the final battle of Armageddon.

Christmas   Christian celebration of the birth of Jesus, expressing the belief that God became human in Jesus of Nazareth, thus connecting humans to God in a new and permanent way.

circle of praxis   A four-step approach to understanding and affecting the world: *Insert* oneself into conditions of poverty and injustice, make a *(descriptive) analysis* of the power relations that cause such a condition, make a *normative (or theological) analysis* of what is desirable and undesirable about the current situation, and make *action plans* to change the situation toward a better, more just one.

class struggle   A Marxist conviction that economic classes are naturally antagonistic; the working class (proletariat) must seize control from the ownership class (bourgeoisie). Liberation theologians do not believe that this is a necessary state of affairs, but do point out that the bourgeoisie in fact often takes advantage of its power to oppress the proletariat.

closed military zone   An area in the occupied areas of Gaza, the West Bank, and East Jerusalem that has been declared closed to Palestinians by military decree, ostensibly for security needs, but often actually as the first stage in appropriating the land for use by Jews only.

coercion   One of the possible outcomes of a nonviolent campaign. Opponents are "coerced" when they remain convinced that they are right and just (and the activists are wrong) and make every effort to maintain their position and their power but find that they are unable to maintain the situation because the people on whom they depend for support no longer give that support.

COINTELPRO   "Counterintelligence Program": a 1956–1971 secret FBI program designed to study activist political organizations in the United States and disrupt their activities, often by spreading false information and promoting dissension within the group. Its targets ranged from violent groups like the Weathermen and the Ku Klux Klan to nonviolent groups like the Southern Christian Leadership Conference of Dr. Martin Luther King Jr.

Communism   According to Karl Marx, the final stage of the historical evolution of society.

Communist Manifesto   A short, 1848 book by Karl Marx and Friedrich Engels, laying out the program of the communist party.

comparative cause   The just war principle insisting that one must balance one's own grievances against the grievances of one's opponent. Only if there is a preponderance of justice on one side is that side justified in carrying on war.

conscientization   Becoming aware of how political, economic, and social forces, structures, and convictions affect people's lives, and how things got to be that way.

Conservative Judaism   A 20th-century form of U.S. Judaism seeking a middle position between Orthodox and Reform Judaism.

constructive program   Gandhi's plan to build strong, self-reliant local communities in India, ending dependence on British colonizers.

conversion   One of the possible outcomes of a nonviolent campaign. Opponents are "converted" to the activists' point of views when they come to believe that the activists' positions are right and just (and they themselves have been wrong) and, as a result, change their actions to meet the activists' demands.

conversion of the head   Coming to see (understand) people and things as God sees them.

conversion of the heart   Coming to love people and things as God loves them.

corporative state   Pope Leo XIII's proposal that the political and economic structures of society itself should promote worker-management cooperation. Rather than representing geographic areas, legislators would represent economic, agricultural, industrial, and professional sectors of society, such as the steel industry. Fascist Italy established twenty-two such groupings. Pope Pius XI objected that the Fascist form did not conform to Pope Leo's intention.

counting coup   Native American practice of showing bravery in battle by riding through a hail of arrows, touching one's enemy with a "coup stick," and galloping safely away.

covenant   Ancient Near Eastern form of political association between two or more kings and their people, usually one dominant and the other subordinate, adopted by God in God's relationship with the Hebrew, later Israelite, people.

Crusades   Early second-millennium Christian campaigns to seize control of the Holy Land from its Muslim rulers.

Cultural Revolution   Movement in Communist China initiated by Mao Zedong to reestablish his authority, which he believed was being threatened by younger and more liberal leaders. He organized a "Red Guard" or militia of activist youth to purge "counterrevolutionaries." Intense struggles produced a disastrous purge of leadership.

cultural Zionism   A movement seeking to bring Jews to Palestine, not to create a Jewish state, but rather to restore and renew Jewish cultural and religious life in Palestine, where history, geography, climate, and other natural factors were regarded as most suitable to that project.

Dakota   Minnesota tribe, thirty-eight of whose members were hung in New Ulm, Minnesota, after an uprising protesting unfulfilled treaty obligations.

Dalit   The name that "untouchables" or "outcastes" in India prefer to use in reference to themselves—it means "oppressed."

Dalit theology   A form of theology inspired by Latin American liberation theology, developed in India by Dalits.

Das Kapital   Classic book by Karl Marx and Friedrich Engels, giving a communist interpretation of political economy and a critique of capitalism.

Day of Atonement   *Yom Kippur*, a day of fasting and atonement for sins, the last day of the Jewish ten-day new year celebration.

Days of Awe   The ten days of the Jewish new year celebration, beginning with *Rosh Hashanah* and ending with *Yom Kippur*.

decade of development   President John F. Kennedy declared the decade 1960–1970 as a time to bring poor countries closer to rich countries in economic development.

declared   The just war principle that requires one initiating a war to state clearly the grievances that are giving rise to the war and what the opponent could do to avoid war.

Deir Yassin   Palestinian village on the edge of Jerusalem committed to neutrality where an informal Israeli army massacred more than 200 villagers in 1948.

dervish   Persian term for one who seeks spiritual poverty for the sake of Allah. One group (the "whirling dervishes") seeks to induce ecstatic trance through stylized dance.

descriptive analysis   The second step in the circle of praxis outlined by liberation theologians. It uses economics, political science, psychology, sociology, and similar disciplines to explain the power relations that shape the current situation, and history to explain how the current situation has come about.

deva   Hindu term for a god or a powerful and good supernatural being.

dharma (Buddhist)   The totality of the Buddha's teachings.

dharma (Hindu)   Responsibilities or duties that one has because of one's place in the caste system.

dialectic   Marxist (and Hegelian) term for the three-stage process that produces historical change: thesis, antithesis, and synthesis.

dialectical materialism   Marx's term distinguishing his form of dialectic from that of Hegel: whereas Hegel thought that dialectic was driven by Spirit, Marx insisted it was driven by the material conditions of production.

Diaspora   Jews living outside Israel/Palestine.

dictatorship of the proletariat   The transition period between capitalism and communism where workers take over the governance of society.

dilemma   The conflict caused when a single actor wants to achieve two incompatible goals.

discrimination   The just war principle requiring that only those who are actually causing or threatening unjust violence can be attacked. Such uninvolved bystanders as captured soldiers, civilians, children, and future generations must not be harmed.

dispensationalism   The Christian theology holding that God deals with humans according to different rules in different periods of time, usually seven, the seventh and last being the millennium.

dispute   The conflict caused when two or more actors want to achieve a single goal that cannot be shared.

dog strap soldier   A Native American warrior who attaches himself to a stake driven into the ground as a sign that he will not retreat in battle.

Dome of the Rock   The Muslim shrine, built around 690 in the Noble Sacuary in Jerusalem, enclosing the rock from which Muhammad is believed to have ascended to heaven in the night journey in 620.

dukkha   In Buddhism, suffering that arises from attachment to and craving for what is temporary and passing.

Easter   The Christian celebration of Jesus' rising from the dead to a new state of existence that includes life in the body. It includes the conviction that faithful Christians will share a similar experience.

economic hit men   Advisors who project unrealistic economic growth as a result of major investments in infrastructure funded by loans that must be used to hire U.S. construction firms, intended to keep third-world nations perpetually in debt and thus forced to supply their raw materials to the United States at bargain prices, to allow U.S. military bases on their territory, to vote as the United States directs in the UN, and in general to follow U.S. directives.

Eid al-Adha   The Muslim feast that commemorates Ibrahim's willingness to sacrifice his son Ismael to God. It is celebrated toward the end of the annual hajj to Mecca.

Eid al-Fitr   The Muslim feast celebrated at the new moon that ends Ramadan.

encyclical   A circular papal latter sent to all Catholic bishops of the world dealing with some problem of common interest to the Catholic Church.

Engaged Buddhism   A movement that uses Buddhist principles to justify and empower social action on behalf of justice.

enlightenment (Buddhism)   Awakening to the true nature of the universe; the experiential discovery that everything is impermanent and that the four noble truths show the way to end suffering.

Enlightenment (period of history)   18th-century movement that gave authority to reason rather than religious faith as the basis for understanding reality.

epistle   Letter written to a group rather than to an individual, or understood to have relevance beyond the individual to whom it was addressed. Christian epistles make up about a third of the New Testament.

Eucharist   The Christian celebration of the Lord's Supper—the final meal Jesus shared with his disciples before he was crucified—in which the elements of bread and wine are variously understood to be, or to signify, the body and blood of Jesus and the loving sacrifice of his death.

Evangelicals   Protestant Christians who emphasize personal conversion, the Bible as the sole religious authority, salvation through the death and resurrection of Jesus, the reality of miracles, and active efforts to convert nonbelievers and affect the larger society. Sometimes used as a less pejorative term for Fundamentalists.

exaltation   The raising of Jesus of Nazareth to a position of power and authority "at the right hand of God."

exploitation   Unjust employment of other human beings for one's own enrichment without fair sharing of the wealth.

extrinsic motivation   Reasons for engaging in an activity other than the natural results of the activity itself, for example, to receive a reward or to avoid punishment.

facts on the ground   Infrastructure, such as settlements, constructed so as to promote one political reality (Jewish control of the West Bank) and make another impossible (a viable Palestinian state).

faqir (*fakir*)   Arabic term for one who seeks spiritual poverty for the sake of Allah.

Fatah   *See* al-Fatah.

five pillars   The five key requirements for Muslims: shahada (profession of faith), salat (prescribed daily prayer), saum (fasting during Ramadan), zakat (annual tax on surplus wealth), and hajj (pilgrimage to Mecca).

Five Civilized Tribes   Five Native American tribes of the east coast of North America (Cherokee, Chickasaw, Choctaw, Creek, and Seminole) that adopted many customs of the European colonists. Except for part of the Seminole nation that was never conquered and still lives in Florida, they were moved west to "Indian territory," mostly Oklahoma. The most famous of these moves was the "trail of tears" transfer of the Cherokee.

Fundamentalists   U.S. Protestant Christians who, in reaction to liberal Protestantism in the early 20th century, committed themselves to traditional articles of faith: the five "fundamentals" of biblical inerrancy, the Virgin birth, the physical resurrection of Jesus, atonement by the sacrificial death of Christ, and the Second Coming of Jesus.

Gaza withdrawal   In 2005, without consulting the Palestinians, Israel removed Jewish settlers and their supporting Israeli soldiers from Gaza, an area considered of less importance than the West Bank, so as to strengthen their hold on the West Bank settlements, which were considered more important.

Gemara   The sections of commentary which, added to the Mishnah (and generally printed as a margin around it), make up the Talmud.

ghetto   An urban area reserved (sometimes voluntarily, sometimes by force, usually protected by walls) for members of one particular ethnic or racial group. Originally used with reference to Jewish areas, it is sometimes used more generally of any poor urban section.

ghost dance   A Native American dance, based on visions received by the Paiute Indian Wovoka, reputed to give miraculous power to bring dead Native warriors back to life, protect them from bullets, bury the whites, and restore the prairies.

Golan Heights   The western plateau of Syria overlooking the Sea of Galilee from which Syrian guns could control the border with Israel. It was captured from Syria by Israel in 1967, fought over in 1973, and is currently in the hands of Israel.

Gramdan   A land redistribution program promoted by Vinoba Bhave involving voluntary donations of villages to their poor inhabitants to heal the wealthy of their slavery to money, and to help the poor stand on their own feet with productive resources of their own.

Great Leap Forward   Chinese communist centrally planned program to promote industrialization. When it failed, resulting in widespread famine, Mao Zedong launched the Cultural Revolution to reestablish his authority.

great tradition   A term that applies to all world religions. It refers to the form in which a particular tradition is taught by its most enthusiastic leaders and practitioners, developed by its major writers and apologists (propagandists), and contained in its sacred and classic texts.

Gush Emunim   "Block of the Faithful"—a group of Israeli settlers seeking to "redeem the land" or establish Jewish control in all of historic Israel, which they believe God promised to Jews, by building Jewish-only settlements throughout the occupied territories and then expanding the areas those settlements control.

Gush Shalom   "Block of Peace"—a group of Israeli Jews and other supporters seeking a just and nonviolent settlement to the Israeli-Palestinian dispute. It supports a two-state solution within the borders determined by the 1948 cease-fire line that prevailed until 1967 (except for small, mutually agreed land swaps), with both nations sharing Jerusalem as a capital, and makes use of strong nonviolent activism to further its cause.

Hadith   Collections of noninspired traditions about Muhammad and his companions relating to his words and actions.

Haganah   The quasi-official underground Jewish army established to protect and promote Jewish settlers in Palestine when it was under British control.

Haggadah   Parables, homilies, and other narrative materials found in the Talmud. It contrasts with Halakah—the legal or prescriptive materials.

hajj   The once-in-a-lifetime pilgrimage to Mecca and Medina required of all Muslims who can afford it by their own resources.

Halakah   Legal materials in the Talmud (and in the Mishnah).

Hamas   Islamic Resistance Movement—a Palestinian movement to regain control of Palestine from Israeli Jews and establish an Islamic state. It is noted for community development, relief work, and armed attacks including suicide bombs.

Hanukkah   Jewish holiday commemorating the recapture and rededication of the Jerusalem temple by the Maccabees in 165 BCE after it had been desecrated by Syrian Hellenists of the Seleucid Empire. It celebrates the miracle that one day's supply of oil burned for all eight days of the original dedication.

Harijan   "Children of God"—the name that Gandhi coined for the "untouchables" or "outcastes."

Hasbuna Allah   A common Islamic exclamation meaning, "God is my enough" (that is, God is all I need).

Hasidism   Now a particularly conservative form of Orthodox Judaism. The 18th-century leader the Baal Shem Tov emphasized ecstatic piety.

herem   A dedication to destruction applied to certain groups whom God directed the ancient Hebrews to kill: man, woman, and child.

Hezbollah   "Party of God"—a Lebanese Shi'ite political and militant movement, founded during the 1982 Israeli invasion of Lebanon, it seeks to end Western colonization of Lebanon (including Israeli occupation), punish war criminals, and create an Islamic government for Lebanon. It carries on numerous social, health, and educational activities.

hijra (Hegira)   The flight of Muhammad and the first Muslims from Mecca to Yathrib, renamed Medina, in 622 CE. It marks year one of the Islamic calendar, *Anno Hegirae*.

Hinayana   "Little vehicle"—pejorative Mahayana term for Theravada Buddhism. *See also* Theravada.

Histadrut   The Israeli Jewish "General Federation of Labor," founded in 1921, which also fills numerous social support functions. It is a mainstay of the Labor Party, owns numerous businesses and the largest Israeli bank, and at its high point counted about 85% of Israeli workers as members. It began accepting Arab members in 1959.

Holocaust   Nazi Germany's program during World War II to kill everyone within Germany and the territories occupied by Germany who had at least one Jewish grandparent. For this purpose, Germany constructed labor-extermination camps that made use of Jewish labor, killed the Jews in gas chambers, and cremated their bodies.

Holy Spirit Third "person" of the "blessed Trinity" of God who came in flames of fire to the disciples on Pentecost and to their converts through the "laying on of hands," empowering them to spread the "good news" of the death and resurrection of Jesus of Nazareth in the face of lethal opposition with the help of numerous supernatural charisms (gifts of power).

Hopi Native American tribe of the southwest United States noted for having largely maintained its traditional way of life under the pressure of European settlement.

ideology (Marxist) Explanations developed to justify (unjust) existing power relations and economic/political/religious structures.

ihsan Justice as *restoring* balance by making up for a loss or deficiency; *ihsan* is to *adl* in Islam more or less as charity is to justice in Christianity.

iman Right faith or belief in Allah.

imperialism Control of weaker nations by stronger nations. In the modern period, control of nonindustrialized societies by industrialized nations through colonization or other means of exploitation, typically in search of cheap raw materials and new markets for manufactured goods.

Inca Native American tribe that controlled an empire around Lake Titicaca in what is today Peru, Bolivia, and Chile.

incarnation The embodiment of a spiritual being in physical flesh, usually human. Christians celebrate the incarnation of the Second Person of the Blessed Trinity (God) in the human being Jesus of Nazareth, who was thus both divine and human.

Indian giver One who freely gives what another member of the community needs, without fear of the future, knowing that, if the giver later experiences need, someone else from the community will meet their need. European settlers distorted the phrase to mean "give something, then take it back."

indwelling A good spiritual being other than the soul living within a human being without violating its freedom. Christians believe that God—Father, Son, and Spirit—indwells faithful Christians.

ingathering Jewish notion that Jews worldwide should come together in Israel to restore the ancient state and society and protect themselves from hostile non-Jews.

Injil Arabic word for "gospels," generally referring to the entire New Testament, which Muslims believe is inspired by God but has been corrupted in its current form.

Inquisition An effort to deal with religious dissent through judicial examination, trial, and punishment of those unwilling to repent, including capital punishment. As was also true in regular secular courts, torture was sometimes used in the examination.

insertion   The first step in the circle of praxis outlined by liberation theologians: one seeks to experience, first-hand or vicariously, the problem one wishes to alleviate.

inspired   The conviction that God is in some sense the author of Sacred Scripture (the Jewish and Christian Bible and the Quran). There is wide variation among churches as to the extent and form of that authorship, from word-by-word dictation to various forms of divine-human cooperation.

intention   The just war principle regarding the aims and goals of a particular war: restoration of justice and peace is regarded as acceptable— plunder and domination are not.

interim ethic   The notion that Jesus expected God to end this world soon with a general judgment, so that extreme demands could be made for the short time left. If he had realized that the world would continue for thousands of years, he would not have made such difficult demands in the Sermon on the Mount.

International Solidarity Movement   Palestinian movement founded in 2001 to resist Israeli occupation through direct nonviolent action, supported by the presence of international observers whose presence would reduce Israeli violence and report the situation to a wider public.

intervention   Third of the three major forms of nonviolent action, the other two being (1) protest and persuasion and (2) noncooperation. One intervenes by getting in the way of another's unjust action—by doing something that interferes with it.

intifada   "Shaking off"—Palestinian resistance to the Israeli occupation of Gaza, East Jerusalem, and the West Bank. The first intifada, from 1987 to 1993, was largely nonviolent on the Palestinian side. The second, from 2000 to the present, has made use of violence as well.

intrinsic motivation   Reasons for engaging in an activity based on the natural results of the activity itself; for example, satisfaction at producing a good result that is helpful for others.

Inuit   Arctic Native American tribes of Alaska, Canada, and Greenland noted for avoiding conflict; they have organized themselves into the Inuit Circumpolar Conference.

Irgun   Unofficial underground Jewish strike force established to attack British police and government installations and Palestinian resistance to Jewish expansion.

Iroquois   Confederation of five Native American nations, noted for its influence on the U.S. Constitution.

Islam   Religion originating in 7th-century Arabia; the word means self-surrender to Allah.

isnad   The chain of transmitters that passed on a particular hadith orally, used to validate its authenticity.

Israel Defense Forces   The Israeli army, navy, and air force.

Jataka Tales   Stories of the Buddha's previous lives, used to inspire good behavior in Buddhists.

Jewish home   What the Balfour Declaration promised to Lord Rothschild. Some Jews interpreted it to be a state under Jewish control encompassing all of Palestine and Transjordan, but Britain clarified that, while it intended the home to be a safe refuge for Jews, it did not intend it to be the sole authority in Palestine.

Jewish settlements   Communities constructed in Gaza, East Jerusalem, and the West Bank since 1967 that only Jews can legally inhabit. They are connected to each other and to Israel by roads that only Jews can legally use.

Jewish state   Ideally, a Western-style democratic state dominated by Jews, Jewish traditions, and Jewish customs, where Jews can live securely and practice their traditions without interference. For such a state to embrace all the territory that the Tanakh designates as promised to the Israelites, most non-Jews would have to be transferred out, voluntarily or involuntarily.

Jibril   Arabic form of the angelic name Gabriel, who revealed to Mary that she was to be the mother of Jesus and revealed the Quran to Muhammed.

jihad   Striving in Allah's cause; it can include inner struggle and outer warfare to defend Islam or to spread the conditions that allow for its faith to be embraced.

jihad, greater   The inner struggle within an individual to overcome one's evil inclination to develop one's good tendencies.

jihad, lesser   The external struggle to overcome injustice and unbelief, particularly to overcome structures and forces that prevent humans from surrendering to Allah according to the revelations of the Quran.

jnana   Knowledge, especially the ultimate knowledge of the nature of reality: that atman and Brahman are identical.

JOCists   Young Christian workers who met in small groups and were very influential in both North and South America.

ju-jitsu, moral or political   Throwing the opponent off balance and bringing his violence out into the open by maintaining nonviolence in the face of his violent repression. The more violent the opponent becomes, the more that opponent loses the cooperation he or she needs from supporters.

juche   Absolute loyalty to the leader of North Korea and the Party, emphasizing Korean military and economic self-reliance.

Judea   In Roman Palestine, the area south of Samaria, including especially Jerusalem, Bethlehem, and Hebron. Modern Jewish settlers use the term for that part of the West Bank to make the claim that it should be under Jewish control.

jus ad bellum Those just war principles that answer the question when an appropriate authority would be justified in *starting* a war.

jus in bello Those just war principles that answer the question what practices wartime leaders would be justified in using to *carry out* a war.

just cause The just war principle specifying what grievances would be grave enough to justify going to war. In modern times, the acceptable causes are two: (1) resistance to an actual unjust invasion and (2) a military action authorized by the UN.

Kaabah The foremost Muslim pilgrimage shrine, it consists of a black stone within a cubical structure covered with a black cloth and set inside a large courtyard in the city of Mecca, Saudi Arabia. Muslims traditionally believe that Abraham built the Kaabah with his son Ismail for the worship of the one God, but it became corrupted as a pilgrimage shrine for (pre-Islamic) Arabian pagans.

Kabbalah Medieval Jewish mysticism represented textually by the *Zohar.*

Kadima Party A new Israeli political party formed by Ariel Sharon before the Israeli withdrawal of settlers from the Gaza Strip in August 2005 and after the Likud party had objected to the proposed withdrawal. *Kadima* is Hebrew for "forward."

Kapital, Das See Das Kapital.

Karbala The site in present-day Iraq where Husayn, son of the fourth Muslim caliph, Ali, was murdered with his companions, in 680 CE. The martyrdom of Husayn marks the beginning of the division between Sunni and Shia Muslims.

karma Actions and their natural effects in present and future lives. One's current status (human, animal, and so forth) results from the good or evil intentions of acts in previous lives.

kerygma The contents of the earliest Christian mission speech, which can be reconstructed from Peter's and Paul's speeches in the Acts of the Apostles. It consists of six key elements.

Ketuvim The third section of the Hebrew Bible (Tanakh), "the Writings," which include the book of Job, Ecclesiastes, and the Song of Songs, among others.

Khudai Khidmatgars Literally, "servants of God"—members of the nonviolent Muslim liberation movement against British imperial rule over India, led by Khan Abdul Ghaffar Khan.

kibbutz A cooperative type of community originally introduced in Palestine by socialist or Marxist Zionist immigrants; members held all property in common. *See also* moshav.

Knesset In modern Israel, the parliament, both building and legislative body, based on the Hebrew word for "assembly."

Kristallnacht   The "Night of Broken Glass," which took place on November 9–10, 1938, in Germany and Austria; orchestrated by the Nazi government, it consisted of Jewish homes, shops, synagogues, and persons being physically attacked, leaving death and destruction in its wake.

Kshatriya   In the Hindu caste system, the second (twice-born) caste, comprising warriors, politicians, and civil authorities.

Labor Party   A major political party in modern Israel. Although left-wing compared to the Likud Party, its policies toward the Palestinians have not proved radically different; for example, it has supported settlement construction. Key Labor Party leaders include Shimon Peres and the late Yitzhak Rabin.

last resort   The just war principle that requires leaders to seriously consider all nonviolent ways to achieve justice and redress their grievances before resorting to war.

League of Nations mandate   Authorization given to Britain and France by the League of Nations after World War I to control, respectively, Palestine, Transjordan, and Iraq (Britain), and Lebanon and Syria (France). The British gave up their Palestine mandate in 1948.

Lebanese Phalange   A Fascist Christian political faction. Members of this group, with Israeli support, perpetrated the massacre of up to 3,000 Palestinians in the camps of Sabra and Shatila in 1982.

Lehi   Unofficial underground Jewish strike force established to attack British police and government installations, and Palestinian resistance to Jewish expansion. *See also* Stern Gang.

likely success   The just war principle that forbids one to enter a war that one is likely or sure to lose or that is likely to lead to a stalemate.

Likud Party   The foremost right-wing political party in modern Israel. Recent Likud prime ministers include Menachem Begin, Benjamin Netanyahu, and Ariel Sharon. In its platform, it "flatly rejects the establishment of a Palestinian Arab state west of the Jordan River." It openly supports settlement activity and initiated the construction of the separation barrier or wall.

little tradition   A term that applies to all world religions, referring to the way ordinary people—often only vaguely committed to its principles—live out the worldview that is enshrined in sacred texts, taught by leaders, and developed by writers.

Lord's Supper   In the Christian Gospels, Jesus' last meal with his disciples just before his arrest, during which he instituted the "new covenant" and the Eucharist.

Mahabharata   In Hinduism, one of the two great national epics (*see also Ramayana*). The *Bhagavad-Gita* is a section of it.

Mahayana   "Greater vehicle"—a school of thought in Buddhism that modifies the older Theravada form by noting that, if all reality is illusory, we shouldn't have to leave the world and join a monastery to gain enlightenment. It also claims that bodhisattvas, by delaying their entry into nirvana, can help others to progress toward enlightenment.

Maya   Central American indigenous tribes noted for their monumental cities, sophisticated writing system, astronomy, and mathematics.

maya   In Hinduism, a "playful illusion" that deceives us into thinking that what we see in our everyday experience is ultimate reality.

Mecca   The Arabian city where Muhammad was born in 570 CE. It was significant as a growing commercial center and as the pilgrimage site of the shrine called the Kaabah.

Medina   In Islam, the Arabian city located north of Mecca where Muhammad and the first Muslims fled in 622 (the hijrah) to escape persecution in Mecca and where they settled.

mendicant orders   Medieval Christian religious orders of "beggars" who owned nothing but lived and worked in the cities, challenging contemporary ideas about riches.

Messiah   In Judaism and Christianity, God's anointed one sent to rescue or save oppressed humans. For Christians, the messiah was Jesus of Nazareth.

metta   Loving-kindness, a key Buddhist virtue.

metta bhavana   In Buddhism, "kindness meditation"—a five-stage meditation extending loving kindness to all beings throughout space and time.

Midrash   Expansions and explanations of the Tanakh serving as commentaries on the sacred text.

millennium   Among Fundamentalist and Zionist Christians, the thousand-year period during the end-time when Christ will reign. In the book of Revelation, it precedes the final defeat of Satan, the last judgment, and the new heaven and earth.

minaret   In Islam, the proclamation tower from which the muezzin issues the call to prayer. It is a regular (usually detached) architectural feature of mosques in Muslim countries, analogous to the bell tower of a Christian church.

Minjung theology   A Korean form of liberation theology seeking social justice and human rights for the downtrodden common people—the "Minjung"—by interpreting the Bible (around the centenary of its first translation into Korean, the language of the common people) with attention to Korean concepts like *han*: the indignation and grief of common people in the face of historic and current injustice.

Mishnah   The first written collection of the oral traditions of the Pharisees.

moksha   In Hinduism, escape from the cycle of rebirth or reincarnation.

moshav   A semi-cooperative type of rural community originally set up in Palestine by socialist or Marxist Zionist immigrants. Present-day moshavim practice communal purchasing, marketing, and in some cases production. *See also* kibbutz.

muezzin   In Islam, the one who calls Muslims to prayer five times each day from the minaret of the mosque.

mujahid   A person who strives in Allah's cause; one who practices jihad.

Mujerista theology   Hispanic feminist liberation theology.

mumin   In Islam, one who practices *iman*, or right faith in Allah and in the basic teachings of Islam; a person of faith.

Muslim   A person of faith who surrenders himself or herself to the will of Allah.

Muslim Brotherhood   A prominent neo-revivalist movement founded in Egypt in 1928 by Hassan al-Banna. Although occasionally in the past it has used or approved of violence, it has espoused nonviolence since 1970, sponsors numerous social service projects, and seeks to participate in politics.

Nakhba   *See* al-Nakhba.

Neviim   In Judaism, the "Prophets," meaning the middle section of the Tanakh (Hebrew Bible), beginning with the book of Joshua and ending with the book of Malachi.

Night Journey   In Islamic tradition, Muhammad's miraculous transport to Jerusalem from Mecca in 620, followed by his ascension to the presence of God, where he conversed with other prophets.

nirvana   The blissful state of freedom from rebirth realized when we gain insight into the illusion of our present existence and let go of our separate personality.

Noble Sanctuary   In Arabic, "al-Haram al-Sharif," the Muslim name for the great esplanade in Jerusalem that Jews call the Temple Mount, on which the Islamic Dome of the Rock and the Al-Aqsa mosque are situated.

noncombatant immunity   The just war principle that forbids attacks on those who are not threatening injustice or harm. It is part of the principle of *discrimination*.

noncooperation   Second of the three major forms of nonviolent action, the other two being (1) protest and persuasion and (3) intervention. One withdraws cooperation by refusing to do something that one is normally expected to do and that is required for the injustice to continue. For example, one refuses to work by striking, or refuses to purchase through a boycott.

nonviolence of the strong   Practice of nonviolence based on the principle of respecting opponents and causing no harm. One practices nonviolence even if one could prevail through the use of violence.

nonviolence of the weak   Practice of nonviolence motivated by the fact that one is too weak to prevail violently. If one could prevail violently, one would do so.

normative analysis   The third step in the circle of praxis outlined by liberation theologians. It raises value questions, asking what is good about the current situation and what is bad about it, then proposes a better or more just situation.

numinous   Something that is terrifying yet draws us toward itself; a dual experience.

Ojibwa   Native American tribe pushed by European settlers west from the Lake Ontario region into Minnesota.

oppression   The suffering of the poor in situations of structural violence, as a consequence of societal injustice; liberation theologians assert that both oppressor and oppressed need to be liberated.

original sin   A key doctrine of Christianity that attempts to express and explain what within human beings resists goodness, generosity, courage, and trust.

Orthodox Judaism   A major branch of modern Judaism that seeks to preserve all the historical Jewish traditions and beliefs, to be distinguished from Conservative Judaism, Reform Judaism, and Reconstructionist Judaism.

Oslo Accords   The Declaration of Principles negotiated in Norway and then signed in Washington, DC, in 1993 by Yasser Arafat and Yitzhak Rabin, which established the Palestinian Authority and promised a permanent Israeli-Palestinian peace settlement within five years.

Ottoman Empire   One of the great medieval Muslim empires. Lasting through the first world war, it was based in Turkey.

Our Lady of Guadalupe   A Catholic shrine in Mexico City dedicated to the Virgin Mary. Inside the shrine a cloak is displayed with an image of Mary as an Indian woman, which was miraculously imprinted on it in a 1531 appearance to the indigenous peasant Juan Diego.

outcastes   In the Hindu caste system, another term for the untouchables, or scheduled caste, or Dalits: those who fall below the three "twice-born" castes and the Shudra (fourth caste).

Palestine Liberation Organization (PLO)   Secular Palestinian movement to return refugees to their former homes, led by Yasser Arafat, which at first made use of terror attacks to resist Israeli expansion and later evolved toward a Palestinian government willing to live alongside a Jewish state of Israel.

Palestine National Congress   The legislative branch of the Palestinian government, originally under the Palestine Liberation Organization and, since 1994, under the Palestinian National Authority.

pan-en-henic   The experience of unity with nature—of feeling lost to self but united to the cosmos around one.

Papal States   States in central Italy where the pope was the civil ruler and administrative functions were carried on by priests.

parinirvana   In Buddhism, the mysterious state in which the Buddha ended his life, never to be reborn into this world, in which he neither exists nor does not exist. Thus, the final state of nirvana that an enlightened person reaches at death.

Passover   *See* Pesach.

pastoral plan   The fourth step of the circle of praxis, as developed by liberation theologians. It develops concrete policies and actions designed to transform the situation from what the descriptive analysis reveals toward the better or more just situation that normative analysis recommends.

Peace Churches   Anabaptists who follow the Sermon on the Mount literally—Mennonites, Amish, Church of the Brethren—plus (non-Anabaptist) Quakers with the same commitment.

Peace of God   A medieval attempt to reduce the savagery of war by exempting certain groups from warfare (for example, clergy and peasants).

peace teams   Attempts to realize Gandhi's dream of teams of nonviolent activists seeking positive social change. In the Israeli-Palestinian conflict, peace teams consist of Palestinians, Israelis, and internationals. They include the International Solidarity Movement, Christian Peacemaker Teams, Muslim Peacemaker Teams, and the Michigan Peace Team.

Pentecost   For the Jewish festival, *see* Shavuot. The first *Christian* Pentecost is described in Acts of the Apostles, chapter 2, as the descent of the Holy Spirit on the first believers in Christ, empowering them to inaugurate the Christian mission. *See also* Holy Spirit.

Pequot   The Native American tribe, living in what is now southern Connecticut, which was the first to resist European settlers who had treated them unjustly.

Pequot War   A war waged in southern New England in 1637–1638 between the Pequot tribe and European settlers. The Pequot were defeated.

persuasion   With protest, the first of the three major forms of nonviolent action, the other two being (2) noncooperation and (3) intervention.

Pesach   The Hebrew word for Passover, the first of three pilgrimage feasts in the Jewish liturgical calendar. It takes place at the beginning of the spring grain harvest and commemorates God's rescue of the ancient Israelites from slavery in Egypt.

PLO   The Palestine Liberation Organization.

pogrom   An active Christian persecution of Jews; a Russian word.

political Zionism   A form of (modern) Zionism that pursued the goal of Jewish colonization outside of Europe by means of international support or the authorization of powerful states. Its goal was the eventual formation of a Jewish state in the colonized region.

praxis   Activity that is reflected upon and consciously chosen to produce a particular effect—a transformation of society.

principle of double effect   The principle, basic to just war theory, that one can carry out an action that produces both good and bad effects provided that (1) the good effect is not caused by the bad effect, (2) one intends only the good effect, and (3) the good effect greatly outweighs the bad effect.

proportionality   The just war principle that requires the good results of a war or any part of a war to significantly outweigh the bad results, considering the effects on all sides, including future generations. Sometimes it is wrongly defined as producing no more harm than necessary to achieve one's objectives.

Prosperity Gospel   Invest generously in God and God's work, then trust God to meet your needs.

protest   With persuasion, the first of the three major forms of nonviolent action, the other two being (2) noncooperation and (3) intervention.

Pueblo   Native American tribes living in communal, apartment-like stone or adobe structures in the southwestern United States that largely succeeded in maintaining their society, culture, and religion in the face of European settlers and missionaries. The Hopi are one of these tribes.

Purim   A Jewish festival commemorating the story told in the biblical book of Esther, in which Jews take revenge on a royal Persian enemy, killing him and numerous other Gentiles.

Qassam rockets   Crude projectiles fired by Palestinians in the Israeli-occupied Gaza Strip across the border into Israel. In a recent two-year period, fourteen Israelis were killed by these rockets. The corresponding Israeli weapons include F-16s and Apache helicopters.

Quechua   Originally the language of the Incan empire, it is spoken today by more than eight million people living in Bolivia, Peru, Equador, Columbia, and Argentina.

Quran   The holy scripture of Islam; the word means "recitation." Muslims traditionally regard the Quran as divinely inspired in every detail.

Radical Reformation   A movement within the Protestant Reformation that believed the Lutheran and Reformed movements did not go far enough. It condemned elite leadership, called for adult baptism (Anabaptists), taught that only fully-committed believers were true members of the church, expected an imminent end of the world, and attacked the corruption of wealth and power. As the world and the more traditional churches continued to exist, the movement tended to create separatist communities of believers.

Ramadan   The ninth month of the Muslim lunar year, when observant Muslims fast from all food, drink, and sexual activity from dawn until dusk. Muhammad received his first revelation near the end of Ramadan.

Ramayana   One of Hinduism's two great national epics narrating the adventures of Prince Rama of Ayodhya when the demon king of Lanka abducts his wife. It is counted among the noninspired traditions known as the Smriti.

rapture   In the ideology of Fundamentalist and Zionist Christians, the first event of the end-time, the airlifting of believers in Jesus out of this world, thus rescuing them from the tribulation.

rasul   The Arabic word for "prophet." The Muslim profession of faith (shahada) refers to Muhammad as the (final) prophet of God.

Reconstructionist Judaism   An American form of Judaism, founded in 1983 as a progressive alternative to Conservative Judaism. In contrast to Reform Judaism, it holds that one should practice Jewish laws, traditions, and customs unless there is positive reason not to. But it considers halakha to be "folkways" rather than laws.

redemption of land   The idea, held by religious Zionists, that the biblical "land of Israel" must be returned in its entirety to exclusively Jewish ownership, so individual seizures of land by Jews from non-Jews are encouraged.

reductions   Jesuit utopian communities for indigenous people in Paraguay early in the 17th century, designed to evangelize them and protect them from Spanish and Portuguese slave traders. They have been criticized by some as patriarchal, although they gave the natives far more freedom than the other colonial settlements did.

Reform Judaism   A 19th-century European movement attempting to bring Jewish life and belief more in line with modern thought.

refugees   Persons forced to flee from their homes and communities because of war or for other catastrophic reasons. *Internal* refugees remain in their native country, while *international* refugees flee from the country itself, especially to escape lethal political repression.

Refuseniks   Officers and soldiers in the Israel Defense Forces who refuse to serve in the Occupied Palestinian Territories (and when applicable, in Lebanon) and in doing so risk imprisonment for their stand.

reincarnation   In Hinduism, the rebirth of a human soul in another human body. Compare with the wider "transmigration of souls" that includes rebirth in animal or vegetable form. Some use the two terms as synonyms with this wider sense.

religious Zionism   A form of Zionism that asserts that God wants Jews to "redeem" all of the "land of Israel" for their exclusive possession, in effect ethnically cleansing it of its non-Jewish inhabitants.

resurrection   The raising of Jesus to life by God after his death and burial. Early Christians understood the resurrection to be God's vindication of Jesus and expected to experience a similar resurrection after their own deaths. They gained this confidence from the outward appearances of Jesus in his body to his disciples and from their inner experience of the risen Jesus alive within them.

Revisionist Zionism   A type of Zionism promoted by Ze'ev Jabotinsky, beginning in the 1920s, that urged the Jewish community to seize control on both sides of the Jordan River by force of arms and declare a Jewish state, which he expected would be backed by Britain, confining Arab resistance behind an "iron wall" of invincible force.

Rosh Hashanah   Hebrew for "head of the year"—in the Jewish liturgical calendar this is the first day of the New Year celebration.

Sabra and Shatila   Two Palestinian refugee camps located in southern Beirut, Lebanon, where in September 1982 as many as 3,000 Palestinians were massacred by the Lebanese Phalange under Israeli auspices during an Israeli invasion of Lebanon.

sadaqa (**plural** *sadaqat)*   In contrast to the formal, annual tax of zakat, this is a more private, spontaneous form of almsgiving in Islam.

salaam   Arabic greeting equivalent to the Hebrew shalom. *See also* shalom.

salat   The second pillar of Islam, obligating Muslims to observe a prescribed prayer ritual to Allah five times each day on a carpet or prayer mat facing Mecca.

Samaria   In Roman Palestine, the area between Judea in the south and Galilee in the north where the group known as Samaritans lived and worshiped. Modern Jewish settlers use the term for that part of the West Bank to make the claim that it should be under Jewish control.

samsara   The cycle of rebirth or reincarnation, from which Hindus seek liberation (moksha).

sangha   The community of the Buddha's disciples.

satyagraha   Truth-power, active nonviolence as developed by Mohandas Gandhi.

saum   The fourth pillar of Islam: fasting from food, drink, and sex during daylight hours of the month of Ramadan.

scheduled castes   The name that the government of India coined for "untouchables" or "outcastes." It indicates that they enjoy certain legal benefits.

scheduled tribes   A term used by the Indian government to refer to indigenous tribes in India that continue to follow an animist, hunter-gatherer way of life.

security/separation barrier/wall   In urban parts of the Palestinian West Bank, a concrete wall twenty-six feet high, and in rural parts of the West Bank, a razor-wire and electronic fence, flanked by patrol roads and equipped with gun towers. Under construction since 2002, it is projected to extend well over 400 miles (700 kilometers) upon completion. Despite its alleged purpose of protecting Israelis from Palestinian terrorists, this Israeli structure has been built mainly on Palestinian land, often leaving Palestinians on the Israeli side of the barrier, intruding up to ten kilometers into the West Bank to include Jewish-only settlements, reducing the land and water available to West Bank Palestinians, and hindering Palestinian movement within the West Bank.

Sephardic   Adjective describing Jews (and their culture) who were strongly influenced by Spanish and Arabic cultures.

Sephardic   Adjective describing Jews (and their culture) who were strongly influenced by Spanish and Arabic cultures.

Sermon on the Mount   The words of Jesus in the Gospel according to Matthew chapters 5–7, including such challenging passages as the beatitudes, the antitheses demanding nonviolence and love of enemies, and other core teachings. The parallel passage in the Gospel according to Luke is called the "Sermon on the Plain."

shahada   The first pillar of Islam. It is the Muslim profession of faith: "There is no god but God, and Muhammad is his Rasul (prophet)."

shalom   "Peace, victory, security and prosperity" in the broad sense: what politicians promise to give their constituents. The Arabic form is salaam.

shaman   A person who, because of his or her special personality, can make contact with the supernatural world through a trance or other means, returning to the everyday world to help others.

Sharia   Literally, the "straight path"—the revealed law of God, of which there are traces in the Quran, to be distinguished from *fiqh*, its application in jurisprudence.

Shavuot   The Hebrew name for Pentecost or the "Feast of Weeks," the second pilgrimage feast in the Jewish liturgical calendar. It occurs fifty days after Passover, at the end of the spring grain harvest. It commemorates God giving the Torah to Moses at Sinai.

Shia   Based on the Arabic word for "party," this designation refers to the approximately 15% of Muslims worldwide who believe that Muhammad chose his cousin Ali to succeed him, and that the office of caliph should not have gone to anyone unrelated to the Prophet.

shirk   In Islam, the only unforgivable sin—that of associating anyone or anything with God, equivalent to idolatry.

Shoah   The Hebrew word for Holocaust, referring to the Nazi program to exterminate European Jews that was attempted in the 1930s and 1940s.

Shruti   General name for the inspired Hindu scriptures, especially the Vedas, Brahmanas, and Upanishads.

Shudra   In the Hindu caste system, the fourth (servant) caste, situated below the three "twice-born" castes and above the untouchables, or scheduled caste.

Smriti   Noninspired traditions that complement the inspired scriptures of Hinduism.

social sin   *See* structural sin.

socialism   According to Karl Marx, the stage in the historical evolution of society coming after capitalism and before full communism. Since he believed that it would come about through the automatic operations of dialectic, he thought that one could not predict what form it would take and so made no effort to describe it in detail.

socialist Zionism   A form of (modern) Zionism that advocated ongoing Jewish immigration into pre-1948 Palestine and socioeconomic development of the Jewish community, with the aim of eventually founding a Jewish state there.

solidarity   A word made famous by the Polish movement for an independent union. It emphasizes our need for each other and its spiritual implications: going beyond justice, we share with our brothers and sisters. There is only one form of human nature—we all have innate dignity and an eternal destiny; we depend on each other.

Son of God   A title found in the Hebrew Bible and applied by New Testament authors to Jesus. Christians believe that the humanity of Jesus is intimately and mysteriously united with the second "person" of the Trinity.

Special Night Squads   Divisions of the Zionist Haganah trained by British military personnel, which attacked Palestinian villages during the Arab Revolt of 1936–1939 in British Mandatory Palestine.

state capitalism   A term used by critics of the Russian Communist system who wished to make the point that the economic system that developed under Stalin and his successors in the Soviet Union was state-owned capitalism rather than Marxist communism.

Stern Gang (Lehi)   Unofficial underground Jewish strike force established in 1940 to attack British police and government installations in the Middle East when the Irgun and Haganah chose to cooperate with Britain against Germany. Later, it attacked Palestinian resistance to Jewish expansion. Best known for assassinating Lord Moyne in Cairo, bombing the Cairo-Haifa train, and cooperating in the attack on Deir Yassin.

strong medicine   Spiritual power. In Dakota Indian warfare, it effectively protected a warrior from harm in situations of danger.

structural sin   Unjust laws, customs, situations, and habitual ways of doing things that result in economic, political, social, or environmental harm, especially to marginalized people, in such a way that no individual person can be directly blamed for the specific harm. However, a range of people do carry responsibility for initiating, supporting, and failing to confront the unjust laws, customs, situations, and habits.

structural violence   *See* structural sin.

subsidiarity   Higher levels of political organization should not take over responsibilities that lower levels can accomplish. Higher levels should give aid to lower levels when needed.

Suffering Servant   A figure found in Second Isaiah (Hebrew Bible) who suffers for the sins of others. Early Christian interpreters used this figure to explain the ministry, death, and resurrection of Jesus the messiah.

sufficiency   A social norm proposed by the Evangelical Lutheran Church in America that confronts unjust disparities in income and wealth. It highlights the sharp contrast between those who do not have enough and those who have far more than they really need. God calls for mutual generosity, support of the common good, and release from the bondage of consumerism and endless accumulation.

Sufism   Islamic mysticism, which originated in the 8th century and remains a vibrant component of Islam. Sufi orders first arose in the 11th century. Among the most famous Sufis were Rabia, Al-Ghazali, and Jalal al-Din al-Rumi.

sun dance   An important four- to eight-day-long ceremony celebrated by North American Plains Indians around the time of the summer solstice. Participants fast, pray, dance, and suffer (from self-inflicted pain) for the sake of the people, to purify themselves and the community, to gain insight through visions, and to renew the community's strength.

Sunna   "Trodden path"—in Islam, recommended behavior based on the reported teachings and actions of Muhammad, which are recorded in the Hadith.

Sunni   The shortened term for about 85% of Muslims taken from the longer phrase "the people of the custom and the community," as distinguished from Shi'ite Muslims.

sura   A chapterlike unit of the Quran that contains 114 suras. Each sura is in turn divided into *ayat* (verses), of which there are more than 6,000.

Sykes-Picot Agreement   A secret agreement between France and Britain signed in 1916, where France was promised control over southeastern Turkey, Syria, Lebanon, and northern Iraq after the war, and Britain control over the rest of Iraq, Transjordan, and a corridor to Haifa. Palestine was to be internationally governed, but after the war Britain assumed complete control over it. Lenin caused an international outcry when he published the agreement.

synthesis   The third stage in the Marxist dialectic of history: the compromise that results from the tension between thesis and antithesis. As the synthesis becomes established and accepted, it becomes itself a new thesis.

Tabernacles   In Hebrew, Sukkot: the last of the three Jewish pilgrimage festivals. It comes at the time of the final fall harvest and commemorates the Israelite period of wandering in the desert.

Talmud Expanded commentary on the Mishnah, existing in both a Palestinian and a Babylonian form.

Tanakh The Hebrew sacred scripture, roughly equivalent to the Christian "Old Testament."

taqwa An Islamic (Arabic) term denoting awareness of Allah, which is also prominent in Muslim liberation theology, where it means responsibility to God and to other human beings.

Targums Free translations of the Tanakh into Aramaic, originally oral, for the benefit of common people who no longer understood Hebrew.

tawhid An Islamic (Arabic) term meaning the unity of God. In Muslim liberation theology, it is used in opposition to the dualism of sacred and secular.

Temple Mount The Jewish name for the artificially leveled hilltop in Jerusalem that Muslims call the Noble Sanctuary. On it the second Jewish temple stood until the first century CE. *See also* al-Aqsa Mosque.

terrorism Killing or wounding civilians to advance a political agenda in the expectation that they will withdraw cooperation from their government (or some other group) or pressure it to yield. Often limited by government apologists to nonstate actors, the concept ought to apply equally to state-sponsored military or paramilitary action against civilians, often called "state-sponsored terrorism."

theory of value The Marxist theory that the value of a product is based on the worker hours used to produce it.

Theravada "The Doctrine of the Elders"—a school of thought in Buddhism that tries to hold to the original teaching without adding new elaborations and insists that each individual must accomplish his or her own enlightenment: No one can do it for another. This branch of Buddhism remains prevalent in Sri Lanka and Southeast Asia, except for Vietnam.

thesis The first of three stages in Marx's dialectical theory of history, dominated by the status-quo forces and the ideas held by the privileged elites whom the productive processes of a particular moment in history have produced.

tikkun Hebrew word meaning "repair." The 16th-century Jewish mystic Isaac Luria used the term to describe the human task of restoring God's creation.

Torah Also called the Pentateuch; the first five books of the *Tanakh*, sometimes inaccurately called "The Law."

trail of tears The forcible removal by the State of Georgia, which violated a ruling of the U.S. Supreme Court, of the Cherokee Indian tribe in 1830 from its territories in Georgia (where gold had been discovered) to Oklahoma. About 4,000 of the 15,000 displaced Cherokee died on the four-month trek.

transfer   In the Israel-Palestine conflict, the illegal, forcible removal of the indigenous Palestinians from their historic homeland, which Zionists call the "land of Israel."

transmigration of souls   The widespread belief among Hindus that after death a person's soul is reborn in another body, whether vegetable, animal, human, or deva. The passage from one human body to another human body is normally called "reincarnation."

tribulation   According to Fundamentalist and Zionist Christians, an anticipated end-time period of seven years following the so-called rapture, during which those "left behind" will suffer. The tribulation will be followed by the battle of Armageddon.

Truce of God   A Medieval attempt to reduce the savagery of war by limiting the number of days on which war could be fought (for example, forbidding war during Lent, Advent, Sundays, feast days, and so forth).

tzaddik   In Hasidic Judaism, a holy man or charismatic leader, as distinguished from an ordinary Hasid, whose values include humility and love.

ummah   The global community of Muslims: those who submit to the will of Allah and the message of the Prophet (*rasul*).

universal destination of the earth's goods   The principle that we are all related members of one human family, so the riches of the earth are intended to be shared fairly among all humans.

untouchables   In the Hindu caste system, the category so low as to be outside the system entirely. The name alludes to fear by others of pollution from physical contact with them. Gandhi tried to raise their status by calling them "Harijans" or "children of God." The secular government of India calls them the "scheduled" caste. They prefer to call themselves "Dalits," meaning "oppressed."

Upanishads   Part of the Shruti that give a philosophical reinterpretation of the Vedas. Each of the eleven Upanishads accepted as Shruti, or inspired, is associated with one of the four Vedas.

utilitarianism   An ethical system developed by the British philosopher John Stuart Mill (1806–1873), it was based on the criterion that one should choose what would produce the greatest good for the greatest number of people.

Vaishya   In the Hindu caste system, the third of the three "twice-born" castes, consisting of merchants, artisans, and farmers.

Vajrayana   A school of thought in Buddhism that uses mantras and ritual practices to put the worshiper into contact with spiritual powers. It is the dominant form of Buddhism in Tibet.

Vedanta   "End of the Vedas." In Hinduism, it refers to the contents and wisdom of the Upanishads. As a school of Hindu philosophy, it can take both nondualistic (Advaita) and dualistic (Dvaita) forms.

Vedas   The part of the Shruti that consists of inspired hymns used by the Brahmins in their ritual sacrifice and intercessory prayer.

vision quest   Among American Indians, an initiatory experience undergone by adolescent males. The seeker fasts and stays awake outdoors wearing minimal clothing, for two to four days, awaiting contact by a guardian animal spirit that will share some of its spiritual power, revealing the seeker's character and revitalizing his spiritual resources.

Wahhabi   The conservative form of Islam officially practiced in Saudi Arabia, it is named after Muhammad ibn Abd al-Wahhab (1703–1792), an early revivalist Muslim scholar. The Taliban of Afghanistan were strongly influenced by Wahhabi traditions.

waqf   In Islam, an inalienable religious endowment committing a building or piece of land and its income for religious or charitable purposes. Income from the waqf might support a mosque, school, hospital, orphanage, or other institution of social service.

Western Wall   The retaining wall supporting the west side of the artificially leveled hilltop of the (Jewish) Temple Mount or (Muslim) Noble Sanctuary in Jerusalem. The lower courses of stone date from the reconstruction by Herod. Since Orthodox Jews avoid the top of the mount for fear of accidentally walking on the site of the former Holy of Holies, they center prayers and devotions at the Western Wall.

Womanist theology   Black feminist theology by black women theologians. They explore the theological implications of race and class as well as gender.

Women in Black   Now an international women's nonviolent peace movement, it was founded in 1988 by a group of Israeli women; they demonstrate against the Israeli occupation of Palestinian territory each Friday in Tel Aviv and Jerusalem.

Women in Green   "Women for Israel's Tomorrow." A conservative grassroots Israeli Jewish group convinced that Arabs intend to destroy the Jewish state. It wants Israel to annex the occupied territories and transfer Palestinians to Arab countries, and complains that the Israeli government is too weak in its policy toward the Palestinians.

Wounded Knee   The site in South Dakota where the last major confrontation between U.S. soldiers and American Indians took place in 1890. In 1973, the American Indian Movement occupied the site to force the government to observe its 1868 treaty and in protest against strip mining on the Pine Ridge reservation that was polluting their water sources. The occupation was broken up by federal forces after a few months.

Yesh Gevul   Organization of Israeli Refuseniks who, on moral grounds, refuse to serve in territories illegally occupied by Israel such as southern

Lebanon, the West Bank, and the Gaza Strip, even though many of them are imprisoned for their refusal.

yetzer ha ra'   The evil inclination, and *yetzer ha tov*, the good inclination, represent two basic tendencies within human beings, according to Jewish ethical thought.

Yishuv   The Jewish community in Palestine before the establishment of the state of Israel in 1948.

yoga   The search for God and for union with God, in Hinduism.

yogi   One who searches for God and for union with God, in Hinduism.

Yom Kippur   The Day of Atonement—a day of fasting and repentance for sin. In the Jewish liturgical calendar, it is the last of the ten "high holy days."

zakat   The third pillar of Islam, the obligatory almsgiving of 2.5% annually of one's assets over and above what is needed for daily living. The proceeds are used for community support, especially of the poor.

Zionism (Christian)   *See* Christian Zionism.

Zionism (Jewish)   A modern nationalist movement within Judaism that originated in 19th-century Europe and was largely secular until 1967. Originally conceived in colonial terms but in diverse forms (political, socialist, cultural, religious), its goal became the establishment of a Jewish state in most or all of Palestine.

Zohar   A Hebrew word meaning "way of splendor." It is the title of the foremost medieval text representing Jewish Kabbalah.

Bibliography

Ackerman, Peter. *A Force More Powerful: A Century of Nonviolent Conflict*. New York: St. Martin's, 2000.

Aho, James Alfred. *This Thing of Darkness: A Sociology of the Enemy*. Seattle: University of Washington Press, 1994.

Akçam, Taner. *A Shameful Act: The Armenian Genocide and the Question of Turkish Responsibility*. Translated by Paul Bessemer. New York: Henry Holt, 2006.

Ali, Abdullah Yussuf, ed. *The Holy Qur'an: Text, Translation, and Commentary*. Translated by Abdullah Yusuf Ali. Elmhurst, N.Y.: Tahrike Tarsile Qur'an, Inc., 1987. Also available at www.sacred-texts.com/isl/quran/00101.htm (accessed March 3, 2007).

Antonio, Edward. "Black Theology." In *The Cambridge Companion to Liberation Theology*, edited by Christopher Rowland, 63–88. Cambridge; New York: Cambridge University Press, 1999.

Aquinas, Thomas. *Summa Theologica* 2-2 Q 40 and 2-2 Q 42 A 2, reply to 3rd objection. Translated by Fathers of English Dominican Province. Numerous publishers. Second and Revised Edition, 1920, available on the web at www.newadvent.org/summa/ (accessed March 9, 2007). Online edition © 2006, Kevin Knight.

Arendt, Hannah. *Eichmann in Jerusalem: A Report on the Banality of Evil*. New York: Viking Press, 1963.

Ariyaratne, A. T. *Buddhism and Sarvodaya: Sri Lankan Experience*. Edited by Nandasena Ratnapala. Bibliotheca Indo-Buddhica Series, vol. 168. Delhi: Sri Satguru Publications (Indian Books Centre), 1996.

Ateek, Naim Stifan. *Justice, and Only Justice: A Palestinian Theology of Liberation*. Maryknoll, N.Y.: Orbis, 1989.

Ateek, Naim, Marc H. Ellis, and Rosemary Radford Ruether, eds. *Faith and the Intifada: Palestinian Christian Voices*. Maryknoll, N.Y.: Orbis, 1992.

Augustine of Hippo. *The City of God*. Available online at *New Advent*, www.newadvent.org/fathers/1201.htm (accessed March 9, 2007).

Augustine of Hippo, *Reply to Faustus the Manichean.* Translated by R. Stothert in *The Nicene and Post-Nicene Fathers* (1st series) 4. Available online at www.new advent.org/fathers/1406.htm (accessed March 9, 2007).

Aung San Suu Kyi. *The Voice of Hope.* Conversations with Alan Clements. New York: Seven Stories, 1997.

Avishai, Bernard. *The Tragedy of Zionism: Revolution and Democracy in the Land of Israel.* New York: Farrar Straus Giroux, 1985.

Avnery, Uri. *Israel and the Palestinians: A Different Israeli View.* New York: Breira, 1975.

——. *My Friend, the Enemy.* Westport, Conn.: L. Hill, 1986.

Baker, Joharah. "How to Fight Back." *Palestine Report* 8, no. 34 (2002). www.jmcc.org/media/reportonline/article4.htm (accessed July 6, 2006). The journal's home address is www.palestinereport.org/ (accessed July 6, 2006).

Ballou, Adin. *Christian Non-Resistance in All Its Important Bearings, Illustrated and Defended.* (Reprint of: Philadelphia: J. Miller M'Kim, 1846.) The Peace Movement in America: A Facsimile Reprint Collection. New York: Jerome S. Ozer, 1972.

Banerjee, Mukulika. *The Pathan Unarmed: Opposition & Memory in the North West Frontier.* World Anthropology. Oxford: Oxford University Press, 2000.

Barbour, Hugh. "Quakers." *Encyclopedia of Religion.* Vol. 11. 2nd ed. Edited by Lindsay Jones. Detroit: Macmillan Reference USA, 2005, 7546–7550.

Begin, Menachem. *The Revolt: Story of the Irgun.* New York: Henry Schuman, 1951.

Beit-Hallahmi, Benjamin. *The Israeli Connection: Who Israel Arms and Why.* New York: Pantheon, 1987.

——. *Original Sins: Reflections on the History of Zionism and Israel.* New York: Olive Branch, 1993.

Bennis, Phyllis. *Understanding the Palestinian-Israeli Conflict.* 2nd ed. Lowell, Mass.: TARI, 2003.

Berndt, Hagen. *Non-Violence in the World Religions: Vision and Reality.* London: SCM Press, 2000.

Berryman, Phillip. *Liberation Theology: Essential Facts about the Revolutionary Movement in Latin America—and Beyond.* London: I. B. Tauris, 1987.

Bhave, Vinoba. *Revolutionary Sarvodaya: Philosophy for the Remaking of Man.* Bombay, India: Bhartiya Vidya Bhavan, 1964.

——. *Shanti Sena.* Varanasi: Sarva Seva Sangh Prakashan, 1963.

——. *Talks on the Gita.* New York: Macmillan, 1960.

Bloomfield, Maurice, trans. *Hymns of the Atharva-Veda. Sacred Books of the East, Vol. 42* [1897]. www.sacred-texts.com/hin/av/index.htm (accessed March 3, 2007).

Bondurant, Joan V. *Conquest of Violence: The Gandhian Philosophy of Conflict.* New revised ed. Princeton, N.J.: Princeton University Press, 1988.

Borelli, John. "Christian-Muslim Relations in the United States: Reflections for the Future after Two Decades of Experience." *The Muslim World* 94 (July 2004): 321–33. Also at www.blackwell-synergy.com/doi/pdf/10.1111/j.1478-1913.2004 .00056.x?cookieSet=1 (accessed March 9, 2007).

Bottomore, Tom, ed. *A Dictionary of Marxist Thought.* Cambridge, Mass.: Harvard University Press, 1983.

Boyd, Doug. *Rolling Thunder: A Personal Exploration into the Secret Healing Powers of an American Indian Medicine Man*. New York: Random House, 1974.

Brecht, Bertolt. *The Caucasian Chalk Circle*. Rev. English version and introduction by Eric Bentley. New York: Grove Press, 1966.

Brilliant, Joshua. "'Rabin Ordered Beatings,' Meir Tells Military Court," *Jerusalem Post*, June 22, 1990, news section.

——. "Officer Tells Court Villagers Were Bound, Gagged and Beaten. Not Guilty Plea at 'Break Bones' Trial." *Jerusalem Post*, March 30, 1990, news section.

Brown, Dee Alexander. *Bury My Heart at Wounded Knee: An Indian History of the American West*. New York: Holt, Reinhart and Winston, 1971.

Bryde, John F. *Modern Indian Psychology*. Rev. ed. Vermillion: Institute of Indian Studies, University of South Dakota, 1971.

Buber, Martin. *Between Man and Man*. With an afterword by the author on "The History of the Dialogical Principle." Introduction by Maurice Friedman. New York: Macmillan, 1965.

——. *I and Thou*. With a postscript by the author. Translated by Ronald Gregor Smith. 2nd ed. New York: Scribner, 1958.

Buddha Educational Foundation. *Twelve Principles of Buddhism*. Taipei, Taiwan: Buddha Educational Foundation, n.d.

Burrows, Robert J. *The Strategy of Nonviolent Defense: A Gandhian Approach*. Albany: State University of New York Press, 1996.

Cannon, Dale. *Six Ways of Being Religious: A Framework for Comparative Studies of Religion*. Belmont, Calif.: Wadsworth, 1996.

Carter, Jimmy. *Palestine: Peace Not Apartheid*. New York: Simon and Schuster, 2006.

Casas, Bartholomé de Las. *Tears of the Indians*. Williamstown, Mass.: J. Lilburne, 1970. (Originally published 1656).

Catholic Church, Archdiocese of São Paulo (Brazil). *Torture in Brazil: A Report by the Archdiocese of São Paulo*. Translated by Jaime Wright. Edited by Joan Dassin. New York: Vintage, 1986.

Cavanaugh, William T. *Torture and Eucharist: Theology, Politics, and the Body of Christ*. Challenges in Contemporary Theology. Oxford: Blackwell, 1998.

Chacour, Elias. *Blood Brothers: A Palestinian Struggles for Reconciliation in the Middle East*. Grand Rapids, Mich.: Chosen Books, 1984.

Chappel, David W., ed. *Buddhist Peacework: Creating Cultures of Peace*. Somerville, Mass.: Wisdom Publications, 1999.

Chomsky, Noam, and Edward S. Herman. *Middle East Illusions: Including Peace in the Middle East? Reflections on Justice and Nationhood*. Lanham, Md.: Rowman & Littlefield, 2003.

Ciszek, Walter J. *He Leadeth Me*. With Daniel Flaherty. Garden City, N.Y.: Doubleday, 1975.

Clark, Katerina, and Michael Holquist. *Mikhail Bakhtin*. Cambridge, Mass.: The Belknap Press of Harvard University Press, 1984.

Cohen, Michael J. *Truman and Israel*. Berkeley: University of California Press, 1990.

Congregation for the Doctrine of the Faith. *Instruction on Certain Aspects of the "Theology of Liberation."* Vatican: Congregation for the Doctrine of the Faith, 1984.

Cooney, Robert, and Helen Michalowski, eds. *The Power of the People: Active Nonviolence in the United States*. Philadelphia, Pa.: New Society, 1987.

Copeland, Kenneth. *The Laws of Prosperity*. Greensburgh, Pa.: Manna Christian Outreach, 1974.

Cory, Catherine A., and David T. Landry, eds. *The Christian Theological Tradition*. 2nd ed. Upper Saddle River, N.J.: Prentice Hall, 2003.

Cromartie, Michael. *Religion, Culture, and International Conflict: A Conversation*. Lanham, Md.: Rowman & Littlefield, 2005.

Curle, Adam. *True Justice: Quaker Peacemakers and Peacemaking*. London: Swarthmore, 1981.

Curran, Charles E. *Catholic Social Teaching, 1891–Present: A Historical, Theological, and Ethical Analysis*. Washington, D.C.: Georgetown University Press, 2002.

Dalai Lama, His Holiness the fourteenth (Tenzin Gyatso). *The Buddhism of Tibet*. Translated by Jeffrey Hopkins. The Wisdom of Tibet series. Ithaca, N.Y.: Snow Lion, 1975.

Dart, Martha. *Marjorie Sykes, Quaker Gandhian*. Birmingham, U.K.: Sessions Book Trust in association with Woodbroak College, 1993.

Day, Dorothy. *The Long Loneliness: The Autobiography of Dorothy Day*. Illustrated by Fritz Eichenberg. Introduction by Daniel Berrigan. San Francisco: Harper & Row, 1952.

Deloria, Vine. *God Is Red*. New York: Grosset & Dunlap, 1973.

Denny, Frederick Mathewson. *An Introduction to Islam*. 2nd ed. New York: Macmillan, 1994.

Diamond, Jared. *Collapse: How Societies Choose to Fail or Succeed*. New York: Penguin Books, 2005.

Doherty, Catherine de Hueck. *The Gospel without Compromise*. Notre Dame, Ind.: Ave Maria Press, 1976.

Dolci, Danilo. *A New World in the Making*. Translated by R. Monroe. Westport, Conn.: Greenwood Press, 1965.

———. *Outlaws*. Translated by R. Monroe. New York: Orion, 1961.

Domhoff, G. William. *Changing the Powers That Be: How the Left Can Stop Losing and Win*. Lanham, Md.: Rowman & Littlefield, 2003.

———. *Who Rules America? Power, Politics, and Social Change*. 5th ed. Boston: McGraw Hill, 2006.

Dwyer, Judith A., ed. *The Catholic Bishops and Nuclear War: A Critique and Analysis of the Pastoral, The Challenge of Peace*. Washington, D.C.: Georgetown University Press, 1984.

———. *The New Dictionary of Catholic Social Thought*. Collegeville, Minn.: Liturgical Press, 1994.

Dyck, Cornelius. "Mennonites." *Encyclopedia of Religion*. Edited by Lindsay Jones. Vol. 9. 2nd ed., 5860–5861. Detroit: Macmillan Reference USA, 2005.

Easwaran, Eknath. *Nonviolent Soldier of Islam: Badshah Khan, a Man to Match His Mountains*. 2nd ed. Tomales, Calif.: Nilgiri, 1999.

Ebbott, Elizabeth. *Indians in Minnesota*. Edited by Judith Rosenblatt. 4th ed. Minneapolis: University of Minnesota Press, 1985.

Eliade, Mircea, et al., eds. *The Encyclopedia of Religion*. New York: Macmillan, 1987.

Ellis, Marc H. *Beyond Innocence and Redemption: Confronting the Holocaust and Israeli Power: Creating a Moral Future for the Jewish People*. San Francisco: Harper & Row, 1990.

———. "Jews, Christians, and Liberation Theology." In *Judaism, Christianity, and Liberation: An Agenda for Dialogue*. Edited by Otto Maduro. Maryknoll, N.Y.: Orbis, 1991.

———. *Toward a Jewish Theology of Liberation: The Challenge of the 21st Century*. Expanded 3rd ed. Waco, Tex.: Baylor University Press, 2004.

Eppsteiner, Fred, ed. *The Path of Compassion: Writings on Socially Engaged Buddhism*. Revised 2nd ed. A Buddhist Peace Fellowship Book. Berkeley, Calif.: Parallax Press, 1988.

Erikson, Erik H. *Gandhi's Truth: On the Origins of Militant Nonviolence*. New York: W. W. Norton, 1993.

Esack, Farid. *Quran, Liberation and Pluralism: An Islamic Perspective of Interreligious Solidarity against Oppression*. Oxford, England: Oneworld, 1997.

Esposito, John L. *Islam: The Straight Path*. 3rd ed. New York: Oxford University Press, 1998.

Esposito, John L., and John O. Voll. *Islam and Democracy*. New York: Oxford University Press, 1996.

Fadiman, James, and Robert Frager, eds. *Essential Sufism*. San Francisco: Harper San Francisco, 1997.

Fahey, Joseph J., and Richard Armstrong, eds. *A Peace Reader: Essential Writings on War, Justice, Non-Violence and World Order*. Revised ed. New York: Paulist Press, 1992.

Farber, Seth. *Radicals, Rabbis and Peacemakers: Conversations with Jewish Critics of Israel*. Monroe, Maine: Common Courage, 2005.

Fellman, Gordon. *Rambo and the Dalai Lama: The Compulsion to Win and Its Threat to Human Survival*. With a foreword by the Dalai Lama. Global Conflict and Peace Education. Albany: State University of New York Press, 1998.

Ferguson, John. *War and Peace in the World's Religions*. New York: Oxford University Press, 1978.

Fernandes, Walter, ed. *The Emerging Dalit Identity: The Re-Assertion of the Subalterns*. New Delhi: Indian Social Institute, 1996.

Fernando, Tarcisius, and Helene O'Sullivan. *Launching the Second Century: The Future of Catholic Social Thought in Asia*. Hong Kong: Asian Centre for the Progress of Peoples, 1993.

Flannery, Austin, ed. *Vatican Council II: More Postconciliar Documents*. Vatican Collection. Vol. 2. Collegeville, Minn.: The Liturgical Press, 1982.

Flapan, Simha. *The Birth of Israel: Myths and Realities*. New York: Pantheon Books, 1987.

———. *Zionism and the Palestinians*. London; New York: Croom Helm; Harper & Row, 1979.

Frossard, André. *I Have Met Him: God Exists*. New York: Herder and Herder, 1971.

Galtung, Johan. *Buddhism: A Quest for Unity and Peace*. Colombo: Sarvodaya International, 1993.

———. *Peace by Peaceful Means: Peace and Conflict, Development and Civilization*. London: SAGE, 1996.

———. "A Structural Theory of Imperialism." *Journal of Peace Research* 8 (1971): 81–117. Reprinted in *Approaches to Peace: A Reader in Peace Studies*, edited by David P. Barash, 42–45. New York: Oxford University Press, 2000.

Gandhi, M. K. *All Men Are Brothers: Life and Thoughts of Mahatma Gandhi: As Told in His Own Words*. Paris: United Nations Educational, Scientific, and Cultural Organization, 1958.

———. *An Autobiography: The Story of My Experiments with Truth*. Translated by Mahadev Desai. Boston: Beacon Press, [1993], 1957.

———. *The Bhagvadgita*. New Delhi: Orient Paperbacks, 1980.

———. *Non-Violence in Peace and War*. Ahmedabad: Navajivan Publishing, 1942.

———. *Non-Violent Resistance (Satyagraha)*. New York: Schocken, 1951.

Gautama, Siddhartha. "The Sermon at Benares." In *Buddha, the Gospel*. Edited by Paul Carus. Chicago: The Open Court Publishing Company, 1894. Available at www.sacred-texts.com/bud/btg/btg17.htm (accessed March 3, 2007).

Gertner, Jon. "The Futile Pursuit of Happiness." *The New York Times*, September 7, 2003, section 6. Available at query.nytimes.com/gst/fullpage.html?sec=health&res=9E0DEFD61538F934A3575AC0A9659C8B63 (accessed March 8, 2007).

Gill, Sam D. "Native American Religions: An Introduction." In *Religious Life in History*. 2nd ed. Belmont, Calif.: Wadsworth/Thompson Learning, 2005.

Glasse, Cyril. *The Concise Encyclopedia of Islam*. San Francisco: Harper San Francisco, 1991.

Glossop, Ronald J. *Confronting War: An Examination of Humanity's Most Pressing Problem*, 4th ed. Jefferson, N.C., and London: McFarland & Company, 2001.

Gopin, Marc. *How Religion Can Bring Peace to the Middle East*. New York: Oxford University Press, 2002.

Gordon, Haim, and Leonard Grob. *Education for Peace: Testimonies from World Religions*. Maryknoll, N.Y.: Orbis, 1987.

Gorospe, Vitaliano, S.J. *Forming the Filipino Social Conscience: Social Theology from a Filipino Christian Perspective*. Makati City, Philippines: Bookmark, 1997.

Gray, J. Glenn. *The Warriors: Reflections on Men in Battle*. New York: Harper Colophon, 1970.

Greeley, Andrew. *Death and Beyond*. Chicago: Thomas More Press, 1976.

Gregg, Richard. *The Power of Nonviolence*. New York: Schocken, 1960.

Gregory, Bishop Wilton D, and the United States Conference of Catholic Bishops. "Letter to President Bush on Iraq." www.usccb.org/sdwp/international/bush902.htm (accessed July 11, 2006).

Gremillion, Joseph, ed. *The Gospel of Peace and Justice: Catholic Social Teaching since Pope John*. Maryknoll, N.Y.: Orbis, 1976.

Grey, Mary. "Feminist Theology: A Critical Theology of Liberation." In *The Cambridge Companion to Liberation Theology*. Edited by Christopher Rowland, 89–106. Cambridge: Cambridge University Press, 1999.

Grossman, Dave, Lt. Col. *On Killing: The Psychological Cost of Learning to Kill in War and Society*. Boston: Little, Brown and Company, 1995.

Gutiérrez, Gustavo. *A Theology of Liberation: History, Politics, and Salvation*. Rev. ed. Maryknoll, N.Y.: Orbis, 1988.

Halley, Henry Hampton. *Halley's Bible Handbook: An Abbreviated Bible Commentary*. 24th ed. Grand Rapids, Mich.: Zondervan, 1965.

Hallie, Philip Paul. *Lest Innocent Blood Be Shed: The Story of the Village of Le Chambon, and How Goodness Happened There*. New York: Harper Colophon Books, 1980.

Hallock, Daniel. *Hell, Healing, and Resistance: Veterans Speak*. Foreword by Thich Nhat Hanh. Preface by Philip Berrigan. Farmington, Pa.: Plough, 1998.

Hasek, Jaroslav. *The Good Soldier Schweik*. Translated by Paul Selver. New York: Penguin, 1942.

Hass, Amira. *Drinking the Sea at Gaza: Days and Nights in a Land under Siege*. Translated by Elana Wesley and Maxine Kaufman-Lacusta. 1st American ed. New York: Henry Holt, 1999.

Heinberg, Richard. *The Party's Over: Oil, War, and the Fate of Industrial Societies*. Revised and updated. Gabriola Island, British Colombia: New Society Publishers, 2005.

——. *Power Down: Options and Actions for a Post-Carbon World*. Gabriola Island, British Colombia: New Society Publishers, 2004.

Herzl, Theodor. *The Complete Diaries of Theodor Herzl*. Translated by Harry Zohn. Edited by Raphael Patai. New York: Herzl Press and Thomas Yoseloff, 1960.

——. *The Jewish State*. Edited with a preface by Ami Isseroff. PDF e-book. Adapted from the edition published in 1946 by the American Zionist Emergency Council. www.mideastweb.org/Jewishstate.pdf (accessed July 2, 2006).

Hiatt, Stephen, ed. *A Game As Old As Empire: The Secret World of Economic Hit Men and the Web of Global Corruption*. San Francisco: Barrett-Koehler, 2007.

Hillesum, Etty. *Etty: The Letters and Diaries of Etty Hillesum, 1941–1943*. Translated by Arnold J. Pomerans. Edited by Klaas A. D. Smelik. Grand Rapids, Mich.: William B. Eerdmans, 2002.

Hinde, Robert A., and Helen E. Watson, eds. *War: A Cruel Necessity? The Bases of Institutionalized Violence*. London: I. B. Tauris, 1995.

Holmes, Arthur F., ed. *War and Christian Ethics*. 2nd ed. Grand Rapids, Mich.: Baker Academic, 2005.

Holmes, Robert L. *On War and Morality: Studies in Moral, Political, and Legal Philosophy*. Princeton, N.J.: Princeton University Press, 1989.

Holmes, Robert L., and Barry L. Gan. *Nonviolence in Theory and Practice*. 2nd ed. Long Grove, Ill.: Waveland, 2005.

Hood, Robert E. *Social Teachings in the Episcopal Church: A Source Book*. Harrisburg, Pa.: Morehouse Publishing, 1990.

Hovannisian, Richard G., ed. *The Armenian Genocide in Perspective*. New Brunswick, N.J.: Transaction Books, 1986.

James, William. *The Varieties of Religious Experience: A Study in Human Nature*. New York: Collier, 1961.

Jews for Justice in the Middle East. *The Origin of the Palestine-Israel Conflict*. 3rd ed. San Rafael, Calif.: Jews for Justice in the Middle East, 2001.

Johnson, Elizabeth. "Imaging God, Embodying Christ: Women as a Sign of the Times." In *The Church Women Want: Catholic Women in Dialogue*, edited by Elizabeth Johnson, 45–59. New York: Crossroad, 2002.

Johnson, James Turner. *The Holy War Idea in Western and Islamic Traditions*. University Park: Pennsylvania State University Press, 1997.

———. *Just War Tradition and the Restraint of War: A Moral and Historical Inquiry*. Princeton, N.J.: Princeton University Press, 1981.

Johnston, Douglas, ed. *Faith-Based Diplomacy: Trumping Realpolitik*. Oxford: Oxford University Press, 2003.

Johnston, Douglas, and Cynthia Sampson, eds. *Religion, the Missing Dimension of Statecraft*. New York: Oxford University Press, 1994.

Jordens, J. T. F. "Gandhi and the *Bhagavadgita*." In *Modern Indian Interpreters of the Bhagavadgita*, edited by Robert N. Minor, 88–105. Albany: State University of New York Press, 1986.

Juergensmeyer, Mark. *The New Cold War? Religious Nationalism Confronts the Secular State*. Comparative Studies in Religion and Society. Berkeley: University of California Press, 1993.

Katz, Shmuel. *Days of Fire*. London: W. H. Allen, 1968.

Kelsay, John. *Islam and War: A Study in Comparative Ethics*. Louisville, Ky.: Westminster/John Knox, 1993.

Khadduri, Majid. *War and Peace in the Law of Islam*. Baltimore: Johns Hopkins Press, 1955.

Khalidi, Walid, ed. *From Haven to Conquest: Readings in Zionism and the Palestine Problem until 1948*. Beirut: The Institute for Palestine Studies, 1971.

King, Martin Luther Jr. *A Testament of Hope: The Essential Writings and Speeches of Martin Luther King Jr.* Edited by James M. Washington. San Francisco: Harper San Francisco, 1986.

Kohn, Alfie. *Punished by Rewards: The Trouble with Gold Stars, Incentive Plans, A's, Praise, and Other Bribes*. With a New Afterword by the Author. Boston: Houghton Mifflin, 1999.

Kotb, Sayed. *See* Qutb, Sayyid.

Kropotkin, Prince Peter. *Memoirs of a Revolutionist*. Montreal: Black Rose Books, 1989.

Lash, Nicholas. *A Matter of Hope: A Theologian's Reflections on the Thought of Karl Marx*. Notre Dame, Ind.: University of Notre Dame Press, 1981.

Lebacqz, Karen. *Justice in an Unjust World: Foundations for a Christian Approach to Justice*. Minneapolis: Augsburg Publishing House, 1987.

———. *Six Theories of Justice: Perspectives from Philosophical and Theological Ethics*. Minneapolis: Augsburg Publishing House, 1986.

Leigh, David. "General Sacked by Bush Says He Wanted Early Elections." *The Guardian/UK*, March 18, 2004. www.commondreams.org/headlines04/0318-01.htm (accessed June 14, 2006).

Lenin, Vladimir Ilich. *The Lenin Anthology*. Edited by Robert C. Tucker. New York: Norton, 1975.

———. *What Is to Be Done? Burning Questions of Our Movement*. New York: International Publishers, 1969.

Lindsey, Hal. *The Late, Great Planet Earth*. With the assistance of C. C. Carlson. Grand Rapids, Mich.: Zondervan, 1970.

London Sunday Times. *The Yom Kippur War, by the Insight Team of the London Sunday Times*. Garden City, N.Y.: Doubleday, 1974.

Lucas, Noah. *The Modern History of Israel*. London: Weidenfeld & Nicolson, 1974.

Luther, Martin. "Doctor Luther's Bull and Reformation." In *Against the Spiritual Estate of the Pope and the Bishops, Falsely So Called* (1522) in *Luther's Works,* Vol. 39: Church and Ministry I. Edited by H. T. Lehmann and E. W. Gritsch. Philadelphia: Fortress Press, 1970.

Luxemburg, Rosa. *Reflections and Writings*. Amherst, N.Y.: Humanity Books, 1999.

Maalouf, Amin. *The Crusades through Arab Eyes*. New York: Schocken, 1984.

Macdonald, Duncan Black. *The Religious Attitude and Life in Islam*. New York: AMS Press, 1970.

MacNair, Rachel. *The Psychology of Peace: An Introduction*. Westport, Conn.: Praeger, 2003.

Macy, Joanna Rogers. *Despair and Personal Power in the Nuclear Age*. Philadelphia: New Society Publishers, 1983.

Maduro, Otto, ed. *Judaism, Christianity, and Liberation: An Agenda for Dialogue*. Maryknoll, N.Y.: Orbis, 1991.

Mahfouz, Naguib. *Midaq Alley*. Translated by Trevor Le Gassick. New York: Anchor Books, 1992.

Marx, Karl, and Frederick Engels. *The Communist Manifesto: Annotated Text*. Edited by Frederic L. Bender. New York: W.W. Norton, 1988.

———. *Karl Marx: Selected Writings*. 2nd ed. Oxford: Oxford University Press, 2000.

———. *Karl Marx, Frederick Engels: Collected Works*. New York: International Publishers, 1975–2004.

———. *The Marx-Engels Reader*. Edited by Robert C. Tucker. 2nd ed. New York: Norton, 1978.

Mason, John. *A Brief History of the Pequot War*. Boston: S. Kneeland and T. Green in Queen Street, 1736. Available at bc.barnard.columbia.edu/~rmccaugh/earlyAC/readings/pequot/pequot.pdf (accessed January 27, 2004).

Massaro, Thomas. *Living Justice: Catholic Social Teaching in Action*. Franklin, Wis.: Sheed & Ward, 2000.

Maurin, Peter. *Easy Essays*. Chicago: Franciscan Herald Press, 1977.

McAllister, Pam. *You Can't Kill the Spirit*. Philadelphia, Pa.: New Society Publishers, 1988.

McDonald, Di. "A Way of Life." *SGI Quarterly* (April 2005). Available at www.sgi.org/english/Features/quarterly/0504/feature7.htm (accessed July 12, 2006).

McGovern, Arthur F. *Liberation Theology and Its Critics: Towards an Assessment*. Maryknoll, N.Y.: Orbis, 1994.

McKenzie, John. *Myths and Realities*. Milwaukee, Wis.: Bruce Publishing Co., 1963.

McLellan, David. *Karl Marx: His Life and Thought*. New York: Harper & Row, 1973.

————. *Marx before Marxism*. New York: Harper & Row, 1970.

McManus, Philip, and Gerald Schlabach, eds. *Relentless Persistence: Nonviolent Action in Latin America*. Philadelphia: New Society Publishers, 1991.

Merton, Thomas. *The Nonviolent Alternative*. New York: Farrar, Straus & Giroux, 1980.

Mich, Marvin L. Krier. *Catholic Social Teaching and Movements*. Mystic, Conn.: Twenty-Third Publications, 1998.

Mill, John Stuart. *Utilitarianism*. London: Longmans, Green and Co., 1901.

Minor, Robert N., ed. *Modern Indian Interpreters of the Bhagavadgita*. SUNY Series in Religious Studies. Albany: State University of New York Press, 1986.

Moody, Raymond A. *Life After Life: The Investigation of a Phenomenon—Survival of Bodily Death*. New York: Bantam Books, 1976.

Morris, Benny. *The Birth of the Palestinian Refugee Problem Revisited*. Cambridge: Cambridge University Press, 2004.

————. *Righteous Victims: A History of the Zionist-Arab Conflict, 1881–2001*. New York: Vintage Books, 2001.

Muhaiyaddeen, M. R. Bawa. *Islam and World Peace: Explanations of a Sufi*. Philadelphia, Pa.: Fellowship Press, 1987.

Munif, Abd al-Rahman, and Peter Theroux. *Cities of Salt*. Translated by Peter Theroux. New York: Vintage, 1987.

Nanda, B. R. *Mahatma Gandhi: A Biography*. Abridged ed. London: Unwin, 1965.

National Conference of Catholic Bishops, United States Catholic Conference. *Economic Justice for All: Pastoral Letter on Catholic Social Teaching and the U.S. Economy*. Tenth anniversary. Washington, D.C.: National Conference of Catholic Bishops, 1997.

Neihardt, John G. *Black Elk Speaks: Being the Life Story of a Holy Man of the Oglala Sioux, As Told through John G. Neihardt (Flaming Rainbow)*. Illustrated by Standing Bear. Lincoln: University of Nebraska Press, 1961.

Nelson-Pallmeyer, Jack. *Harvest of Cain*. Washington, D.C.: Epica Task Force, 2001.

Nhat Hanh, Thich. *Being Peace*. Edited by Arnold Kotler. Berkeley, Calif.: Parallax Press, 1987.

————. *Interbeing: Commentaries on the Tiep Hien Precepts*. Edited by Fred Eppsteiner. Berkeley, Calif.: Parallax Press, 1987.

————. *Vietnam: Lotus in a Sea of Fire*. New York: Hill and Wang, 1967.

Nicholson, Reynold A. *The Mystics of Islam*. London: Routledge and Kegan Paul, 1966 [1914]. Also available at www.sacred-texts.com/isl/moi/moi.htm (accessed March 9, 2007).

Olson, Lynne. *Freedom's Daughters: The Unsung Heroines of the Civil Rights Movement from 1830 to 1970*. New York: Scribner, 2001.

Paige, Glenn D., Chaiwat Satha-Anand, and Sarah Gilliatt, eds. *Islam and Nonviolence*. Honolulu: University of Hawai'i, 1993.

Palackapilly, George, and T. D. Felix. *Religion and Economics: A Worldview*. New Delhi: AIDBES, 1996.

Perkins, John. *Confessions of an Economic Hit Man*. San Francisco: Berrett-Koehler, 2004.

Peterson, Anna L. *Martyrdom and the Politics of Religion: Progressive Catholicism in El Salvador's Civil War*. Albany: State University of New York Press, 1997.

Pieris, Aloysius. *An Asian Theology of Liberation*. Maryknoll, N.Y.: Orbis, 1988.

———. *Love Meets Wisdom: A Christian Experience of Buddhism*. Faith Meets Faith. Maryknoll, N.Y.: Orbis, 1988.

Pontifical Council for Justice and Peace. *Compendium of the Social Doctrine of the Church*. Città del Vaticano: Libreria Editrice Vaticana, 2004.

Pope John XXIII. *Mater et Magistra: On Christianity and Social Progress*. Libreria Editrice Vaticana: Vatican, 1961. Also available at www.vatican.va/holy_father/john_xxiii/encyclicals/documents/hf_j-xxiii_enc_15051961_mater_en.html (accessed March 4, 2007).

Pope John XXIII. *Pacem in Terris: On Establishing Universal Peace in Truth, Justice, Charity, and Liberty*. Libreria Editrice Vaticana: Vatican, 1963. Also available at www.vatican.va/holy_father/john_xxiii/encyclicals/documents/hf_j-xxiii_enc_11041963_pacem_en.html (accessed March 4, 2007).

Pope John Paul II. *Centesimus Annus: On the Hundredth Anniversary of Rerum Novarum*. Libreria Editrice Vaticana: Vatican, 1991. Also available at www.vatican.va/edocs/ENG0214/_INDEX.HTM (accessed March 4, 2007).

Pope John Paul II. *Laborem Exercens: On Human Work*. Libreria Editrice Vaticana: Vatican, 1981. Also available at www.vatican.va/edocs/ENG0217/_INDEX.HTM (accessed March 4, 2007).

Pope John Paul II. *Sollicitudo Rei Socialis: On the Twentieth Anniversary of Populorum Progressio*. Libreria Editrice Vaticana: Vatican, 1987. Also available at www.vatican.va/edocs/ENG0223/_INDEX.HTM (accessed March 4, 2007).

Pope Leo XIII. *Rerum Novarum: On Capital and Labor*. Libreria Editrice Vaticana: Vatican, 1891. Also available at www.vatican.va/holy_father/leo_xiii/encyclicals/documents/hf_l-xiii_enc_15051891_rerum-novarum_en.html (accessed March 4, 2007).

Pope Paul VI. *Evangelii Nuntiandi: On Evangelization in the Modern World (Apostolic Exhortation)*. Libreria Editrice Vaticana: Vatican, 1975. Also available at www.vatican.va/holy_father/paul_vi/apost_exhortations/documents/hf_p-vi_exh_19751208_evangelii-nuntiandi_en.html (accessed March 4, 2007).

Pope Paul VI. *Octogesima Adveniens: Apostolic Letter to Cardinal Maurice Roy*. Libreria Editrice Vaticana: Vatican, 1971. Also available at www.vatican.va/holy_father/paul_vi/apost_letters/documents/hf_p-vi_apl_19710514_octogesima-adveniens_en.html (accessed March 4, 2007).

Pope Paul VI. *Populorum Progressio: On the Development of Peoples*. Libreria Editrice Vaticana: Vatican, 1967. Also available at www.vatican.va/holy_father/paul_vi/encyclicals/documents/hf_p-vi_enc_26031967_populorum_en.html (accessed March 4, 2007).

Pope Pius XI. *Quadragesimo Anno: On Reconstruction of the Social Order*. Libreria Editrice Vaticana: Vatican, 1931. Also available at www.vatican.va/holy_father/pius_xi/encyclicals/documents/hf_p-xi_enc_19310515_quadragesimo-anno_en.html (accessed March 4, 2007).

Potok, Chaim. *The Chosen: A Novel*. New York: Simon and Schuster, 1967.

Prabhupada, A. C. Bhaktivedanta Swami. *Bhagavad-Gita As It Is*. Los Angeles: The Bhaktivedanta Book Trust, 1984.

Queen, Christopher S., ed. *Engaged Buddhism in the West*. Boston: Wisdom Publications, 2000.

Queen, Christopher S., and Sallie B. King, eds. *Engaged Buddhism: Buddhist Liberation Movements in Asia*. Albany: State University of New York Press, 1996.

Quigley, John. *Palestine and Israel: A Challenge to Justice*. Durham, N.C.: Duke University Press, 1990.

Qutb, Sayyid [Sayed]. *Milestones*. India: Islamic Book Service, 2006. Also available at www.youngmuslims.ca/online_library/books/milestones/hold/index_2.asp (accessed March 9, 2007).

———. [Kotb, Sayed]. *Social Justice in Islam*. Translated by John B. Hardie. American Council of Learned Societies Near Eastern Translation Program, Vol. 1. New York: Octagon, 1970.

Radhakrishnan, S. *Indian Philosophy*. 2nd ed., 738. The Muirhead Library of Philosophy, Vol. 1. New York; London: The Macmillan Company; George Allen & Unwin Ltd., 1929.

Radhakrishnan, S., ed. *The Bhagavadgita, with an Introductory Essay, Sanskrit Text [Transliterated], English Translation and Notes*. New York: Harper and Brothers, 1948.

Rahman, Fazlur, *Major Themes of the Qur'an*. 2nd ed. Minneapolis, Minn.: Bibliotheca Islamica, 1994.

Ramsey, Paul. *The Just War: Force and Political Responsibility*. Reprint of 1968 edition. Lanham, Md.: University Press of America, 1983.

Ratzinger, Cardinal Joseph. *Instruction on Certain Aspects of the "Theology of Liberation."* Sacred Congregation for the Doctrine of the Faith, 1984. Available at www.vatican.va/roman_curia/congregations/cfaith/documents/rc_con_cfaith_doc_19840806_theology-liberation_en.html (accessed July 10, 2004).

———. *Instruction on Christian Freedom and Liberation*. Rome: Congregation for the Doctrine of the Faith, 1986. Also available at www.vatican.va/roman_curia/congregations/cfaith/documents/rc_con_cfaith_doc_19860322_freedom-liberation_en.html (accessed July 10, 2006).

Rawls, John. *A Theory of Justice*. Cambridge, Mass.: The Belknap Press of Harvard University Press, 1971.

Restall, Matthew. *Seven Myths of the Spanish Conquest*. Oxford: Oxford University Press, 2003.

Rinpoche, Samdhong. *Selected Writings and Speeches: A Collection of Selected Writings and Speeches on Buddhism and Tibetan Culture*. Jamtse Series. Alumni of Central Institute of Higher Tibetan Studies, 1999.

Roman Synod of Catholic Bishops. "Justice in the World." In *Proclaiming Justice and Peace,* edited by Walsh and Davies, 268–83. Mystic, Conn.: Twenty-Third Publications, 1991.

Rosenberg, Marshall B. *Nonviolent Communication: A Language of Compassion*. Encinitas, Calif.: PuddleDancer Press, 1999.

Rowland, Christopher, ed. *The Cambridge Companion to Liberation Theology*. New York: Cambridge University Press, 1999.

Roy, Beth. *Some Trouble with Cows: Making Sense of Social Conflict*. Berkeley: University of California Press, 1994.

Rubenstein, Richard L. *After Auschwitz: Radical Theology and Contemporary Judaism*. Indianapolis, Ind.: Bobbs-Merrill Company, 1966.

Rubenstein, Richard L., and John K. Roth. *Approaches to Auschwitz: The Holocaust and Its Legacy*. Atlanta, Ga.: John Knox Press, 1987.

Ruether, Rosemary Radford. "False Messianism and Prophetic Consciousness." In *Judaism, Christianity, and Liberation: An Agenda for Dialogue*, edited by Otto Maduro, 83–95. Maryknoll, N.Y.: Orbis, 1991.

Ruether, Rosemary Radford, and Herman J. Ruether. *The Wrath of Jonah: The Crisis of Religious Nationalism in the Israeli-Palestinian Conflict*. New York: Harper & Row, 1989.

Ruether, Rosemary Radford, and Marc H. Ellis, eds. *Beyond Occupation: American Jewish, Christian, and Palestinian Voices for Peace*. Boston: Beacon Press, 1990.

al-Rumi, Jalal al-Din. *Mathnawi.* Available at www.sacred-texts.com/isl/masnavi/index.htm (accessed June 8, 2006).

Saadawi, Nawal. *A Daughter of Isis: The Autobiography of Nawal El Saadawi*. Translated by Sherif Hetata. London: Zed Books, 1999.

——. *The Hidden Face of Eve: Women in the Arab World*. Translated by Sherif Hetata. Boston, Mass.: Beacon Press, 1982.

——. *Memoirs from the Women's Prison*. Translated by Marilyn Booth. Berkeley: University of California Press, 1994.

Samuel, Dorothy T. *Safe Passage on City Streets*. Expanded ed. Richmond, Ind.: Liberty Literary Works, 1991.

Sanford, Agnes Mary White. *The Healing Light*. 8th ed. St. Paul, Minn.: Macalester Park Publishing Co., 1949.

Satha-Anand, Chaiwat, et al., eds. *The Frontiers of Nonviolence*. Honolulu: International Peace Research Association (IPRA)'s Nonviolence Commission, Center for Global Nonviolence, 1998.

Schall, James V., ed. *Out of Justice, Peace: Winning the Peace*. San Francisco: Ignatius Press, 1984.

Schiff, Ze'ev, and Ehud Ya'ari. *Intifada: The Palestinian Uprising: Israel's Third Front*. Translated by Ina Friedman. New York: Simon and Schuster, 1990.

Schuhmacher, Stephan, Gert Woerner, and Kurt Friedrichs, eds. *The Encyclopedia of Eastern Philosophy and Religion: Buddhism, Hinduism, Taoism, Zen*. Boston: Shambhala, 1989.

Scofield, C. I., and Henry G. Weston, eds. *The Scofield Reference Bible. The Holy Bible, Containing the Old and New Testaments. Authorized King James Version*. Scofield Facsimile Series No. 2. New York: Oxford University Press, 1917.

Second Vatican Council. *Gaudium et Spes: Pastoral Constitution on the Church in the Modern World*. Libreria Editrice Vaticana: Vatican, 1965. Also available at www.vatican.va/archive/hist_councils/ii_vatican_council/documents/vat-ii_cons_19651207_gaudium-et-spes_en.html (accessed March 4, 2007).

——. *Lumen Gentium: Dogmatic Constitution on the Church*. Rome: Vatican, 1964. Also available at www.vatican.va/archive/hist_councils/ii_vatican_council/

documents/vat-ii_const_19641121_lumen-gentium_en.html (accessed March 4, 2007).

———. *Nostra Aetate: Declaration on the Relation of the Church to Non-Christian Religions*. Libreria Editrice Vaticana: Vatican, 1965. Also available at www.vatican .va/archive/hist_councils/ii_vatican_council/documents/vat-ii_decl_19651028_ nostra-aetate_en.html (accessed March 5, 2007).

Shahak, Israel. *Jewish History, Jewish Religion: The Weight of Three Thousand Years*. Forewords by Gore Vidal and Edward Said, with a new introduction by Norton Mezvinsky. London: Pluto Press, 2002.

Shahak, Israel, and Norton Mezvinsky. *Jewish Fundamentalism in Israel*. New ed. Pluto Middle Eastern Studies. London: Pluto Press, 2004.

Sharp, Gene. *Gandhi as a Political Strategist: With Essays on Ethics and Politics*. Boston: Porter Sargent, 1979.

———. *The Politics of Nonviolent Action*. Boston: Porter Sargent, 1973.

———. *Waging Nonviolent Struggle: 20th Century Practice and 21st Century Potential*. Boston: Porter Sargent, 2005.

Silouan, Staretz, and Archimandrite Sofronii. *Wisdom from Mount Athos: The Writings of Starets Silouan, 1866–1938*. Translated by Rosemary Edmonds. Edited by Archimandrite Sophrony. Revised ed. Crestwood, N.Y.: St. Vladimir's Seminary Press, 1974.

Sivaraksa, Sulak. *Conflict, Culture, Change: Engaged Buddhism in a Globalizing World*. Boston: Wisdom Publications, 2005.

Sivaraksa, Sulak, ed. *Socially Engaged Buddhism for the New Millennium: Essays in Honor of the Ven. Phra Dhammapitaka (Bhikkhu P.A. Payutto) on His 60th Birthday Anniversary*. Bangkok: Parallax Press, 1999.

Smart, Ninian. *The World's Religions*. 2nd ed. Cambridge: Cambridge University Press, 1998.

———. *Worldviews: Crosscultural Explorations of Human Beliefs*. 3rd ed. Upper Saddle River, N.J.: Prentice Hall, 2000.

Smith, Preserved. *The Life and Letters of Martin Luther*. London: John Murray, 1911.

Solzhenitsyn, Aleksandr I. *The Gulag Archipelago 1918–1956: An Experiment in Literary Investigation*. Translated by Thomas P. Whitney. New York: Harper & Row, 1975. [Copyright © 1974 by Aleksandr I. Solzhenitsyn.]

———. *One Day in the Life of Ivan Denisovich*. Translated by Ralph Parker. Harmondsworth, Middlesex, England: Penguin, 1963.

Spiro, Melford E. *Buddhism and Society: A Great Tradition and Its Burmese Vicissitudes*. New York: Harper & Row, 1972.

Strain, Charles R., ed. *Prophetic Visions and Economic Realities: Protestants, Jews, and Catholics Confront the Bishop's Letter on the Economy*. Grand Rapids, Mich.: William B. Eerdmans, 1989.

Suttner, Bertha von. *Lay Down Your Arms: The Autobiography of Martha von Tilling*. Translated by T. Holmes. With a new introduction for the Garland ed. by Irwin Abrams. New York: Garland, 1972.

Ten Boom, Corrie. *The Hiding Place*. With the assistance of John and Elizabeth Sherrill. Old Tappan, N.J.: Fleming H. Revell, 1971.

Tessler, Mark A. *A History of the Israeli-Palestinian Conflict*. Bloomington: Indiana University Press, 1994.

Thurman, Robert. "Nagarjuna's Guidelines for Buddhist Social Action." In *The Path of Compassion: Writings on Socially Engaged Buddhism*, edited by Fred Eppsteiner. Revised 2nd ed., 120–44. Berkeley, Calif.: Parallax Press, 1988.

Tolstoy, Leo. *Writings on Civil Disobedience and Nonviolence*. Philadelphia, Pa.: New Society, 1987.

Topel, L. John. *The Way to Peace: Liberation through the Bible*. Maryknoll, N.Y.: Orbis, 1979.

Trotsky, Leon. *The Revolution Betrayed: What Is the Soviet Union and Where Is It Going?* Garden City, N.Y.: Doubleday, Doran, and Co., 1937.

United States Catholic Conference. *The Challenge of Peace: God's Promise and Our Response. A Pastoral Letter on War and Peace by the National Conference of Catholic Bishops*. Washington, D.C.: United States Catholic Conference, 1983.

van Braght, Thieleman J., ed. *The Bloody Theater: Or, Martyrs Mirror*. Scottdale, Pa.: Herald Press, 1992 [1660].

Vasto, Lanza del. *Gandhi to Vinoba: The New Pilgrimage*. Translated by Philip Leon. New York: Schocken Books, 1956.

Victoria, Daizen. *Zen at War*. New York: Weatherhill, 1997.

———. *Zen War Stories*. London: Routledge, 2003.

Vorspan, Albert, and David Saperstein. *Tough Choices: Jewish Perspectives on Social Justice*. New York: UAHC Press, 1992.

Wakin, Malham M., ed. *War, Morality, and the Military Profession*. 2nd ed. Boulder, Colo.: Westview, 1986.

Walsh, Michael, and Michael Davies, eds. *Proclaiming Justice and Peace: Papal Documents from Rerum Novarum through Centesimus Annus*. Mystic, Conn.: Twenty-Third Publications, 1991.

Walzer, Michael. *Just and Unjust Wars: A Moral Argument with Historical Illustrations*. 3rd ed. New York: Basic Books, 2000.

Watterson, Kathryn. *Not by the Sword: How the Love of a Cantor and His Family Transformed a Klansman*. New York: Simon and Schuster, 1995.

Weaver, Mary Jo, David Brakke, and Jason Bivins. *Introduction to Christianity*. 3rd ed. Belmont, Calif.: Wadsworth, 1998.

Weber, Max (Darth). *The Protestant Ethic and the Spirit of Capitalism*. New York: Charles Scribner's, 1958.

Weber, Thomas. *Gandhi's Peace Army: The Shanti Sena and Unarmed Peacekeeping*. Syracuse, N.Y.: Syracuse University Press, 1996.

Weigert, Kathleen Maas, and Alexia K. Kelley, eds. *Living the Catholic Social Tradition: Cases and Commentary*. Lanham, Md.: Rowman & Littlefield, 2005.

Weyler, Rex. *Blood of the Land: The Government and Corporate War against First Nations*. Revised ed. Philadelphia, Pa.: New Society Publishers, 1992.

Wielenga, Bastiaan. "Liberation Theology in Asia." In *The Cambridge Companion to Liberation Theology*, edited by Christopher Rowland. Cambridge: Cambridge University Press, 1999.

Wiesel, Elie. *Night*. Translated by Stella Rodway. Toronto: Bantam Books, 1960.

Wigoder, Geoffrey. *Everyman's Judaica: An Encyclopedic Dictionary.* Jerusalem: Keter Publishing House, 1975.

Wilson, Boyd H. "Vinoba Bhave's Talks on the *Gita*." In *Modern Indian Interpreters of the Bhagavadgita*, edited by Robert N. Minor, 110–30. Albany: State University of New York Press, 1986.

Wink, Walter. *Engaging the Powers: Discernment and Resistance in a World of Domination.* Minneapolis, Minn.: Fortress Press, 1992.

———. *Unmasking the Powers: The Invisible Forces That Determine Human Existence.* Philadelphia, Pa.: Fortress Press, 1986.

Yarrow, C. H. Mike. *Quaker Experiences in International Conciliation.* New Haven, Conn.: Yale University Press, 1978.

Yoder, John Howard. *What Would You Do? A Serious Answer to a Standard Question.* Scottdale, Pa.: Herald Press, 1983.

Yogananda, Paramahansa. *Autobiography of a Yogi.* 12th ed. Los Angeles, Calif.: Self-Realization Fellowship, 1993.

Zaehner, R. C. *Hinduism.* New York: Oxford University Press, 1966.

Zahn, Gordon Charles. *In Solitary Witness: The Life and Death of Franz Jägerstätter.* 3rd ed. Collegeville, Minn.: The Liturgical Press, 1964.

Zunes, Stephen, Lester R. Kurtz, and Sarah Beth Asher, eds. *Nonviolent Social Movements: A Geographical Perspective.* Malden, Mass.: Blackwell, 1999.

Index

Cold War, 180–81
Columbus, Christopher, 163–64
Combatants for Peace, 216
Communism, 169–88; active nonviolence
 and, 284–85; Catholicism and, 176;
 primitive, 177, 178*t*
The Communist Manifesto, 169, 171
community, Islam on, 124
comparative cause, 308*t*, 311–13
Cone, James, 269
Conference of Churches in Asia, 270
Conferencia Episcopal Latino-
 Americana (CELAM), 238–39, 258
conscientization, 257
Conservative Judaism, 70–71
Constantine, 86
Constantinian Judaism, 267
constructive program, Gandhi and,
 17–18
consumerism, Ariyaratne on, 46–47
contradiction, 314
Contras, 184
conversion, 283; of head, 94; of heart,
 94; as intention, 315
cooperation, 279; and power, 278
Copeland, Kenneth, 107
corporative state, 230
Corrie, Rachel, 217
costs, labor theory of, 175
counsels of perfection, 97–98
counting coup, 157, 161
covenant, 59
CPT. *See* Christian Peacemaker Teams
Crusades, 102, 133–34, 194
Cuba, 184
Cuban missile crisis, 171
cults, xxvi, 181
cultural change, Catholic Church on,
 241
Cultural Revolution, 171
cultural Zionism, 73, 79
Custer, George, 155

Dakota, 154–55, 157–60
Dalai Lama, 33, 46

Dalits, 10
Dalit theology, 271
Damascus, Islam in, 118
dana, 19
dance: in Islam, 132; Native American
 worldviews and, 151*f*; in religion,
 xxxvi
Darwin, Charles, 106
Das Kapital, 170
Daughters of the American Revolution,
 288
David, king, 59–60
Day, Dorothy, 110–11
Dayan, Moshe, 204
Day of Atonement, 66–67
Days of Awe, 66–67
death, fear of, and active nonviolence,
 286
decade of development, 233, 255–57
declaration, 309*t*, 321–22
Declaration of Principles (DOP), 208–9
Deir Yassin, 202
de Las Casas, Bartholomé, 163–64, 229,
 254
de Leon, Moses, 69
demonstrations, 305
Deng Xiaoping, 171
dervish, 127
descriptive analysis, in circle of praxis,
 256
deva, 36
devekut, 70
development, decade of, 233, 255–57
de Vitoria, Franciscus, 304
dharma, 9, 27, 52n6
dialectic, 172–73
dialectical materialism, 172
Diaspora, 57, 60, 192
Dickens, Charles, 172
dictatorship of proletariat, 177–79
Diego, Juan, 150–51
dilemma, 314
discrimination, 309*t*, 324–26
Dispensationalism, 98, 108
dispute, 314